797,885 Books
are available to read at

Forgotten Books

www.ForgottenBooks.com

Forgotten Books' App
Available for mobile, tablet & eReader

ISBN 978-1-330-64907-7
PIBN 10087288

This book is a reproduction of an important historical work. Forgotten Books uses state-of-the-art technology to digitally reconstruct the work, preserving the original format whilst repairing imperfections present in the aged copy. In rare cases, an imperfection in the original, such as a blemish or missing page, may be replicated in our edition. We do, however, repair the vast majority of imperfections successfully; any imperfections that remain are intentionally left to preserve the state of such historical works.

Forgotten Books is a registered trademark of FB &c Ltd.
Copyright © 2015 FB &c Ltd.
FB &c Ltd, Dalton House, 60 Windsor Avenue, London, SW19 2RR.
Company number 08720141. Registered in England and Wales.

For support please visit www.forgottenbooks.com

1 MONTH OF FREE READING

at

www.ForgottenBooks.com

By purchasing this book you are eligible for one month membership to ForgottenBooks.com, giving you unlimited access to our entire collection of over 700,000 titles via our web site and mobile apps.

To claim your free month visit:

www.forgottenbooks.com/free87288

* Offer is valid for 45 days from date of purchase. Terms and conditions apply.

Similar Books Are Available from
www.forgottenbooks.com

A Syllabus of Modern European History, 1500-1919
by Herbert Darling Foster

Revolutionary Europe, 1789-1815
by H. Morse Stephens

An Account of Denmark
As It Was in the Year 1692, by Robert Molesworth

The Emperor William and His Reign, Vol. 1 of 2
by Edouard Simon

The Royal Marriage Market of Europe
by Princess Catherine Radziwill

History of the Netherlands
Holland and Belguim, by Alexander Young

France Under Louis XV, Vol. 1 of 2
by James Breck Perkins

The Cabinet of History
History of Switzerland, by Dionysius Lardner

History of the House of Austria
From the Accession of Francis I. to the Revolution of 1848, by Archdeacon Coxe

Balkan Problems and European Peace
by Noel Buxton

Norway and the Union With Sweden
by Fridtjof Nansen

The French Revolution and First Empire
An Historical Sketch, by William O'Connor Morris

Germany in the Nineteenth Century
Five Lectures, by J. H. Rose

The Great Condé and the Period of the Fronde, Vol. 1
A Historical Sketch, by Walter Fitz Patrick

The Historical Development of Modern Europe
From the Congress of Vienna to the Present Time, by Charles M. Andrews

Modern France, 1789-1895
by André Lebon

The Evolution of Prussia the Making of an Empire
by J. A. R. Marriott

Modern Spain, 1788-1898
by Martin Andrew Sharp Hume

Since Waterloo
A Short History of Europe and of the British Empire, 1815-1919, by Robert Jones

Italy
From 1494 to 1790, by Mrs. H. M. Vernon

THE BIRTH OF MODERN ITALY

POSTHUMOUS PAPERS OF
JESSIE WHITE MARIO

EDITED, WITH INTRODUCTION,
NOTES AND EPILOGUE BY THE
DUKE LITTA-VISCONTI-ARESE
AUTHOR OF "THE SOUL OF A PRIEST"

ILLUSTRATED

T. FISHER UNWIN
LONDON: 1 ADELPHI TERRACE
LEIPSIC: INSELSTRASSE 20
1909

(All rights reserved.)

Italia ! by the passion of the pain
That bent and rent thy chain,
Italia ! by the breaking of the bands,
The shaking of the lands :
Beloved, O men's Mother, O men's Queen,

rne, "A Song of Italy"

CORNELL
UNIVERSITY
LIBRARY

GIFT OF
Dudley Schoeles

PUBLISHER'S NOTE

AT her death Madame Mario left a large pile of manuscript, the unrevised draft of her memoirs of the Italian Risorgimento. The work was a complete whole, but lacked the arrangement, the curtailment, and the finishing touches which the author would no doubt have given to it had she lived. It was felt that, as might be expected from Madame Mario's unique knowledge of the Risorgimento and the men who made it, the manuscript contained valuable historical and biographical material which ought to be given to the public; but at the same time the form necessary for publication was lacking. In these circumstances, the Duke Litta-Visconti-Arese, whose family played an important part in the Revolution and who is thoroughly versed in its history, kindly consented to edit the work. He has retained as far as possible Madame Mario's own words, deleting passages which seemed to be of small interest or to interrupt the flow of the narrative, and adding where necessary, connecting and explanatory matter.

Important assistance in the preparation and revision of the book has been given by Mrs. E. F. Richards, who, as a close friend of Madame Venturi and a keen student of Mazzini's life and work, has been able to elucidate many obscure passages in Madame Mario's manuscript, and to whom are due the notes signed "E. F. R."

In the matter of the illustrations, thanks are due to the Mayor of Milan (1908) for his permission to reproduce a large number of portraits from the Museo del Risorgimento; to Dr. Lodovico Corio, Keeper of the Museo, for his kind help and advice in the choice of these portraits; to Madame Villari, who lent the three interesting photographs of Alberto and Jessie White Mario, and of Agostino Bertani; and to Capitano Ferri and the Sidoli family for the loan of the valuable portrait of Giuditta Sidoli.

CONTENTS

	PAGE
INTRODUCTION	xix

THE FIRST STRUGGLE (1830-1834)

Influence in Italy of the French Revolution—Carbonari—Mazzini's parentage and youth—First imprisonment and exile—Letter to Charles Albert—" Young Italy "—Giuditta Sidoli—Betrayal—Executions in Piedmont—Jacopo Ruffini's suicide—All exiles expelled from Marseilles—Mazzini and Signora Sidoli—Gavioli and the Paris *Moniteur*—Difficulties of correspondence.

II

VAIN ATTEMPTS . . . 21

Savoy Expedition—General Ramorino—Mazzini a foot soldier—Foresees disaster—Failure—Garibaldi—" Young Europe " (1834)—Switzerland rejects the exiles—Mazzini's mental suffering—Resigns the leadership of "Young Italy"—First months in London—Mademoiselle de Mandrot—No. 9 George Street—Death of Francesca Mazzini—Mazzini writes for *Le Monde*, the *Monthly Review*, the *Westminster*, the *Foreign Quarterly*, the *Monthly Chronicle*.

III

MAZZINI AND THE CARLYLES (1838-1840) . . 31

Acquaintance with the Carlyles—Review of the French Revolution—Letters home—The Chartists—Chelsea "too

CONTENTS

PAGE

far" from London—Mazzini's appreciation of Carlyle—John Stuart Mill—Lamennais—Carlyle and Chartism—Mazzini's views differ from Carlyle's—Working-men's Association—The *Apostolato Popolare*—Evening- and Sunday-schools—Mazzini works for the idea of One Italy—His view of Charles Albert—Changes in Mazzini's household—Harriet Martineau—To St. Paul's with Mrs. Carlyle—Mrs. Carlyle and Giovanni Ruffini—Mazzini moves to Chelsea—Mrs. Carlyle sends a keepsake to Mazzini's mother—Dr. Mazzini's uneasiness—Mazzini's reassurances—Carlyle's theory of silence — The Bullers.

IV

MAZZINI'S LIFE IN LONDON (1841–1844) .   50

Signora Mazzini and Mrs. Carlyle—Lady Byron and the school for organ-boys—Mrs. Carlyle loses her mother—Mazzini's faith in immortality — Mrs. Carlyle's surprising references to Mazzini—Lady Harriet Baring—Mazzini requires a dress-coat—Failure of Gambini's bank—Mazzini's allowance from home—Carlyle, the Barings, and Mazzini—Mazzini's letters of counsel to Mrs. Carlyle—Mazzini leaves Chelsea—He is watched by the Austrian Embassy—Attempts to break up his school—Gisquet's *Mémoires* revive the Gavioli libel—Prosecution of Gisquet—Mazzini's faith in the honour of the English Government.

V

THE BANDIERA BROTHERS (1843–1845) .   66

Mazzini's letters opened in the English Post-office—His correspondence with the Bandieras—Thomas Slingsby Duncombe gives notice of a motion in the House of Commons—Sir James Graham's admission—Lord Aberdeen the betrayer of information to Austria—Interest aroused throughout England and Scotland—England not responsible for the Bandieras' death—Nicola Fabrizi—Baron Bandiera's sons conspire—Domenico Moro—Attilio Bandiera writes to Mazzini—Treachery of Micciarelli—Attilio contrives to warn his brother and Moro—

CONTENTS

PAGE

Writes to his wife and mother—Escapes to Syria—Emilio visits his mother and sister-in-law on the eve of his escape to Corfù—Betrayal by a stewardess—Incautious letters handed by a false friend to the Austrians—Mazzini, deprecating small risings, preaches patience—Fabrizi organising a large movement—Ricciotti—Treachery in Paris—Ricciotti liberated—Reaches Corfù—Refugees embark for Calabria—A trap—Assailed and defeated—Death—Sir James Graham denounces Mazzini as an assassin—Carlyle's letter to the *Times*—Sir James Graham's *amende honorable*.

VI

WEARY WAITING (1845)   84

Mazzini's gratitude to Englishmen—Medals presented to Mr. Duncombe—Mazzini brought prominently into notice—Demands from editors for articles—English and Italian friends—Lord Ashley President of the Society for the protection of Italian boys—Joseph Cowen—Peter Taylor—An impostor deceives Dickens and Cobden—The Ashursts—Lloyd-Garrison—Caroline Ashurst Stansfeld—Emilie Ashurst Hawkes (afterwards E. A. Venturi).

VII

MAZZINI IN LONDON (1846–1847)   94

The Moderates and the Rimini insurgents—Interest felt for Italy in England—Anti Corn-law League—Peel's return to power—Russell's Ministry—Palmerston's services to oppressed nations—Mazzini and Browning's poetry—Mrs. Browning—Mazzini's feeling for the Poles—Mazzini reports Garibaldi's deeds in South America—Accession of Pius IX.—Italian enthusiasm—Attitude of Piedmont—Mazzini's New Year letter for 1847—Sir Ralph Abercromby—Metternich—Italy a "geographical expression"—Annexation of Cracow—International League—Its influence—Mrs. Milner-Gibson and the Ashursts—A successful bazaar—Grisio and Mario sing at school concert—The Pope and Charles Albert.

CONTENTS

VIII

THE EVE OF THE REVOLUTION (1847) . 112

Resentment at Austria's occupation of Ferrara—Palmerston's frank *communiqué*—His opposition to Guizot and Louis Philippe—England the disinterested friend of Sardinia—Cobden—Popular feeling in Genoa—A sequestrated letter of Mazzini's—Nino Bixio voices popular enthusiasm—Charles Albert's desire for a War of Independence—Belief in Pius IX.

IX

GEORGES SAND AND LONDON FRIENDS (1847) 121

Letter to Lizzie Biggs—Mazzini and the Ruffinis in Paris—Visit to Madame Sand—The Ashursts and Madame Sand—The affair of Favizzano—Mazzini back in London—Margaret Fuller — The Whittington Club and the Metropolitan Athenæum—Condition of Italy in 1847—The idea of Union—Mazzini's "Instructions and Methods"—His New Year letter for 1848.

X

THE GREAT REVOLUTION (1848) . 137

Milan's "Self-denying Ordinance"—Palermo's ultimatum—The Sicilian rising—Determination to regain the Constitution of 1812—Flight of the Governor—De Sauget abandons the Molo—Triumph of the revolution—Mazzini and Sicily—English interest—Louis Philippe's abdication—Mazzini in Paris—Lamartine's speech—Ledru-Rollin — Mazzini's influential position — Giovanni Ruffini—Mazzini's arrival in Milan—Cattaneo's efforts to form a Lombard army—Treatment of volunteers and of Garibaldi—Lack of military maps—Luciano Manara and Pietro Arcioni—Incapacity of the Provisional Government—False confidence—Pius IX.'s *volte face*—Its effect—Count Pompeo Litta's protest against the Government's intentions—The Plebiscite—Decree of the 12th of May—Disasters in the field.

CONTENTS

XI

THE GREAT REVOLUTION—*continued* (1848)   162

Count Casati — The question of the capital — Mazzini's neutrality—Protest against the decree of the 12th—Riotous demonstration—Democratic journals burnt—Question of the capital postponed—Appointment of a Lombard "Consulta"—Venice—"Fusion" voted — Garibaldi offers his sword to Charles Albert—Appointed head of the Volunteers in Milan—Ferrara occupied by the Austrians—Charles Albert willing to abandon Venice—Radetzky pushes his advantages—The alarmed "Consulta" summon Mazzini and Cattaneo—Defence Committee formed—Superseded by a military Commission—Mazzini joins Garibaldi's force as a foot soldier—Charles Albert enters Milan—Secret terms with Radetzky—Fury of the populace—Escape of the King—The Austrians enter Milan Garibaldi's heroic efforts and defeat.

XII

VENICE, ROME, AND SISTER CITIES (1848–1849) .   177

Radetzky—Cattaneo—Venice—Manin keeps the Austrians at bay—Palmerston and France—Kossuth supports Radetzky—Palmerston deaf to Venice's plea—Radetzky ravages Lombardy—The Pope summons Rossi to form a Ministry—Sicily appoints Settimo head of an independent Government—Death of Mazzini's father—Rossi stabbed—Pius IX. flies to Gaeta—Mazzini and Saffi—The Chartists in England—Registration of Aliens Bill—Cavaignac despatches Oudinot to receive the Pope—Garibaldi cries "Vive la Republica"—Mameli summons Mazzini to Rome—First Triumvirate—Carlo Pisacane—The Republic decides to aid Piedmont—Charles Albert's abdication—Mazzini and Garibaldi in Rome—Second Triumvirate—Garibaldi's desire to invade the Kingdom of Naples—Oudinot advances on Rome—Roman victory of April 30th—Armistice—De Lesseps—King of Naples driven to retreat—Ancona and Perugia—De Lesseps recalled to Paris—Oudinot announces that he will attack on June 4th.

CONTENTS

XIII

THE DEFENCE OF ROME (1849)   195

Mazzini's opinion—Oudinot's treachery—The night surprise of the 2nd and 3rd—Goffredo Mameli—Heroism of men and women—Pisacane's tribute to the Government—Garibaldi deprecates further "useless butchery"—His difference with Mazzini—Manara's influence—His death—Garibaldi's last effort—Death of Aguyar—The three alternatives—Garibaldi summoned to the Assembly—Cernuschi's resolution—Mazzini's protest—Carlyle's diary—Garibaldi, Anita, and about four thousand march out by the Porta San Giovanni—The Tuscans refuse them hospitality—San Marino—Garibaldi disbands his followers—Attempts to reach Venice—Betrayed by the moon—Gorzkowsky's ferocity—Death of Anita—Dom Giovanni Verità—Garibaldi imprisoned in Genoa—Mazzini's journey from Rome—Reaction general—Napoleon's dupes—Thiers—Victor Hugo—Arago—Frenchmen decree the death of the Roman Republic.

XIV

THE WEARY INTERVAL (1849-1851)   212

Ledru-Rollin and Barbès—Letters from Georges Sand to Mazzini—*L'Italia del Popolo*—Mazzini's letter to Tocqueville and Falloux—Georges Sand's estimate of the French spirit—Her adhesion to Communism—Mrs. Stansfeld visits her—Law restricting suffrage in France—Mazzini's foresight—His return to England—Hartmann's description of Mazzini—"Italian National Committee"—"European Democratic Committee" Death of Mme. Ashurst Bardon.

XV

EUROPEAN POLITICS (1850-1852) .   224

Lord Palmerston's courageous policy—The Porte and the Hungarian and Polish Exiles—Palmerston's action—Kossuth, Mazzini, and Ledru-Rollin—"The judicious Bottle-

CONTENTS

PAGE

holder"—Lord Stanley's attack on Palmerston—Death of Sir Robert Peel—General Haynau and Barclay's draymen—"The Friends of Italy"—Louis Napoleon's Coup d'État—Palmerston's dismissal.

XVI

SORROW AND GRIEF (1852-1854) . 232

Death and the galleys—Mazzini and the Socialists—Georges Sand stands by the Socialists—Mazzini's last letter to his mother—Her sudden death—Emilie Ashurst Hawkes breaks the news—Signora Mazzini's wise legacies.

XVII

THE RISE OF THE HOUSE OF SAVOY (1853) 241

Abortive insurrectionary attempt in Milan, February 6, 1853—Kossuth's Manifesto—Monarchical influence ascendant—Cavour becomes Premier—His hostility to the Mazzinian party—Garibaldi in England—The Crimean War—Piedmont a party to the peace negotiations—Garibaldi challenges Rosselli—A duel averted—Miss White accompanies Garibaldi's betrothed to Italy and Sardinia.

XVIII

MISS WHITE MAKES THE ACQUAINTANCE OF STANSFELD AND MAZZINI (1855-1856) . . 253

Ricciotti Garibaldi—Mr. Stansfeld—Pietro Fortunato Calvi—Garibaldi at Portsmouth—English Ambassadors and "Bomba's" prisoners—Felice Orsini—His escape from prison—Acclamations for Cavour—The words "British subject" held to refer to males only—Mazzini at Cedar Road.

CONTENTS

XIX

THE MARTYRS OF SAPRI (1857–1858) . 263

Mazzini in Genoa—Attempts in 1856—Letter from Garibaldi—Pisacane and Pilo—Pisacane's first venture—He goes to Sicily—Second expedition—Three days of suspense—Terrible news—Pisacane's fate—Nicotera—Miss White imprisoned—Attempts to prove her insane—Cavour appeals for an expert French *agent* to unearth Mazzini—Mazzini eludes the police—Reaches Hastings.

XX

THE SHADOW OF COMING EVENTS (1858–1860) 276

Change of Ministry in England—Orsini's attack on Louis Napoleon—Cavour at Plombières—Cavour and Garibaldi—Piedmontese-French alliance—Exiles return to be enrolled in the Piedmontese regular army—Louis Napoleon vacillates—Cavour's determination to declare war—Austria invades the Sardinian States—French army corps crosses the Alps—Mazzini morally triumphant—Napoleon suddenly resolves to end the war—He writes to the Emperor Francis Joseph—Palmerston's foresight—Diplomacy—Napoleon and Francis Joseph at Villafranca—Humiliating position of Victor Emmanuel—Cavour's fury—His resignation—Desire of the Italians for unity—Army of Central Italy—Military League to be commanded by Garibaldi and General Fanti—Both deprived of their commands—Garibaldi determines to resume revolutionary methods—Cavour again Premier—Cession of Nice and Savoy—Mazzini discovers the secret—Formal act of cession.

XXI

THE "THOUSAND" (1860–1861) 299

Crispi's work in Sicily—Rosalino Pilo—Parts played by the King and Cavour—Cavour's embarrassment—Garibaldi fixes the

CONTENTS

number of volunteers at a thousand—He starts for Sicily—His intention to invade Naples—Five days of suspense—Pilo's death after six weeks of heroic struggle which kept the way open for Garibaldi—Castelfidardo—Volturno—Garibaldi hands over eleven millions of Italians to King Victor Emmanuel.

XXII

THE KINGDOM OF ITALY   309

The Moderates and Mazzini in Naples—Garibaldi's indignation—Napoleon's petty revenges—Garibaldi elected to Parliament—February 6, 1861—Cavour's death—Rumours as to the cession of Sardinia—Lord John Russell warned—Baron Ricasoli succeeds Cavour—Lord John Russell deprecates the habit of looking upon Italy as the mere vassal of France—"Emancipation Committees."

XXIII

ROYALTY AND THE PEOPLE'S HERO   314

Garibaldi presides at the Plenary Assembly—Campanella voices the aspirations of the Democracy—The Moderates overthrow Ricasoli—Garibaldi arranges a "Dalmatian" scheme with the King and Rattazzi—He enrols volunteers—A stormy meeting at Trascorre—Arrest of certain volunteers—The people attack their prison—Garibaldi returns to Caprera—The condition of the Southern Provinces—"The eagle flies southward"—Garibaldi in Palermo—Louis Napoleon threatens to march on Rome—Victor Emmanuel orders Garibaldi's movement to be suppressed—General belief in a secret understanding between Garibaldi and the King—Garibaldi evades the Government troops and crosses into Calabria—A terrible march—A royal bullet strikes Garibaldi to the ground at Aspromonte—Mazzini and Cattaneo—Hopeless misery—Subscription in England—Dr. Parkins—Professor Zanetti extracts the bullet—Lady Palmerston's gift—Mazzini, the Greco plot, and the Moderates—Mazzini's correspondence with Victor Emmanuel only interrupted.

CONTENTS

XXIV

GARIBALDI IN ENGLAND (1864) 332

Extraordinary reception—Stay in the Isle of Wight—Entry into London—Dinner-party at Stafford House—Lord Palmerston gives an official dinner—Visit to Mazzini—Banquet of Revolutionaries—The Duke of Sutherland opportunely concerned for Garibaldi's health—Provincial tour given up—The Prince of Wales visits the General—Departure—Mazzini warns Menotti of a "friendly" scheme which Garibaldi thwarts.

EPILOGUE . . 338

INDEX . 343

LIST OF ILLUSTRATIONS

GARIBALDI (WITH DEDICATION TO MADAME MARIO)	*Frontispiece*
	FACING PAGE
JESSIE WHITE MARIO	xix
MAZZINI'S BIRTHPLACE AT GENOA	3
CARLO ALBERTO	9
(By Horace Vernet)	
GIUDITTA SIDOLI	10
(From a painting by Appiani. Lent by the Sidoli family, and here reproduced for the first time)	
JACOPO RUFFINI	14
GARIBALDI'S DEATH SENTENCE	23
MAZZINI'S MOTHER	57
NICOLA FABRIZI	69
ATTILIO BANDIERA	72
EMILIO BANDIERA	72
FACSIMILE OF MAZZINI'S HANDWRITING	88
(From a letter lent by Mrs. E. F. Richards)	
PIUS IX.	101
(From a painting by Metzmach)	
MASSIMO D'AZEGLIO	102
MAZZINI	110
(From a painting by Emilie Ashurst Venturi)	
NINO BIXIO	118
ENRICO CIALDINI	152
LUCIANO MANARA	154
UGO BASSI	154
GOFFREDO MAMELI	154

LIST OF ILLUSTRATIONS

	FACING PAGE
POMPEO LITTA	159
CATTANEO (Bust by Vela)	165
DANIELE MANIN	167
AURELIO SAFFI	185
VICTOR EMMANUEL II.	188
GIULIA CALAME MODENA	197
AGOSTINO BERTANI	200
ANITA GARIBALDI	204
NOTE OF ITALIAN NATIONAL COMMITTEE	220
ADRIANO LEMMI	222
EMILIE, YOUNGEST DAUGHTER OF W. H. ASHURST, MARRIED TO SIDNEY HAWKES, AFTERWARDS TO CARLO VENTURI	239
CAMILLO CAVOUR	243
CARLO PISACANE	270
GIOVANNI NICOTERA	270
JESSIE WHITE MARIO IN THE YEAR OF HER MARRIAGE (From a photograph kindly lent by Madame Villari)	272
ALBERTO MARIO (From a photograph kindly lent by Madame Villari)	276
BETTINO RICASOLI	282
URBANO RATTAZZI	287
FRANCESCO CRISPI	299
GARIBALDI AND MAZZINI (Taken for the Emancipation Committee)	313
MAZZINI ON HIS DEATH-BED	342
MAZZINI'S TOMB	342

JESSIE WHITE MARIO.

To face p. xiv]

INTRODUCTION

JESSIE WHITE MARIO

IN great historical events, in the memorable struggles which from time to time have taken place on the world's stage, certain personages have appeared who, though not entitled to rank among the chief actors or even the supernumeraries of the tragedy, possess a certain interest, because unconsciously their lives have been profoundly influenced by constant and intimate association with the protagonists. Though intercourse with giants of thought and of action may have biased the equanimity and objectiveness of their judgments, still their opinions are entitled to a certain amount of consideration, as explaining and justifying the irresistible fascination exercised by the great actors with whom they came in contact. The psychologist must always find a pathetic interest in examining channels of thought and sentiment through which absolute surrender of self has been attained.

Jessie White Mario was one of those figures, destined by circumstances to move in the orbit of many of the great men who have thrown an imperishable light on the epos of the Italian Resurrection—that extraordinary succession of events which still awaits its narration by an historian worthy of the lofty theme. When this long-looked-for historian does arrive, he will certainly not ignore the testimony of this remarkable woman, who seemed to blend in her character the staunch tenacity of the Anglo-Saxon race with the poetic enthusiasm of the Latin. Fate dealt somewhat cruelly

INTRODUCTION

with her, and she was doomed to be a stranger both in her adopted and in her native land, as her manners and ideas, partaking of the idiosyncrasies of the two races, made it impossible for her to be thoroughly comprehended and appreciated by either.

Born at Gosport, May 9, 1832, she was a daughter of Thomas White—eldest surviving member of the well-known family of yacht builders—and of Jane Meriton. Her mother was of American origin; her uncle, Thomas Leader Harman, being the owner of a great part of the land upon which New Orleans was built. Mr. Harman, in the early twenties, liberated all his slaves, evidently from humanitarian principles, and by his will ordered that the land he possessed should not be alienated until his youngest child should be of age. This child, Charlotte, Jessie's second cousin, was educated by the Meritons, and married Mr. Eaton, the great China-silk importer, who, in 1887, was created Lord Cheylesmore.

According to a pamphlet, issued by the "Garibaldi Unity Committee," and printed in Newcastle by Robert Todd, of the *Newcastle Chronicle*, probably in December, 1861, Jessie White was educated in various private schools, among others, in "one conducted by two kind-hearted and most respectable ladies, at Birmingham" (*sic*). It appears that these ladies, thoroughly and rigidly orthodox though they were, could not suppress the girl's innate tendencies towards freedom of thought, so she never lost an opportunity of attending the lectures of that most popular of "heretical" preachers, George Dawson, whose principles of municipal reform found, later on, in Mr. Chamberlain, a powerful and eloquent advocate. This liberty of thought naturally horrified many of Jessie's straight-laced and intensely "respectable" friends.

At the age of twenty-one, she had rendered herself independent, and was able to earn her own living by teaching and writing. About this period she went to Paris for the double purpose of learning French and supervising the education of her sisters. There she made the acquaintance

INTRODUCTION

of Henri Martin, Cousin, Lamartine, and Thierry, and, for the first time, wrote for publication. "Alice Lane; a story of Humble Life in Yorkshire" was accepted by Eliza Cook, and published in her magazine, October, 1853. Having been present at the funeral of Lamennais, by whose principles and spirit she was greatly attracted, she wrote an article about him, and also, later, one about Bèrenger, both of these studies being published in the *Biographical Magazine*. Her first attempt in the political field was a tale entitled " Brotherhood *versus* Nationality."

In 1854 a lady friend offered her the post of companion in a journey to Italy, which she accepted, and thus entered for the first time what was to be her second country. As chance willed, this lady rented for a few months the Maison Garibaldi in Nice, and there she met the hero, with whom both Jessie and her friend became so intimate that they eventually spent a month together in the mountains of the island of Sardinia. During this trip Garibaldi must have spoken much of his life in South America, and of the siege of Rome, and have expressed his hopes for Italy's future. Friendship with him evidently had a powerful influence on Miss White's destiny. It is certain that Garibaldi entertained the greatest respect for his young English friend, and, later on, it was to her care that he confided his son Ricciotti, who was a most delicate child, requiring intelligent and devoted attention.

Jessie White now visited Florence, becoming acquainted, and afterwards intimate, with Elizabeth Barrett Browning, another great Englishwoman, whose name is a household word in Italy. When she returned to England, in the spring of 1856, Paolo Fabrizi, Garibaldi's friend and physician, introduced to her Felice Orsini, who had just escaped from the dungeons of Mantua, and she undertook to translate and edit his "Memoirs," just accepted for publication by Mr. George Routledge. On this occasion she made the acquaintance of Mazzini. From the very first interview, her fate was decided: she had found her leader, and, henceforth, her unswerving allegiance was passionately

INTRODUCTION

dedicated to the great Apostle of Unity and Liberty. This devotion never swerved, and it explains and excuses all that might be considered partisan in her judgments.

From the hour of her acquaintance with Mazzini she devoted herself body and soul to his great work, and, having placed Ricciotti at a school in Liverpool, she returned the same year (1856) to Genoa, to aid Mazzini in the organisation of Pisacane's expedition to Naples. She remained there, however, only for a short time, and returned almost immediately to England. A new society of Italian sympathisers having been formed, comprising most of Mazzini's best and most faithful friends, she, with Aurelio Saffi, the ex-triumvir of Rome, was commissioned to lecture in the English provinces on the subject of Italy. Her first lecture was delivered at Derby in December, 1856, and met with remarkable success; then the death of her brother momentarily interrupted her activity. In the following year she visited Newcastle, Glasgow, Edinburgh, Paisley, &c., and in these cities a considerable sum was collected, which served to complete the ill-fated expedition of Pisacane.

Shortly after, Jessie White wrote a series of articles for the *Daily News*, entitled "Italy for the Italians," in which she expounded the views and aspirations of the National Party. Weir, the then editor of the paper, was so struck by them that he offered her the post of correspondent in Genoa. In those days such an offer being made to a woman was without precedent, so we may easily imagine how eagerly she accepted it, especially being well aware that grave events were maturing there at that time. The Genoese received her enthusiastically; when called upon to appear at the balcony of her hotel and address the cheering crowd, she characteristically advised the multitude to "reserve their strength for the coming conflict with Austria."

It was on this occasion that she met Alberto Mario. A compatriot of hers who knew her well describes her as "a handsome young woman, with a lovely complexion, and masses of shining reddish hair crowning an eager, intelligent face, and with a magnetic personality, expressive of strong

INTRODUCTION

mental power and goodness." Alberto Mario was one of the handsomest men in Italy, and was furthermore surrounded by a romantic halo of mystery, persecution, and heroism. It must assuredly have been a case of love at first sight, as they became engaged almost at once. As they were both soon afterwards imprisoned, their marriage only took place in England in December, 1857.

The Pisacane expedition, begun with inadequate means, was, from its very inception, destined to failure. Cavour, whose great genius was essentially practical and matter-of-fact, could never find an excuse for it. Leaving apart his dislike and distrust of revolutionary methods, which were quite incompatible with his duties as a minister, the neighbouring Powers were menacingly demanding the suppression of these subversive attempts, and insisting that Mazzini and his followers should be so restrained as to render them powerless to put their ideas into execution.

The conspirators had arranged a *coup-de-main*, by which they would seize the city of Genoa, the ships in the harbour, arms and ammunition, and thus give all possible assistance to Pisacane and his companions. But the plot failed, almost before it could be carried out, and hundreds were imprisoned. Jessie White, though having an English passport in perfect order, was peremptorily commanded to quit the town: she declined to do so, and appealed to the English ambassador in Turin, Sir James Hudson, not for protection, but to see that she obtained a fair trial. It seems that Sir James, whose admiration and affection for Cavour are matters of history, did not protect her sufficiently, so the young woman was placed in prison, and remained there until the end of November. Although subjected to four searching examinations, nothing was found against her, "much to the discomfiture of the Attorney-General, a silly, spiteful old man, who, incensed by her declarations that Mazzini was the greatest man and truest patriot Italy ever possessed, would have sent her to the galleys if he had dared," as the Newcastle pamphlet, already quoted, somewhat naïvely describes the events.

INTRODUCTION

She was then set free, together with almost all her companions in captivity : Mazzini and five others, all in contumacy, were condemned to death, nine to twenty, and many others again to thirteen, ten, and seven years' imprisonment. But here we must note a remarkable circumstance, as it casts a most peculiar light on the actions and intentions of Cavour. Mazzini, during all this time, had been hiding in the house of Marchese Pareto, which was repeatedly ransacked and searched by the police without any result, and he was able besides always to warn his associates. Even Saffi asks with some reason how all this blindness was possible, especially as it was well known that Mazzini left the Pareto palace with a lady of Genoa, Christina Profumo, on his arm, in full daylight, passed through the police surrounding it, and even asked one of the men for a light to his cigar. Jessie White never forgave Sir James Hudson, and still less Cavour, so the most prejudiced and partisan judgments to be found in these memoirs are those concerning the great Piedmontese statesman.

After their marriage, the Marios left for the United States, where they lectured in New York, Washington, Philadelphia, and Baltimore, obtaining considerable success. On their return to Europe, Madame Mario, as war correspondent to the New York *Times* and *Evening Post*, hastened back to Italy with her husband, but the campaign was practically over, for the famous, or rather infamous, Peace of Villafranca, had been stipulated. The Marios then went to Ferrara to be near the Venetian provinces, in which most of Alberto's relatives were living, but their revolutionary activity soon giving umbrage to the "liberal" Italian Government of the day, both were arrested by order of Colonel Cipriani at Pontelagoscuro, and imprisoned in the Castle of Ferrara. However, as nothing could be proved against them, they were conveyed by the *carabinieri*, first to Lodi, then to Milan, *en route* for the Swiss frontier.

As exiles, they remained some time in Lugano, busying themselves mostly with purely literary work ; but when

INTRODUCTION

Garibaldi's expedition of the "One Thousand" started on its adventurous and glorious enterprise, notwithstanding the orders of Cavour to General Medici, to the Governor of Cagliari in Sardinia, and to Garibaldi himself, that the Marios should not be allowed to land in Sicily, and should be sent back, they reached Palermo in safety. From that moment, Jessie White Mario dedicated all her energy to nursing the many wounded, first under Dr. Ripari, the chief of Garibaldi's medical staff, and then under Dr. Cesare Stradivari at Barcelona, in the "Convent on the Hill," where the severest cases had been gathered. The young woman's unfaltering and loving devotion to her charges was so conspicuous, that the thankful patients, quite unofficially, as their pathetically ungrammatical address is there to prove, offered to the "nurse of Garibaldi's wounded" a gold medal.

When the Garibaldian troops triumphantly arrived at Naples, after the bold landing at Pizzo, near Reggio, Calabria, in which Alberto Mario played a prominent part, the good nurse found her hands full, as there were in this city sixteen or eighteen hospitals to attend to, and means were very limited. With the help of the English Committee presided over by Lady Shaftesbury, she managed to alleviate much suffering; but however great had been her merits during the entire campaign, everything pales into insignificance beside her conduct on the memorable 1st of October (battle of the Volturno), when Jessie Mario remained thirty-six hours in the first-aid hospital, and, as related by the *Times* correspondent, made not less than fourteen journeys under fire to bring back the wounded, displaying unparalleled courage and devotion.

Thus, as it were in an apotheosis of purest light, ended what may be called the "heroic" part of Jessie White Mario's existence, and only once did she sally forth from her seclusion, in 1870, to follow Garibaldi in France, where she nursed the wounded at Dijon. Her private life, henceforward, escapes the biographer, and of it we can only say that nothing could have been more simple or more dignified.

INTRODUCTION

To the end she was compelled to make her livelihood by writing and teaching; for many years she was the Italian correspondent for English and American papers, notably the New York *Nation* and the London *Daily News*. She wrote lives of Mazzini, Garibaldi, Cattaneo, and Bertani, and several pamphlets on social questions. Unlike many of those who had taken an active part in the struggle for Italian Independence under the banner of Mazzini, she and her husband never bent their knee to the monarchy, triumphant though it was; Alberto Mario even refused to take his oath of allegiance to the King and thus lost his seat in Parliament, an example of coherence and dignity which many Republicans of the day have conveniently forgotten in order to accept from the Government high and lucrative positions.

Alberto Mario died poor and almost forgotten, and his widow was forced to teach until shortly before her death, at the "Scuola di Magistero" (Provincial Normal School) of Florence. On March 5, 1906, she died, a victim to her keen sense of duty, as, ill and feeble, she insisted upon resuming her work, notwithstanding the entreaties of her friends and medical advisers. According to her testamentary dispositions, she was cremated, and, with a purely civil ceremony, her ashes were transported to Lendinara and placed beside those of her husband. All the authorities were present, and Professor Pasquale Villari pronounced an eloquent speech on the occasion. By a remarkable and pathetic coincidence, her funeral cortège passed before "Casa Guidi," decorated with flowers and banners for the inauguration of a memorial to her dear friend and companion in the love of Italy, Elizabeth Barrett Browning.

Carducci said in his "Confessioni e Battaglie" that Jessie White Mario was "a great woman, to whom we Italians owe a great debt," and it is shameful that Italy made no attempt to sweeten and console the failing years of the stranger who had sacrificed so much for its Independence. In the frantic rush of the twentieth century, in its mad chase after material enjoyment, her figure seems vague and

INTRODUCTION

shadowy, out of place and out of time. But if one day those who know not how to forget, and who keep sacred in their hearts the cult of the glorious past of Italy, in striking contrast to its actual political degradation and lack of high ideals moral and social, erect one day a monument to her memory, no pompous inscription should mar its pedestal. Her name alone would be the greatest homage to the woman who accomplished her unrequited labour of love with simplicity and in silence.

Before closing this brief Introduction, it is advisable to state that we do not indiscriminately endorse all the opinions of the writer. We have no polemical or political intent in view, and have accepted the honour and responsibility of editing these papers, with the sole aim of presenting to the public what we conscientiously consider a living and precious record of the most striking event of the nineteenth century, the Liberation and Unification of Italy.

LITTA VISCONTI ARESE.

BIRTH OF MODERN ITALY

I

THE FIRST STRUGGLE

1830–1834

Influence in Italy of the French Revolution—Carbonari—Mazzini's parentage and youth—First imprisonment and exile—Letter to Charles Albert—"Young Italy"—Giuditta Sidoli—Betrayal—Executions in Piedmont—Jacopo Ruffini's suicide—All exiles expelled from Marseilles—Mazzini and Signora Sidoli—Gavioli and the Paris *Moniteur*—Difficulties of correspondence.

AN appreciation of those early movements which, with a rapidity of result unprecedented in the world's history, culminated in the unification of Italy, is only possible to those who are acquainted with the conditions of Europe on the morrow of the great French Revolution. It is a striking and peculiar fact that events, comparatively so recent that a man of eighty could easily have been an eye-witness of some of them, may appear as remote as occurrences of centuries ago. This is partly due to the rapid rate at which we live, and partly to the fact that the sentiments which inspired those ideals were caused by a huge convulsion in the social and political body, the effects of which, though for some purposes permanent and lasting, have, on the whole, given proportionately poor ethical results.

The victorious armies of Napoleon I., in their triumphal marches over Europe, had been the most powerful agents in the dissemination of the principles of the French Revolution: their action in Italy was especially potent because of old republican traditions lurking in the obscure sub-

THE BIRTH OF MODERN ITALY

stratum of the popular consciousness, and fanned to a greater intensity by the foundation of the Ligurian, Cisalpine, Parthenopean, and Etrurian Republics. This culminated in the resurrection of the Kingdom of Italy—a name unheard since Arduino of Ivrea[1] in the eleventh century—and the coronation of Napoleon with the Iron Crown of the old Longobard kings. The Emperors of Germany and of Austria had often styled themselves "Kings of the Romans," but the genius of Napoleon called to a new life the long-forgotten appellation. Thus a great number of the historic landed aristocracy accepted positions and honours at the Court of the "King of Italy," and "Italy" became later the battle-cry of thousands of heroes, the green-white-red flag of the new monarchy having received in the campaign of Russia its glorious baptism of fire.

This kingdom created by Napoleon was as meteoric as his own career, and when he fell, everything apparently returned to the *statu quo ante*. But the seed that had been sown had taken deeper root than the shrewd diplomats of the Congresses of Paris and Vienna—Metternich and Talleyrand not excepted—ever imagined. The veteran officers of the "Great Emperor," abruptly dismissed on half-pay, and with the rank and file returning to their homes, resorted in self-defence to conspiracy and propaganda, for they found themselves the butt of police persecution and in danger of being murdered by an ignorant rabble instigated by the fanaticism of clergy who were tools of the Jesuits. From this sprang the Carbonari Association, organised in *vendite* or lodges, and widely distributed all over Italy. In 1821 this work of propaganda was so successful that a plot, having ramifications in the entire Peninsula, broke out in Romagna. The Romagnoli, a strong, bold, proud, independent race, ill supported the corrupt and tyrannical Papal Government and rose in arms against it. Unable to withstand the popular revolt, the Papal Government immediately appealed to Austria, and Metternich, only too pleased at the opportunity of extending Austria's hegemony

[1] Arduino, Marquis of Ivrea, last Italian "King of Italy" (1002–1012).

MAZZINI'S BIRTHPLACE AT GENOA.

over the rest of Italy, immediately sent a strong army to "restore order." Bologna, Imola, Ravenna, Forli, Rimini, and other cities were militarily occupied, and the spies and "judicial commissions" began their tragic work on the patriots.

This insurrection gave rise to conspiracies and agitations all over the country; in Piedmont, even a prince of the Royal house, Carlo Alberto di Savoia Carignano, not far removed from succession to the throne if the Salic law were respected, was undoubtedly aware of the movement, though perhaps he did not actually take part in it; in Lombardy, men of high position and great intellectual value, such as Confalonieri,[1] Pellico,[2] Montanelli,[3] and others, were arrested, condemned to death, and being reprieved, sent for years to the horrid dungeons of Spielberg.[4] Henceforth, no year passed without bringing its contingent of martyrs to a cause the popularity of which was fostered by the blood of the best and of the noblest.

No city in the whole of Italy was more imbued with liberal and republican ideas than Genoa, and it was there, on June 22, 1805, that Giuseppe Mazzini, the purest hero of the Italian "Risorgimento," was born. His father, Dr. Giacomo Mazzini, Professor in the University, was an earnest and rather stern personality; his mother, Maria, née Drago, a woman of high moral virtue and great intellect, educated him with unceasing care, because as a child, he was especially delicate and sensitive. At fifteen he entered the University with the intention of studying medicine, but he soon found that his highly impressionable

---

[1] Confalonieri, Conte Federico (1776-1846), attempted to raise a Revolution in Lombardy in 1821; was condemned to death, respited, and imprisoned in the fortress of Spielberg. Later was for two years exiled in America and died in exile in Switzerland.

[2] Pellico, Silvio (1788-1854), patriot, writer, and poet, author of "Le Mie Prigioni," implicated in Confalonieri's movement, condemned to death, respited, and for nine years a prisoner in the Spielberg.

[3] Montanelli, companion to Pellico in the Spielberg.

[4] Spielberg, fortress in Moravia, famous for its dungeons, in which many Italian and Hungarian patriots have languished.

nature could not withstand the ordeal of the dissecting-room and the operating table. So he decided to study law, and in 1827 took his degree. He was only sixteen when his soul was for the first time stirred by the impulse of patriotism: he saw his native city literally thronged with gaunt and famished fugitives, escaping from all parts of Italy, forced into exile for having taken part in the Revolution of 1821. In 1827 he was affiliated to the "Carboneria" and at once dedicated all his energies to the ends of the Association. He also contributed to a small Genoese paper, the *Indicatore Genovese*, originally destined for trade and shipping advertisements. His articles, however, soon attracted the attention of the Censors, and the paper was summarily suppressed. He then went to Leghorn, and together with Carlo Bini [1] and Guerrazzi,[2] founded the *Indicatore Livornese*, which also purported to be a trading and advertising medium. This paper, however, having aroused suspicion, was suspended by the Tuscan police. He next travelled through Tuscany as an emissary of the Carboneria, doing excellent work as a propagandist, and acquainting himself thoroughly with the condition and aspirations of the people.

When he returned to Genoa, a traitor, Cottin, denounced him to the Piedmontese Government as a dangerous agitator, and he was imprisoned at Savona. However, notwithstanding the strictest researches, nothing could be proved against him and after about six months he was liberated, being given the choice between confinement in a small village of Piedmont and exile. He unhesitatingly chose the latter, and on January 10, 1830, young Joseph Mazzini passed through Turin and crossed the Alps radiant with hope and energy, for central Italy was in Revolution, and no doubt was entertained as to the sympathy of France for oppressed

[1] Bini, Carlo (1806-1842), born at Leghorn, distinguished patriot and writer.

[2] Guerrazzi, Domenico (1804-1873), great patriot and writer, born at Leghorn. His novels, "L'Assedio di Firenze," "Beatrice Cenci," "Veronica Cybo," &c., were considered "as so many victories over the oppressors of Italy."

1831] ACCESSION OF CHARLES ALBERT

nationalities. Was not Lafayette the chief mover in the "three days"—were not Guizot, whose historical lessons, and Cousin, whose philosophy was founded on the doctrine of progress—the teachers of their youth—now the leading men of France? On arriving at Lyons he found that an expedition into Savoy (which formed part of a new conspiracy in Turin to wring a constitution from Charles Felix) had been dispersed by the prefect of Lyons, but the revolution in central Italy seemed triumphant, so giving the slip to his uncle, who had him in charge, he went to Marseilles with some of the exiles of 1821, and arriving in Corsica, joined the "2,000 Corsicans and exiles who were to sail for Ancona." But there were no means of embarkation, and when he returned to Marseilles the city was crowded with fugitives, victims of their own mistake in trusting to the non-intervention proclaimed by France, instead of uniting all the forces of the provinces in revolution and calling upon the rest of Italy to make common cause with them. Meanwhile, just as Charles Felix had commenced the military trials of the new conspirators—among whom were some future notabilities: Brofferio,[1] Cadorna,[2] Durando,[3] Ribotti[4]—the King died and the Prince of Carignano, Charles Albert, the conspirator of 1821, succeeded to the throne (1831). Being fully aware that the conspiracy had been "Albertist and Constitutional," he refused permission to the Special Committee to continue their researches. The belief in Charles Albert's intention to wage war against Austria and to grant a constitution was universal. Among the papers of Jacopo Ruffini were found

---

[1] Brofferio, Angelo (1802–1866), Piedmontese writer, statesman, and jurist, took part in the Revolution of 1821, and was later one of the chiefs of the Democratic party, adverse to Cavour.

[2] Cadorna, Conte Carlo (1809–1891), Piedmontese statesman; constitutional monarchist; Italian ambassador in London, 1868–1875. Afterwards President of the Council of State in Italy.

[3] Durando, General Giacomo (1807–1894), Piedmontese officer and statesman, belonged in his youth to the "Giovane Italia."

[4] Ribotti, Admiral, distinguished sailor and Minister of Marine, born in Nice, also belonged in his youth to the "Giovane Italia."

notes of a letter calling upon him to fulfil pledges which, as a prince, he had been unable to redeem. Pecchio,[1] from Brighton, and other exiles of 1821, appealed to their fellow-countrymen to rally to his standard. Mazzini was but the voice of the community when he addressed his letter to Charles Albert, with the motto adopted by the Sicilian patriots after the "Vespers," "SE No, No."

The endless discussions as to whether Mazzini wrote that celebrated letter in "good faith" seem to us absurd. Profoundly convinced that no revolution could be successful until the multitudes should be permeated with a spiritual sense of their rights and duties, Mazzini was no visionary. That Italy could, must, and should be created was his conviction, and that material instruments were necessary was obvious. How else could Austria, encamped in Lombardy and dominating the whole Peninsula, be ousted? Charles Albert had an army, the Piedmontese and the Genoese hated Austria; the Central Provinces, now crushed by her intervention, thirsted for revenge. Mazzini had studied every line of the Piedmontese Revolution, and he could not therefore attribute its failure to Charles Albert's desertion. Of effective betrayal he never accused him, nor could any one reasonably do so for had he betrayed the conspirators before the action commenced the King (Victor Emmanuel I.) would have had them arrested—had he betrayed them afterwards, Austria would not have waited an entire year to arrest Confalonieri and the other Lombard conspirators, whose actions were discovered by accident. The failure was clearly due to the incapacity of the military leaders, who, after the Constitution was proclaimed, were unable to hold their own against the troops who remained loyal, before the Austrians came upon the scene (April, 1821). The fact that Charles Albert had fought against the Liberals at the Trocadero was easily accounted for, as he desired to become King

---

[1] Pecchio, Conte Giuseppe (1785-1835), born in Milan, conspired with Confalonieri, exiled in England, was professor at York, and later at Brighton, where he died.

of Piedmont, and naturally did all in his power to frustrate Austria from transferring the crown to the Duke of Modena, whose wife was the daughter of old King Victor. Mazzini knew Charles Albert to be ambitious, and the moment seemed auspicious, for Louis Philippe had not yet shown himself in his true colours, Poland was not yet crushed, Belgium was in arms against Holland. If Charles Albert would only dare, he must win. Every one believed in him; it was certain that no other plan for ousting Austria would be listened to until he had made manifest his intentions. And it was at least well that he should be aware that if his plans led to a crusade against the Austrians he would not lack devoted followers. Referring to the past, Mazzini writes:—
"Fate was the only traitor. We are anxiously waiting to see if the King will maintain the promises of the Prince." The picture of the times is a faithful one:—
"The battle is commenced between the old world and the new, between the despots, fighting for the maintenance of their usurped dominions, and the people, conscious of their rights, of their centuries of slavery and of suffering, resolute to undergo active martyrdom, but never again to slavishly submit. The people remember their past glories. You ascend a throne that has no prestige of glory, no solemn memories to make it venerated or feared. . . . What will you do, Sire? Two paths are opened to you, two systems between which despotism still oscillates, represented by two powers: Austria and France, with one of which Piedmont will be called to ally herself. . . . Austria represents crime, blood, terror. An alliance with Austria will compel you to be and to act as a monster, to live and die a tyrant, to bandage your eyes and advance, brandishing your sword to right and to left, to drop the mask of a man and steep yourself in blood. The second system, that of concessions, is no longer available, is a mere postponing of the evil moment. The people are bent on liberty, independence, and union, with guarantees for

their permanence; they have faith in their power to acquire these, given a favourable opportunity. Can things last in France? Are the corpses of ten thousand martyrs to serve as the footstool of seven Ministers? Périer, Sire, has signed a bond with infamy, not with eternity! But the French Nation has not signed that bond; the French Nation, with its blood, has signed its alliance with the people."

All the first part of the letter is reasoned out coldly and logically. Then, when the writer thinks of what might be the future of Italy and of Charles Albert if he would "dare to do," he warms to his subject. There is a third ally, the Italian people; a crown, nobler and costlier than the crown of Piedmont, for which he has but to stretch out his hand: the crown of Italy—engemmed with twenty centuries of historical glory—the land of genius, endowed with natural defences, peopled with sturdy hearts, ready to follow to the death a leader against the foreigner. "Have you studied this people, realised its glorious destinies? Despite the servitude which bows it down, it is great with instinctive life, with the light of intellect, by the energy of its passions, now fierce and blind because circumstances have afforded it no ennobling vent, but resolute and indomitable, for even misfortune has not extinguished its hopes. These are the elements that form nations. Does not the idea of creating a nation from these elements inspire you to the work which will enable you to say: 'Italy is happy and she is mine!'— to hear twenty freed millions cry: 'God is in Heaven, Charles Albert on Earth'? Sire, you have dreamt this dream and the blood boiled in your veins; for this idea you conspired, nor need to blush in remembrance. Times were adverse then, they are more favourable now. Italy awaits your call, one word suffices to make her yours; throw down the glove to Austria, turn your back on France, bind Italy in one unity of combatants. Place yourself at the head of the Nation, write upon your banner: Union, Liberty, Independence. Proclaim the

CARLO ALBERTO.

(By Horace Vernet.)

To face p 9]

sanctity of ideas, declare yourself the champion of the rights of the People, the regenerator of Italy. Free Italy from the Barbarians! Build up her future! Give your name to a Century! Become the Napoleon of Italian Liberty! It is a general belief that kings have nothing in common with Humanity, and History confirms that belief. Disprove it! Act so that beneath the names of Washington and Kosciuszko—citizens born—shall be written: 'There is a name greater than these, there is a throne built by twenty millions of free men; on its base is inscribed: To CHARLES ALBERT BORN A KING, ITALY REBORN BY HIM.' ."

Here follow minute particulars of the forces existing in Italy, of the indomitable, universal will to do or die. Should Charles Albert fail to seize his opportunity, other leaders will arise; to him will remain Napoleon's remorseful cry: " I have rejected the idea of the age, and I have lost everything! . . . "

Charles Albert read the letter and ordered that the writer should be prevented from crossing the frontier. Mazzini, who had judged rightly in assuming that the aspirations of the Prince's youth were still latent in his soul, had no knowledge of his strangely complicated nature, swift to conceive, irresolute in carrying out his conceptions, overpowered by mystical, supernatural terrors, and at times completely subjected to the Jesuits, whose one object was to keep Piedmont in thrall so that with Austria, the Pope, and the Bourbons, Italy should remain subjected to the hierarchy of the altar and the throne. Neither did he take into account the influence of ten years of misery, of the hatred engendered in Charles Albert's unforgetting nature by the insults poured upon him by the revolutionists and conspirators of 1821, who had chosen the *esecrato Carignano*[1] as the scapegoat who was to bear the burden of their follies, their incapacity and their cowardice. Charles Albert hated Austria

---

[1] *Esecrato Carignano*, "execrated Carignano," was the name applied to Charles Albert by the Italian revolutionary poet, Berchet, in an ode on the Revolution of 1821 which became famous.

with undying hatred; ambition and pride, not unmixed with a sense of his Italianhood, kept alive his resolve to free Italy from her yoke, but this he would do as a king, a king by Right Divine; never by the aid of rebels; never by alliance with the Revolution.

Meanwhile Austria, with the tacit consent of France, crushed the Revolution in the Central Provinces (1833) and exiles by the hundred thronged Marseilles and Switzerland, there to consider the causes of their failure and to prepare for a renewal of the combat.

Very soon an Association called "Young Italy," instituted by Mazzini in 1831 with the aim of replacing Carbonarism, which for many reasons had ceased to be a useful and active force, was able to number its adherents by the thousand. In Genoa, Jacopo and Giovanni Ruffini, Federico Rosazza and Campanella, and in Tuscany, Carlo Bini, were the active chiefs. Mazzini, the beloved and revered head of the Association, fearing no failure, believing not only in the ultimate but in the speedy realisation of his "idea," enjoyed for once the happiness of loving and of being beloved. With the first band of exiles from Modena had come a youth, Lamberti, and the one woman whom Mazzini grew to wholly love—*dum vivimus et ultra*—and whose sole rival in his heart was Italy, the supreme sovereign of his being. This lady, Giuditta Ballerio, of Milan, beautiful as Appiani's brush depicted her, had been married at fifteen to Giovanni Sidoli, a Reggian patriot who, being condemned to death by the Duke of Modena, had fled with his young bride and infant to France, where he died, leaving her a widow with four little children. She immediately returned to Reggio, where the Duke, hoping to supplant Charles Albert and thus to unite the whole of Northern Italy under his sceptre, had masked his hatred under a feigned conversion to liberal measures. The beautiful and enthusiastic Giuditta remained faithful to the principles for which her husband had lived and died, and for which her only brother had also been condemned to death.

She became the soul of the patriotic movement in Reggio,

GIUDITTA SIDOLI.

(From a painting by Appiani lent by the Sidoli family, and here reproduced for the first time)

and in 1831 it had its headquarters in her house. When the Revolution had been crushed and the false Duke had executed his too-trusting accomplice, Ciro Menotti,[1] "la Giuditta," leaving her children with her father-in-law, fled with numerous other conspirators, and accompanied by her faithful friend, Lamberti. Arriving in Marseilles, she enthusiastically embraced the doctrines of " Young Italy," being swept the more completely into their current because of the overwhelming passion with which she felt suddenly inspired for " Young Italy's " chief.

All those who knew Mazzini at that time of his life speak of his exceeding beauty. Enrico Mayer, the Tuscan educator, dwells on the freshness of his clear olive complexion, shaded by long black hair, the chiselled delicacy of his regular and beautiful features, his noble forehead, his sweet, though vivacious, expression of steadfast resolution and inflexible determination, and the bright flashes of his dark eyes, as all combining to render him the "most beautiful being, male or female, he had ever seen." So his college friends spoke of him. So Campanella,[2] grim and stern, would describe him, adding that his humour was unsurpassed and constituted one of his principal charms. His convictions were so intense that he easily inspired others with them ; in fact, the fascination of the man was irresistible. The very *connotati* on his passport confirm the general testimony. Small wonder that this man who, besides his personal fascination, was the exponent of that idea to which Giuditta had from childhood devoted herself and for which she was suffering exile from home and separation from her children, should have won her love, and have given in return the rare treasure of his own. Mazzini's studious life, his concentration on one idea, had saved him from those light

[1] Menotti, Ciro (1788–1831), born near Modena, patriot and martyr, condemned to death and executed by the orders of the Duke of Modena, who had infamously lured him to his death.

[2] Campanella, Federico (1804-1884), patriot and writer. Took part in all the Italian Conspiracies beginning in 1821, and remained to the end an uncompromising Republican. He reformed and reorganised Italian Freemasonry.

attachments which weaken the root of love; so for Giuditta was reserved the treasure of his virgin soul, and this he poured out to her during the year and a half they spent together in Marseilles. Love, in their case, far from proving a hindrance to their work, redoubled the powers they dedicated to the redemption of that land to which both were so self-sacrificingly devoted. Mazzini felt no jealousy of his friend's past, and he was prepared to love her children, orphaned for Italy's sake, hoping that in a free country they would be able to reap the fruits of his sacrifice, and mature them. No doubts then beset the young leader: he felt as certain of success as did Moses, and believed that he would get more than a Pisgah view of the Promised Land into which he wished to lead his people. If he should fall fighting, death would, he believed, open up a new life, where fresh work would await him, the connection with life " here-down " (*quaggiù*) being not entirely severed, for faith in immortality was not an instinctive, but an intellectual certainty for him.

Giuditta and Lamberti acted as chiefs of Mazzini's staff, and later as his best and most active agents. After the decree of expulsion promulgated by the French Government, he decided to risk remaining in Marseilles, hidden in the home of Domenic Ollivier, father of the Emile Ollivier who was to be the last Prime Minister of Napoleon III.

Until April, 1833, all the schemes of " Young Italy " seemed to prosper. Its publications and its journal (bearing the name of the Association) flooded the Peninsula. Arms and ammunition were smuggled into the Italian seaports, and a general rising was being organised in every province. The rallying cry of the insurrection was to be: " Italy, one, free and independent." The first aim was to get rid of Austria and all its satellites. Charles Albert was to be invited to put himself at the head of the movement, and if he refused he was to be forcibly accompanied to the frontier and expelled. If the uprising should achieve its aim the nation was to be called upon to name representatives to a " Constituent Assembly." Republican propaganda was advised, but on no account would a republic be imposed upon a people freed by their own unaided valour.

The influential positions, the names, the numbers of the party, afford ample proof, not only of the possibility but of the probability that success awaited them. But while the exiles and their correspondents in Italy believed their secret intact, spies had been actively at work. A box, with a secret receptacle, sent from Marseilles, was detained at the Custom House in Genoa, and the documents it contained, including the secret cipher and its key, were read and copied by the Piedmontese police. The contents were then carefully replaced in the box, which was despatched to Andrea Gambini, the friend of the Mazzinis to whom it had been addressed, and by him it was consigned to Mazzini's mother. But as soon as Charles Albert was in possession of the copies, he sent them to his brother-in-law, Archduke Rainieri, Viceroy of the "Lombardo Veneto," and in recent years these copies have been found in the State Archives of Milan. Published in 1884, they have solved a very vexed question.

At first, no great importance was attached by Charles Albert and the Archduke to the discovery, but the frontier was well guarded and spies set to watch all suspected persons. It was not until a mere chance revealed the extent of the propaganda in the army that Charles Albert realised the gravity of the danger. In that army, which he was organising so carefully—secretly hoping, it cannot be doubted, that he would lead it at some future day against his ancient foe—there were men who, under Napoleon, had fought, conquered, and humiliated Austrian battalions, and who later had conspired for the renewal of the crusade. Were they now preparing to re-enact the past, under another leadership than his own—under revolutionary chiefs? The bare suspicion filled his soul with fury. He became for a moment "the monster; rushed ahead blindfold, brandishing his sword right and left."

The attempt to whitewash Charles Albert and lay the blame of the Piedmontese massacres on Jesuits, Generals, and reactionary Ministers, is absurd. He was an absolute sovereign and used his power to the uttermost. None dared to advise or to oppose him.

Complete silence was maintained until it seemed that words were ripening into action. Precisely because of the propaganda in the army, the chiefs of the movement, and especially Dr. Jacopo Ruffini, Mazzini's fervent co-operator, his *alter-ego* in Genoa, had warned him that action must commence immediately or the secret would no longer remain such. "Not yet, the Southern Provinces are unprepared," was the advice given verbally to Ruffini at the frontier (by Lamberti?). "We must act or we are lost," Ruffini replied, and this answer was taken back to the chief, who redoubled his efforts to get the Southern Provinces into line.

Suddenly at midnight, hundreds of arrests were made in all the provinces of Piedmont; terror and desolation spread in every family. Then the Government organs, inventing unthought-of horrors, affirmed that the conspiracy, vast and deep, had for its object the extinction of the Royal family. They suggested that the Royal palace was undermined, that the barracks were to be blown up, the wells poisoned; that the banks and the palaces of the wealthy were to be pillaged, the army disbanded, and that anarchy would reign supreme. A special Military Commission was created in Turin towards the end of April, 1833. Its members vied with each other in seconding the King's commands. He resolved to strike before the conspirators could begin to act. He was not willing, for obvious reasons, to bring his army into contact with the populace, but, martial law having been proclaimed, the military tribunals were ordered to make short shrift of a sufficient number of conspirators to serve as an example to the rest. Between the 22nd of May and the 22nd of July, twelve young men, against whom nothing could be proven excepting that they had read publications of "Young Italy," were tortured to induce revelations, and, as they could not or would not reveal anything, they were, "after invocation of Divine aid," condemned to ignominious death and at once publicly executed.

JACOPO RUFFINI.

But Charles Albert was not satisfied with these executions. He considered the example insufficient to subalterns, as those hitherto condemned were only civilians and non-commissioned officers. Effisio Tola, a lieutenant in the 1st Infantry, was therefore condemned to death and shot "for having been seen with seditious books in his hands" and " for not denouncing the same to his superiors."

Charles Albert was successful. Prisons and fortresses were crowded and terror reigned throughout his dominions, though, fortunately, many of the real leaders escaped. Spies freely mixed with the prisoners, many of whom, to escape moral and physical tortures, either revealed what they knew or invented fables to save their lives.

Austria rejoiced ; though aware that her Italian subjects were hostile to her rule and that although many wealthy Lombards had crossed over to Switzerland numberless "suspects" still remained in Venice and Lombardy, not one single arrest was made by her, for political reasons, in 1833. And though many had been condemned to death for previous revolutions, not a single sentence had been executed. Charles Albert was now doing all that severity could do to inculcate fear of the results of plots and rebellions, so Austria, with subtle policy, saw that she might afford to be clement.

When the arrests began under Charles Albert, Jacopo Ruffini gave swift and peremptory instructions that all affiliated to "Young Italy" should seek refuge without delay in France or Switzerland, and he was obeyed by those reasonably fearing arrest ; but, though urged by his anguished mother and friends to practise what he preached, he himself refused to fly, saying that "he, the standard-bearer, must hold the flag aloft or fall with it in his grasp." Arrested early in May, it would seem that the high position of his father—a stern magistrate—and of his many friends induced his judges to treat him leniently, in the hope of obtaining revelations. He had one trusted confidant who had received numerous benefits from his family, and who alone was in possession of the real secrets of the plot and of

THE BIRTH OF MODERN ITALY

the key to the cipher used with Mazzini and changed every month. This Dr. Castagnino, unsuspected till long after Mazzini's death, turned traitor, revealed everything, and was allowed to escape unnoticed. When the judges had failed to obtain any revelations from Jacopo, they placed before him a document in which every fact and project of the conspiracy was detailed, the key to the last cipher given, and names hitherto unsuspected written out in full. Ruffini recognised the signature as Mazzini's, saw, though probably with instinctive incredulity, ostensible proof that his own familiar friend had betrayed him, and simply said to the judge: "You shall have my answer to-morrow." Next day he was found by the gaoler dead, weltering in blood on the floor of his cell. Upon the wall, with that blood, was written: "This is my answer. To my brethren the vengeance."

Doubt has been cast on Jacopo's suicide; his elder brother, Ottavio, chose to believe he had been murdered. But there was no motive for such a crime; and the judge had expected "revelations" on the morrow. The gaoler who found him dead, took from his finger a ring that had been given to him by the beautiful Laura de' Negri, and restored it to her, describing the suicide as committed with "a bit of iron torn from the door and sharpened on the stones"; telling also of the words written on the wall. Ottavio, remembering his mother's anguish when her other son Vittorio had killed himself, perhaps did his utmost to spare her this second trial; but no evidence has ever been brought to invalidate the truth of the first account.

The effect of Jacopo's suicide on Mazzini was so terrible that Giuditta and Lamberti feared for his reason—even for his life. That he was eventually saved is due to them, but the iron had entered into his soul never to be withdrawn, for nothing could remove from his mind the certainty that his own signature had been forged, and that his first, dearest, most trusted and most trusting friend, believing him the betrayer, had, fearing to be overcome and turn traitor also, desperately ended a life void of all trust and hope, a life which, shorn of these, would be worse than worthless.

Within a month of Jacopo's death his bereaved mother arrived in Marseilles with her youngest son Agostino, and was led by Giuditta to Mazzini's retreat. Her other son, Giovanni, who though condemned to death had escaped through his eldest brother, Ottavio, allowing himself to be arrested by "mistake," joined them almost immediately.

Misfortune, however, seldom comes alone. All exiles were ordered to quit Marseilles at once, and many set sail for America. The Prefect, who had hitherto chosen to ignore Mazzini's hiding-place, now warned Ollivier that his guest had better depart, as he was compelled to order his arrest. Change of residence being indifferent to Mazzini and the projected expedition into Savoy being more easily organised and effected from Switzerland than from Marseilles, he decided to go there (1833).

But to add to his troubles, news came that Giuditta's only son was perilously ill; nevertheless that she would not be allowed to enter Modena, nor, indeed, to set foot in Italy at all without danger. That she resolved then and there to run the risk is evident from a note she wrote to Mazzini's mother, though in order to see him safely into Switzerland, and also probably to throw the police off their guard, she delayed her attempt for some weeks. Maria Mazzini advised her son to go to England, and in his letter to her' of the 28th of June of that year he gives his reasons for refusing:—

"Heaven knows if I would content you! . . . I feel all your anxiety, but, believe me, I cannot. I should die were I to go far from Italy. All my passions, inflamed by the horrible catastrophes that have overtaken me, are centred there and compel me to remain near. But do not exaggerate the danger. I have strong supporters, and will be well informed. Despite all their researches, I remained a whole year undiscovered. The French Government has just made a raid in rue Choiseuil, and found a Masini, a musical composer, another in Usiglio's house in Marseilles, where I had never set foot; other searches were made in Lyons . 'fiasco' all along the line."

Giuditta's note says :—

"In a moment of bitterness such as this of my separation from Pippo, I feel the need of turning to you, and to your promise of affection. I did not answer (before ?), but the discourtesy was merely apparent ; tenderness, deep tenderness filled my heart. Remember me and love me. I love you and shall never forget you. I did not write because Pippo forbade me to tell you the truth about his health, and I had not the heart to betray the trust you have in me and to deceive you. Now, though terribly weak, Pippo is a little better, but he has need of the utmost care ; he will recover. The affection of his friends, whom he calls 'brothers,' and of their mother [the Signora Ruffini and her sons] will be a substitute for other affections, and will aid him to bear up under such heavy misfortunes. It is a comfort to me in this enforced separation to see him surrounded by them. The *singulti* [sobs, probably the consequence of his nervous prostration] are growing rather less. I do not however think that the climate of England would be beneficial. On the contrary, I believe that it would be most hurtful, physically and morally. I embrace you with deep affection.—GIUDITTA."

The efforts of the French Government to possess themselves of Mazzini's person failing, they forged their first calumny, which was destined to pursue him to the end. In October, 1832, a certain Emiliani had been attacked and wounded at Rhodez, in the Department of Aveyron. In the spring of 1833 this same Emiliani and another refugee, Lazzareschi, were mortally wounded by one Gavioli. The Paris *Moniteur* invented a sentence of death, said to be signed by Mazzini and Cecilia, respectively President and Secretary of an imaginary "Secret Tribunal of Young Italy." This sentence, teeming with orthographic and grammatical errors, could have deceived no one. Mazzini, through his French friends, protested, challenging the *Moniteur* to produce the original of the sentence. No notice whatever was taken of his protests, and, in the meanwhile, the Tribunal of Rhodez gave its verdict, viz., that the crime had been committed by Gavioli, without premeditation, in a drunken brawl. In spite of this the *Moniteur* kept silent, and as Mazzini thought that sentence sufficient, the matter dropped. But, as we shall see, this sentence was ignored, while later on the calumny was revived and twice repeated in the British Parliament (1844 and 1864) in order to degrade Mazzini in the eyes of the civilised world.

Then his separation from Giuditta took place. To his mother Mazzini writes :—

"She left me the day after she wrote to you. This separation is to me a bitter grief. But it is better so. There are times when I could have wished that even you were not left to me. I longed to make you all happy, and I have made all miserable, myself, first of all, but for myself I care not. What hurts me is that I may in the course of my life be compelled to bring other sorrows on those whom I love. Life is a chain, and one action is linked to another, as links in a chain."

Their old friend, Andrea Gambini, refusing to act any longer as intermediary in the correspondence between mother and son, their difficulties increased, and Mazzini, anxious to know "who had been arrested and who had escaped," was obliged to address his mother as his "aunt." The Signora Mazzini evidently urged her son to marry Giuditta, for he answered :—

"Your wish, if it were possible of realisation, would form the greatest consolation of my life. But it is impossible, believe me, it is impossible for me to be happy or to make others happy. But I love her, love her truly ; it is something, after all, in my isolation to be able to love and to know myself beloved. . Write to her : she is wretched ; a line of love from you will do her good."

In another letter, he tells his mother that "la Giuditta is committing an act of real madness, so that I . . . am in constant alarm."

Poor Giuditta ! When she heard of the illness of her

boy she was "delirious for a whole night," then, though that danger passed, she resolved to get back her children at any cost, and for this purpose went under another name through Italy to Reggio, where she demanded of the Duke permission to see them. But her father-in-law, entirely under the influence of the Jesuits, had them and their fortune in his possession, and as he hated his daughter-in-law he thwarted all her attempts. She was forbidden to set foot in Modena; orders for her arrest were out and she had to take refuge in Tuscany, from whence, after a brief arrest in her own house, she escaped by the help of the British Consul in Florence. She wandered to Naples, then to Rome, then back to Parma, pleading, threatening all in vain. Once she wrote to the Duke of Modena: "I will pass the gates: I will see my children, arrest me if you choose." For one half day she succeeded. Then her boy was placed in the military college directed by the Jesuits, and the girls in a convent. In the Archives of Modena we found letters, running through the years from 1836 to 1842, imploring permission to visit them. She generally seems to have succeeded in doing so about twice a year, until the father-in-law died; then she obtained her heart's desire. The children idolised her, and she brought them up in their father's and her lover's faith. To the latter she wrote constantly, generally through his mother, often purposely leaving him without her address when she was in "dangerous" quarters.

They loved deeply, faithfully, but each had a rival in the heart of the other. The children reigned supreme in hers, Italy in his. They never met again till 1849 in Florence, when Giuditta gave Mazzini her one son to fight, and if need be to die, for Rome and the Republic. He fought valiantly under Medici at the Vascello, and still lives, reverencing his mother's memory. Mazzini and Giuditta often met in after-life at Turin, she retaining her faith in him, in the Flag, the Republic, in God, and Immortality. She died only one year before he died, his last letter consoling her on her death-bed. That was forty years after their separation.

II

VAIN ATTEMPTS

Savoy Expedition—General Ramorino—Mazzini a foot soldier—Foresees disaster—Failure—Garibaldi—" Young Europe " (1834)—Switzerland rejects the exiles—Mazzini's mental suffering—Resigns the leadership of " Young Italy "—First months in London—Mademoiselle de Mandrot—No. 9 George Street—Death of Francesca Mazzini—Mazzini writes for *Le Monde*, the *Monthly Review*, the *Westminster*, the *Foreign Quarterly*, the *Monthly Chronicle*.

THE expedition which was being prepared by the Liberals as a response to the persecution of Charles Albert, was from its inception destined to failure. It was hastily and faultily planned and worse executed. The choice, by the men who had failed in the revolution of 1821, of General Ramorino as military leader, proved a terrible mistake. They believed in him because he had seen much fighting, first in the great school of Napoleon I. and then in Poland during the insurrection of 1830. But he was truly a fatal leader: he squandered much time and money in Paris, only coming to Geneva after repeated and peremptory intimations from the Committee, finally taking the field with the mere handful of men left, devoid of enthusiasm or even of any belief in success. Four days later he disbanded his force without striking a blow.

Was Ramorino a traitor? Had he been paid by the French Government to act as he did? His subsequent conduct, which brought him fifteen years later to an ignominious death, when, as a commanding officer in the Piedmontese army, he abandoned his post on the eve of the battle of Novara, goes far to suggest the affirmative.

The failure of the Savoy expedition was, and even still is, laid at Mazzini's door—first and foremost of his "fatal errors" or "crimes," in sacrificing everything to his "chimera." In truth, he was but one among hundreds of exiles who believed in the possibility of an Italian revolution. His error, if any, was common to numbers of men of note and experience, wealth and position, who unhesitatingly sacrificed their liberty for their country, and, like the Marchese Rosales and the wealthy brothers Ciani, volunteered to provide the sinews of war. The choice of Ramorino was not his; indeed, he protested against the selection as strongly as he could, though without avail, as the prestige of a name was clamoured for; so his efforts were concentrated upon the thankless task of endeavouring to sterilise the errors of others. He who at the cost of endless labour and heavy personal sacrifice, collected the funds needed for the enterprise, had to see them squandered by Ramorino in a few weeks in Paris. Finally, exhausted by prolonged work, and almost driven to despair by the premonition of inevitable disaster, he started as a simple foot soldier, keeping foremost in the ranks until, unconscious and delirious, he was carried back to Switzerland by his friends Lamberti and Scipione Pistrucci.

It was on the occasion of the Savoy expedition that the name of Giuseppe Garibaldi first came to public knowledge. He has often been pathetically described as a young enthusiast seduced by Mazzini's wiles to rebel against his lawful sovereign. In 1833 Garibaldi was twenty-six years old, and through eleven years of hardships, dangers, struggles with the elements and all sorts and conditions of men, had worked his way up to the lucrative position of "master" in the merchant service. As such he had been inscribed on the register of the port of Nice, February 27, 1832. Love for his country and hatred of foreign domination were sentiments he had cherished from boyhood, but the massacres of 1833 first aroused in him a desire to gain know-

SENTENZA.

IL CONSIGLIO DI GUERRA DIVISIONARIO

SEDENTE IN GENOVA

CONVOCATO D'ORDINE DI S. E. IL SIG. GOVERNATORE
COMANDANTE GENERALE DELLA DIVISIONE

NELLA CAUSA DEL REGIO FISCO MILITARE

Contro

MUTRU Edoardo del vivente Giovanni d'anni 24, nativo di Nizza Marittima, Marinaro di 3.ª classe al R. Servizio

CANEPA Giuseppe Baldassarre del fu Gio. Batta d'anni 34, nato e domiciliato in Genova, Commesso in Commercio, Sotto Caporale provinciale nel 1.º Reggimento *Savona*

PARODI Enrico del vivente Giovanni d'anni 28, Marinaro mercantile, nato e domiciliato in Genova

DALUZ Giuseppe detto *Dall'Oro* del fu Francesco d'anni 50, nato a Praya dell'isola di Terceira (Portogallo), Marinaro mercantile di passaggio in Genova

CANALE Filippo del vivente Stefano d'anni 17, nato e domiciliato in Genova, Lavorante Litografo

CROVO Gio. Antonio del vivente Gio. Agostino d'anni 36, nativo di Carasco (Chiavari) e domiciliato in Genova, Sostituto Segretario del Tribunale di Prefettura.

GARIBALDI Giuseppe Maria del vivente Domenico d'anni 26, nativo di Nizza Marittima, Capitano marittimo mercantile, Marinaro di 3.ª classe al R. Servizio

CAORSI Gio. Battista del fu Antonio, detto il figlio di *Tognella*, d'anni 30 circa, abitante in Genova.

MASCARELLI Vittorio del vivente Andrea d'anni 25 circa, Capitano marittimo mercantile dimorante nella Città di Nizza

I primi sei dinanzi, e gli altri tre contumaci imputati, — *Di alto tradimento militare*, cioè

Li GARIBALDI, MASCARELLI, e CAORSI

Di essere stati i motori di una cospirazione ordita in questa Città nei mesi di gennajo e febbrajo ultimi scorsi, tendente a fare insorgere le Regie Truppe, ed a sconvolgere l'attuale Governo di Sua Maestà; Di avere li GARIBALDI e MASCARELLI tentato, con lusinghe e somme di danaro effettivamente sborsate, di indurre a farne parte alcuni Bassi Ufficiali del Corpo Reale di Artiglieria, e di avere li CAORSI fatto provvista, a sì criminoso scopo, d'armi, state poi ritrovate e di munizioni da guerra.

E gli altri sei, di essere stati informati di detta cospirazione, di non averla denunziata alle Autorità Superiori, e di essersi anzi associati.

Udita la relazione degli atti, gl'Inquisiti presenti nelle loro rispettive risposte, il R. Fisco nelle sue conclusioni e i difensori nelle difese degli accusati presenti

Il Divino ajuto invocato

Rejetta l'eccezione d'incompetenza opposta dai difensori di alcuni accusati

Ha pronunciato doversi condannare, siccome condanna in contumacia li nominati GARIBALDI Giuseppe Maria, MASCARELLI Vittorio, e CAORSI Gio Batta alla pena di morte ignominiosa, dichiarandoli esposti alla pubblica vendetta come nemici della Patria e dello Stato, ed incorsi in tutte le pene e pregiudizj imposti dalle Regie Leggi contro i banditi di primo catalogo, in cui manda li stessi descriversi.

Ha dichiarato li MUTRU Edoardo, PARODI Enrico, CANEPA Giuseppe Baldassarre, DALUZ Giuseppe e CANALE Filippo non convinti, allo stato degli atti, del delitto ad essi imputato, ed inibisce loro molestia dal Fisco

E finalmente ha dichiarato e dichiara inconsistente l'accusa addebitata all'Andrea CROVO, e lo rimanda assoluto.

Genova 3 Giugno 1834

Per detto Ill.mo Consiglio di Guerra
BREA, *f.f.*

Visto, ed approvato
Il Governatore, Comandante Generale della Divisione

M. Paulucci.

GENOVA — Dai Fratelli Pagano, Stampatori del Governo Generale e della R. Marina.

GARIBALDI'S DEATH SENTENCE.

ledge that would enable him to act in Italy's behalf. At Taganrog, on the Black Sea, during one of his voyages, he met G. B. Cuneo, an early and ardent member of "Young Italy," who recounted the history of the past three years and explained the efforts then on foot for a fresh crusade. Upon his return, Garibaldi went at once to Marseilles, saw Mazzini, heard and approved all the plans for the proposed expedition, and having joined "Young Italy" under the name of Joseph Borel, intimated his intention of entering the Piedmontese navy as a volunteer in order to organise a revolt among the men and officers, believing that the ideals of "Young Italy" would find many a champion in the seamen of the Sardinian States. Much to the dismay of his family, who knew that his status of merchant skipper exempted him from military service, he enlisted under the *nom-de-guerre* of "Cleombroto," it being the custom for sailors to adopt fancy names on joining. It seems that his efforts as a propagandist were crowned with extraordinary success. An outbreak on board the *Eurydice* had been planned by him for February 4, 1834, but twenty-four hours earlier he was suddenly transferred to Admiral De Geneys' flag-ship, probably because some notice of the intended uprising had reached the Admiral. Hearing no good news from Savoy, Garibaldi took advantage of this transfer to escape to the mountains, and thence, disguised as a peasant, he reached Nice and subsequently Marseilles. Having read in a newspaper the sentence of death passed upon him by a court-martial, he embarked for Buenos Ayres, where, later, he formed that "Italion Legion" that was to become the nucleus of his "Army of the Independence."

The expedition of Savoy had been fatal to Mazzini in every sense. He and many others were condemned to death by the Sardinian courts. "Young Italy's" idea, steeped in blood on Sardinian soil, had lamentably failed to "express itself in action"; not only had he spent every farthing he possessed, but he had borrowed largely from friends. In fact, though he had carefully concealed his plans from his parents, he had felt compelled to leave a letter to be delivered to them in case of his death in which he begged them to honour his debts in full.

After the failure of the expedition his friends fell away from him with the exception of two or three. But though he suffered excruciatingly on account of the pain he caused to others, circumstances could work no change of conviction in so intensely subjective a nature as his. With the help of many German exiles he founded a new association, " Young Europe" (April 15, 1834), and pamphlets and newspapers were once more widely circulated. This, of course, caused serious alarm to the Austrian, French, and especially the Sardinian Governments, and terrible threats were conveyed to the Swiss Diet should it not at once expel the exiles. At first the Diet stoutly refused, then wavered, and finally yielded. But Mazzini and the brothers Ruffini remained in hiding in the house of a Protestant pastor, whose family lavished kindness upon them. Once they were arrested at La Grange, but the indignant population quickly caused them to be liberated. Penniless, proscribed, forced for six months to live in an attic, their health failing for want of air and exercise, even the Ruffinis chafed indignantly at Mazzini's persistence in what they called a chimera, for they became utterly sceptical of success.

Here fell upon the burdened leader his hour of Gethsemane, which he afterwards called " the tempest of doubt." Was the presage of his soul, then, only a delusion? Was Italy destined, like other countries, to perish from among the nations? Had he been mistaken in believing that God willed her to live a third life, and that his own work was to assist in the accomplishment of that Will? If so, if his idea were merely a madman's dream, then he was indeed a criminal guiltier than Cain. This anguish of despondency, assailing him when his physical energy was at its lowest ebb, brought him again to the very verge of the precipice, and without even Giuditta or Lamberti to rescue him. But the thought of the trust reposed in him by Jacopo's sorrowing mother, the recollection of the devotion shown him by his own dear ones, the exalted love of Giuditta, still mournfully haunting the gates of Modena, powerfully appealed to him and prevented his liberating himself from his mental torment by a cowardly deed. At length the cloud began to lift. A new and higher conception of life emerged from the darkness—the conception that shows life as a mission, whose aim is to "develop and bring into action all the faculties which constitute and lie dormant in human nature—Humanity—and cause them harmoniously to combine towards the discovery and application of" the law governing life, viz., the law of Progress. No. Italian Independence was no chimera. All the great Italians, from Dante to Foscolo, had prophesied it. If he and his generation could not enter the promised land, they must work to prepare it for their children. "Light dawned," he tells us simply, and it was a light that never faded. Pain and loss, defeat, ingratitude and rejection even during partial triumph, were his accepted doom to the end; but his faith was never again shaken, for he realised that "discouragement is but the temptation of the demon Self." He had fought that demon alone, and had vanquished: his armour was still intact, though his weapons might be blunted. Nothing more could be effected in Switzerland, nor, so far as he could see, anywhere at that moment. He was penniless, the Swiss, to whom he already owed so much, were threatened on every side, and the health of the Ruffinis visibly failing. Coming to a resolution, he wrote to Rosales that he resigned his leadership of "Young Italy," as he meant to retire from action for a time. He says: "This, not because I believe less in the final triumph of the Idea, but because I have not a crown-piece left with which to work for it; but as soon as I have paid my debts I shall return to my post, shall conspire and inculcate in the Italians that their duty is to conspire—to prepare a general revolution—which sooner or later must succeed." He then informed the French Minister in Berne that he was willing to receive, for himself and the two Ruffinis, a passport through France to England. The passport was instantly furnished, and Mazzini and his two friends, accompanied by gendarmes, quitted Pontarlier on the Swiss frontier, embarked at Calais, and landed from the Thames, in London on January 13, 1837.

The first months in England—passed in wretched lodgings in Goodge Street, Tottenham Court Road—were as gloomy for them as the English skies. The English friend upon whom Mazzini had counted, Dr. Bowring, was ill and absent; another, a wealthy Italian merchant and a friend of his family, was dead. A Modenese exile, Angelo Usiglio, joined them, and the four took, later, a little house and furnished it with funds sent by the two families Mazzini and Ruffini. They hoped to live more economically thus than in lodgings, but their utter inexperience in household affairs made daily life a tiresome business.

Soon, also, Mazzini had a new grief to contend with. A young girl whom he had known, but scarcely noticed, in Switzerland, had loved him silently for four years: after his departure her fortitude gave way, and she wrote him despairing letters. This so-called love-affair of Mazzini was first revealed by an article in the *Nineteenth Century* in May, 1895. The young lady, whose name was probably De Mandrot, conceived such a profound passion for him that common friends, and especially Melegari, his companion in the ill-fated Savoy expedition, opined that it was his duty to save her from an early, and what seemed an inevitable, death. Some biographers of Mazzini affect to believe that he felt himself touched by this devotion even to the point of forgetting Giuditta for her. This is disproved by Mazzini's own letters. To Melegari, who, later, became Italian Ambassador, Deputy, Minister of Foreign Affairs, Senator, and pillar of the "Moderate" party, and who was connected by marriage with Mademoiselle de Mandrot, he writes: "Why inflict useless tortures on me? Why propose my writing to Maddalena? and why do so with the words, 'What do you mean to do for this unfortunate child?' You ask me if my intentions are in accordance with the only possible ending of such a pure love, and other things of that sort! . . . Great heavens! . . . Can I in any way console her? Can I have any intentions? Am I free? God knows I am not. . . ." In the same letter he affirms that he only loves Giuditta, and that he is bound to be true to her, not only on account of his love, but because he would never add to the misery of that poor mother, "wandering through Italy in quest of her children," for his betrayal would be the death-blow to "her passionate and vehement nature." With his own mother, Mazzini is still more explicit. He asserts that he never gave one thought to this girl; he says that he "no more imagined inspiring her with affection than of becoming Emperor of the Indies." He does not even remember what she is like, only that she was very beautiful. Her devotion touches him, that is all. He has written her only one letter to tell her "gently, but firmly" that her dream was an impossible one, that he is profoundly grieved to have "been an unconscious cause of unhappiness," and, finally, that he loves another. In the same letter to his mother he tenderly inquires about Giuditta, and asks to have her address; he implores "from his far-away love a little letter of consolation, even if only to say that it must be the last." He ends by saying that he can never love another woman, and that he "will try to become thoroughly antipathetic" to all women. His affections are centred in his father, mother, and sister, the Ruffinis and their mother, and Giuditta. To all he has brought "infinite sorrow," but he will love them, and them only, to the end.

Other affections did come into his life in after years; but no woman ever lived who could say truly, "He promised me love for love." This is but an instance of Mazzini's sensitiveness carried to excess. What fault was it of his if a sentimental girl gave him her love unsought? What business had a friend to appeal to him to perform a chimerical, an impossible duty? What right had any one to bind him to a promise to go to Switzerland to see her once more? He agreed to try to do this, but fate, in the shape of impecuniosity, prevented, perhaps fortunately for all. Any tie would have fettered him in the life of abnegation he had accepted. The idea of incurring such a tie never entered his mind: it would have been unworthy of him, and his letter to Melegari, where he speaks of "the gladness with which he would welcome the possibility of a home-life of love," simply gives us a glimpse of the man within, to whom domestic affection appealed with immense force, and of that haunting sense of the sorrows he brought to others, not only necessarily, but it would seem also unwittingly. The simple truth is that Giuditta never had a successor.

Once established in "their own house," 9, George Street, New Road, where at least the four exiles had a room apiece and a "parlour" in which to receive their friends, the search for work was pursued with steady but unrequited energy. Mazzini read English fluently, could speak it intelligibly, but to write a single sentence that would pass muster with a publisher was quite beyond his powers. He had to compose in French—which he spoke and wrote like a native—then his articles were translated and sent to English reviews and magazines; but during the year 1837, notwithstanding the assistance of Dr. Bowring, a faithful friend through good and evil report, they could not be disposed of.

In the beginning of 1838 a bitter trial awaited him in the loss of his beloved sister Francesca, who had shared his thoughts, understood his aspirations, and who, in his parents' letters, always added some pleasant bits of home news. It was Agostino Ruffini who broke the sad tidings to him, as neither his father nor his mother had the courage to do so. His father afterwards confessed in writing to him that "only the thought of Christ on the Cross kept him from suicide." Of the three, probably the mother suffered least— she was so entirely engrossed in her only son. On this occasion Mazzini wrote one of his most beautiful letters to his parents, in which he speaks of the certitude of a reunion with the loved ones gone before as being the one anchor to which he clings "with ever more tenacious and confident grasp." He solemnly claims that in future no misfortune shall be kept from him, and that "they shall let him have his rightful share of suffering." They promised, and the mother kept her word when the father died, in 1848, without again seeing his only son; but when her own death left him desolate, save for his boundless faith in immortality, it fell to English friends (the Ashursts) to disclose the sad tidings.

During 1838 he wrote for *Le Monde*, a journal established by Lamennais in Paris, some letters on English social and political questions, and from these letters, and those to his mother, it is possible to trace a vivid picture of the epoch.

He always appreciated Lord Ashley's efforts, and in after-years had pleasant intercourse with, and assistance from, him. He says in a letter to his mother: "It is good to shorten the hours (of work) for women and children, but if the wretched wages of the men are not increased, what with a series of bad harvests and the high price of everything, it will be merely substituting death by starvation for death by overwork."

His descriptions of the Queen's coronation, and of life at the Court, are admirable, and he also recognises the high standard of political integrity and honour among English statesmen, as compared with the French. He says: "In England there was once a Walpole, and he was called by his name, but there was only one, while in France there are whole generations of Walpoles." Thiers he heartily despised, and in his article in the *Monthly Review* there is a most unflattering criticism of the "great" French statesman.

Through the influence of John Stuart Mill, who was one of his earnest admirers, he was enabled to write for the *Westminster*, but, alas! Mill went abroad, and Robertson, the real editor, who later so grievously offended Carlyle, led him a dog's life: accepting articles, then postponing their publication, saying that they were "too metaphysical, too mystical, soaring above the head of their readers," and "begging him to write things to amuse people, on Italian carnivals and masques, &c." In a review of recent Italian literature, Robertson asks him "to confine himself to names and dates, and a short biography of each author, with a list of his actual writings, dwelling less on his views, his aims, with fewer criticisms on the writer's failure to transform art into a patriotic mission."

Still, an article on Fra Paolo Sarpi was published by the *Westminster* in 1839, followed by others in the *Foreign Quarterly* in 1840. In the same year he wrote regularly for the *Monthly Chronicle*, which agreed to pay him £10 a sheet, but funds failed, and only £5 could be allowed, which nearly all went to the translator; but his articles Lamennais, Thiers, Georges Sand, Byron, and Goethe, and one on "The State and Prospects of Italy," brought him into notice, so by the end of 1847 he had become a well-known literary contributor.

III

MAZZINI AND THE CARLYLES

1838–1840

Acquaintance with the Carlyles—Review of the French Revolution
  Letters home—The Chartists—Chelsea "too far" from London
  Mazzini's appreciation of Carlyle—John Stuart Mill—Lamennais
  —Carlyle and Chartism—Mazzini's views differ from Carlyle's—
  Working-men's Association—The *Apostolato Popolare*—Evening- and
  Sunday-schools—Mazzini works for the idea of One Italy—His
  view of Charles Albert—Changes in Mazzini's household—Harriet
  Martineau—To St. Paul's with Mrs. Carlyle—Mrs. Carlyle and
  Giovanni Ruffini—Mazzini moves to Chelsea—Mrs. Carlyle sends
  a keepsake to Mazzini's mother — Dr. Mazzini's uneasiness —
  Mazzini's reassurances—Carlyle's theory of silence—The Bullers.

IN 1839 he made the personal acquaintance of Carlyle. His description of his first dinner with the Carlyles at a friend's house is quite enthusiastic, although he bemoans the expense of cabs: "as one can't go among these prim, proper English folk muddy and bedraggled with walking in the slush, and a cab costs from three to five lire, whereas my home dinner only costs me one." Carlyle attracts him by his immense sincerity, his absorption in spiritual things, and his grave anxieties anent the signs of the times.

He writes to his mother: "I am in a fix: I have, at the request of the editor of the *Monthly Chronicle*, written a review of Carlyle's 'French Revolution,' which was to have been printed this month, but owing to the faithless translator was delayed, and now cannot appear till January.

Now, though I admit the grandeur of the work, and here and there praise it highly, on certain points I differ from Carlyle so decidedly that I cannot but criticise severely, though, of course, respectfully. I cannot alter anything, or play the hypocrite. I have sworn to myself to write nothing but the truth or what seems to me to be the truth, and I cannot change. If he respects me as a man of convictions, he will not blame me for expressing them."

Carlyle calls and sympathy increases. Mazzini finds him "a man of heart, of conscience, of genius." To his mother he writes · " He is now a man about forty, but fifteen years ago he wrote with as much talent as at present, though of course he has now acquired much vaster knowledge. Yet, because his literary opinions differed from those of the majority, he was neglected, could find no editor (publisher?) for his articles, was regarded as an unpractical dreamer, by some a fanatic. He had a struggle with actual poverty. To-day the world has begun to admire him, to appreciate his writings; he will soon become a power in England."

The moral he wishes to point is, that to succeed in England one must work and wait patiently, without expecting immediate reward. Clearly, he hopes that his father will take the lesson to heart.

On December 11th he wrote that he had paid a visit to Carlyle and found only his wife, who invited him to dinner: " The usual story." And to dinner " I went and dined and smoked, as Mr. Carlyle smokes, but I was there from half-past four till eleven, and grew weary: talking does weary me. I should tire of Plato after half an hour, if he came down here again. Some fine day I will write an article against invitations to dinner, and send it to all my acquaintances, showing how absurd it is that two decent people cannot meet without consuming four hours dining, taking tea, and so on."

His letters home during 1840 are full of " the Carlyles." He goes to visit them on New Year's Day, but "not to dinner, for I am going to dine with my washerwoman; she is English, married to a poor Perugian exile, who mends old Etruscan vases, and he has prepared an Italian dish, and it will vex him if I refuse."

His article on "The French Revolution" had just appeared, but Carlyle had not seen it. He goes to Chelsea in an omnibus, but returns on foot, as Carlyle wants to finish their conversation. Mrs. Carlyle presents him " with a bottle of eau-de-cologne, I don't know why." He loses the mail, owing to the new regulations—penny post—" which do not lessen the price of our letters, but make the letter-collector pass an hour earlier than before." On January 10th he writes : " Carlyle has read the article ; he takes my blame and praise quite kindly and begs me to come and see him often." They meet continually, and Mazzini's letters are filled with their conversations, varied with news of the Chartists, and with somewhat exaggerated accounts of their doings. " An insurrection may be possible anywhere except in London, but the Government is thinking of dissolving Parliament, and gives the country to understand that its own power must be strengthened to ensure the safety of England. The armed police disperses meetings. It is not yet known whether Frost and his companions will be hung, drawn, and quartered, or whether the young Queen will pardon them. At present she is engrossed by her approaching marriage, and Parliament with the amount of the allowance to be accorded to the Prince Consort, who is not to be King, as William of Orange insisted on being. It is said that Frost will not be pardoned. I will not believe it. That a young woman and a Queen, on the eve of marriage with the man she has chosen, can sign a death-warrant is incredible. Petitions imploring pardon are signed by thousands, but very few of the signers belong to the middle classes."

In another letter he says, after dining again with Carlyle : " Really his village is too far off, and I always lose my way when I go about without Angelo (Usiglio) : some day you will receive a letter from another county where I shall have drifted in my wanderings." On February 10th he writes: "The Queen's wedding-day, but there was far less enthusiasm than at her coronation. Half London drunk, of course. Frost and his two companions are saved, but their sentence is commuted to transportation for life, and Frost's poor wife was not even allowed to see him before sailing. Still, he lives, and they may meet again here down sooner than many think."

Later we find · "Another invitation to dine with Carlyle. I lose too much time. He is good, good, good : his wife is good, we dine without ceremony, but he insists on introducing me to this, that, and a third person . he does it out of kindness . . . wishing to make me known to people who may want me to write for them."

It is evident from his letters that Mazzini was more powerfully attracted by Carlyle than he had ever been by any human being, save through his affections. He had personally known some men whose writings he admired—Guerrazzi, for instance, whom he had visited in 1829 in his enforced domicile at Montepulciano while he was composing his "Siege of Florence," but whose egotism and contempt for men, with their " paltry, futile strivings," had repelled him. Sismondi also failed to satisfy because he "merely took a surface view of Italy and her old Republics, of Europe in her present chaotic state." He had been attracted by John Stuart Mill, whose views were far more in accord with Mazzini's own ideas than the latter imagined, for Mill's modest, timid nature prevented his fully revealing his sympathies. To Mazzini, therefore, Mill was "simply a Utilitarian, a Benthamite, a seeker after happiness." In this judgment Mazzini was evidently wrong. It will be long before humanity finds a nobler example of the searcher after the best means of social improvement.

Mill, who has done more than any other disciple of Bentham to spread and popularise "Utilitarianism" in ethics and politics, exalts the "moral hero" for voluntarily sacrificing his own happiness to promote that of others, a phenomenon which, according to Bentham's views, is not even possible. This proves that he had outgrown

Benthamism, which admits "that the only interests a man is at all times sure to find adequate motives for consulting, are his own" · that man, being universally and solely governed by self-love, the so-called moral judgments are merely the common judgments of any society as to its common interests, and that the most effective moralist is the legislator who acts on self-love through legal sanctions, thus moulding human conduct as he chooses. The new "Utilitarianism" of Mill represents the right middle path between the extremes represented by Bentham on the one side, and on the other by Comte, whose general conception pictured human progress as consisting in an ever-growing preponderance of the distinctly human attributes over the purely animal. So, according to Mill, it is the development of benevolence in man and the habit of "living for others" which should be the ultimate aim and standard of practice rather than the mere increase of happiness. It has been rightly said that "no calculus can integrate the innumerable pulses of knowledge and of thought that Mill has made to vibrate in the minds of his generation." That Mill admired and respected Mazzini, and would often try to be useful to the Italian exile, is evident in many of his letters to Robert Barclay Fox. Among the men admired by Mazzini, Lamennais also held for some time a conspicuous place. He used to call him his "saint," though later, despite Lamennais' courage and imprisonment, he felt unable to condone his retraction.

But in Carlyle he saw a man "highly gifted with genius, inspired by an imagination full of true poetry and power, who had also such a big tender heart that he was racked and tortured" by the wrong, misery, and oppression that he witnessed around him.

In December, 1839, "Chartism" appeared in pamphlet form, and was reviewed and abused alike by Tories, Whigs, and Radicals; the latter being disgusted that a writer who demanded even more strenuous reforms than they did themselves, should scout the remedies proposed "by their isms and fisms." These articles of Carlyle's had, two years previously, been offered to and refused by Mill, or, more probably, by his sub-editor, the "clever dodger" Robertson, who used to impress on contributors that they "must consult the taste of his readers and not attempt to impart new knowledge." Lockhart had accepted, but "dared not print" them. Mill would have accepted them later, but "wife and brother John" deemed them too precious a cargo to go down in the ignoble wreck of the *Westminster Review*.

After having read "Chartism," Mazzini collected all the former writings of his new friend and set to work on a review, in which he promised himself that neither friendship nor admiration of their merits should prevent his pointing out their defects, though he would strongly advocate their merits.

At that period Carlyle had not yet assumed for his heroes "unlimited powers," and Mazzini had not yet returned to a militant revolutionary attitude ; in many points therefore they were altogether in agreement. But while Carlyle insisted "that God in His own good time would send a new teacher," so that men needed only patiently to watch and wait, "working each in his own groove in humble expectancy," Mazzini maintained that God would reveal His New Word to "the People, who in their collective intelligence would propound it." One can imagine the sarcasms and explosions that greeted Mazzini's suggestion. "The people !" Carlyle exclaimed ; "the ignorant, blind, vicious masses, chiels and fools, to be regarded as teachers, leaders, guides ? . . . No ! . . . In verity, they were to be taught, led, guided, if need be constrained to obey the superior wisdom and virtue of the chosen few !" To this Mazzini answered · "At any rate they must all be free first : space and liberty must be secured for leaders and teachers, for followers and pupils." And he believed that this could be attained in England if only the ruling classes came to a sense of their duties, but in Italy it would never be achieved without a revolution. According to Carlyle the French Revolution of 1793 had closed a cycle, and

England would profit by the lesson "only when God wills it, as no one can hasten His time or alter His methods." He thought that Italy and other oppressed nations would arise by the agency of "some God-sent Cromwell," and, nursing a profound contempt for conspiracies, he regretted that Mazzini and men of his kidney, "endowed with intelligence and a sense of duty, should be monomaniacs" on the subject.

In his letters home Mazzini gives the pith of these discourses, begun in the pleasant dining-room at Cheyne Row, together with comments and criticisms. In one he says : "Carlyle sees only the individual, sympathises with each, with all individuals, but the true sense of their unity escapes him ; otherwise he would not ridicule the idea of the progress of the species, speak so ironically of the perfectibility of philosophy, nor so bitterly and violently condemn all who seek to transform the social system as it exists. Should they succeed he would applaud their victory. . . . Let all suffer (he says) in silence, purify their own souls, consume their anguish, and hope each in his own fashion. . . ."

Mazzini's father endorsed Carlyle's opinions, applying them in a peculiar and personal sense to his son's efforts. He bade him trust in God to get His own will done. But Mazzini replies to his mother : "I also pray God's will be done, but the point is to find out what that will is, not to confound it with the will of the devil: God's will is to be 'obeyed on earth as it is in heaven' ; does father think that what goes on on earth to-day is God's will? Our duty is to transform things till conformity is brought about, and that as speedily as possible. We must begin by securing the equality of all His children here-down, by clearing away the obstacles that prevent them from developing their faculties and using them in His service ; this they cannot do while suppression of free thought and speech continues : tyranny, oppression, aristocratic privileges will not take themselves away without our efforts. God will not remove them by a miracle when He has put into our hands the instruments for removing them. Father says that 'I delight in argument, that I never let a word pass without an observation.' If he could hear me argue and dispute with Carlyle, and contradict him often, he would be confirmed in his opinion. But let him remember that I never argue except with people whom I love and esteem, and who have deep convictions. I try to believe theirs, or persuade them to believe in mine."

Mrs. Carlyle invited him one night to dinner and afterwards to accompany her to the theatre. He writes to his mother: " Mary Stuart—by somebody—was given, but Macready was the only good actor. A Scotch lord, speaking of Rizzio, asks : ' What can you expect of a low Italian ? ' Rizzio reminds the lord that Italians civilised Europe, and names all our great men, asking · ' Were these low fellows ? ' and the whole audience clapped their hands and applauded lustily. Well, I confess that I was moved and delighted, yet a moment later I reflected : ' Poor Rizzio speaks in the tragedy as we speak to-day ! ' We try to hide the cowardly present under the mantles of our illustrious dead ; we erect a statue to Galileo or Dante, and are as elated as if we had performed a noble action. It would be better to keep silent about our past glories and strive to do something to lessen our present ignominy."

On the occasion of a commemoration of the Polish martyr Konarski, during which Mazzini was requested to pronounce a short speech, some Italian working men who were present told him " that they had held a little meeting and discussed methods to obtain for themselves some sort of national education," and that they were willing to pay a small monthly sum if he would help them to get a paper printed which would give them some notions about their country. Mazzini accepted with enthusiasm, as " the Italian working men form here a numerous class, entirely uncultured, but intelligent and earnest."

So then and there began the series of efforts made in England by Mazzini to rally his countrymen round the flag of Italian Unity and Independence. The Italian Working

Men's Association was founded and the *Apostolato Popolare* started. Evening and Sunday schools for organ boys and image vendors were set on foot, and he was often brought into contact with their brutal employers, or rather masters. Not infrequently he penetrated into dens and slums of Whitechapel in order to bring some exploiting scoundrel to book, and was generally successful. Now, also (1839), he sternly recommenced work on the old lines, and reprinted articles written for the Young Italy Society. He formed " Central Congregations " in Paris, New York, and Montevideo, for the purpose of disseminating news and instructions, and of sending messengers into all the provinces of Italy—not to promote partial revolts, which he insisted were useless, but to focus agitation, to convince all Italians who impotently raged against their condition that they must unite their efforts, agree on a common programme—the expulsion of foreigners and the establishment of " One Italy " under whatever form of government the majority of the nation should choose—in order to render success certain. He was not hoping for a Messiah, nor expecting a heaven-born leader to arise in Piedmont, but the anxiety with which he watched every faintest sign of progress there, such as the penal code, the foundation of a newspaper, &c., shows that he never lost sight of the possibilities latent in the House of Savoy. That Charles Albert would ever take the initiative Mazzini no longer hoped ; nay, he severely rebuked those writers who urged him to such a course, for by them the populations were confirmed in inertia through a nebulous belief that he could and would strike the blow for them. He said : "Only a manifestation of the popular will, within and without the Austrian possessions in Italy, that Austria must and shall 'quit the premises '—a resolute effort to drive them out—will ever induce Charles Albert to place himself at the head of a national war. Soon he will find himself in the dilemma : either he must lose his provincial crown or risk it for the national crown of Italy."

This plain and practical programme, preached incessantly,

monotonously, for eight years, was at last put into practice by the Milanese in 1848, when the people arose in their omnipotence and drove the Austrians away. Charles Albert did then unsheathe his sword and risk his little crown for "the proud crown of towers," not winning it for himself, but securing it for his son and his descendants.

People accused, and still accuse, Mazzini of halting between two opinions, which he never did. He was a constant, profound, intellectual believer in a republic founded on the will of the people, carried on by them through their combined choice of the wisest and most virtuous citizens to govern, and to the last he believed that Italy would become a republican nation in the future. But the immediate problem was the creation of *a nation*, and his keen observation of facts, his insight into human nature, whose instincts teach man to choose the line of least resistance, his knowledge of the state of Europe, convinced him that an unarmed people could not succeed alone. Hence his "aut aut": "Arise! call Charles Albert to help you if you choose: if he does his duty, reward him as you deem fit: but see that he does it, see that he does help you to become an independent nation. Till then, by offering him a crown and a throne which do not exist, you only make him ridiculous, and prove yourselves cowards who deserve slavery. . . ."

Meanwhile changes took place in Mazzini's little house hold. Agostino Ruffini went to Edinburgh with a fair chance of getting lessons, for the Carlyles furnished him with valuable letters of introduction. Then Mazzini and Giovanni Ruffini changed their house, as Tancione, the Perugian exile, a true, good, feckless fellow, with his brave, bright English wife Susannah—the "washerwoman" with whom Mazzini dined on New Year's Day—undertook to lodge and feed them for £40 a year each. The Carlyles urged him to come to Chelsea, a "cheap, quiet, fresh-aired village," but for three months at least he and Giovanni settled at 26, Clarendon Square.

The "Working Men's Association" made rapid progress

and Mazzini became more busy than ever. He writes to his mother · "I work all day and part of the night, but people come at all hours and interrupt me. I have told Susannah that I mean to be dead for everybody except the Carlyles." He went, however, to a parting banquet given to Geoffrey Cavaignac, brother of the General, who in consequence of an amnesty returned to France, and remarked that Frenchmen, however good, must make a noise. Innumerable bottles of champagne were drunk, "but for me half a glass is sufficient."

In his letters to his mother he speaks often of the great care his housekeeper, Susannah, takes of him, and once adds that "many ladies send me flowers, and I am grateful to them, but your thyme-leaves are dearer to me than all the flowers of Florida."

He duly attends Carlyle's second series of lectures, and becomes acquainted with Harriet Martineau—"deaf as a post, but who consoles herself for her infirmity by remembering how much stupid 'talk-a-talk' she is spared, for, you see, she herself can choose who shall talk into her ear-trumpet, and for how long a time." Miss Martineau is most favourably impressed by him, and he speaks of her as "the woman with the broadest views and most cultivated intellect" in England. In this same letter he announces a "Chelsea and St. Paul's day for next Friday," and on June the 18th gives an account of his jaunt. "Well, so I took Mrs. Carlyle up to the 'Ball,' the cupola of St. Paul's, the highest point in London. It occupied the entire day. First I went to Chelsea, then we came back into the City along the Thames in a steamboat. I enjoyed the trip and so did my companion, exceedingly, though of all people unadapted for escorting ladies I am the most famous ; still, as I do try to be courteous, they probably give me credit for that. When we landed from the boat and got into the hustling, bustling crowd—for St. Paul's is in the very heart of this vast city of business—we lost ourselves. I did not know where St. Paul's Street (? Churchyard) was, nor did Mrs. Carlyle :

THE BIRTH OF MODERN ITALY

I always do lose my way in London, unfortunately for those who trust to me as their guide. I asked quite ten persons. They only laughed, for we were not ten steps from St. Paul's itself; we entered what seemed hardly to be a church, it was so filthy and disorderly. We climbed up to the 'Ball,' escorted by an old crone, who explained all that she thought most interesting, and which we did not find interesting at all. Nothing bores me like a human machine prating set phrases about places and rare sights, so the poor old soul must have been scandalised at our inattention to most of the things she pointed out, and our attention to those she passed over. Fortunately, she left us in the 'Ball.' We remained there three-quarters of an hour alone, with the wind howling most diabolically; the view is most imposing, but, as at that hour the vapours of the atmosphere and the dense smoke rising from the manufactories and the houses dim it considerably, it ought to be seen at dawn. The city, built on a level plain, is vast, immense, and the form of the roofs and the red chimneys give it the appearance of a sea on fire, like that in which they paint the lost souls who have been petrified in Purgatory. We returned by water to Chelsea, and then I walked home."

Carlyle seems to have been much amused by the account of their expedition. Many more follow. One day Mazzini arrives with a bad toothache and a swollen face. Mrs. Carlyle, after some commiseration, " proposed a walk." He says: "I note that people who do not suffer from toothache, sea-sickness, or such minor evils, treat them lightly. It was dark, and we walked to the middle of a bridge and stood watching the Thames, the steamers, boats, &c. What with the damp of the river, and the cold, and the furious wind which raged around us, I expected a night of torture. On the contrary, I slept well, and this morning feel all right." Another evening Mrs. Carlyle takes him to a literary lady (Lady Morgan?), a friend of hers, and on returning they lose their way, miss the boat in which they were to cross the river, and have to walk five or six miles and cross Battersea Bridge, then built of wood.

He is introduced to a number of literary people, and Giovanni Ruffini, who often accompanies them, is enthusiastic about Mrs. Carlyle—" the only person who has taken any interest in or tried to help him, and who has found him some pupils."

Mr. and Mrs. Carlyle pressed Mazzini to remove to Chelsea, and Carlyle himself went to see "a beautiful house in a garden," too dear, however. Mrs. Carlyle and Giovanni Ruffini examined others. At last they decided to let Tancione and Susannah take a house and lodge and feed them as in Clarendon Square. And then intercourse with the Carlyles ripened into intimacy. Carlyle often went with Mazzini for a walk; Mrs. Carlyle asked him frequently to accompany her to the City. In August he writes: "I have walked more in this than in all the years that I have been in London." This was an excellent thing for his health and spirits, which improved vastly, partly, however, because he was at work for Italy and really hopeful that the Italians were beginning to awake in earnest. Mazzini tells his mother that Mrs. Carlyle is going to write to her and send her a little token of loving admiration. "All those who like me, love you. I do not know what the present is to be, but yesterday she cut off a lock of my hair." The present was a brooch, with Mazzini's and Mrs. Carlyle's hair entwined in it, with the motto "Ora e Sempre" (Now and Ever).

Mazzini's mother was, of course, enchanted, but his father seemed seriously anxious to know more about the lady, so Mazzini writes: "Father seems much preoccupied and says that all the women with whom I have come in contact have felt a great sympathy for me, which is curious, as I do nothing to excite it. I dress badly, worse now than in Genoa, I smoke from morning till night, and ladies don't like the smell of smoke. I have no small-talk, I don't know how to be '*galant*,' if I hand a cup of tea I upset it. I am what the French call '*gauche*,' in the fullest sense of the word. I only can suppose that women see that I have a good and affectionate heart, and as women are generally surrounded by men who pay compliments and flatter them, perhaps they find my different behaviour an attraction. Then, too, I do really deserve women's liking, for I always stand up in their defence; I deny the accusations men make against them, and I abhor the treatment to which they are often subjected."

But his father wants to hear more about this particular lady, whose letters to the Signora Mazzini may fairly have passed with him for exaggerations, though he also had a very exalted opinion of his son's genius and moral qualities. "Well," Mazzini replies, "I will do my best to satisfy your natural curiosity. Mrs. Carlyle is still young; she is not beautiful and she is not plain; her eyes are dark, and her hair, as you will have seen, is as dark as mine. She is tall, thin, vivacious, but of very delicate health, suffering terribly from headaches and other ailments. But do not, because I say she is still young, go off on a wrong tack." He further explains the sisterly devotion she bears him— undoubtedly "sisterly, though perhaps tenderer and more demonstrative." He reminds his father that Carlyle is a friend whom he loves and who loves him, so that "an entanglement is out of the question. . ."

At this time Mrs. Carlyle translated an essay of Mazzini's, presenting Austria under her true colours, and destined for *Tait's Magazine* in Edinburgh. This translation is perfect, but translations by others of Mazzini's articles— the originals of which are preserved—are often so execrable that one can only wonder an English publisher ever accepted them. [Mrs. Mario must not here be understood as referring to the subsequent translations of Mazzini's writings by Mrs. Emilie Ashurst Venturi, which possess every merit, including that of having been read and approved by Mazzini himself.—E. F. R.]

Not only the exile's father, but Giovanni Ruffini, was much exercised, not about Joseph, but about Mrs. Carlyle. She was four years older than he, having been born in 1801, "but," Giovanni writes to his mother, "I tell him that a man with his fascinating qualities, his gifts of mind and intellect, his winning ways, ought not to indulge in intimate friendships with women and then expect them not to fall in love with him." Of course, Giovanni knew, as did his mother, of Mazzini's talisman; they were perfectly aware that "la Giuditta" was his one and only love, and that though he could never claim her for his own, no other woman would ever call him hers. And the fears of Giovanni for Mrs. Carlyle, and of the father for his son, were groundless. Mazzini never lost sight of the fact that Mrs. Carlyle's life was centred in her husband, that her sole ambition was for his success, her clearly accepted mission to

> "Keep space for his genius to soar to its height
> Unfettered, unsullied, fresh-winged in its flight."

That Mazzini was at times amused, at times really wrathful, at Carlyle's grumblings and ragings over cockcrowing, pianos, clatter and indigestion is true, but he probably considered that Mrs. Carlyle's stinging and often cruel witticisms, under which her husband winced, did not improve matters. The friendship was beneficial on both sides, for the year in Chelsea freshened up Mazzini, and Carlyle, who enjoyed his society, certainly made him look at facts more analytically than he had been accustomed to do. The long talks on Cromwell, then Carlyle's chief preoccupation, greatly interested Mazzini, as his letters home prove.

To Elia, an enthusiastic member of "Young Italy" who had crossed and recrossed the Peninsula distributing clandestine tracts and papers, and who, though arrested once, had been allowed to return to his native city, Mazzini often wrote of the Carlyles. Enrico Nencioni,[1] who had it directly from Elia, told us of a scene described in one of these letters, in which " a certain poor devil," who had come a long way to visit him, ventured to say that, after all, the first thing to do was to ensure the happiness of the people. The unfortunate was assailed by a torrent of

[1] Enrico Nencioni, poet, writer, and critic, recently deceased.

invectives, thunder following on lightning, till he got up to go, crushed, deafened, more dead than alive. Mrs. Carlyle, vexed and hurt, accompanied him to the door, murmuring words of apology, but Carlyle went on, soliloquising, as he walked up and down the room like a raging lion in a cage, shaking his forest of grey hair : " Happiness ! . . . Happiness ! the fools ought to be chained up ! . . . man is born to work, not to enjoy ! . . . Shut up your Byron and open your Goethe ! . . . The ideal is within us, the ideal lies in the present moment ; work with all your might, and to the best of your abilities. Work, and produce even the least atom ! . . . Every kind of work, whether intellectual or manual, is sacred and gives peace to the human soul. Be silent and work—these are the cardinal virtues of Humanity. Silence ! Yes, only silence is grand ; we live suspended between two silences : the silence of the stars and the silence of the grave ! . . . Nations, too, should be silent until genius speaks for them—genius is their voice and interpretation. How great was the silence of the ancient Romans ! The Middle Ages, too, had a solemn silence, which was broken by the sublimest song, human or divine, ever sung—the poem of Dante. These are the true voices of the nations, and when one of them is heard, the nation for which he spoke is a consecrated nation ; it is redeemable even if oppressed, divided, humiliated. Your Italy, oppressed as it is by Austria, is actually a great nation, because Italy has Dante. One day she, too, will be allowed to speak, and will be listened to."

According to Carlyle, only "the great *blagueurs* made a loud noise, but renewed nothing, created nothing, exploding like cannon loaded only with powder," so that when the noise had ceased, " a simple breath of wind swept away all their smoke," and the universe remained undisturbed, as before. Then, looking to Mazzini, Carlyle, with his imperial, scrutinising smile, slowly added : "You . you have not succeeded yet, because you have talked too much : the fundamental preparation is wanting ! . . . " Mazzini, according to Elia, must have answered only with another smile, that subtle Genoese smile, a mixture of admiration and benign irony, that seemed to say : " Your theory of silence would suit Austria most admirably."

Probably the smile was caused by the humour of the doctrine of silence thus illustrated. But on certain occasions Mazzini let Carlyle talk on, not only because he liked to hear his paradoxes, but because he always got his own turn, when he would prove that Dante's message, spoken five hundred years before, was a command to translate thought into action, a command which he was humbly but resolutely striving to obey and to induce others to obey. Mazzini had an immense interest in listening to and reading Carlyle's utterances. Both of them had outgrown the "clothes" of Christianity, though both used biblical language to express their deepest thoughts, and longed to see Christ's humanity embodied in the social life of the world ; but Mazzini hoped for some clear expression from Carlyle of the new faith, which, according to him, would bring order out of chaos, and hoping, he waited and listened, reading in manuscript and in proofs the new work, "Past and Present," which Carlyle, while still thinking of Cromwell, had begun to write, and to talk out, and which Mazzini reviewed with his other works, "Sartor Resartus," "Essays," &c., in 1843.

The Carlyles introduced him to all their literary friends, among whom the Bullers, mother and son, took amazingly to him, as he did to them, and from Charles Buller he must have gained some of the intimate and accurate knowledge of English political affairs that is so remarkable in his letters. Mrs. Buller, journeying later to Italy, went to Genoa on purpose to see his home and his mother, and brought back to Mazzini a very precious ring from her.

Towards the end of that year the exiles were greatly alarmed by news of what seemed the fatal illness of the Ruffinis' mother, and Mrs. Carlyle was unremitting in her kindness to Giovanni. Knowing that Mazzini regarded "la Signora Eleonora" as his "second mother," for she was "the saintly mother of the martyr Jacopo," her anxiety was great for him also. But on New Year's Day, by the earliest post, good news arrived.

Mazzini wrote home: "Already, before I was up, came from Mrs. Carlyle a letter, a present, and some hot tarts (mince-pies?), but I was too wretched to think of anything; then Nina's [the married sister of the Ruffinis] letter came with the good news, and I, happy as a boy, ran over to Mrs. Carlyle, who, from some Scotch superstition, wished mine to be her first visit, and I was in time to be her 'first foot.' Then I bought some wine for Giovanni, and we had our usual Polish friends and Angelo to dinner, and then your letter came. Ah! if all the days of the year were to be like this first, one would never be tired of living"

1841 was one of the most miserable years for Carlyle, and so, of course, for Mrs. Carlyle, who, however, chaffs Mazzini for *his* spleen and *his* sadness, for which, poor man! he had far more real excuse than either of them. He sends his mother a drawing of Chelsea and the Thames; his house "is behind those on the bank, so they must be inundated before mine, and the names of the steamers are real names. There are ten of them; they start, and take you to London Bridge for 4d., every quarter of an hour. The row where the Carlyles live looks on to the avenue on the right, not where the church is."

In June the elections were discussed at Carlyle's—"£20,000 to £30,000 spent for one election—a nice system, truly, for choosing the representatives of the people. Carlyle and I agreed in this, that Tories and Whigs are the inside and outside of the same coat, and that neither the one nor the other have the will or the power of doing any good; that they would go on butting at each other for some time, and then that the people would send them both to the devil. While we were talking, in came a famous Tory, one of the principal managers of the *Times*. I said to him, 'Well, are you triumphant?' 'Of course, of course,' and thinking me deeply interested, he set himself to prove the absolute certainty of Tory victory. I listened gravely; just then Mrs. Carlyle turned and looked at me, and thinking of our previous conversation, we tried to keep serious, but suddenly and most inopportunely we both burst into a roar of laughter. The poor man gazed from one to the other in bewilderment; we turned the matter off as best we could, and he went away pacified. Joking apart, the aristocratic party is getting the upper hand not only here, but everywhere; here the Tories are sure to win,[1] in Switzerland the Jesuits and the foreign ambassadors are preparing reaction. In Spain, the Carlists; in France, worse and worse; but something else progresses, and that is the people. The Carlyles are off to Scotland next week, not for all the summer, I hope."

[1] The Whig Government had been beaten by a majority of one on June 5th, on Sir Robert Peel's resolution that they did not possess the confidence of the House. Parliament was prorogued on the 23rd, and the elections gave a majority of ninety to the Tories. Sir R. Peel's administration, including Lord Aberdeen and Sir James Graham, and later Mr. Gladstone, lasted till 1846, the Duke of Wellington sitting in the Cabinet without office.

IV

MAZZINI'S LIFE IN LONDON

1841-1844

Signora Mazzini and Mrs. Carlyle—Lady Byron and the school for orga boys—Mrs. Carlyle loses her mother—Mazzini's faith in imm< tality.— Mrs. Carlyle's surprising references to Mazzini — La Harriet Baring—Mazzini requires a dress-coat—Failure of Ga bini's bank — Mazzini's allowance from home — Carlyle, t Barings, and Mazzini — Mazzini's letters of counsel to M Carlyle—Mazzini leaves Chelsea—He is watched by the Austri Embassy—Attempts to break up his school—Gisquet's *Mémoi*. revive the Gavioli libel—Prosecution of Gisquet—Mazzini's fa in the honour of the English Government.

ON her return to London in October Mrs. Carly found awaiting her a beautiful bouquet of eve lastings, and in the evening Mazzini brought h a ring, both gifts from his mother. She thanked t] giver in the following letter in her quaint Italian, of whi< we append a literal translation ·

LONDRA, 30 *Ottobre*, 1841.

CARA MADRE,—Dio vi benedica per mandarmi i fiori e l'anell In vita mia non ho ricevuto un dono così stimato ! Molto tempo nella sciocchezza del mio cuore di giovanetta, io desideravo tanto vezzo di perle, ed uno zio mi diede inaspettatamente uno superbo.] ricordo quanto era giojosa di sollevare il coperchio della cassetta, ecco la mia segreta voglia adempiuta ! E mi ricordo come più ta. io divenni un giorno piu grande di tutto un piede, al ricevere gioiello e versi da Goethe ! Ma, nè la vana giovanetta, godeva de sue perle, nè la fiera moglie del suo regalo del grande Goethe, com' l'amica di vostro figlio, godo dei miei fiori ed anello da voi !

1841] A LETTER TO SIGNORA MAZZINI

Fui tornata da casa, dopo due mesi passati in Scozia, nella mia patria, e pur vorrei dire in esiglio! Fui ritornata mezzo morta di fatiche e di noie, e, caduta sul mio letto, ebbi dormita qualche ora, svegliando la prima cosa chi miei occhi incontrarono fu il vostro mazzetto di fiori! La serva mi lo recò in letto, dicendo con piccol'aria di trionfo, "Voi sapete da chi? Non è bello? e durerà per sempre!" S'io non avessi temuta di guastar i graziosi fiori, di certo li avrei stretti al mio seno, come cosa vivente, tanto in quel momento vennero cari e di buon'augurio! La medesima sera, mio amico mi diede stesso l'anello, con scuso, piu modesto che ragionevole, per "la parole di madre vi intagliate!" Come se quelle parole non mi valessero più che oro!... come se non facessero dell'anello d'oro uno vero talismano di affetto! Si in momenti d'abbattimento, di che tanti mi prendono, mi sentirò incoraggiata a vista di quell'anello, portando la vostra benedizione sull'amore che mi ha reconciliata colla vita!... "Ama il martir di Italia!" Non bisogna comandarmelo!... Non posso far altro!. Oh! se voi sapeste come l'amo!... Non *bisogna*, dico, ma mi goda!... Quindi innanzi potro dirmi in amarlo: "E la volontà di una madre!..." e credo non è ipocrisia piu cara a noi donne che il dar ai nostri diletti una vernice di dovere!!!

"E vi sei figlia," oh! cara, vi sono, vi sarò sempre figlia, solamente come egli in esiglio. Che l'amore dunque che voi portate a lui si stenda sopra me, e in pregare Dio per lui, pregatelo per me ancora!!.

Non aggiungerò più, perchè io scrivo male, e, ch'è peggio, con difficoltà. Il studio d'Italiana ch'io m'aveva promesso ed anche cominciato da davvero, fu dolorosamente sparso ai venti per progetti di mio marito, che non mi lasciavano un momento di pace. M'al presente che quei minaccievoli progetti hanno mancati, e tutto il danno è stato un assenza di due mesi, voglio ricominciare e spero di scrivervi lungamente in poche settimane, e senza la mortale compagnia del dizionario.

Addio, cara, e credete nel tanto che vorrei dirvi, oltre il poco che vi ho imperfettamente detto.

Vostra
Jane Carlyle.

"I minaccievoli progetti," of which the writer tells, derived from the fact that in 1841 Carlyle had serious thoughts of returning to Craigenputtoch to live. Here is the translation:

Dear Mother,—God bless you for sending me the flowers and the ring. I have never in my life received such a precious gift. Long ago, in the foolishness of my girlish heart, I longed for a pearl necklace, and an uncle unexpectedly gave me a splendid one, and I

remember how delighted I was when, on lifting the cover of the lit(tle)
box, lo! my secret longing was gratified. And I remember ho(w)
later, I grew a whole foot taller on receiving a jewel and verses fr(om)
Goethe. But neither did the vain girl rejoice in her pearls, nor t(he)
proud wife in the great Goethe's gift, as I, the friend of your s(on,)
rejoice in this gift of flowers and ring from you.

I had returned home after two months spent in Scotland, my o(wn)
country, or rather, in exile! I had returned half dead with fatig(ue)
and worry, and, falling on my bed, had slept for a few hours; the fi(rst)
thing which met my eyes in awakening were your flowers. T(he)
servant brought them to my bedside, saying with a little air (of)
triumph, "Do you know who sends them? Are they not beautifu(l)
and they will last for ever!" If I had not feared to spoil the love(ly)
flowers, I should have clasped them to my bosom as a living thi(ng)
so welcome and of such good augury they seemed to me in t(he)
moment. In the evening, my friend gave me the ring with (an)
apology more modest than reasonable for the words inscribed by (his)
mother, as if those words were not more precious than gold to m(e)
as if they did not transform the gold ring into a precious talisman (of)
affection. Yes!! in the moments of discouragement to which I a(m)
prone, I will feel cheered by the sight of that ring, bringing yo(ur)
blessing on the love that has reconciled me to life. "Love Ital(y's)
martyr!." No need to bid me do so. I cannot do otherwi(se.)
Ah! If you knew how I love him! . It is no case of *must*, I a(m)
happy in doing so. Henceforth I can say in loving him: "A mot(her)
bids me love him," and I think there is no hypocrisy dearer to
women than to give to our delights a varnish of duty.

"Be a daughter to me," ah! dear, I am and always shall be o(ne)
but even as he is, in exile, so let the love you bear him be extended (to)
me, and when praying for him, pray for me also.

I do not write more, as I write badly, and, what is worse, wi(th)
difficulty. The study of Italian which I had promised myself (to)
pursue, and which I had begun in earnest, was unhappily dispersed (to)
the winds by my husband's projects, which did not leave me (a)
moment's peace; now that these threatening plans have failed, and
the harm has been an absence of two months, I mean to recommen(ce)
and I hope to write a long letter in a few weeks without the dea(d)
company of the dictionary.

Adieu, dear, and believe in the much that I would say, besides t(he)
little I have imperfectly said.

Your
JANE CARLYLE.

Mazzini's school for Italian organ and plaster-ima(ge)
boys throve apace. Mrs. Carlyle presented it with (a)
beautiful atlas, and three guineas were contributed

Lady Byron, who seems to have been greatly touched by Mazzini's article on her husband—certainly one of the most just and appreciative ever written on our great poet. About that time Mazzini finished his second article on Carlyle, "when lo! . . . the publisher goes mad." He sadly adds · "A fatality follows all those who have something to do with me! ."

In 1842 Mrs. Carlyle's mother died. Mazzini relates in his home letters how she received the tidings, and how, though unable to answer his letter, she had sent him a note from Liverpool, through her cousin, sealed with his seal, the motto "*Ora e Sempre*." Though Mrs. Carlyle believed in a future life this was no consolation to her, and Mazzini could not instill into her his own absolute, palpable, visible certainty in immortality and reunion. He says: "Sad! .·. . Sad! . . . Dwelling on all the little things in which she [Mrs. Carlyle] did not fall in with her mother, unable to feel that she is not dead, but knows all, and loves more, and watches and waits, intercedes and hovers over her child, to help and strengthen her."

Mrs. Carlyle was not the only friend whom Mazzini tried to comfort with the consolation which sufficed him, even in the bitterest hour of his life, when he too found himself motherless and the world "a barren waste." His lasting grief was that he could not impart his belief to others as a solace to their despair. But, whether he succeeded or not, it was impossible to come in contact with such a lofty soul, knowing his immeasurable sufferings and the serene manner in which he bore them, without striving to hope and to believe even as he did.

Mazzini's friendship was a treasure in itself, and Mrs. Carlyle availed herself of it to the fullest extent, especially during the three years in which he resided in Chelsea; hence when in 1881 her letters were published in the "Reminiscences" ("Letters of Jane Welsh Carlyle," edited by J. A. Froude; Scribner's, New York), her impertinent satires and the flippant tone in which she alludes to him were bitterly resented by the large circle of Mazzini's English friends, who had held his friendship as their highest privilege, and who, when they lost him in 1872, felt an aching void the world could never fill.

A remarkable instance of Mrs. Carlyle's strange conduct can be found in her letter to her husband of August, 1843 ("Reminiscences," vol. i. p. 186), in which she tells him that "the Italian Revolution has begun and also, I suppose, ended." According to her, Mazzini "has been in a state of violent excitement . . really forcibly reminding one of Frank Dickinson's goose with the addled egg," and she could not help "telling him that a Harrow or Eton schoolboy who uttered such nonsense" as his alleged plan of persuading a (Neapolitan?) frigate then in England to revolt openly and take him to Italy, "would be whipped and expelled from the community as a mischievous blockhead." These and similar expressions, though quite typical, are not only cruel, but wholly unjust and untrue. But there is even worse. She considers quite seriously whether it is not her duty as "Mazzini's friend" to warn the Austrian Government of the plans which he has confided to her, "to save his head, and those of the many at the sacrifice of a few." And she would have certainly done it, she adds, if she had not been convinced "that it would be, like the Savoy expedition, stopped by some providential toll-bar."

Here is exaggeration, even in the narration of facts, which is unpardonable. In that year, throughout Italy, especially in Calabria and the Papal States, conspiracies were rife though no organised plan of revolution was concerted. The Constitutionalists took no part therein, protesting against any action not concerted with their ideal chief, Charles Albert. The movement did not, as Mrs. Carlyle asserts, go into Sicily to act there alone; all attempts were known to Mazzini and to Fabrizi,[1] who

[1] Fabrizi, Nicola (1805-1885) born in Modena, one of the noblest

constantly endeavoured to prevent partial and unconnected risings as being mere waste of lives and resources. Mazzini may have told Mrs. Carlyle of the revolts that had already taken place, but unquestionably he never entrusted her with the names of men preparing any movement, nor of the places where they might be intending to go. This he never did to his most confidential friends; even his coadjutors only knew the part which each was to take in plans that they had concerted with him. Nothing, then, that she knew, could have harmed or saved any one, even had she communicated all to Radetzky himself.

The letter therefore may be considered as a fling off in her satirical vein, probably sharpened by Mazzini's resolution to leave Chelsea in the following month. Take again her account (*op. cit.*, vol. i. p. 160) of Mazzini's first interview with Lady Harriet Baring, so unlike his own in his letters to his mother. He was certainly not the man to ridicule any one who had received him kindly, or who had in any way shown interest in Italy. The fact that he had made the acquaintance of a lady, who, in all probability unconsciously, had a serious influence on the lives of the Carlyles, is worth noting, as it casts an astonishing significance on two letters of Mazzini's— given by Froude—to Mrs. Carlyle, who, despite all her flippant satires, appealed to him as the one counsellor to whom she could go for help and advice in her fantastical, Wertherian woes.

In 1842 Mazzini had been asked by Lady Harriet Baring, who knew the Italian language well, to give her a course of lectures on Italian literature. Most likely this offer came through the Bullers, who were increasingly attracted not only to Mazzini but towards his struggling and suffering country; and Charles Buller, an intimate friend of Lady Harriet, probably talked to her of both.

figures in the history of the Italian Risorgimento. Incessantly at the head of all the revolutionary movements, he fought during the sieges of Venice and Rome and as one of Garibaldi's Thousand. He was a faithful friend and co-operator of Mazzini.

But the departure of the Barings for the country prevented the lectures from taking place, as well as some others which Mazzini had intended to deliver publicly on "The Spirit of the Age."

In 1843 Lady Harriet again wrote to Mazzini, asking him to come and see her "not as a professor," but as one whose acquaintance she and her husband desired to make. Overburdened with work as he was, he seems to have demurred, but John Stuart Mill, always anxious that Mazzini and his cause should be known by influential persons in England, advised him to pay the visit, telling him that the Barings, though they would not be offended by his refusal, were genuinely anxious to know him. This, added to his father's desire that "he should enter into society in high circles," and the constant hope of interesting people of influence in Italy's behalf, made him consent to go, but he fixed "some evening a fortnight hence," pleading extra work for his school and a concert to be given in its behalf as an excuse for delay. "But the real reason," he writes to his mother on May 8th, "will make you both laugh. I am told that you can't go to these aristocratic houses in a frock coat or an overcoat, but only in a dress-coat, a *marsina*, a swallow-tail, and I have never possessed such a thing. To the Carlyles, and to most literary people in other houses, I go in my frock-coat, but to accept this invitation and to go dressed differently from other guests would seem an affectation of democracy which I dislike, as I do the republican pretence of calling every one *citoyen*. If any lord or lady ask what my opinions are, I shall tell them that I am a republican, but I shall not leave it to my clothes to proclaim my creed, nor excite attention by going —in trifles—against accepted usages, so I will be measured for a *marsina*, and pay this visit, hoping that father will give me credit for the same."

Circumstances put the visit off for two months. Work for the concert and school was really exhausting, as he had to do everything himself; and then the great banking-

MAZZINI'S MOTHER.

To face p. 57

1843] FAILURE OF GAMBINI'S BANK

house of the Gambinis, where Professor Mazzini's savings were mainly invested, failed, and he lost 65,000 francs (£2,600). He took his loss philosophically, as did his son, whose chief concern seems to have been for Andrea Gambini, the friend of his childhood, the recipient of the famous box of contraband documents, and who now, though "timid to cowardice," is "still the man who loves me best outside my own family." This failure entailed much correspondence, though all persons concerned seem to have taken the misfortune with equanimity except the Signora Mazzini, and she fretted because the loss might deprive her beloved son of his income. This, however, was not the case, as the father, in spite of all, never failed to send him his regular remittance, and did not even curtail his generous New Year's gift of £50 to £100.[1]

---

[1] Madame Mario has here fallen into a pardonable error. She made the acquaintance of Mazzini in 1856, and never personally knew his mother, who died in 1852. For the truth concerning the pecuniary assistance which the exile received from his family we can turn to Mrs. Emilie Ashurst Venturi, who was for many years intimate with Signora Mazzini. That lady greatly desired her young friend to write a life of her son, and for this purpose gave her (in 1851) the complete collection of his letters home, and caused her to make notes and to record anecdotes of his early years. The work was not, however, undertaken, owing to insuperable difficulties; but after Mazzini's death Mrs. Venturi wrote a memoir to accompany a volume published by Mr. P. A. Taylor, in which every statement regarding Mazzini was made from absolute knowledge. On p. 61 Mrs. Venturi says: "Since all who could have been pained by the revelation are dead, it appears not unworthy to relate how nobly the mother took her share in the life of silent abnegation chosen by her son. When Mazzini was first banished, his father, in the hope of inducing him to make such submission . . . as might ensure a pardon, resolved to refuse him all means of support. The mother . . . unable to modify her husband's determination, continued, unknown to him, secretly to forward to her son throughout the whole period of their weary separation a quarterly remittance sufficient to supply his frugal necessities . . . and by one of those sacred deceptions on which the angels smile, to keep him in ignorance of the constant personal abnegation and restriction by which the necessary sum was gathered together, to be forwarded always in the name of the father who had denied it. In all the contrivances and sacrifices necessary to accomplish this she was greatly

THE BIRTH OF MODERN ITALY

At last he went to see the Barings on the 25th of July, and on the 29th he wrote to his mother, ". . . They are going abroad this week and will probably take Italy on their travels. Both received me with hearty kindness. Lady Baring is a woman of spirit, and highly cultured, very tolerant of other people's opinions. It was not a regular full-blown party, or I should have been bored; there was one I knew there (John Stuart Mill) and I was not bored at all. I avowed myself a republican and a revolutionist, and we joked about the risk they would run if a revolution should break out in Italy while they were there."

On their return the Barings again invited him, and he gave his mother a most amusing description of how he lost one whole evening in *not* finding Bath House, and of another spent there, and of his political discussions with several members of Parliament, among them Monckton-Milnes. In September, 1844, when the famous letter-opening affair was on hand, he wrote to his mother: " Carlyle has been staying with the Barings in the country. Their invitations to me have made quite a hubbub. Lord Brougham has been talking horrors of Lady Harriet. Lord Ashburton, her father-in-law, has written reproving them for fraternising with a revolutionist, and the Ministers have upbraided Mr. Baring." The matter became public, and the *Pictorial Times* had caricatures of Lord Brougham and of Mazzini (with a kindly notice) which he sent home, adding that Lady Harriet declared she would never receive or speak to Lord Brougham again.

Though Mazzini was the truest democrat ever born, he

---

aided, during her short life, by her daughter Francesca, who regarded every privation undergone for the dearly loved exile as light and easy. The details of the manifold secret privations by which the mother and sister maintained this loving and truly pious fraud would fill a volume. Some of them were related to the present writer many years after, with mingled tears and laughter, . . . by the noble old mother herself, on the condition that the beloved object of such care and devotion should ever be kept in ignorance of the trials endured for his sake and of the paternal harshness which had rendered them necessary."—E. F. R.

appreciated intelligence, culture, and integrity in persons of exalted birth, and his artistic nature derived great pleasure from beautiful and tasteful surroundings ; therefore, excepting dinner-parties, which always bored him to death—for he said he " could not eat with servants placarded all over the wall "—he must have enjoyed his evenings at the Baring's, despite all Mrs. Carlyle's caricatures, and would have enjoyed them even more if from 1844 to 1848 he had not been so absorbed in work for Italy. Quite a number of the highest intelligences and of the deepest thinkers met at Lady Harriet's, and he was always delighted to see a woman holding her own, as this lady certainly did. She must have possessed great charm for the Princess Lieven to have declared " qu'il vaudrait bien s'abonner pour entendre causer cette femme." And when we remember that she had lost her only child under very painful circumstances ; that her health was never good, her suffering often acute, yet that she never intruded her grief and pain upon others, that she was devoted to her husband and anxious above all things to make her own great social position subserve his public fortunes, that he took a loverlike delight in the display of her genius and in the effervescence of her gaiety, it really seems as though Mrs. Carlyle ought to have felt thankful that her " roaring lion," her " raging bear," should come under the softening influence of such society. But she only felt aggrieved.

Mazzini, after moving with his faithful Tencionis from Chelsea to Devonshire Street, Queen's Square, in September, 1843, visited the Carlyles regularly once a week, and it is evident that he was made the confidant of griefs which, groundless as they were, rendered poor Mrs. Carlyle's life a burden to herself and others. To Mazzini, who knew Lady Harriet, and Carlyle's position at the Grange, and who appreciated the deep tenderness that underlay his rugged exterior, the whole story must have appeared astonishing. However, not a single word transpires in his letters to his mother of the cloud hanging over the house where he is made so welcome ; he has often, instead, some kindly deed

THE BIRTH OF MODERN ITALY

of Mr. Carlyle's to record, and he never fails to visit him most regularly.

The two following letters show how Mazzini endeavoured to advise and console Mrs. Carlyle :—

My Dear Friend,—I was yesterday almost the whole day out, and did not receive your notes except in the evening, when it was too late to answer them. Your few words sound sad—deeply, I will not say irreparably sad ; and the worst is, that none can help you but yourself. It is only you who can, by a calm, dispassionate, fair re-examination of the past, send back to nothingness the ghosts and phantoms that you have been conjuring up. It is only you who can teach yourself that, whatever the *present* may be, you *must* front it with dignity, with a clear perception of all your duties, with a due reverence to your immortal soul, with a religious faith in times yet to come, that are to dawn under the approach of other cloudless suns. I could only point out to you duties, fulfilment of duties which can make life—not happy ; what can ?—but earnest, sacred, and resigned ; but I would make you frown or scorn. We have a different conception of life, and are condemned here-down to walk on two parallels. Still it is the feeling of those duties that saves me from the atheism of despair, and leads me through a life every day more barren and burdensome, in a sort of calm, composed manner, such, I repeat, as the consciousness of something everlasting within us claims from every living mortal. For I now most coolly and deliberately do declare to you, that partly through what is known to you, partly through things that will never be known, I am carrying a burden even heavier than yours, and have undergone even bitterer deceptions than you have. But, by dint of repeating to myself that there is no happiness under the moon, that life is a self-sacrifice meant for some higher and happier thing, that to have a few loving beings, or, if none, a mother watching you from Italy or from heaven, it is all the same, ought to be quite enough to prevent us from falling, and by falling, parting. I have mustered up, thank God, strength enough to go on till I reach the grave—the grave for which the hour will come, and is fast approaching, without my loudly calling for it. Awake and arise, dear friend. . . Bent by pain or not, we must go on with a sad smile and a practical encouragement from one another. We have something of our own to care about, something Godlike that we must not yield to any living creature, whoever it be. Your life proves an empty thing, you say ! . . . Empty ? . . . Do not blaspheme ! . . . Have you never done good ? . . . Have you never loved ? . . . Think of your mother, and to do good, set your eye to Providence. It is not as a mere piece of irony that God has placed us here ; not as a mere piece of irony that He has given us those aspirations, those yearnings after happiness, that are making us now both unhappy. Can't you trust Him a little longer?

How long will you remain at Seaforth ? Does he himself propose to go anywhere? I was coming to see you on Saturday, but the exertions for the concert have quite knocked me down. Write when and if it does good, even homeopathically, to you, and be assured that to me it will always do.

Ever yours,
Joseph Mazzini.

Mrs. Carlyle seems to have made some efforts to send back "into nothingness the ghosts and phantoms," as Mazzini justly calls them, for she writes "a good little letter" to her husband, that lifts "a mountain from his inner man" (see "Thomas Carlyle : A History of His Life in London," 1834–1881, by J. A. Froude, vol. i. pp. 381–382), but again she must have sent a mournful letter to Mazzini, to which he replies as follows:—

To Jane Welsh Carlyle.

Seaforth, *July* 15.

My Dear Friend,—I could not write yesterday, as I intended, on account of the death of Scipione Pistrucci's wife.

Yes: sad as death, but not basely sad! . . . That is what you must be, and what a single moment of truly earnest thought and faith will cause you to be. Pain and joy, deception and fulfilled hopes are just, as I often said, the rain and sunshine that must meet the traveller on his way. Bless the Almighty if He has thought proper to send the latter to you. Button or wrap your cloak around you against the first, but do not think a single moment that the one or the other has anything to do with the *end* of your journey. You know that; but you want the *faith* that would give you strength to fulfil the task shown by the intellect. These powers will give you that too, if you properly apply to them affection, a religious belief, and the dead. You have affection for me, as I have for you; you would not shake mine ? You would not add yourself to the temptations haunting me to wreck and despair ? You would not make me worse than I am by your example, showing yourself selfish and materialistic ? You believe in God. Don't you think, after all, that this is nothing but an ephemeral trial; that He will shelter you at the journey's end under the wide wing of His paternal love ? You had, have, though invisible to the eyes of the body, your mother, your father too. Can't you commune with them ? I know that a single moment of true, fervent love for them will do more for you than all my talking. Were they now what you call living, would you not fly to them, hide your head in their bosom, and be comforted and feel that you owe to them to be strong, that they may never feel ashamed of their Jane ? Why, can you think them to be *dead*, gone for ever, their loving, immortal soul annihilated ? Can you think that this vanishing for a time has made you less responsible

THE BIRTH OF MODERN ITALY

to them ? *Can you, in a word, love them less because they are far from sight ?* I have often thought that the arrangement by which loved and loving beings are to pass through death is nothing but the last experiment appointed by God to human love, and often, as you know from me, I have found that a moment of true soul-communing with my dead friend has been a source of strength for me, unhoped for here-down. Did we not often agree about these glimpses of the link between ours and the superior life ? Shall we now begin to disagree ? Be strong then, and true to those you loved, and proud, nobly proud, in the eyes of those you love or esteem. Some of them are deeply, silently suffering, but needing strength too, needing it perhaps from you. Get up and work ; do not set yourself apart from us. When the Evil One wañted to tempt Jesus, he led Him into a solitude ! . . .

Believe me, my dear friend, ever yours,
JOSEPH MAZZINI.

Mazzini, in abandoning Chelsea, where he had spent three quiet years, evidently sought solitude and isolation. Instead of renting rooms for a longer term, he took them only by the week, so that at any moment when the exigencies of his schemes demanded, he might vanish from London without attracting notice.

He remained alone, for Agostino Ruffini had gone to Edinburgh, where he was doing fairly well, and his brother Giovanni had decided to seek employment in Paris, Mazzini having written to Georges Sand to introduce and recommend him. Those two, Giovanni and Mazzini, were unable to agree on many vital points, so that their relations had gradually become strained. Though this separation was necessarily painful, it really relieved both parties from a false situation. The worst feature of it, and one that left its mark on Mazzini, was that, during a short visit of the brothers to their mother in Montpellier, they brought her to their way of thinking ; and her subsequent silence was extremely painful to him, acutely renewing the morbid remorse about Jacopo that never wholly ceased to torment him. The Signora Mazzini and the Signora Eleonora must have also had a difference, but Mazzini, in his letters, persistently defended the brothers of Jacopo.

His letters continue as usual to portray English life · he whimsically describes the Queen's visit to the Château d'Eu, the "bread, cheese, and beer" offered by Louis Philippe with his usual affectation of *bourgeoisie*, and the pleasure she experienced in seeing Guizot again. Then he expresses his concern that England's might should be used to strengthen King Money. He finds that the Golden Calf is all powerful in France, and that Rothschild could be King there if he conspired. The misery is shocking in London, but in Ireland it is a hundred times worse. There, starvation and the trial of O'Connell are fanning the spirit of agitation towards rebellion. He sympathises greatly with Ireland—though he cannot help thinking that she would gain nothing by separation from England—but not much with O'Connell, whom, on account of his speeches about Spain and Italy, he finds to be "simply and solely dominated by the clergy, and a retrograde who did not understand what Liberty meant."

His desire for solitude was not attained. An article of his in the *Apostolato Popolare* against a microscopic party in Lombardy who wished to exalt the Russian Prince Leuchtemberg, the son of Prince Eugene, ex-Viceroy of Italy under Napoleon I., created quite a sensation in diplomatic circles, and an English ex-Ambassador to Constantinople, who was a confirmed Russophobe, called upon him for further information. He adds in his letter: "So goes the world! ... a little Court intrigue excites more interest than the slavery and misery of twenty millions of men."

With a supper of macaroni, fish (it being Friday), and beer, price one shilling for strangers and free for the boys, he celebrated the anniversary of the foundation of his school. As Mazzini was then suffering from an abscess which tormented him for over six months, he could not speak, but in his place their old teacher Pistrucci improvised, and an English gentleman "spoke heartily to the many English present." This seems to have excited the jealous attention of the Sardinian Embassy, whose agents, notably Baldaccone, the chaplain, closely watched his movements and tried by all means, fair and foul, break up the school. 'Roughs' were paid to disturb t proceedings, the pupils were threatened, and so was po old Pistrucci, who even feared for his own life. Mazz narrated these disgraceful incidents in the English pre and one Sunday evening he personally arrested a fello who was trying to cut off the gas, handed him over the police, and next day appeared in court against him

Through his articles in the English magazines Mazz had by this time contrived to create a growing inter in the British people for the cause of Italy; ubiquito Austrian spies, however, presently fathoming its gravi and extent, Austria diplomatically remonstrated with t English Government for allowing this "pernicious activi of dangerous individuals." Soon the Austrian press teem with calumnies of all kinds against Mazzini, much to t anguish of his father, who repeatedly begged him to d prove them in the English papers; but this he pers tently refused, feeling that to do so would "give und importance to such ribaldry."

A climax, however, was reached with the publication the "Mémoires" of a certain Gisquet, an ex-Prefect the French service, in which the Rhodez affair was revive These "Mémoires" were translated into English, and t *Athenæum* reviewed them at length, in a manner mo hostile to Mazzini. Letters poured in from all par clamouring for particulars, so that Mazzini decided prosecute Gisquet for libel. He engaged as counsel t Avocat Benoit (a relation of Lamennais), who proved mo zealous and disinterested, and prepared to demand a sa conduct to Paris. His father approved of his action a sent him £40 for the journey and £80 for law expense The trial dragged on for a whole year, though excelle testimonials as to Mazzini's character were collected Benoit in England, Italy, and Switzerland. Carlyle, perha at the instance of Giovanni Ruffini, wrote a very nol

[1] See note, p. 57. In all probability Signora Mazzini supplied t money.—E.F.R.

letter without Mazzini's knowledge ; so also did Dr. Bowring, and his old tutor, a priest in Genoa. These were read in court, as well as the sentence passed by the "Cour d'Assises de l'Aveyron" upon Gavioli, so of course Mazzini was acquitted, but Gisquet was not condemned, for he not only pleaded that "the Mazzini mentioned in his book was not the Joseph Mazzini whom all the world knew as a talented and honourable gentleman," but that furthermore he had been ignorant of the trial and condemnation of Gavioli.

Benoit wished to carry the case to the Court of Cassation, seeing that this Gisquet, though acquitted in the "Correctionnel" for a libel on the Duke of Brunswick about a diamond, had been sentenced by the "Cassation" to a fine and the expenses of the trial. Dr. Mazzini expressed the same desire, but his son unfortunately, assured by his English friends that his reputation was safe and his honour above suspicion, refused. Benoit returned the £80 for law expenses intact, and only accepted as a token of gratitude a ring from Dr. Mazzini. But it was a grievous mistake to have neglected his advice, for the scotched snake's poisoned fangs inflicted other dangerous wounds before it was finally killed. Much to Dr. Mazzini's disgust, the *Athenæum* and other English papers that had repeated the calumny were not prompt to publish its disproval, and he hints in his letters that as regards liberty the world is "much of a muchness," England being quite as bad as France. To which the son replies : "There is no possible comparison between liberty in England and liberty in France. English surpasses French liberty ten thousand times. The English Government is neither venal nor immoral, it never violates individual liberty nor attempts to corrupt individuals, whereas French Ministers are both venal and immoral, corruptors and oppressors."

V

THE BANDIERA BROTHERS

1843–1845

Mazzini's letters opened in the English Post-office—His correspondence with the Bandieras—Thomas Slingsby Duncombe gives notice of a motion in the House of Commons—Sir James Graham's admission—Lord Aberdeen the betrayer of information to Austria—Interest aroused throughout England and Scotland—England not responsible for the Bandieras' death—Nicola Fabrizi—Baron Bandiera's sons conspire—Domenico Moro—Attilio Bandiera writes to Mazzini—Treachery of Micciarelli—Attilio contrives to warn his brother and Moro—Writes to his wife and mother—Escapes to Syria—Emilio visits his mother and sister-in-law on the eve of his escape to Corfù—Betrayal by a stewardess—Incautious letters handed by a false friend to the Austrians—Mazzini, deprecating small risings, preaches patience—Fabrizi organising a large movement—Ricciotti—Treachery in Paris—Ricciotti liberated—Reaches Corfù—Refugees embark for Calabria—A trap—Assailed and defeated—Death—Sir James Graham denounces Mazzini as an assassin—Carlyle's letter to the *Times*—Sir James Graham's *amende honorable*.

TOO soon, alas! was his boundless faith in the integrity of the English Government, and its respect for the liberties of all individuals domiciled in the British realm, destined to receive a rude shock. Proof of his robust faith in England is found in his continued refusal to believe direct evidence that his letters were tampered with, not only in the French and Sardinian, but in the British Post Office, and that his movements were watched in the interest of Austria; probably also in that of the King of Naples. The

Austrian papers boasted of the fact, but Mazzini wrote to his father: "Do not believe a word of it; the English Government has sent no note, given no pledge to Austria. There exists no political police in England, no office, no chief, no agents, so it cannot exercise espionage; if I found myself shadowed I should get some member of Parliament to make an interpellation."

And to this expedient he was compelled to resort after repeated trials and exhaustive tests had proved that all his letters, whether from abroad, from Scotland, the provinces, or even from London, were opened, reclosed, and, of course, delayed in delivery.

During 1843 and 1844 agitations and revolts in the Neapolitan provinces, especially in Calabria and the Papal States, had incessantly broken out. Austria sent four thousand troops to occupy Bologna, affirming that when disturbances approached the Po it was her bounden duty to protect her Italian provinces. And no doubt the authorities were greatly alarmed by the spirit of insubordination that was spreading in the Venetian fleet and by the desertion of naval officers of high rank, such as the sons of Admirals Bandiera, Nugent, and Paolucci, besides numerous Hungarian cadets. One young officer, Attilio Bandiera, had written to Mazzini, under an assumed name, towards the close of 1842, before he deserted, and continued in direct communication with him; hence the bare suspicion that his correspondence was opened at the British Post Office filled Mazzini with consternation. Communicating his fears to Dr. Bowring and Thomas Duncombe, the latter assured him that it was by no means impossible, as there existed precedents for such an outrage. His own correspondence, for instance, had been violated during the Irish troubles. He offered, when proof should be established, to bring the matter before the House of Commons; so, at the suggestion of his friends, Mazzini resorted to certain contrivances which left no doubt that his letters were systematically tampered with. Accordingly, the chain of evidence being complete, "Tom" Duncombe, the exponent of popular and unpopular grievances, gave notice in the House of his motion (July 1st).

Sir James Graham at first refused any explanation, but when hard pressed he admitted that the letters had been opened, though he denied that their contents had been communicated by Lord Aberdeen to the Austrian ambassador in London or to any foreign Government; he justified his action by a statute of Queen Anne, which he insisted had been frequently put in practice by Ministers of both English political parties. Mr. Duncombe's accusation, brought at the moment when the suppression of the first revolt in Calabria was reported in the press, created a sensation in the House, which, in questions relating to foreigners and foreign affairs, has scarcely had a parallel. Later in the month, when the Bandiera brothers and seven of their companions were sentenced to death by a military tribunal of the King of Naples and shot at Cosenza, a flame was lit throughout the country that at first seemed to threaten the existence of the Cabinet. Throughout England and Scotland Sir James Graham was spoken of, somewhat unjustly, as the "assassin of the Italian patriots." As a matter of fact, it was Lord Aberdeen who had had the letters opened and who had (as he was finally constrained to own) transmitted their contents to the Austrian ambassador. For many years it was the belief of most right-minded Englishmen that the information thus obtained led to the arrest and execution of the patriots, but now evidence to the contrary is happily attainable. Permitted to burrow in the secret recesses of the State Archives of Milan by their venerable keeper, Cesare Cantù, we came upon documents which, while confirming the fact of the transmission of the letters to the Austrian Embassy in London (demonstrating that Lord Aberdeen lied), proved that Austria had obtained earlier and independent knowledge of the plans of the Venetian patriots. As it may still be grateful to English hearts to know that the blood of the Bandieras and their companions does not rest on England's head, we will give a short sketch of their brief life and tragic end.

NICOLA FABRIZI.

[To face p. 60.]

Every year revolts had been breaking out, mostly in the Neapolitan provinces and Sicily, and numbers of exiles in Spain, and notably in Montevideo, where Garibaldi had organised a "legion," were looking hopefully for the moment to return and take part in a general revolution. In 1841 Nicola Fabrizi, a believer in "Young Italy," and one of the leaders of the Savoy expedition who had been condemned to death by the Duke of Modena (1831), came back from Spain. He considered Sicily the theatre where an initiative would have the greatest chance of success. Mazzini, however, differed from him in this, believing that the Sicilians would rest content with autonomy for themselves and disregard the claims of Italy. Still, he and Fabrizi were at one in condemning the projects of the Federalists, Gioberti's League of Princes with the Pope at their head, and the plans of the Albertists for a union of all northern Italy with the duchies under the crown of Piedmont; both believed strongly in the doctrine of union, so when Fabrizi settled at Malta to become the connecting link between Italian conspirators and the exiles in London, Paris, Spain, Montevideo, and New York, Mazzini corresponded with him. Fabrizi collected funds and smuggled both arms and ammunition, leading an austere, retired life, which gave no pretext for suspicion. His doings were thoroughly known only to Mazzini in London and to Lamberti in Paris, and these both sent emissaries to him for instructions.

The good seed sown by "Young Italy" had taken root: the sense of Italianhood was springing up in the hearts of the new generation; children felt proud of fathers who had suffered for the cause and were ashamed of such as had deserted or betrayed it. This was the piteous case of Attilio and Emilio Bandiera. They were the sons of Baron Bandiera, commander of the Austrian fleet, who, after the failure of the revolution in Central Italy in 1831, and despite the formal capitulation, had captured the schooner *Isotta* in the Adriatic and taken the insurgent General Zucchi, with several chiefs of the movement who were on board, to Venice as prisoners. There, after a long confinement, Zucchi and twelve others were condemned to death; but their sentences were in the end commuted to *carcere dure* for life. Attilio was fond of his profession, and Emilio—nine years younger and devoted to his brother—followed in his steps. Emilio was a daring, reckless lad, always in punishment at college for heading the Istrian and Italian students in their school frays against the Austrians. Attilio, of a reserved and serious disposition, for a time felt himself bound by his oath of allegiance and his duty to his father. But in all the ports at which Attilio touched between the years 1838 and 1840 he became increasingly aware of the hatred of the entire population of the Peninsula for Austria, and found that his father's name was generally held in abhorrence. At the bombardment of St. Jean d'Acre in 1840 he met Domenico Moro, a friend of Emilio's, who had decided to quit the Austrian service and devote himself to the task of freeing Italy from foreign dominion. Then and there the struggle in Attilio's mind between patriotism and the powers that were, ceased. He and Moro decided to commence a propaganda among their fellow-officers, intending, when possible, to carry off a couple or more of Austrian warships, descend upon some part of the Italian coast, and give the signal for a general uprising.

This was before the Bandieras had had any intercourse whatever with Mazzini. For two years the three friends laboured ardently but cautiously in different centres, Attilio on board the *Bellona*, Emilio in Venice, and Moro on the *Adria*. In 1842, at Smyrna, Attilio came across some of Mazzini's writings and a copy of the last number of the *Apostolato Populare*, which of course strengthened his views and made him resolve to put himself in touch with their author. This he did, sending a letter by a safe hand to Mazzini in London. A correspondence with both the brothers ensued. At that period the whole of Central Italy was in a condition of ferment, produced not only by misgovernment and oppression, but by ill-considered, rash promises made by conspirators not acting in concert, and which remained unfulfilled. The elements of disaffection were strong enough, had they been daringly and wisely focussed, to have opened the way for an Italian movement, and not a few significant portents fed the Bandieras' hope and energy.

In June, 1843, a secret meeting of those who were keeping in touch with Fabrizi, took place at Naples, when it was decided to bring about simultaneous revolts in Romagna and Calabria. And then began for the Bandieras one of those destructive experiences that either ruin men's faith or precipitate them into desperate action. Delays, disappointments, crippling counsels of caution, the difficulty of obtaining promised money, undermined all plans. Presently treachery added its hateful quota to the growing tragedy.

Attilio wrote to Mazzini on the 19th of March : " Events of great importance, not more to ourselves than to our cause, have taken place here since last January. A certain T. V. Micciarelli, whom perhaps you know by reputation, betrayed all my plans, . . . but I, having from previous causes learnt the perfidy of Micciarelli, and fearing that this first blow might be followed by another less easy to avert, had secretly prepared to fly ; and on the 29th of last month I started on my escape, and after an eventful pilgrimage succeeded during the last few days in accomplishing it. I succeeded in sending word to my brother, then in Venice—who was also known to my betrayer—in order that he might follow my example, but as yet I have no news of him. How will my mother and my wife bear the news of these misfortunes—they who are so delicate and, it may be, unable to endure such sorrows ? Ah ! the idea of serving humanity and my country ever was, and I hope ever will be, my first desire ; but I must confess it costs me very dear."

In those days spies swarmed and flourished ; no man in Italy knew whether he could trust his own brother. Mazzini makes a terrible comment on contemporary domestic life in his unfortunate country. " The unhappy mothers of Italy, victims themselves of the worst possible species of education and deprived of all fitting influence in the social organisation, tremblingly teach their sons . . . submission to those in power. . . . The fathers of Italy, well aware that every family counts probably one spy among its members, educate their sons to a life of isolation and distrust." It is not, therefore, surprising to find in the informer who first betrayed the Bandieras, a brother-officer recruited to their secret banner by Emilio himself. This man, cognisant of every detail of the nascent conspiracy, going to Smyrna and Constantinople, revealed all to the Austrian Minister in each place. But, prompted perhaps by some movement of conscience, as soon as the price of his infamy was safely in his pocket, he warned Attilio.

Attilio advised Moro and his brother. He then asked his father for permission to go to Venice to visit his wife, and suggested a change of service, saying that by remaining so long the Admiral's aide-de-camp he might engender jealousy among his brother-officers and cause his father to be accused of favouritism. The Admiral, according the permit, promised to consider this suggestion. Attilio's mother, hearing that he was to leave the *Bellona* on the 28th of February, naturally expected him in Venice, but he wrote to say there might be some delay, as he should take a sailing-boat instead of coming by the more expensive steamer. Then undated, touching letters reached both wife and mother. "Near or far, happy or unhappy, I shall ever love and desire thee, my Marianna, but I wish for thine own sake that thou shouldst love me less and so suffer less.   . If only instead of writing I could wake up in thy arms!" Attilio had married Marianna Graziana, the daughter of a naval officer, and was not only a husband, but a father. He had made his wife privy, as far as he dared, to his plans, and nobly she responded, bravely carrying her gnawing anxiety, though it sapped her strength and presently brought her young life to its close.

To the Baroness the fugitive wrote in much the same vein, ending with the words: "You are ever my first thought." It seems that in this missive the mother saw merely the usual expressions of fervid love, but the young

EMILO BANDIERA

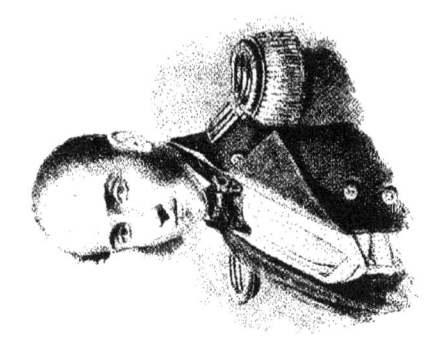

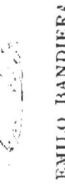

ATTILIO BANDIERA

wife trembled. Emilio had warned her of her husband's projected flight, and she maintained an outward show of calmness during the awful uncertainty of the days that followed; but the tension was so great that when news of his safety at last reached her she sank under the reaction of relief. Death spared her, perhaps mercifully, the knowledge of his second betrayal, of his heroism, and of his ultimate execution. At the moment when Attilio wrote the letter to Mazzini above quoted she was already dead. All who have known Marianna Bandiera describe her as remarkable not only for her beauty, but for her high intellectual and moral qualities.

While Attilio was achieving his perilous flight towards Syria, Radetzky, informed by the Austrian Consul at Constantinople of Micciarelli's delation, sent an express ordering Rear-Admiral Paolucci to recall the squadron from Trieste, to keep a sharp watch over the entire fleet, and only to reveal privately to Admiral Bandiera the delinquencies of his sons. Emilio escaped by a miracle. The despatch arrived while Paolucci happened to be absent, and Emilio, being empowered as private secretary to open all his correspondence, concealed it. When Paolucci returned he asked and received permission to go to Venice for forty-eight hours, as it was Carnival time. He passed the last evening with his mother and his sister-in-law—the latter already ill through anxiety about her husband, and whose worst suspicions were confirmed by this departure of Emilio in the midst of the Venetian Carnival. His mother, conveniently for him, gave him 112 florins to pay his tailor.

At Trieste, through a friend, he obtained a passport under the name of Consiglio; but though he disguised himself, he was recognised by the Austrian stewardess of the Lloyd steamer in which he took his passage, and she told the captain his name. The captain, however, perhaps imagining that the young man might have been despatched on some secret mission, decided not to interfere with him; seeing which, the stewardess, with a persistency that seems to smack of the spy, warned the Austrian Consul in Corfù, who at once communicated with the authorities in Venice. Emilio's place of refuge therefore became known, and his movements could be checked. Believing that he had a safe address, he wrote several incautious letters to his sister-in-law, telling her that he had no news of Attilio, though he had lingered fifteen days in the hope of obtaining tidings, and that now he shall go on to London to see Mazzini, or to Valenza to confer with Colonel Alduino. "A few days since I received letters from London warning us of the danger hanging over our heads."

Mazzini, who somehow got to know most things, had received tidings, not of the actual treachery of Micciarelli, but of his disappearance and of mysterious movements on the part of the Austrians.

None of these letters reached their destination, for the friend to whom they were sent, under cover, handed them all to the Austrian officials. They may still be seen in the State Archives of Milan, and afford proof of the way in which the Austrian authorities obtained information of the whereabouts of the deserters, their plans and correspondents. Other reports also show that although Sir James Graham and Lord Aberdeen did their servile best for Austria—although they descended to falsehood and the cowardly arm of calumny—they did not actually set the mark of Cain on England's brow. Lord Staton, Governor of Corfù, refused to interfere with the exiles.

Rumours of general and increasing discontent in Italy reached both Emilio and his brother in Syria, and fired their already intense longing for action to fever pitch. An *émeute* took place at Cosenza, which, though quelled in blood, awakened a widespread desire in the populations to be up and doing. Sicily was burning to revolt, and an attempt would certainly have been made if those well-meaning but timid voices which so constantly pour lukewarm wisdom upon the initiative of the *people*, had not prevailed.

In a letter to Mazzini, Emilio gives a very frank estimate of those over-cautious plotters who, doubting the judgment of the more enthusiastic spirits, bidding them, "like vegetables, wait for the spring," allowed the dynamic power of the popular excitement to sink down almost beyond reach :—

"I only required a few thousand francs. My brother answered that they were denied him. . . . May the evil consequences be on the heads of those who denied and despised us. *Do not speak any more of your friends.* Forgive me if I have allowed myself to use the language of one forsaken; I do so because I know how innocent you are of all the delay and neglect to which we have fallen a sacrifice."

Mazzini and Fabrizi alike were certainly innocent of delay and neglect, but it always had been, and always continued to be, Mazzini's policy to deprecate small risings that could only end in waste of precious lives; and when he saw that a possible opportunity had gone by, he earnestly counselled patience and prudence.

Before Attilio joined him in Corfù, poor Emilio had to undergo the greatest trial of his life. Once in possession of Emilio's letters, the military tribunals of Venice had commenced investigations. The *Bellona*, together with the rest of the fleet, was recalled from Trieste and the officers subjected to rigorous examinations, over which Radetzky presided in person. But neither Radetzky, Paolucci, nor Archduke Raineri, Viceroy of the Lombardo-Venetian provinces, desired to lend conspicuous importance to these aristocratic deserters by punishing them. For diplomatic reasons they hastened to declare that they only "desired the return of the erring sheep to the fold," and the convenient formula of "youthful indiscretion" should be made to explain their irregular absence. The Baroness Bandiera (to whom both her sons were tenderly attached) was commissioned to go in person to Corfù and assure Emilio of the Emperor's absolute pardon if he would return with her, adding that the clemency of the Emperor might also be extended to Attilio, notwithstanding the fact that his age rendered his crime more heinous. The description of the interview with his mother given in Emilio's letters is pathetic in the extreme: " My mother, tortured, blinded by anguish, cannot comprehend me; she upbraids me as unnatural, impious, a murderer. Her tears break my heart; her reproaches—though undeserved—are to me as the wounds of a dagger; but my misery cannot deprive me of my reason. I know that the responsibility of her tears and of her anger rests upon our tyrants, and if hitherto I was animated by love of country alone, I am now inspired as much by hatred against the despots and usurpers whose infamous ambition reduces families to such misery as this. . . ."

While Emilio was chafing in Corfù because unable to join the rumoured insurrection in Calabria, Attilio and Domenico Moro arrived in the island, Moro having effected his escape from the *Adria*. Reports of fresh movements in the Pontifical States made them all anxious to rush to Italy, but Mazzini put them in correspondence with Fabrizi, impressing upon them to follow his instructions. In March Emilio wrote to Mazzini that Fabrizi was keeping them inactive, refusing them supplies, that he, Emilio, feared that he and his brother might have made useless sacrifices. Fabrizi, however, thoroughly understood the situation, and, counselling caution, advised them that for the present every symptom of revolt had been crushed; he entreated them to have patience and not to throw away their own and other lives in useless attempts, for he was in a position to assure them that fresh plans were maturing.

Fabrizi could at that moment give no further information, but it is now known that a better organised insurrection was being contemplated in the Papal States, and that another patriot, Ricciotti, had started from London with funds and passports from Mazzini, intending, should all go well, to bid the Bandieras, Moro, and others join him at a given moment. Unfortunately, in passing through Paris, Ricciotti revealed his plans to one of the foulest of the spy tribe, Attilio Partesotti, who, himself an exile and living among the exiles as their friend, was all the while a paid instrument of the Austrian Embassy. This man's crimes remained unsuspected by his victims until after his death—from blood-poisoning occasioned by the corrosive acid he used for erasing names from passports, &c. He denounced Ricciotti, who was arrested by the French authorities and detained at Marseilles. On his liberation he got back to England, then started joyfully for Malta and Corfù.

Attilio, who had already written with imprudent explicitness to Mazzini, "*trusting to the known loyalty of the English post,*" says in a letter dated the 6th June, "We have seen Ricciotti and we will do our best to help him. . . ." The next day Emilio wrote: "I thank you for the affectionate lines brought me by Ricciotti. The friendship you grant me I have felt for you . . . ever since the day I contrived to procure some copies of *Young Italy*, and repeat them to my companions. . We are endeavouring to solve the intricate problem with Ricciotti. At all events I hope soon to be in action with him. . . . "

On the 8th of the same month Ricciotti writes: "For the moment there is no embarkation for where you know (Ancona), but I hope for one shortly." Thus, up to that date, all idea of an expedition to *Calabria* was abandoned.

How was it, then, that within *three* days, on the 11th of June, the intentions of the exiles were entirely changed? How was it that, without consulting Mazzini or Fabrizi, the two brothers Bandiera, Ricciotti, Moro, and sixteen others started for Calabria, where the insurrection had been crushed, military tribunals having made short shrift of such captives as they did not imprison or exile?

It would occupy too much space to translate all the denunciations and other explanatory documents which throw a sinister light on this subject. The facts are that a schooner, bearing money, arms, and ammunition, appeared as by a miracle in the waters of Corfù. French and Maltese papers affirmed that the King of Naples, weary of revolts and insurrections, desired above all things to grant a constitution, and to govern as a liberal monarch, but that he was kept in check by Austria and his Austrian consort. The captains of two merchant vessels arriving within a day of each other at Corfù from Calabria narrated that the mountains around Cosenza, Scigliano, and San Giovanni in Fiore swarmed with armed insurgents, who were receiving regular rations from fellow-conspirators in the cities; they declared that the shores were not patrolled, and that the insurgents only needed military leaders who represented the popular feeling of other provinces, for a national insurrection to result. At the same time, a fictitious " Committee of Paris" —probably Attilio Partesotti—assured the exiles that the news from Calabria was true, and sent them two proclamations, one to the Calabresi and one to the Italians, to be exhibited when they should land in the insurgent district.

It is easy now to marvel at the credulity of the exiles; but when one remembers that they were furious with the lukewarm patriots who had preached patience to their youthful ardour, refused promised succour, and prevented them from carrying out the ideal to which they were willing to sacrifice all that made life worth living, we see nothing unnatural or exaggerated in their belief. And now, where we are bereft of direct evidence, we must resort to hypothesis. Who sent the schooner, the funds, and the false news? In default of proof one seeks for a motive. To whose interest was it that such dangerous conspirators should be put out of the way? Clearly, the Power most interested was Austria.

During the revolution of 1821, when complicity was proved against numbers of Milanese, no death sentences were pronounced. The horrors of the Austrian Spielberg, as revealed by Silvio Pellico, were light in comparison with those of the prisons of the Papal States and the kingdom of Naples. The policy of Metternich was to make believe that the populations under the direct rule of Austria were contented and loyal, but in the States where Austria could exercise armed control or moral pressure, she put the screw on to induce the Governments to arrest and imprison all suspects, and to show no leniency either in their sentences or in their execution.

To get such dangerous conspirators, such audacious deserters, as the Bandiera group despatched to another world by the King of Naples, Austria, in the meanwhile, retaining her character for clemency, exactly suited both Metternich and Rainieri; and nothing short of Austria's acuteness could have successfully improvised such a *coup*.

On June 11th the exiles embarked with eighteen companions, among them being an unsuspected traitor named Boccheciampi. This man had been imposed upon them by an unfrocked priest, who had for some time aired his "patriotism" in England, and who it is now shrewdly suspected had no small share in luring the Bandieras to their fate. Boccheciampi was assisted by the Neapolitan Consul in Corfù, who also employed a second spy named Compagnoni to consort with the exiles. Another wolf in sheep's clothing connected with the little band passed as a political refugee under the name of Battistino Nivari. In reality this man was one of the most notorious brigands of the Sila. Ten years before he had fled from Calabria after committing at least one murder, but in Corfù had conducted himself respectably as the factor of a wealthy citizen.

The little party landed near Cotrone, in Calabria, knelt down, and kissing the Italian soil exclaimed, "Thou hast given us life; we give our lives to thee." Boccheciampi immediately sent secret information to Del Carretto, who despatched a courier to the Governor of Otranto and spread the tidings that a famous brigand, with a band of desperadoes, had returned to renew his former exploits. Then Boccheciampi disappeared.

The insurgents expected by the Bandieras were, of course, not forthcoming, and the band returned to the shore intending to re-embark, but the captain of the schooner had already set sail—to receive the price of his freight. The little party presently being assailed by gendarmes and the urban guard, fought valiantly, killed one man, wounded another, and actually put the rest to flight; but later, four miles from San Giovanni in Fiore, two of their number, Miller and Tesei, were killed by the regular troops; Nardi, Moro, and Emilio Bandiera were wounded; all were arrested and carried to Cosenza, where they were imprisoned with those insurgents who had been condemned to death for the rising of March 15th. At the court-martial before which they were brought they again saw Boccheciampi, also cited; but the accusation against him was simply that of not having revealed their project. It is, perhaps, unnecessary to add that this man was not shot.

The Bandieras refused counsel for defence, but were compelled to submit to having the office performed for them, the line of defence being that they had landed in the belief that the King was willing to grant a constitution and place himself at the head of an Italian movement. From the first they foresaw, and were resigned, to their fate, only hoping that some of their numbers might be spared. But the sentence of death was passed upon all, though for three —Manessi, Pacchioni, and Osmani—the sentence was commuted to the galleys. Pacchioni, an artist, took portraits of the Bandieras during their twenty days' imprisonment, and afterwards made public the pathetic details of the last hours spent in their company. At dawn on July 25th Attilio and Emilio Bandiera, with seven companions, were led barefooted, a black veil covering their faces, to the Vallone di Rovito, all chanting the chorus of "Donna Caritea," *Chi per la patria muore vissuto ha assai* (Who dies for his country, has lived long enough). On the place of execution they kissed each other, and exhorted the weeping soldiers to do their duty. They alone were calm. The people assembled on the surrounding heights wept and muttered curses low and deep; the soldiers, unwilling executioners, fired badly. "Courage," cried Ricciotti; "do your duty; we too are soldiers." A second volley killed several and horribly wounded Attilio and two others; but until their last breath all cried "Viva l'Italia!" Emilio, in one of his letters to Fabrizi, had written: "And if we do lose our lives what matters? Italy will never live till Italians learn to die." And to teach the lesson Attilio and Emilio Bandiera, Domenico Moro, Anacarsi Nardi, Francesco Berti, Domenico Lupatelli, Giovanni Venerucci, Giacomo Rocca, Nicola Ricciotti cheerfully laid down their lives. And from these consecrated martyrs, these hearts devoted unto death, the Italians learnt the lesson, practising it in increasing numbers in every province of Italy, till sixteen years later Garibaldi and his Thousand, after liberating Sicily and Naples, knelt and gave thanks in the church of Sant Agostino, where the martyrs were buried. Some of the last letters of the victims, published in the *Times* and other newspapers, produced a profound sensation. Mazzini's pamphlet on the Bandiera brothers was widely read, and his wonderfully exhaustive article in the *Westminster Review*, September, 1844, revealing the methods of the letter-opening system, filled Englishmen with indignant shame.

At the re-opening of Parliament in 1845, " Tom " Duncombe demanded the nomination of a second Commission, with public sittings and all facilities for examining witnesses on oath, in order that facts concealed by the previous Commission should be revealed. In his speech he narrated the history and tragic end of the Bandieras, and said that when free Italy erected a monument to their memory, on it would be inscribed : " They died for their country, betrayed by the British Government of the day." This, as we have shown, was hardly the case ; but the conduct of the Government on this occasion surpassed in infamy even their letter-opening exploits. Lord Aberdeen, with all the proofs of the contrary in his hands, denied that the " Bandieras and consorts " had been arrested by the troops of the King of Naples, insisting that they had been assailed by the population. It was, however, left for Sir James Graham to fill up the cup of iniquity by gratuitously denouncing Mazzini as an assassin and a hirer of assassins, and by reading to the House the spurious sentence declared to have been passed by Mazzini and Cecilia on Emiliani and Lazzareschi, in 1833. The demand for a second Commission was vetoed, Ministers refusing to admit the proposal for the abolition of the law enabling the Government to open letters, even those of foreigners. Monckton-Milnes said that if the House divided he must go with the adversaries of the Government, and Dr. Bowring would not allow the discussion to close without bearing testimony to the character of Mazzini, so unjustly attacked by Sir James Graham. It was neither charitable nor honourable, he said, to level the most terrible and criminal accusations in a place where a man could not be present to defend himself. He demanded that Sir James Graham should acquaint himself with the real character of Mazzini, and if he found, as he would find, that he had been misinformed, he would appeal to his sense of justice to decide whether Mr. Mazzini should be left in that abyss of degradation to which he had been cast by the aspersions publicly thrown upon him in that House. Other members also strongly censured the Under-Secretary for producing from certain newspapers trumped-up charges which he ought to have known were not true, and for stating that Mazzini had never attempted to clear himself when, if he had taken the trouble to ascertain the facts, he would have found that Mazzini had brought one or two actions against the papers by which his character had been aspersed.

Carlyle, who by his genius and integrity had then attained a powerful position, had in the preceding summer sent the following letter to the *Times*:—

To the Editor of the *Times*.

Chelsea, *June* 15, 1844.

Sir,—In your observations in yesterday's *Times* on the late disgraceful affair of Mr. Mazzini's letters and the Secretary of State, you mention that Mr. Mazzini is entirely unknown to you, entirely indifferent to you, and add, very justly, that if he were the most contemptible of mankind it would not affect your argument on the subject.

It may tend to throw further light on this matter if I now certify you, which I in some sort feel called upon to do, that Mr. Mazzini is not unknown to various competent persons in this country, and that he is very far indeed from being contemptible.

I have had the honour to know Mr. Mazzini for a series of years, and, whatever I may think of his practical insight and skill in worldly affairs, I can with great freedom testify to all men that he, if I ever have seen one such, is a man of genius and virtue, a man of sterling veracity, humanity, and nobleness of mind, one of those rare men, numberable, unfortunately, but as units in this world, who are worthy to be called martyr souls, who, in silence, piously, in their daily life, understand and practise what is meant by that. Of Italian democracies and " Young Italy's " sorrows, of extraneous Austrian Emperors in Milan and chimerical old Popes in Bologna, I know nothing and desire to know nothing: but this other thing I do know, and can here declare publicly to be a fact, which fact all of us that have occasion to comment on Mr. Mazzini and his affairs may do well to take along with us, as a thing leading towards new clearness, and not towards new additional darkness, regarding him and them.

Whether the extraneous Austrian Emperor and miserable old Chimera of a Pope shall maintain themselves in Italy, is not a question in the least vital to Englishmen. But it is a question vital to us that sealed letters in an English post-office be, as we all fancied they were, respected as things sacred; that opening of men's letters, a practice near of kin to picking men's pockets, and to other still viler and far fataler forms of scoundrelism, be not resorted to, in England, except in cases of the very last extremity. When some new Gunpowder Plot may be in the wind, some double-dyed high treason, or imminent national wreck, not avoidable otherwise, then, let us open letters: not till then. To all Austrian Kaisers, and such-like, in their time of trouble, let us answer, as our fathers from of old have answered: "Not by such means is help here for you! Such means, allied to picking of pockets and viler forms of scoundrelism, are not permitted in this country for your behoof."

The Right Honourable Secretary does himself detest such, and even is afraid to employ them. He dare not: it would be dangerous for him!.. All British men that might chance to come in view of such a transaction would incline to spurn it, and trample on it, and indignantly ask him what he meant by it.

I am, sir, your obedient servant,
THOMAS CARLYLE.

Sir James Graham, presently finding himself pushed to the wall, made a virtue of necessity and offered to Mazzini, as far as it was possible, the *amende honorable*. On a subsequent day he stated that if he had known of the trial of Gisquet and the impressions received during that trial by the judge and public prosecutor, so far from committing himself to the statement he had made, he would have religiously abstained from noticing the matter. As the accusation had been public Sir James thought it was due to Mazzini that the retractation should also be public, and he added that he hoped what he had said would be considered satisfactory.

Thus ended the memorable debate which, owing its origin to the heroic attempt of the brothers Bandiera, completely cleared the good name of Mazzini.

VI

WEARY WAITING

1845

Mazzini's gratitude to Englishmen—Medals presented to Mr. Duncombe—Mazzini brought prominently into notice—Demands from editors for articles—English and Italian friends—Lord Ashley President of the Society for the protection of Italian boys—Joseph Cowen—Peter Taylor—An impostor deceives Dickens and Cobden—The Ashursts — Lloyd-Garrison — Caroline Ashurst Stansfeld — Emilie Ashurst Hawkes (afterwards E. A. Venturi).

DEEP thankfulness that the cause of Italy remained uninjured, and might even be benefited, by the result of the protracted discussion, and gratitude to the Englishmen who had championed his country and himself both in the House of Commons and the press, overflows in the letters Mazzini wrote home after Sir James Graham's retractation.

Dr. Mazzini had had very scant hopes of his son's triumph in the matter, and in a letter dated May 5th wrote that the Minister " would never retract his accusation : it is not possible that he could retract " ; but with the careful translation of Sir James Graham's speech before him he was at last reassured. Both parents would now cease to tremble lest their son might be banished from England and condemned to his old life of hiding, running the constant risk of imprisonment and even of ignominious death—a prospect which they had begun to fear, in spite of his assurances that he could not be expelled from British soil without the renewal of the " Alien Bill," a measure which the English people would not tolerate. Mazzini had rightly estimated the relief that his letter would convey to the dear anxious ones in Genoa. So great was that of his father that the old gentleman announced his intention of writing to Sir J. Graham, to thank him for having cleared his son's name from the horrible imputations cast upon it.

Mazzini wrote back post-haste to his mother : " Dissuade my father from writing at all to the Minister, who is the cause of all the evil, who has acted throughout basely and in bad faith : his retractation was compulsory, for he could not have kept silent any longer after the repeated interpellations." In this same letter he sends his father extracts from his recent article on " Italy, Austria, and the Pope," ironically dedicated to Sir J. Graham. Dr. Mazzini yielded, but disapproved of the extracts, and urged his son to discontinue expressing erroneous opinions which only caused trouble to himself and sorrow to his parents, and which could do no good to the cause he had at heart. But Mazzini replied that his convictions were unalterable, and that he felt it to be a duty to express them, believing that by so doing he furthered the great cause for which he lived. In every letter he narrated the good that public discussion had produced ; he sent reviews of the Bandiera pamphlet, and told of the people who, in consequence of the revelations made concerning the real state of Italy, had written or come in person to offer help towards his school and towards the publication of his views.

Dr. Mazzini was especially pleased that the Italians resident in London should have shown their gratitude to Duncombe by presenting him with two medals coined in honour of " the Martyrs of Cosenza." Exquisite works of art, they had been designed by old Scipione Pistrucci, sculptor, painter, and teacher in Mazzini's school. They bore the names of the martyrs on the verso, and a wreath of cypress, palm, ivy, and oak, with the motto " ORA E SEMPRE (Now and forever)—YOUNG ITALY TO HER MARTYRS," on the recto. The medals were artistically set in black velvet, with the following inscription in silver letters: "To Thomas Slingsby Duncombe, M.P., Italians offer this slight but affectionate token of gratitude because he, in the British Parliament, commemorated with generous words our brothers who died for the Italian faith in Cosenza: because he staunchly upheld the rights of exiles, basely and for base purposes violated by the British Government: because he disproved the calumnies launched in order to justify the betrayal of British hospitality by its members against one of our countrymen."

Some time afterwards Mazzini wrote that the address and Duncombe's beautiful reply to it had been published in the papers, adding that he had declined the invitation to a public meeting and banquet in honour of Duncombe and other champions of the rights of the exiles, "first because I do not care to appear in England as an agitator, and secondly because I should be called upon to make a speech in English, which would be a terrible infliction to me." Later he feared that Lord Ashley, because he voted with the Government in the letter-opening debate, would withdraw from the presidency of the society for the protection of the Italian organ-boys, but that noble-hearted gentleman, "*though voting as a Tory, acted as a Christian*," and abated none of his efforts in favour of those poor little white slaves, sold by their own parents to worse than Egyptian taskmasters.

Thus, so far from having damaged the cause of Italy or his own usefulness in her behalf, Mazzini might, on the morrow of Sir J. Graham's retractation, have said with Byron, "I woke up and found myself famous." From all parts of England, Scotland, and even Ireland, letters expressive of indignation, sympathy, and congratulation poured upon him, taxing his modesty and his purse on account of the needed replies. Editors of London and provincial papers wrote to him for particulars of his own life and work, for a history of Italy's martyrs, for details of the actual state of Italy, her hopes and chances; and he who had hitherto found difficulty in getting his articles accepted because they were "too transcendental," "too synthetical," "too theoretical," even for Reviews destined for cultured readers, could now hardly satisfy the demand for literary contributions.

From his letters to his mother we make out a long list for the years 1844-5-6-7, some of which we have never been able to find.

It is easy to discern which are translations and which are written by himself in English, owing to favourite idioms of his own and to the use of the verb "to do," persisted in, in spite of criticism, when he wished to emphasise an admonition or to repel a contradiction. The translations are not much to boast of, nor, indeed, was justice ever done to his incisive yet poetic prose, until Mrs. Stansfeld (Caroline) took it in hand, and, later, Emilie, the youngest of Mr. Ashurst's daughters, who became proficient in the Italian language. All this daily work, added to his Italian correspondence, to his toil for the school and for the working men, was a sad hindrance to his labours on Foscolo's writings, and, together with subsequent events, deprived Italy for ever of the true life of Foscolo, which remains yet unwritten. And his time was further "cut up by visitors and the tiresome teas and dinners that one can't always avoid, even miles out of town, entailing cabs and a late return home." From the most importunate, the people who came out of mere curiosity, "Susannah," his landlady, defended him to the best of her ability, but he says, "There are some who really wish to know me in order to understand our Italy better, to try and help her in some way or other," and these brought gifts for the school or would assist in forcing the rascally slave-drivers of poor little organ-boys into the police courts.

To a friend Mazzini writes: "Some Englishwomen ask to come to me that they may take counsel as to the best means of helping their own most miserable poor, their toiling, starving, distracted working men, by other methods than almsgiving and useless strikes and violence. Though I can do little save counselling them . . . to promote associations among the sufferers and by urging them to avoid the '*isms*' and '*fisms*' of the communistic and socialistic schools, never to separate the social from the political question, and, while exposing the errors of the capitalistic system, to avoid attacks on individual capitalists or in any way excite the bitter passions of the populace, I cannot refuse to see them without discourtesy, without appearing to care alone about the misery and needs of my own country. This is by no means the case ; it is for the people and all the peoples that I work, and if you could see the awful misery of England you would be appalled. We have nothing like it at home. But all this tends to consume my time, and so you must have patience for the continuation of the article on the 'Academy of the Pythagorics.' . . ."

In comparing the misery of England and Italy Mazzini wrote from his remembrance of the poor in Genoa, where work or charity rarely failed to alleviate their sufferings. He knew nothing of the pellagra breeding rice-fields of Lombardy, of the ague-stricken marshes of the Maremma, nor of the caves and dens where the Neapolitan poor swarmed and rotted.

Though the time consumed by English acquaintances was a real loss to him, and though he was saddened and disillusioned by the sundering and loosening of early friendships, he struggled against contracting new ties ; yet there gathered round him men and women who gradually became part and parcel of his life, replacing to a certain degree the home that he had lost and bringing to his heart fresh sensations of individual joy and sorrow, such as could not be derived from devotion to an " ideal " alone or from the vaguer love of " humanity."

From the time of his first arrival in England he made many friends among the Italian residents. Then had begun his life-long friendship with the Rossellis and the Nathans, men hitherto devoted to " business," but whom he won over to " the cause." He transformed them into true patriots, willing to make pecuniary sacrifices and to take risks in smuggling his letters and papers into Italy. They remained unshakenly faithful to him, and no woman in Italy can

My Dear Friend,

Can you doubt me? Can you doubt my watching from afar with an eager eye and a blessing soul the efforts of brave and earnest british women struggling for the extension of the suffrage to their sex or for the repeal of the Contagious Diseases Acts, which is only an incident in the general question? Is not the question, Equality between man and woman, sacred for any sensible, logical and fearless man who fights for any question involving equality to whatever class or section of mankind it applies? Could I even feel safe in my right and duty to struggle for equality between the working men and the so-called upper class of my own country, if I did not deeply and warmly believe in your own right and duty? Is your question less sacred than that of the abolition of slavery in America or

FACSIMILE OF MAZZINI'S HANDWRITING.
(From a letter lent by Mrs E F Richards)

compete for devotion, sacrifice, and energy in promoting the triumph of independence and unity with Mrs. "Sarina" Nathan. She trained up her children in the religion of patriotism, and verily she has had her reward.

Before 1844, besides his Italian friends and the Carlyles, Dr. Bowring, and a Scotch lady named Mrs. Fletcher, Mazzini became intimate with Charles Buller and his mother, with Joseph Toynbee, W. J. Linton, and Frank Dillon; he was also acquainted with J. S. Mill and many literary men. In 1844 William Shaen offered Mazzini his services in any capacity that might be found useful. Besides taking a deep and intelligent interest in Italian affairs, Mr. Shaen materially assisted in many disputes between Italian organ-boys and their masters, bringing some of the latter to court and repatriating three or four of the former.

On April 10, 1845, Mazzini announced the formation of a Society for the Protection of Italian Boys, with a committee of nine Italians and fifteen Englishmen, Lord Ashley again consenting to act as president. We have no list of the fifteen Englishmen, but we think that Milner Gibson, M.P., and William Shaen were members from the first.

Joseph Cowen, then a student at the University of Edinburgh, after expounding the rights and wrongs of the exiles in the Debating Club and in the newspaper of his native Newcastle, wrote an enthusiastic letter to Mazzini, enclosing the radical resolutions of his fellow-students. Referring to this in one of his last letters to us (February 28, 1899), Mr. Cowen says in his modest way: "Later I visited him to give him some information about the means of transmitting contraband political publications to the Continent." These *means* were the retorts and other fireclay utensils invented by Mr. Cowen, sen., and manufactured at the Blaydon-Burn Works, famous not only in England, but throughout the Continent. Young Joseph Cowen utilised the commercial relations of his father's firm for the purpose of smuggling into the great seaports and populous centres of Europe, the newspapers, pamphlets, and other "forbidden fare" sent by the exiles. The despotic continental Governments could not for a long time discover how the chief cities of Italy became inundated with this revolutionary lore. The refugees were, therefore, carefully watched; many of them were tracked to "Stella House," and so the culprit was discovered. Spies were sent to Newcastle, Joseph Cowen, jun., became a "suspect," his name was placed on the black list, and when his father, who intended to visit the Continent on business, took his passport for the *visé* of foreign ambassadors it was refused. We do not think the genial old Radical ever reproached the son for whose delinquencies he thus had to suffer. Cowen's devotion to Mazzini became a consecrated worship, and assuredly no one made more pecuniary sacrifices or devoted more time and toil to the emancipation of Italy than he until "Rome was ours."

In 1845 Peter Taylor, jun., made Mazzini's acquaintance through Worcell, the beloved and revered Polish exile, whose society had been a great solace—indeed, a source of inspiring hope—to the great Italian during the first dreary years of his life in London. Here was a real stroke of fortune, for Mr. Taylor, a keen man of business, held in high esteem in the City and already a noted champion in the Anti-Corn Law agitation, was destined to become a power in the ever-widening circle of Italy's well-wishers. He was not one to give his friendship or his moral support lightly, and only after long years of intimate acquaintance with Mazzini did he accept his judgment on all Italian and many English affairs. At first he measured every step, weighed every word that might commit himself and his friends to a given course. A constant expression of his— "I don't see my way clear"—earned for him the irreverent surname of "the wet blanket," but once convinced of the wisdom and equity of a measure, Taylor's purse was kept open for its furtherance. His wife added her gentle and persuasive enthusiasm to the service of poor Italy's friends, and for Mrs. Taylor there came to exist only one being in the world besides her husband whose words and deeds must never be questioned by common mortals, and that was Mazzini.

Gradually Taylor interested his father (President of the Anti-Corn Law League of London) and his father's partners, the Courtaulds (great crêpe manufacturers), in Mazzini and his cause, so that in 1846 Mazzini writes home that Mrs. Courtauld has come forty miles from the country to be present at the anniversary supper of his school. Others followed suit, among them the Mallesons, and some still remain (1906) of the little circle who have clasped Mazzini's hand and can, from their own reminiscences, prove what manner of man he was.

All the results, however, of this sudden notoriety were not as pleasant as the process of gaining friends for Italy. On one episode Mazzini dwells with exceeding ire in more than one of his letters to his mother. A man presented himself to Charles Dickens with the pamphlet which Mazzini had dedicated to Graham, and exhibited a letter purporting to be written by Mazzini which stated "that having spent my all for the liberation of my country, .
l am compelled to live by my pen from hand to mouth, and shall be thankful for whatever you like to pay for the pamphlet." The letter was signed "Unhappy Exile," and Dickens gave the man £2, then spoke to some friends of "Mazzini's unhappy case." Fortunately, he came upon a lady who knew the exile well, and who, by comparing this letter with one Mazzini had written to her, convinced Dickens that he had been imposed upon.

"The villain had not even made an attempt to imitate my handwriting!" Mazzini exclaimed when recounting the incident to his mother. He was furious when, a day or two later, he received a letter from Cobden enclosing £1 for "the poor exiles, regretting that it was so little," as "who knows," he writes, "to how many people the wretch has applied?" Though Dickens's servant described the beggar and would have helped to spot him, Mazzini's "advocate" (Shaen) told him that it was impossible to have the man arrested on suspicion only. Mazzini then wrote to the papers, but the impostor, a certain Scuri, evidently in ignorance of this, went with his old story to Mr. Hume,

THE BIRTH OF MODERN ITALY

M.P.; there he was taken and handed over to the police. In court it turned out that Scuri was only a tool in the hands of a so-called Count Bertola, chief of a band of rogués and sharpers, and so cunning a knave that it was impossible to bring him to justice. Scuri was condemned to six months' hard labour, notwithstanding Mazzini's efforts to get the sentence mitigated in consideration of the fact that Bertola was the real culprit. Bertola not only escaped scot free, but threatened Mazzini with a libel suit if his name should appear in the criminal proceedings or the papers. Later, however, in Italy, Mazzini had the satisfaction of exposing Bertola as a spy masquerading under the garb of a patriot.

It is uncertain whether it was at this time that Mazzini made the acquaintance of Dickens, of whose writings he was a great admirer, but probably their friendship developed subsequently, when Dickens was living in Tavistock House —afterwards the residence of the Stansfelds and the Hawkes.

It is only towards the end of 1845 that in Mazzini's letters home we come upon allusions to new friends, the Ashurst-Stansfeld family. In 1845 Mazzini merely alludes to a visit "from a young English girl who has brought me flowers, and is translating Georges Sand's 'Spiridion.'" This was evidently Eliza Ashurst, who had been probably introduced by Shaen. Only in 1846 begins the real intimacy between the Ashurst-Stansfeld family and Mazzini. Lloyd Garrison, in his beautiful introduction to Mazzini's writings, says that "it was in the summer of 1846, at the charming residence of my honoured friend the late William H. Ashurst, an eminent solicitor of London, at Muswell Hill, that I had the first interview with the great Italian patriot, where he impressed me very favourably, not only by the brilliancy of his mind, but by the modesty of his deportment, the urbanity of his spirit, and the fascination of his conversational powers. There our personal friendship began, which revolving years served but to strengthen. . . ."

On July 24, 1846, Mazzini for the first time tells his

mother of the "excellent family" whose acquaintance he has made : "one of them, as you know, brings me flowers and takes tea with me ; she and her three sisters all smoke, a capital crime in English society ; you shall have a full description later. These sisters and their husbands are all deeply interested in all social, and especially the "Women's," questions." Very soon, from Caroline Stansfeld's letters, we see that Mazzini has become "Mazz," and "The Angel," names that were retained by the Ashursts as long as he lived.

When Caroline Stansfeld wished to go to Paris, Mazzini wrote to his mother that he had given her letters of introduction to Lamberti and Giannone (the historian). To Lamberti he wrote : "This letter will be brought to you by an English lady, who is travelling with her sister and their two husbands. Mrs. [Caroline Ashurst] Stansfeld and Mrs. [Emilie Ashurst] Hawkes are quite exceptional persons, and in thought and sympathy free from all English conventionalism. You will please me exceedingly if you see them and render them any service ; they are very fond of me and sympathise with our cause. I esteem and am very fond of them, and but for my work, and circumstance, and the distance between our homes, I could live among them as among brothers and sisters."

By the end of October, 1846, James and Caroline Stansfeld were back in Lancaster Place, having brought Mazzini letters and papers from his friends, who had evidently been most kind, for Sidney Hawkes, who visited him at once, had no end of good things to say about Lamberti. To his mother Mazzini wrote : "I shall see the ladies on Sunday ; they have a sister even better and more attached to me than they are (Eliza). I have many of such women here and there, who some day will help on our cause."

VII

MAZZINI IN LONDON

1846-1847

The Moderates and the Rimini insurgents—Interest felt for Italy in England—Anti Corn-law league—Peel's return to power—Russell's Ministry—Palmerston's services to oppressed nations—Mazzini and Browning's poetry—Mrs. Browning—Mazzini's feeling for the Poles—Mazzini reports Garibaldi's deeds in South America—Accession of Pius IX.—Italian enthusiasm—Attitude of Piedmont—Mazzini's New Year letter for 1847—Sir Ralph Abercromby—Metternich—Italy a "geographical expression"—Annexation of Cracow—International League—Its influence—Mrs. Milner-Gibson and the Ashursts—A successful bazaar—Grisi and Mario sing at school concert—The Pope and Charles Albert.

UNFORTUNATELY we have no letters of this period from the English circle concerning their intercourse with Mazzini. A few conversations with Mr. Stansfeld and Mr. Shaen after Mazzini's death, together with his letters to his mother, alone enable us to trace the rise and growth of English sympathies with Italy in those days.

Just before the election of Pius IX. he wrote to his mother: "Public attention is attracted by the state of the Peninsula, and the atrocious misgovernment of the Two Sicilies and the Papal States is admitted; the constant risings in different provinces are no longer attributed to outside agitators, but to the absolute impossibility of submitting to such an abnormal existence."

A rising of some five hundred youths in Rimini was

frustrated by the " Moderates "—the party who cared more for local reforms than for the national question—and a hundred or so of the young insurgents sought refuge in Piedmont, but by order of Charles Albert they were prevented from crossing the frontier. They managed to reach Marseilles, where, however, they were arrested and shut up in the Chartreaux. Learning of their dire poverty, Mazzini collected 1,200 lire (£48) for them. In the first letter which Dr. Mazzini wrote after a severe illness which had prostrated him, he drew the usual moral from this fresh insurrectionary failure, but his son triumphantly pointed out that " the national idea is gaining ground " and that Italians " are beginning to see that unless they can unite as a nation, they never will be able to resist the domestic tyrants or rid themselves of Austria."

At the same time Mazzini is able to record that the Italian question is becoming extensively discussed in the English press. The *Westminster* has a second article on Italy, the *Monthly Chronicle* has taken up the cause of the poor little Italian white slaves, and even *Dolman's Magazine*, though Catholic, endorses Mazzini's article on the " Pope-king." Increased interest is being taken in his school ; a picture, presented by some English ladies for a raffle, has brought in £14. During this period his letters home give the entire history of the Anti-Corn Law agitation. He expresses unbounded admiration for the pecuniary sacrifices of the leaguers, who, he says, " have raised and spent a quarter of a million sterling in the purchase of county qualifications." Their bazaar has proved an extraordinary success, and he means to try to follow their example on a smaller scale for his school. On December 16, 1845, he writes that nothing is talked about " save the ministerial crisis." He doubts whether Lord John Russell will be able to form a Cabinet, and thinks that " Peel, after a short interval, will return to power." According to him, the Whigs cannot hope " to have a majority in Parliament unless they dare to join the Anti-Corn-Law leaguers, take Cobden into the Ministry, dissolve Parliament, and appeal to the country." Indeed, that was Lord John's intention. He offered Cobden the Vice-Presidency of the Board of Trade, but Cobden declined it, believing that as the most prominent leader of the crusade he would serve the people's cause better by retaining his freedom.

Lord John Russell did fail and Peel did return to power. Mazzini at once saw that the Premier's position was very precarious and almost untenable, but he felt convinced of Peel's good faith; in fact, he said, " It cannot be questioned, for it is clear that he has become convinced that the measure [repeal of the Corn Law] is indispensable to the prosperity of England. Though Peel intends to have the honour of affixing his name to this great measure, even if the Bill passes he will not remain long in power. The Protectionist Tories will act against him for what they call his desertion, and as he is contrary to a Reform Bill, which the Liberals are bound to bring in, they will desert him, and he will remain isolated and alone." The forecast was a true one, for never before nor since was a minister baited and bullied and assailed by such scurrilous abuse as was hurled at Peel by Disraeli and Lord George Bentinck. But Peel's testimony to Richard Cobden, " the man whose pure motives, indefatigable energy, unpretending and unadorned eloquence have secured the success of the repeal," places him among the few Ministers of whom England may justly feel proud.

On July 3, 1846, Mazzini announced to his parents the formation of the ministry by Lord John Russell, with Palmerston as Foreign Secretary, Grey, Morpeth, Macaulay, &c., but expressed fears as to its duration on account of the division of the House into three parties : " the Peelites, the Whigs or Russellites, and the Protectionists, who hate the other two parties, although they allied themselves with the Whigs to upset Peel's Government." Nevertheless, the Cabinet remained in office till 1852, and taught Europe the difference between the foreign policy of Liberals and Conservatives. Palmerston, whatever may have been his faults in the eyes of his sovereign or his colleagues, rendered good service to the cause of oppressed nations, and the

Swiss, Hungarians, and Italians have reason to bless his presence in that Cabinet. Fate was against them then, but not England. During those six years England's influence was cast in their favour, and no act sanctioned the re-enthronement of brute force against them.

Mazzini not only informed his family of English political events, but called their attention to every sign of sympathy for Italy that came to his knowledge. He sent his mother, bit by bit, the translation of "a truly beautiful poem, by one of the best poets of the age, 'The Italian in England,' of Robert Browning." Then, suddenly, some one having carried off his Browning, the translation ceased. The family circle asked for more, as the end seemed to them abrupt, but he answers that "the exile is back to his work for Italy." The original translation of the whole poem in his own writing exists in Florence, and for a long time was printed as, and believed to be, an original poem of his own. We do not know whether Browning ever heard of this translation, or of Mazzini's understanding of his poetry, into which he had a deeper insight than most of the poet's English contemporaries. Mazzini's special favourite was "The Lost Leader," and when one of the men he most trusted not only changed sides but became a coercionist minister, we heard him quote:

>   "   one lost soul more,
> One task more declined, one more footpath untrod,
> One more devil's triumph, and sorrow for angels,
> One wrong more to man, one more insult to God! . . . "

When, in another case, the beloved backslider came back to the fold, and an English friend, who did not trust to his repentance, said, "There will be doubt, hesitation, and pain," he retorted instantly: "Yes—' never glad, confident morning again '!" but added, "He is not a leader, only a very hot-headed comrade who is not likely to relapse again."

For Rogers, the poet, to whose famous breakfasts he sometimes went, he felt a kindly affection, for, he said, "he was the first Englishman who foretold that there would yet arise a third Italy."

He delighted in Mrs. Browning's "Portuguese Sonnets," and later admired "Aurora Leigh" for the true views expressed in it on woman and her work, but he asked himself, "Why not have written in prose?" Mrs. Carlyle seemed to think that the Brownings appreciated Mazzini "unduly," but then she thought Robert, despite or because of her husband's liking for him, only a man of "fluff and feathers." It is likewise true that Browning was not one of her worshippers, and not even just to her. "Oh! what a fuss about Mazzini!" she exclaimed one day when she was present at the Brownings' reception of him. When the Brownings went to Paris he gave them letters for Georges Sand. Later Mrs. Browning rendered him a homage in her "Casa Guidi Windows"; but when Napoleon III. became her ideal liberator she, of course, turned against the exile who was his relentless antagonist, and in 1859 she vented a pious hope that Mazzini might be at least captured and "kept out of mischief."

Regarding Tennyson, Mazzini was never an enthusiast, though he admired his lyrics and parts of his "In Memoriam"; but the "Ode to Wellington," and other "bombastic laudations of insular selfishness," displeased him. He often used to say to Englishmen, "You have only one poem expressive of true patriotism, and that is Cowper's; and only one 'War Hymn' with a true ring in it, Campbell's 'Men of England.'" Once when asked to suggest a name for a girl baby, he wrote to a dear friend, "Do not call her 'Maud,' it is too Tennysonian," and, always true to his Byron, he chose "Ada."

Mr. Stansfeld often told us that no Englishman of his acquaintance was more thoroughly versed than Mazzini in English literature and poetry. He and his friends could, however, never be satisfied with Mazzini's strange appreciation of Shakespeare. Of course, he admitted that Shakespeare's great individualistic creations were masterpieces, but he found in his works no forefeeling of the unity of the race, of the continuity of tradition, of the responsibility of the living to future generations. For Mazzini, Shakespeare was "an objective painter."

Again Mr. Stansfeld resented, and could neither understand nor explain, Mazzini's indifference to Shelley. Mr. Stansfeld used to say, "Was it Shelley's pantheism, his horror of dogmas, creeds, and religions, his indifference to political forms, his passion for Nature, equal to, and at times apparently surpassing, his love for the human?" "To me his apathy for 'our divinest' was and remains a mystery. When we first knew him he made us read, and Caroline translated into English, some Polish poetry that had been translated for him into Italian by a Pole in Switzerland, and throughout 1846 his whole soul seemed centred in the Polish struggle. He incited us to write on Poland, to get up meetings of protest; it was one of his first attractions that Italy and her sufferings did not absorb him to the exclusion of those of other peoples. He hoped at that time that Lord Palmerston would do something more than protest against the Powers, violators of the sacred treaties of Vienna."

And Mazzini's letters home during 1846 bore witness to the fervour of his sympathy with the "martyr nation," whose heroism as yet remains latent though unrecompensed. He narrated the heroic struggle of 1846 to his mother. "The Polish insurrection fills my heart and head, mother mine; it is a solemn movement, and whether it succeed or not it is heroic. Their condition is worse than ours, but they have the courage that is wanting in Italians. The insurrection is not crushed. Cracow is an open city without walls or fortifications, and yet, though attacked by the united Powers, the insurgents, who have but three cannon and are only armed with hatchets, are determined to defend it; the women, the priests, encourage and help the men; four hundred Austrian soldiers have passed over to the insurgents and two Italian regiments under Mazzuchelli and Bertolotti have been disbanded, so great was the ferment among the troops. The English papers said that they were composed exclusively of Poles. I wrote to correct this, and send you the article for the circle. If they are not utterly crushed at once all Poland will arise; is it possible that the Italians will not seize this opportunity for attacking Austria in the flank?" 18th March: "All is not ended, but it is going ill for Poland. The Government has tried to turn the peasantry against the proprietors, has put a price of ten florins on the heads of the Polish nobles; a thousand florins on the heads of two Polish exiles. The insolent language of Thiers in the Chambers fills me with loathing. The measures taken by Austria in Gallicia raise immense indignation here. A public meeting is summoned, but protests without cannon are useless." His father seems to think that Lord Palmerston might have joined France in a protest, but he maintains that he is quite right in having nothing to do with Louis Philippe, who was perfectly aware that the three Powers had resolved on the annexation of Cracow, and had tacitly consented, in order to gain them over to his domestic policy. "The English Minister was quite right to send his curt protest separately, but, alas! the Polish insurrection is crushed and the brutal vengeance of her assassins has commenced." He writes an article for the *Monthly Chronicle*, and "another meeting of sympathy for Poland has been summoned, but, alas! words without deeds are useless."

Meanwhile, to be freer from visitors and noises, he went to a little house in Cropley Street, New Road, with Tancione and his wife Susannah, who boarded and lodged him. It took him nearly two hours to get to Chelsea, but he never missed his weekly visit to the Carlyles when they were at home. The school concert went off beautifully this year, the famous violinist Sivori improvising a solo and the audience, chiefly English, becoming enthusiastic.

At this epoch Mazzini received particulars of the heroic deeds of Garibaldi and his Italian Legion at Montevideo and in the Pampas of the Argentine. It is perhaps forgotten that it was at first entirely due to Mazzini, and for a time to Mazzini only, that Garibaldi's wonderful career

PIUS IX.

(From a painting by Metzmach.)

To face p 101.]

in South America became so thoroughly known that when he returned in 1848 he was regarded as a hero and a mighty man of war. Mazzini not only printed reports of his doings in the *Apostolato Popolare*, but managed to have them inserted and widely circulated in the English press.

On June 16, 1846, the Cardinal Mastai Ferretti, after a short Conclave, was elected Pope under the name of Pius IX., and this event proved to be one of capital importance for the destinies of Italy. Just before the death of his predecessor, Gregory XVI., Mazzini had written home that "during the last two years the opinions of England about Italy are singularly altered for the better," and that even the *Times* says that "sooner or later, and perhaps sooner than is generally believed, the whole Peninsula will be in flame." The liberal dispositions of the new Pontiff, though more imaginary than real, profoundly impressed the Italians, who contrasted them with the incredibly tyrannical and corrupt methods of his predecessor. Pius IX., with his historic invocation, "Dio benedici l'Italia!" (O Lord, bless Thou Italy!), with his promise of reforms and his opposition to Austria, became in a very short time the idol of all Italians, and it was with the rallying cries of "Viva Pio Nono!" and "Morte all'Austria!" that the insurrections of the few following years were initiated.

The centennial anniversary of the expulsion of the Austrians from Genoa was blazoned by the lighting up of bonfires all along the Apennines. The populations of Ancona celebrated every slight concession wrung from the Pope with cries of "Viva l'Italia!" "Down with Austria!" and insults to the consular agents of that power. At Ravenna tricolour flags were hoisted, and cries of "Viva i Bandiera!" "Death to Metternich!" "Death to the Emperor!" mingled with those of "Viva Pio Nono!" The authorities made feeble attempts to suppress these manifestations, but in the city of Rome a banquet attended by eight hundred persons was given, where speeches were made expressing hatred to Austria and urging the necessity for

THE BIRTH OF MODERN ITALY

armaments and organic reforms, and they found an echo all over the Peninsula. Arrests followed in Florence, but the prisoners were liberated to the cry of "Viva l'Italia!" "Viva Pio Nono!" There was no question of parties. Moderates, the old Carbonari, and Young Italy, all joined together in harmony.

On the other hand, the King of Naples, old Ferdinand of Bourbon, a despot cruel to the core and a faithful friend to Austria and Russia, filled his awful prisons with patriots, arresting even the son of his own Prime Minister. The Dukes of Parma and Modena, in agonies of terror, followed Ferdinand's example and entreated Austria to send troops to defend them against their rebellious subjects. All these events were duly reported in the English press, Palmerston's paper, the *Morning Chronicle*, being decidedly hostile to Austria.

Mazzini, while rejoicing in these symptoms, anxiously watched the course of affairs in Piedmont, where, though no constitution had been granted or even promised, the King was in contact with the leading Liberals, tolerating the circulation of the writings of d'Azeglio,[1] Gioberti,[2] and Balbo,[3] shunning the Jesuits, and giving Austria, whenever the occasion presented itself (as, for example, in the questions of the exportation of wine and salt), a "Roland for

[1] Azeglio, Marchese Massimo d' (1798–1866), statesman, journalist, novelist, and painter, born in Turin. Was grievously wounded at Novara. He wrote some celebrated novels and pamphlets in defence of the rights of Italians to independence. He was Foreign Secretary and Premier during 1849, and inspired Victor Emmanuel to make the Proclamation of Moncalieri, of which more will be said further on.

[2] Gioberti, Vincenzo (1801–1852), illustrious statesman and philosopher. He took orders and was chaplain of Charles Albert, King of Sardinia. Suspected as a Liberal, was first imprisoned and then exiled. Returning to Italy, he was elected to Parliament and became minister, but was exiled again in 1851. His celebrated work, "Moral and Civil Superiority of the Italians," was a splendid defence of the Italian race and its aspirations.

[3] Balbo, Conte Cesare (1789–1853), statesman and historian. Was Premier in the first Constitutional Ministry in Piedmont. His "Hopes of Italy" had placed him among the most noted men of the Unity party in Italy.

MASSIMO D'AZEGLIO.

To face p 102]

"her Oliver." The Italians had fully realised that Austria was the irreconcilable enemy of the new Pope and of reform; the question now was whether Charles Albert would understand this, share the hopes and aspirations of his own subjects, and throw his sword into the balance for independence.

Mazzini's home letter for New Year 1847 differs strikingly from all his former ones. The new life spreading through Italy and the sympathy of the family of enthusiasts (the Ashursts) who in England had made his cause their own, had restored something of the elasticity of bygone years to his heart. He passed Christmas Eve at Muswell Hill, where all the Ashurst circle were assembled, and his letter, dated December 25th, is most touching: " I think of you always, but more at these times, and I thought of you all last night in the midst of the English family of brothers and sisters where I remained until after midnight. When I think of the sister dead and of your solitude I naturally grow sad at these times. But I will not deny that I write with greater exhilaration and courage and hope this year than in any former one. I feel within me a certain audacity, a redoublement of energy that is inexplicable, for I can assign no cause save a feeling that this year is to usher in happier times, perhaps even to put an end to our separation. . . . Is it a presentiment ? . . . I know nothing, but have strange feelings, like the war-horse scenting powder. . . I tell you this as the best year's wish that I can send you; but if it is an illusion, if this next year is to pass like the others in isolation and sadness, God's will be done, and may our sadness be calm, animated by faith in Him who knows more than we do, and who, here or elsewhere, will reunite us. . . . In the midst of sorrow let us be thankful, and march onwards with patient courage. We have lived without remorse, and without remorse I trust we shall meet, and with the same love that throughout our life created our strength. God bless you all, then, mother, father, sister who have never ceased to love me, and you two who have never ceased and continue to do everything for me, may you be blessed indeed ! " He closes this letter with affecticnate words for each and all of his relatives and friends, beginning with Andrea Gambini, and including the old servant Benedetta, adding : "To meet once more, to embrace you all in the full enjoyment of our freedom, with none to let or hinder, and with the dawn of our country's future before our eyes, would compensate for all these years of exile, for your sufferings as well as mine!" On the outside of this letter his mother wrote, "Lettera Santa del Primo d'anno" (My holy New Year's letter).

It is an undoubted fact that the history of these years is clearly and impartially delineated in the Blue Books. Sir Ralph Abercromby, ambassador in Turin, writing on January 12, 1847, about the Austrian reprisals for the infringement by Sardinia of the Convention of 1751 (concerning the importation of salt to Switzerland), says that they are really only Austria's method of expressing her displeasure at the Piedmontese encouragements to Liberal and Italian ideas. He proceeds : " I look to a continuance of indirect opposition to Austria, rather than to an open intention to lead the party whose object is the national regeneration of Italy. Circumstances might arise when, feeling himself supported by other Powers, his Sardinian Majesty might perhaps be induced to follow a more decided course of action, but failing such support, my expectation is . . . that his Sardinian Majesty will not go beyond the limits I have defined." He adds that there is a marked desire in Sardinia and in the Papal States, on the part of the two sovereigns, to better the conditions of their subjects, though some calculate that the time is fast approaching for the overthrow of Austrian dominion in Italy.

One man, however, saw clearly the goal to which all things were tending, and prepared to oppose the movement by brute force. This was Metternich. He was well aware that while from the hands of the Pope or of Charles Albert —so long as they proved themselves national princes—the people would accept such instalments of liberty as they might feel justified in granting, no concessions, no constitution, not even autonomy, would be accepted from the hands of Austria, and that nothing short of her evacuation of the whole Peninsula would be entertained even for a moment.

In a diplomatic note, which has remained famous, he affirms "that Italy is only a 'geographical expression'; the Peninsula is composed of Sovereign States mutually independent; their existence and limits are based upon principles of general public right, and confirmed by political transactions least liable to be questioned, the inalterable maintenance of which the Emperor intends to enforce."[1] In a second note to all the Courts of Europe he writes: "Central Italy is given up to a revolutionary movement, at the head of which are the leaders of sects who for years past have undermined the States of the Peninsula. Under the banner of administrative reforms, the factions paralyse the legal action of power, and seek to consummate a work which, in order to answer their subversive views, could not remain circumscribed within the limits of the Papal States, or within those of any of the States which encompass the Italian Peninsula. What these sects aim at is the fusion of those States into one body politic, or at least into a confederation of States, placed under the control of a supreme central power."

Can any testimony as to the triumph of the "idea" equal this?

This note closes without any proposition; he merely asserts a fact: "The Emperor has no pretensions of being an Italian Power: he is satisfied with being the head of his own Empire, portions of which are situated beyond the Alps. . . . In the present state of possession, he well knows how to protect himself. He desires to know whether the principal guardians of the political peace share his views."

[1] By a strange irony of Fate, the Parliament of United Italy voted some months ago (May, 1908), a Bill empowering the Minister of Foreign Affairs to acquire the Metternich Palace in Vienna as a seat for the Italian Embassy.

Nothing could be clearer or more logical. But the violation of the treaty of Vienna by the annexation of Cracow admitted of but one answer. Mazzini immediately saw this, and having in January been invited by the *People's Journal* to define the proper line of conduct for England to adopt in presence of the violation of the treaty of Vienna, he boldly advised her to consider those acts as no longer binding, and to give her moral support to the oppressed nationalities.

But Mazzini believed with Byron that " Who would be free, himself must strike the blow."

In 1847 the International League was founded, and almost immediately afterwards Mazzini wrote home that its members " now have reached the number of two hundred." He was asked to draft the first address, but as he suggested in it the re-making of half the map of Europe, it underwent a considerable revision, and Peter Taylor, jun., must have been one of his sternest critics. The address was first read privately in the house of W. J. Linton, and copies were distributed for alterations and suggestions, a process which had to be repeated over and over again. James Stansfeld, in speaking to us of these years, used to say that " Mazzini carried us completely out of ourselves, and transferred his convictions into our hearts and heads; brought home to us that England free, strong, powerful, and capable of giving liberty to her own people, able to extend a helping hand to the struggling peoples beyond her seas, allowed herself to be dominated by a class—a class opposed to her own interests, as proved in the Corn Law struggle. Now that fight had been won it was time to set to work at the real task appointed to her. The question of nationalities had never been brought before us as a question in which we were vitally interested, but as he set it forth no believer in duty and right could avoid the conviction that we had abdicated our rightful position in Europe, become a tacit consenter to the atrocities committed by the absolute Powers, and that even for our own interests we should do well to exert our influence on the politics of Europe in behalf of right and liberty."

1847]   A NEW LEAGUE

After many postponements a public meeting was convened on April 28th at the " Crown and Anchor," Strand, Dr. Bowring in the chair, when it was resolved: "That an association be now formed, to be called the ' People's International League,' the objects of which shall be as follows :—To enlighten the British public as to the political condition and relations of foreign countries; to embody and manifest an efficient public opinion in favour of the right of every people to self-government and the maintenance of their own nationality; to disseminate the principles of national freedom and progress; to promote a good understanding between the peoples of all countries."

Among the officers of the League for the first year, William Ashurst, sen., P. A. Taylor, sen., and Joseph Toynbee were trustees. In the Council were Dr. Bowring, T. S. Duncombe, Douglas Jerrold, William Carpenter, Dr. Epps, W. J. Fox, Peter Taylor, jun., W. Shaen, Sidney Hawkes, J. Stansfeld, H. Vincent, J. Watson, Thomas Cooper, and J. H. Parry. W. J. Linton was the first secretary of the League and proved a most able and active one.

The address, exceedingly quiet and practical in tone and chary in its pledges—none of which, however, have been forfeited, but are even to-day bearing fruit—is well worth quoting, as it gives the basis of the first understanding between Italians and Britons in the sphere of politics. " The insularity of England, her concentration on the affairs of her own country, is admittedly an anomaly, and deprecated because it encourages absolutism to interfere with national rights in a way it would not dare to do were England to object; but England has not hitherto cared even to understand the workings of absolutism in Europe. Now, however, the virtual abrogation of the treaty of Vienna by the recent suppression of Cracow has opened a new era to Europe, especially as the political system established and guaranteed by that treaty has already undergone changes and modifications by the rejection of the elder branch of the Bourbons, the severance of Belgium from Holland, and the formation of a new kingdom of Greece. The three absolute Powers having shown by their usurpation that they are not to be restrained by treaties, however solemnly contracted, is not the professed respect for those treaties a farce and a sham? In any case, the people never accepted them and are daily giving evidence that they intend to substitute living nationalities for the arbitrary divisions imposed by the Powers. Whether the struggle will be fierce and prolonged, or brief and comparatively bloodless, will depend much on England's conduct. But that nothing can avert the struggle is made as clear as daylight by often baffled, never conquered Poland; by the rebirth of Greece, whose growing aspiration is to reunite in one common nationality all the Greek populations now in the hand of Turkey, rallying round her her children of Thessaly, Macedonia, and Candia; by Switzerland, who, disdaining the Constitution imposed upon her by the Allied Powers in 1815, intends to unite in one Federal bond the general Swiss interests, to be represented by some central power not at present existing; and by Germany, still bent on national unity, even as in 1813-15, when her popular spirit was aroused against Napoleon. Betrayed by her Government, Germany is still moved by the same spirit, and lives and works to the same end. In Italy the character of the agitation, descended from the few to the masses, is clearly revealed: concessions, reforms, have been wrested from its Governments as means to an end only: no local remedies nor partial improvements stay its progress. Italy wills to be one. Here is a national question: twenty-four millions of men, tried and disciplined by five hundred years of common bondage and martyrdom, mean to unite in one compact body, to have some weight in the scale of nations, some recognition of their part and mission in the life and destinies of Europe."

All this sounds commonplace to-day, but in 1847, who else spoke in England of a United Germany, of the certainty of a United Italy?

Perhaps the most remarkable paragraph is that relating to the Sclavonians—read in the light of the incessant struggles that have been going on among them from then till now. " A race of eighty millions (including the Poles and Russian Slavs), spreading from the Elbe to Kamtchatka, from the frozen sea to Ragusa on the shores of the Adriatic : five millions of Chekhs in Bohemia ; two millions of Moravians scattered through Silesia and Hungary ; two millions of Slovaks in Hungary ; two millions of Croatians and Slovenes in Styria and Carinthia ; the Serbs, Bulgars, and Bosnians in Turkey ; the Dalmatians, Illyrians and Slavonians in Austria—they, too, are looking to a new era in Europe ; they, too, having arisen from a literary movement unknown to England to a political one equally unknown, are demanding the common life and unity of nationality. From all this the position of Europe, the volcano on which it sleeps, may be discerned. Will not England try to bring on a calm and peaceful evolution?—avert the threatened strife? Is not England ready to welcome any new Power, any new element of activity and civilisation? There are three Powers representing absolutism leagued together for any foul deed that may serve their design ; and none are leagued against them. England, having abdicated her place in Europe, has no hold upon those Powers except through their interests, which may and may not be the same as ours. Besides the atheism and selfishness of the abdication, is it a wise one, even from the point of view of her future influence and material prosperity ? Suppose England persists in her carelessness and apathy, suppose she quietly looks on without uttering a single word of sympathy for the struggling peoples of Europe? The explosion comes. The Austrian Empire vanishes from the map under the combined forces of its Slavonian and Italian subjects. The Mediterranean and the Danube are in the hands of new Powers. Greece lifts up her voice on Eastern questions. Europe is altogether remodelled. What will England do ? Will not her old alliances be shaken ? Will the new nations readily take for their ally, for their partner in commercial activity, for their fellow-worker in the new channels opened to industrial energy, the Power which, while they were suffering and struggling, turned contemptuously away and said, 'I know you not?'"

We think that no small credit is due to the English men of business, of letters and of the learned professions, who dared inevitable ridicule in raising such questions. Yet they did raise them, did repeat them, till they awakened a feeling throughout the land in favour of Italian nationality. And they compelled the Government to secure fair play by forcing the Powers to refrain from intervention. This is a fact which the *Times*, whose writers jeered and protested in 1847, might record with appreciation to-day, when its columns are loud in praise of Italy for her unwritten alliance.

This address was reproduced throughout the provincial press, and provoked comment which, though varied, showed that popular sympathy for the Italians was on the increase. An article in the *Times* appears to have been the most violent on the adverse side.

At that epoch Mrs. Milner-Gibson, conspiring with the "Muswell Hill Brigade" (the Ashursts), held a bazaar at her own house in aid of Mazzini's school, Mazzini knowing nothing whatever of the affair until he was invited to attend. The success, much to his joy, was immense, for the proceeds ensured the school's existence for an entire year. Shortly afterwards a concert, in which Grisi, Mario, and other Italian singers took part, brought in sufficient to ensure it for yet another year. He was so relieved by this good fortune that he wrote home saying he was preparing for a trip " to Kent or Wales," but in reality he intended going to Paris, as coming events were casting their shadows before. Emilie Ashurst Hawkes had finished his portrait, and he thought it more like him than any that had been painted before, but it was so large that he did not know how he could manage to smuggle it over to Italy, "especially," he writes, "as your Government, so popular, so founded in the love and esteem of its people, has forbidden the circulation of my daguerreo-

MAZZINI.

(From a painting by Emilie Ashurst Venturi)

type sent to Leghorn." This, we suspect, is the one that represents him as a large, burly, rather ferocious individual, with nothing of the sad, sweet, or stern expression which alternated with his moods.

As Mario often sent him a box for the opera he was able to offer some pleasures to his friends, among others to Miss Winkworth, the *fiancée* of William Shaen, who after her marriage became devoted to Mazzini and his cause.

In the meanwhile, Austria, in accordance with Metternich's declarations, augmented her forces in Italy, and the British consul in Milan, Dawkins, announced the arrival in that city of two battalions of the Croat Infantry, so especially hated by the people. Then the Austrian troops, sent on the strength of certain treaty rights, occupied Ferrara, which belonged to the Pontifical States, notwithstanding the objections of the Apostolic Delegate, Cardinal Ciacchi, whose written protestation is inserted in the Roman *Official Gazette*. Sir Ralph Abercromby reported to Palmerston that the Pope, after consulting the Cardinals, had officially remonstrated in Vienna and sent a special messenger to Charles Albert, expressing his desire to take refuge in his Majesty's Sardinian territory in the case of the territory of the Church being again violated by Metternich. He (the Pope) also begged that a steamer might be sent to Civitavecchia to await his orders. The intelligent ambassador reported likewise that Count Pellegrino Rossi, the French ambassador, had hastened to the Vatican to offer the assistance of France, which his Holiness refused in terms showing his conviction that France and Austria were in reality acting together in Italian politics. This had been from the first the belief of Lord Palmerston, and it was proved, later, that Louis Philippe had in fact allied himself with absolutism in the Cracow affair, in Switzerland, and then in Italy. Mazzini, who had denounced his intrigues from the first, wrote to his mother, when Rossi was sent to Rome, that the new ambassador had received instructions to advise the Pope to be friendly to Austria and to act most moderately and gradually in the matter of reforms.

VIII

THE EVE OF THE REVOLUTION

1847

Resentment at Austria's occupation of Ferrara—Palmerston's frank *communiqué*—His opposition to Guizot and Louis Philippe—England the disinterested friend of Sardinia—Cobden—Popular feeling in Genoa—A sequestrated letter of Mazzini's—Nino Bixio voices popular enthusiasm—Charles Albert's desire for a War of Independence—Belief in Pius IX.

IN May, 1847, friends begged Mazzini to reprint his letter to Charles Albert in order to demonstrate that the Moderates had espoused the opinions expressed by him in 1831. He consented unwillingly, saying that everything he had published could be reprinted, but he did not advise this particular reprint because he did not wish people to imagine that he hoped anything from their "hero." Whoever is "born a rabbit will die a rabbit," and he is convinced that the King of Piedmont will do nothing effective unless a popular uprising constrain him to act. However, the indignation of the Pope and the general resentment of the Italians at the high-handed occupation of Papal Ferrara by the Austrians had altered the aspect of things, for at any moment a collision between Papal and Austrian troops might prove a match to powder.

On August 22nd, Mazzini told his mother that Lord Palmerston had despatched a *communiqué* hostile to Austria and her projects. He was accurately informed, as exactly ten days previously Palmerston had written to Lord

Ponsonby, ambassador in Vienna, admitting Austria's right to defend her own possessions, " which no one within his knowledge is threatening," but reminding Metternich " of another right which belongs to every Sovereign Power, that of making such reforms and internal improvements as may be judged . . . conducive to the well-being of the people whom it governs." It appears, Lord Palmerston continues, " that some of the Sovereigns of Italy are willing to exercise this power, and her Majesty's Government hopes that Austria may think fit to employ its great political influence . . . to influence and support those Sovereigns in such laudable undertakings. No information has been received as to the existence of a scheme for uniting the now separate States of the Peninsula into a Federal Republic, but it is a certain fact that the present Governments teem with abuses of all kinds, especially in the Papal States and in the kingdom of Naples."

Considering that Austria was aiding and abetting the wanton butcheries in Calabria, the irony of the advice is delightful, and it was not without its effect, for Austria dared not further invade the Papal States, but she justified the occupation of Ferrara by citing a clause in the treaty of Vienna, and the crisis was thus delayed.

With an interest as keen as that of Palmerston, Mazzini watched the trend of affairs in Switzerland. The Swiss Constitution of 1848 embodied the essential principles that Mazzini had propagated in " La Jeune Suisse " (1835–36), for the men who drafted it were his friends ; but had Palmerston not checkmated the designs of France and Austria by refusing, in 1847, to convene a Congress for the forcible modification of the Federal compact, those principles could not have triumphed. The services rendered to European liberty by this English statesman are incalculable, but none were ever greater than his steadfast opposition to the crafty designs of Guizot and Louis Philippe.

When it appeared possible that Austria was meditating an invasion of the Sardinian territory, Lord Palmerston instructed the Earl of Minto " to assure the Government of his Sardinian Majesty of the sincere friendship and good-will of the British Government. You will say that her Majesty can never forget that the crown of Sardinia has been the faithful and steady ally of the crown of Great Britain through periods of the greatest difficulty, through trials the most painful and distressing, and that his Sardinian Majesty may at all times and under all circumstances rely upon finding in her Majesty a true and disinterested friend."

When the Prince of Castelcicala, the Neapolitan envoy in London, begged the Foreign Secretary to prevent communications between Mazzini and the Italian exiles in Malta, "as they are meditating an expedition from Malta to the mainland," Palmerston, having ascertained that no such scheme existed, answered that no military expedition would be permitted, but urged the extreme gratification which her Majesty's Government would derive from learning that the King of Naples intended following the liberal example set him by the Pope, because such a course, more than any orders issued by her Majesty's Government, would ensure the internal peace of his kingdom.

In the same year another great Englishman, Richard Cobden, while more especially bent on spreading his economic doctrines, gave the Italians a magnificent opportunity of expressing, and of interchanging with his countrymen, their patriotic sentiments and hopes.

For Cobden Mazzini cherished a profound esteem, though as both men were almost exclusively absorbed in the furtherance of their own great ideas they never came into direct contact; perhaps, therefore, neither fully appreciated the other. Cobden's tour through Italy may be compared to a triumphal march, Genoa, Milan, Venice, Rome, competing to honour the great apostle of Free Trade. He, with his shrewd sense of humour, doubtless saw behind the scenes much more than he cared to show in the speeches which he made, for he was naturally anxious not to compromise the effective help he was giving indirectly to the cause of Italian Unity. In a letter to George Coombe he writes · "The Italian Liberals have seized upon my presence as an excuse for holding meetings ... to make speeches. They consider this a step gained, and so it is."

These meetings and the public complimentary dinners given to Cobden did not always pass without disagreeable consequences. In Venice arrests and imprisonments followed a great popular banquet at the Giudecca, where patriotic allusions were mingled with Free Trade speeches. At Trieste the poet Dall'Ongaro made such references to United Italy that he was summarily expelled from the city. Austria did her best to impress Cobden with the genial and lenient nature of her government, but there can be no doubt that the great thinker saw clearly enough through the artifice. The cause of Italian Unity had all his sympathies and his valid, though discreet, support.

Meanwhile Austria was preparing to invade Lucca, Parma, Modena, and possibly Tuscany; but suddenly a counter-order was given. Metternich sought to justify his aggressive policy and to disprove the accusation of having connived at a plot to abduct Pius IX. across the Neapolitan frontier. Mazzini's anxiety to secure the arming of civic guards in all the towns was keen, and in one of his letters he wrote: "Among other things that take up my time, the commune of Forli wants to purchase arms in Malta for arming the National Guard. My friends there write that the arms could be purchased from the English military depôt, but that the Governor of Malta cannot accede to their request without the consent of the English Government. So they have written to beg me to find people who may exert their influence with Lord Palmerston to induce him to consent." The intermediary was very possibly Dr. Bowring, but of the result (probably negative) nothing is apparent.

In other letters he noted with satisfaction the growth of hostility towards Austria, telling how the Irish Catholics were getting up subscriptions for the Pope, dwelling on Lord Minto's semi-official mission to Rome, and the favour with which the Pope's reforms were regarded by the English Government.

THE BIRTH OF MODERN ITALY

At Genoa popular feeling was being vented in extraordinary demonstrations; illuminations and processions, in which were carried the Piedmontese and Papal flags, with the *tricolore* here and there introduced, marked the general excitement, while cries of acclamation to Charles Albert, to Pius IX., to the Piedmontese army, and to Italian Independence, resounded enthusiastically before the Royal palace. Hostile cries were raised in front of the Jesuits' College. Sir Ralph Abercromby, writing about the demonstrations, explicitly announces "that they are made with the understanding of the constituted authorities." But his comments are curious. He goes on to say: "There is also another circumstance in the present state of public feeling in Italy which is certainly remarkable, and which shows how much more seriously and deeply the interests of Italy are now considered by the people than they were a few years back. I allude to the total absence in all the various popular demonstrations that have occurred in Italy of any idea of uniting under one Government the various States into which this peninsula is divided."

According to the British ambassador the diminution of the national idea is a sign of progress. But Lord Palmerston did not believe that the national idea had ever existed, though Metternich persisted in affirming that it not only existed but was steadily progressing, and as a proof he sent Lord Palmerston a violent address of the Livornese to the Romans, asking whether they are asleep, "whether the pestilent Moderates have frozen the blood in their veins, whether they are indifferent to the sufferings of the Two Sicilies, whether they still mean to tolerate the Austrian occupation of Ferrara?" And in the same despatch he enclosed a letter from Mazzini which had evidently been sequestrated in the post. This letter, written on October 4th to some friend in Italy, runs thus: "I received your letter to-day, Monday, and write to say goodbye, as I am uncertain whether I shall rejoin you. Affairs in the Papal States are going ill, as you say. But the uncertain or retrograde steps of the Government cannot change the law that rules events. The impulse is given, and, well or ill, the movement will continue to advance : the Italians are children with good instincts, but they have not the shadow of political intelligence or experience. I speak of the masses, not of the few leaders, who fail through want of courage. Nevertheless, if the few really good men will act with calm and prudence and without precipitation, these illusions will all end. Pius IX. is what he appeared to us from the first —a good man, I am willing to believe. I know that his subjects are a little better off than before, *voilà tout*. All the rest is a scaffolding which the so-called Moderates have erected round him, as they have around Charles Albert. The illusions will gradually vanish, but infallibly, and the moment will arise in which the people will understand that if they mean to become a nation they must create that nation with their own hands, and then they will break out into such manifestations as will lead Austria to invade, with or without leave. Then the struggle, if Italy has a spark of courage and sense of honour, will commence. The few good men must prepare for that moment cautiously, accumulate arms, gain influence over the people, allow illusions to die out of themselves without attacking them openly, limit themselves to educate the people, especially the peasantry, instruct the youth in arms, excite ever more abhorrence for Austria, and irritate her in every possible way. I shall be glad to hear from you, and shall be grateful for your efforts to increase the National Fund. Believe, absent or present, in the affection of your Joseph."

Metternich adds the following remarks : " One can but share this judgment which Mazzini passes on the future of his country in this letter, which seems to me sufficiently remarkable to send it to you. It sums up the question that all the scaffolding of Italian liberalism, so-called Moderate, will not be long in crumbling under the blows which will be aimed at it by uncurbed radicalism."

This letter of Mazzini is less hopeful in tone than those written in September, when " in a moment of illusion and youthful enthusiasm" (as he wrote to Lamberti), he had penned on the 8th a letter to Pius IX. About this same letter to the Pope, he wrote on November 25th to his mother: "I do not know whether I told you that last September, one evening, filled with youthful emotion by the thoughts of the immense good the Pope could effect, I wrote a letter to him, which was handed to him in his carriage. I gave it to my friends, who made copies and copies, so it was widely disseminated, and now they write to me that it is going to be published. I could still prevent this, but do not care to do so, as anything that I write even privately may be published. I suppose it will appear this week, and if I get a copy, I shall send it to you."

Mazzini goes on to allude to an incident that had occurred in Genoa during a demonstration of enthusiasm for Charles Albert. A militant young patriot, Nino Bixio, then in correspondence with Mazzini and destined to be one of the generals who led the Italian troops to Rome in 1870, placing his hand on the King's carriage, had cried, "Sire, cross the Tessin and we will all follow you to the death!" Mazzini writes: "The manifestations please me because they indicate the right spirit, but as to hopes, I confess that mine are slight. I have no faith in princes. All this fuss about reforming sovereigns, of leagues of war against Austria, seems to me a sort of magic-lantern, a passing phantom. The princes have an antipathy for Austria, naturally, but they have a greater antipathy for the development of liberty in their subjects, and as they perceive that the one cannot be disjoined from the other, they will not take the initiative. There is too much childishness in Italy. Yesterday all the cry was "Viva Pio IX.!" now it is all "Viva Carlo Alberto!" to-morrow it may be "Viva the Grand Duke of Tuscany," and so on, till the whole round of princes will be gone through. But it is well that these things are: they can only lead to good. So I approve all the demonstrations of fraternal feelings, and also those of gratitude to the King, but I would that all should preserve their *sang-froid*, and not mistake for

NINO BIXIO.

To face p. 118.]

accomplished facts hopes that are yet hopes only, that a caprice, a fright, a physical or moral illness may dispel.

As to my father's remark that the preference should be given to a stable, hereditary chief, it is a question of fact. To prefer him, it is necessary to have him. Let this stable, hereditary, idoneous chief, resolved to secure the welfare of the whole of Italy, show himself, and then we will talk about him."

There is no doubt that Charles Albert was at that time stirred to the very depths of his soul by the demonstrations of affection and trust which greeted him at every step. One of his letters to his secretary, Count di Castagneto, recently published, proves this abundantly, and proves likewise that his youthful aspiration of heading a crusade against Austria had never abandoned him. In this letter the King writes: "I am sending you only a few lines, as there is much yet to do. Austria has sent a note to all the Powers in which she declares that she intends to hold Ferrara, believing that she has a right to do so. On my return to Racconigi I found a great crowd before the palace; it was a perfectly decorous manifestation, and no cries were raised. If Providence should send us a war for Italian Independence I shall mount my horse and place myself and my sons at the head of the army, and act as Shamyl is acting in Russia. What a glorious day will be that in which the cry of 'War for the Independence of Italy' shall resound!"

This letter was handed about among Charles Albert's friends, and they used it largely as an instrument of propaganda, though its authenticity was disputed for a long time. Mazzini heard of it, and though from the first he must have thought it to be the King's and did not doubt its sincerity, he remarked, when writing to his mother about it: "Se saranno rose, fioriranno" (If they are roses, they will bloom).

Mazzini incurred much reproach for the reprint of his "Letter to Charles Albert," and for having addressed another to Pius IX., but he coherently and victoriously held his ground. Charles Albert needed to be spurred on by popular initiative : when the initiative came, he responded to it. Mazzini willingly admitted that if the people had kept the direction of the movement in their own hands things would have ended differently, but then, the people and their leaders "abdicated" in favour of Charles Albert. As to his letter to Pius IX., "it was not written to the Pope, but to the man who was then all powerful in Italy, who, if he had chosen, could have headed a crusade against Austria and driven her beyond the Alps. At that moment I would have gladly hailed him Head of United Italy and its President for life."

Mazzini was by no means the only one who believed in the ability of Pius IX. to unite and free Italy if he had only used his great powers. Garibaldi and his Legionaries in Montevideo regarded Pius IX. as the political Messiah of Italy, and they sent an enthusiastic address to the Papal Nuncio in Uruguay, in which, among other things, they said : " If these hands, used to fighting, would be acceptable to his Holiness, we would most thankfully dedicate them to the service of him who deserves so well of the Church and of our Fatherland. Joyful indeed we, and our companions, in whose name we write, shall be, if allowed to shed our blood in defence of Pius IX.'s work of redemption ! "

IX

GEORGES SAND AND LONDON FRIENDS

1847

Letter to Lizzie Biggs—Mazzini and the Ruffinis in Paris—Visit to Madame Sand—The Ashursts and Madame Sand—The affair of Favizzano — Mazzini back in London — Margaret Fuller — The Whittington Club and the Metropolitan Athenæum—Condition of Italy in 1847—The idea of Union—Mazzini's "Instructions and Methods"—His New Year letter for 1848.

THROUGHOUT the year Mazzini had been preparing his father and mother for his "holiday in the country," hoping to prevent their being anxious during his intended visit to the Continent. His father had written "trusting that his presentiment for the New Year would not lead him to tempt fate in Genoa, as his only consolation was to think him safe in London." Mazzini had now made the acquaintance of Mr. Ashurst's fourth daughter, Matilda, and of her husband, Mr. Biggs, with their young children. The result in their case, as in the case of every one else who had come to know him, was "fascination." "I am going to Muswell Hill," he writes to "Lizzie" (Matilda's little daughter), on August 14th, "and shall talk about you both to your Aunt Eliza. I am leaving London for five weeks, and hope to visit you on my return : let us hope, but not complain too much if it cannot be done. We are here-down, not for our own pleasure, but to do our duty."

It was not, however, until the beginning of October that he left London, and after visiting Switzerland, spent some time in Paris, where, after their long separation, he met Giovanni Ruffini, for whom, though estranged in views, he retained a faithful affection. Agostino Ruffini had sent £3 for the National Fund, and had expressed his opinion that all the exiles ought to arm, and be prepared for the events that were evidently maturing in Italy. Giovanni writes to his brother: " Pippo appears here as a practical man enlightened by experience : he talks quietly, soberly, reasonably, even about politics " ; then, alluding to the series of ovations and triumphs that await him right and left from the Italian exiles and French Liberals who crowded to greet him at 66, rue du Faubourg St. Honoré, where he was the guest of Mario (the great tenor) and Grisi, he adds : " The fact remains that Mazzini is an extraordinary man ; only a being endowed with great qualities could exercise such a fascination as he does."

From Paris Mazzini went down to the " Black Valley " to visit Madame Sand, with whom he had been in correspondence since 1843, and whose works he had reviewed in the English press, while for Eliza Ashurst's translation of " Les Lettres d'un Voyageur " he had written a charming preface. They had read each other's writings and had been mutually attracted by the similarity of their spiritual views. In one of her letters Georges Sand told him that, finding herself in Switzerland during his sojourn there, she had decided on going to him to seek counsel in her own great troubles, but that on reflection she found that she had no right to inflict personal sorrows upon one so heavily burdened already by the sufferings of humanity. She knew of his efforts for oppressed nationalities and had probably read his " Foi et Avenir." This visit of his to Black Valley deepened their spiritual sympathy, but we may suppose that Georges Sand did not expound her social theories, and that Mazzini did not give vent to his disapproval, we may almost say contempt, for the French Liberals of the day. The correspondence that followed is deeply interesting. Most of Madame Sand's letters to Mazzini have been published by her son, but many of them are misdated : Mazzini's will appear in Italian, in chronological order, with those to his mother and other friends. As we have been permitted to select one letter from the collection, we have chosen the following as indicative of the enthusiasm felt in the English circle for the large-brained woman and large-hearted man who so powerfully attracted the Brownings, Matthew Arnold, Emerson, Mrs. Carlyle, and most of the thinkers of England and the Continent. That stern old Puritan, Thomas Carlyle, could, however, never be brought even to tolerate Madame Sand's name.

Mazzini's letter is written from Switzerland, where he remained some time, and runs:

26 Novembre, 1847.

MON AMIE,—Quelqu'un vient d'imprimer une lettre que j'envoyais au Pape, il y a trois mois à peu près, lorsqu'il paraissait hésitant entre les deux routes, et à laquelle il vient de répondre dans un discours à la Consulta, en qualifiant 'd'Utopie' toute chose qui tendrait à diminuer ou à transformer l'autorité pontificale. Je vous l'envoie. Lisez le, si vous en avez le temps, elle est courte. Quant au Pape, 'l'Utopie' un beau jour le devorera, lui et sa chose morte. Mais n'est-ce-pas douloureux que de voir toutes les grandes institutions condamnées à périr ainsi dans la boue, sans nouer la tradition entre ce qui a été et ce qui sera, sans soupçonner ce qu'il y aurait de sublime dans une parole de Vie, prononcée en entrant volontairement au tombeau?

Il me faut vous transcrire quelques fragments de lettres que je reçois de Londres et qui vous concernent. Des amies à nous me demandèrent naturellement de vos nouvelles. Je répondis que je vous avais trouvée telle que vous deviez être, profondément malheureuse et saintement calme. Je n'ai pas, je pense, besoin de vous dire que je ne faisais nullement allusion a vos souffrances intimes. Voici ce que l'une d'elles m'écrit: I can think of nothing but of Mme. Sand. How I wish she would come to England. Affection has a blessed power, when all else fails, of consolation. And we would surround her with such an affection. You would be a friend and support to her, and we would all be her very loving and devoted slaves. I have an immense faith in affection doing for a heart like hers what nothing else can do. Don't laugh at me: I have no insane notion that we could make her happy, but it would be a privilege to afford even the smallest consolation to a soul like hers. Our own home could be her headquarters, where she could have as many rooms as she liked quite her own, and never be disturbed, but be as much her own mistress as in an hotel.

Une autre, pour laquelle vous avez écrit votre nom, aborde le sujet encore plus franchement: This letter is not for you really at all, but to

THE BIRTH OF MODERN ITALY

wish you to do something I have not courage to do for myself. You are, if you do not think it too presumptuous a request from people whom she does not know, to ask Mme. Sand to come to us, if ever she does come to England, to make our house her resting-place, her inn. You, better than any one, can make her understand how welcome, how at-home she can be. You know also that there are three houses (celles de ses sœurs) in town, where her presence would be welcome, in fact you know all we feel, which might appear exaggerated if written to her, but you can vouch for it and us. My father and mother join most warmly in the request. I would have written, only that she would have felt obliged to write a polite note perhaps, and of all things, I should hate to receive a polite note from Mme. Sand. So, you must do everything; make her know that at any time our home, such as it is, is ready for her. I would say our hearts also, but you know she has been enshrined there so long already, that I feel as though we actually had a claim on her.

Je connais intimement les femmes qui écrivent cela, il n'y a pas une seule syllabe qui ne parte pas du cœur. Vous leur avez fait du bien ; elles vous aiment. Vous leur feriez plus de bien encore par votre présence. Et si un jour la fantaisie vous prenait de faire une course en Angleterre, vous vous rappeleriez d'elles, j'en suis sur.

Il ne m'a pas été possible d'avoir un exemplaire de ma lettre au Pape avant aujourd'hui. . . Je ne vous dis rien sur la visite de votre fille et sur vos souffrances. Même en étant près de vous, je ne vous dirais rien, je crois. Ce ne serait que par un regard, par un serrement de main que je chercherais à vous donner de la force. Et ce serrement de main, vous le sentez de loin, n'est-ce-pas ? Vous êtes bien sure, n'est-ce-pas, que je donnerais avec joie quelques années de la vie qui me reste pour vous la ramener tout de suite par l'amour, comme elle vous reviendra un peu plus tard par la souffrance ? Je les donnerais bien toutes, si je n'avais pas ici-bas mon pays et ma pauvre mère. Je pars mercredi, il n'y a rien à faire en Suisse, il n'y aura rien à faire avant l'année prochaine en Italie. Ici je suis surveillé. Le Gouvernement sait où je suis : écrivez moi à Londres à cette addresse : S. Hamilton, Esq., 13, Cropley Street, New North Road. De près, de loin, souffrant ou calme, n'oubliez pas que je suis à vous, que je vous aime comme une sœur, comme une amie, comme une sainte, et que si je pouvais par hazard vous être bon à quelque chose, vous n'avez qu'à dire venez, allez, j'irai, je ferai ce que vous me direz de faire. Adieu, mon amie, aimez moi comme je vous aime.

JOSEPH.

P.S.—Je trouve ici, parmi quelques papiers à moi une courte lettre écrite à un ami quelques heures avant de mourir, par un de ceux qui tombèrent fusillés à Cosenza, avec les frères Bandiera. Je vous envoie une copie. Elle me parait admirable. Rappelez moi au souvenir de Maurice et de vos amis.

The letter alluded to in this postscript was written by

Anacarsi Nardi and had been published by Mazzini in the *Times* while the Cosenza affair was fresh in the public mind.

In her reply Georges Sand thanks his friends for their kind offers, but says that she is writing her memoirs and cannot leave Nohant till they are finished. She tells Mazzini that he has left in her house a ring which he must be sorry to have lost, as inside of it is graven "Let a mother's love console thee." So grieved had he indeed been that he had written to his mother to find some means to send him another ring, as he felt he had lost a talisman. She was able to comply, so he wrote to Georges Sand telling her to keep the one she had found in memory of his mother and himself, and she thanks him affectionately.

He sends his mother a paragraph from the first letter Madame wrote to him after his visit to her :—

"simply to give you pleasure, but do not allow anyone to see it or take copies of it, as I should feel really culpable if the least publicity were to be given to such intimate expressions about myself. 'C'est assez vous parler des autres. Permettez moi de vous parler de vous, et de vous dire tout bonnement ce que j'en pense, à présent que je vous ai vu. C'est que vous êtes aussi bon que vous êtes grand, et que je vous aime pour toujours. Mon cœur est brisé, mais les morceaux en sont encore bons, et, si je dois succomber physiquement à mes peines, avant de vous retrouver, au moins j'emporterai dans ma nouvelle existence, après celle-ci, une force qui me sera venue de vous. Je suis fermement convaincue que rien de tout celà ne se perd, et qu'à l'heure de mon agonie, votre esprit visitera le mien, comme il l'avait fait plusieurs fois avant que nous eussions echangé aucun rapport extérieur. Tout ce que vous m'avez dit sur les morts et sur les vivants est bien vrai, et c'est ma foi que vous résumiez. A présent que vous êtes parti, quoique nous ne nous sommes guère quittés pendant ces deux jours, je trouve que nous ne nous sommes pas assez parlé. Moi, surtout, je me rappelle tout ce que j'aurais voulu vous demander et vous dire, mais j'ai été un peu paralisée par un sentiment de respect que vous m'inspiriez avant tout. Croyez pourtant que ce respect m'exclut pas la tendresse, et, qu'excepté votre mère, personne n'aura désormais des élans plus fervents vers vous et pour vous. J'espère que vous me donnerez de vos nouvelles de Paris, si vous en avez le temps. Je suis en dehors des conditions de l'activité. Je ne puis rien pour tout ce que vous aimez, mais Dieu écoute ces prières-là, et elles ne sont pas sans fruits. Adieu, mon frère, quand vous souffrez, pensez à moi, et appelez mon âme auprès de la vôtre. Elle ira.'"

THE BIRTH OF MODERN ITALY

Georges Sand translated Mazzini's letter to the Pope, but the *Siècle* declined to print it; Pierre Leroux[1] translated some parts of it for his *Revue Sociale*, but he was, at that time, so bent on universal concord and absolute peace that he did not even wish the Austrians to be driven out of Italy by force.

On November the 13th, Mazzini wrote to Mrs. Carlyle from the confines of France and Switzerland:—

DEAR FRIEND,—Here I am after some wanderings through the Departments on my way back: if nothing arises from the present collision in Switzerland, to summon me elsewhere, and without any other inconvenience than a great cold. If nothing arises, I will see you some day during the first week of next month. I have spent a few days with Madame Sand, and left her more *enthousiaste* than ever. She is dreadfully unhappy, and still calm and good, and loving all that is to be loved. There is not a shadow, a single shadow, of vanity or pride about her. There is much of what you like, and much of what I like, combined. But I will tell you all on my first visit: I have seen Lamennais too, and I like him very much. Besides these and a few peasants in the Indre, I dislike almost everything here, and, if I could long for something, I would long for England. As for my main concern, Italy, we are going on tolerably well. It is not a transitory ebullition, nor a feverish moving of the ailing to avoid suffering, but the real awakening of a people to consciousness, to the feeling of its own life and task. I feel hopeful, I could say confident, that before long I shall be able to die in and for my country, the best thing that can befall me.

And you? I left you weak and shattered: shall I find you stronger? I have often thought of you when at Georges Sand's. Carlyle is now, of course, in town. I find, as usual, his name very well known in France, his works very little. Remember me, take care of your health, and believe me, dear friend,

Ever affectionately yours,
Jos. MAZZ.

The certainty that events were preparing the way to action in the sense of independence and nationality was all that he desired. In a letter to his mother he had complained of the servility of the Genoese, who *fêted* Charles Albert as if he had already freed Lombardy, but when he

---

[1] Leroux, Pierre (1797–1871), French philosopher of the Socialistic School: was in 1831 an adherent of the theories of Saint-Simon.

THE AFFAIR OF FAVIZZANO

heard how thoroughly national the demonstration had been, he wrote on November 16th :—

"I have received other letters from Genoa with accounts of the festivals that are more satisfactory, and I retract some, not all, of the bitter things I wrote in my last. Still, it is a game of see-saw, after all; one goes up, and the other comes down. The Pope shows visible signs of retrogression : his refusal to receive the Belgian agent because he was an enemy of the Jesuits; the expulsion of Pescantini[1] by the gendarmes because he was the bearer of a petition from the Swiss to the Pope for the recall of the Jesuits, his general speeches, all prove this, and the people note it, and their enthusiasm diminishes. I have just seen one who visited you in the country, and who saw my father. I am friendly with Agostino and Giovanni [Ruffini], but, naturally, seeing each other so little, there is small opportunity for manifestations, but, I repeat, 'siamo bene assieme' (we are on good terms). . . . Friends write me that a universal amnesty has been signed in Turin. We shall see: send it to me at once, whatever it is, as soon as it appears. I do not believe that it will extend to all, and I am meditating on the steps to be taken. God knows that I thirst to embrace you all. But if, as it is almost certain, there should be declarations to be made and pledges to be given, I could not, cost what it might, submit to make or give them. I wonder if it would be possible to obtain a safe-conduct without any conditions, just to visit you and spend a month with you ? Of course I would promise that for the time being I would not occupy myself with politics. But these are useless conjectures; we must wait and see. Swiss affairs are proceeding slowly. At Favizzano they are fighting. Clearly a crisis is approaching, and I would stake my all that next year the cup will overflow. Why do you so dread the idea of intervention ? Let a few months pass to give time to Time, and I should hail it with joy. I hear that Balbo and Cavour are beginning a new newspaper in Turin. I regret this, as they are behind the times [nevertheless it was Cavour and his *Risorgimento* who first demanded the Constitution]. Genoa, I hope, will become bolder in its ideas. Beg my father to take care of himself, and you do so also. The times are pregnant with events."

He ends this letter with the news that Fribourg has capitulated, that at Favizzano the youth of Tuscany are taking part in the fight, and that the International League in London has held another meeting with two thousand people present.

This affair of Favizzano, the account of which occupies

---

[1] Pescantini, Federico (?–1871), a Romagnol patriot; conspired later with Farini against the Papal power.

about fifty pages (with map) of the Blue Book for 1847, is a fair specimen of the cool fashion in which the petty princelets of the day privately chopped and changed their territories without any regard for the inhabitants. Thus the Sovereigns of Tuscany, Modena, and Lucca had arranged that on the death of the Archduchess Maria Louise, Duchess of Parma (widow of Napoleon I.), the duchy of Lucca should be annexed to Tuscany, barring certain allotments which the Duke of Modena begged for in order to be able to reach to Massa. In Lucca, Charles Bourbon of Modena was so much detested that, before the death of Marie Louise, he actually felt it desirable to make over Lucca to the Grand Duke of Tuscany for " a consideration." Great was the joy of the Lucchesi, but great also was the indignation felt by the inhabitants of the " allotments " who were to be separated from Lucca and handed over in the shape of this " consideration " to the hated Charles. Hence the squabble. The people of Favizzano rose in arms, and the Lucchesi and other Tuscans went to the assistance of their brethren. Radetzky was for rushing to the rescue, but Palmerston requested Metternich to order him to keep his hands off. Then the Archduchess Marie Louise died, the Duke of Modena took possession, and proceeded to shed the blood of his future subjects. Austria, without direct intervention, lent troops to the Duke of Modena, and concluded a secret treaty with him and the Duke of Parma, by which the right banks of the Po and the passes of the Tuscan Apennines passed under the control of the commander of the Austrian forces. On the other hand an amicable convention was made by which Ferrara was to be occupied by combined Papal and Imperial forces, and so, apparently, peace and order reigned in Italy towards the close of 1847. The interest felt by Mazzini and the Nationalists in the squabble centred in the fact that Favizzano was Tuscan, and that it proved the Tuscans to be alive to the rights of their brethren.

At the end of November Mazzini returned to London, where he was warmly greeted by many English friends, who, having visited Paris and Italy, had managed to establish a private postal service on his account. William Shaen, William Ashurst, jun., and his wife, and Emilie and Sidney Hawkes were among these. Mr. and Mrs. Gillman, whom to the last Mazzini always remembered as "of the dear circle of Muswell Hill," came back enthusiastic about the exile's mother, and brought the precious ring above mentioned, besides valuable contributions for a contemplated bazaar, notably a hand-worked rug valued in England at £20. Some of the ladies of the Genoese aristocracy had contributed of their own handiwork, others in Rome, Modena, and Tuscany were also busy for him.

Margaret Fuller (afterwards the Contessa d'Ossoli), who was making a European tour with the Marcus Springs, also visited Mazzini's family, and sent him an album with dried flowers, among which were some from the balcony of his old study, which was kept by his mother just as he had left it. In presenting Margaret Fuller to Enrico Mayer—a sincere patriot and fervid educationalist, once an ardent member of "Young Italy" and still personally attached to its founder, though detached from his theories—Mazzini wrote: "You will receive these lines from Miss Fuller, a distinguished American well known in England and in her own country, the intimate friend of Emerson, rare among women for her active sympathies for all that is great and beautiful and holy. I warmly recommend her to you, and with her, Mr. and Mrs. Marcus Spring, excellent people, and devoted to the cause of negro abolition (*sic*). Help them to love, not only Italy, but the Italians. Introduce Miss Fuller to our friends in Tuscany, and mind that you secure her an interview with Niccolini and Gino Capponi. I shall be really grateful to you." The fact of these last-named introductions to men as hostile to his own especial views as any who could be found in Italy is another proof of Mazzini's unsectarianism, and of his earnest desire that Italians should be known and appreciated at their worth.

Towards the autumn of 1847, possibly in August, the Whittington Club and Metropolitan Athenæum, formed by

Douglas Jerrold, elected Mazzini one of its twenty-two vice-presidents, and he was thus brought into friendly intercourse with Charles Dickens, the Howitts, Monckton-Milnes, Colonel P. J. Thompson, Edward Miall, and Lord John Manners; his old friend Joseph Toynbee, the Earl of Radnor, and Frank Stone also being members. William Shaen was chairman of the council upon which women were admitted without entrance fee to the full rights and privileges of membership, and we find on the list of councillors Mrs. James Stansfeld, Mrs. P. A. Taylor, Eliza Cook, Miss Meteyard, and several other ladies. Two club-houses were established, one at 7, Gresham Street, in the City, and the other at 189, Strand, once the famous "Crown and Anchor Tavern," and there members could breakfast and dine at any hour between 8 a.m. and 12 p.m. There seems to have been a good library and reading-room, taken over, probably, from the People's Association, in which Stansfeld had assiduously worked. Periodical lectures on literature, science and art were delivered; for instance, R. H. Horne (author of "Orion") lectured on the "Spirit of Poetry," Charles Knight on Literature, and George Dawson on "The Natural History of Manners, Habits, Customs, and Forms." This genial teacher and preacher of unsectarian religion was one of the rare ministers of the Gospel who, during the invasion of Rome in 1849, proclaimed the duty of England towards the people who were striving to emancipate their land from Popedom.

In literary and artistic circles the club was popular as a meeting-place for social and debating purposes. It was not a political centre, but its members, at one time numbering more than a thousand, all held Liberal, many of them extremely Radical, views. Mazzini joined it in order to enlarge the sphere of his Italian propaganda, and went sometimes after dinner, as he tells his mother, for a game of chess: "the only diversion—excepting music with the Rossellis and the Nathans—in which I indulge." An old friend of ours and a member of the club told us that Mazzini frequently discussed the Italian question in a most persuasive and, on the whole, convincing fashion, but woe to the listener who ventured to suggest that moral means would be more likely to effect Italian emancipation than an appeal to physical force ! Then he would protest vehemently, asking if Cromwell and his followers had won liberty for England by moral force. Were revolts, revolutions, cutting off the heads, or getting rid of kings and their minions in other summary fashions, moral methods? He had England's revolutionary history on his finger-tips ; he would count up the " fences " that we had put round monarchy to prevent kings from ever again encroaching on our national liberties, and then he would conclude : "*You* can now multiply reforms and introduce improvements without revolutions," but he would add : " Even *you* are forcing your fellow-countrymen into using physical force, because you won't grant their very reasonable demands, and the Chartists and Repealers will give you trouble yet : but this ought not to be, this need not be. By justice and the concession of their rights you can avoid revolution : with us, the use of muskets and cannon is a necessity. Do you think we can *pray* Austria out of Italy ? Preach that doctrine to the Pope. He could, if he would, by placing himself at the head of a holy war, and if war there must be, he could make it short and swift. But to preach passive resistance to a people which has suffered passively for three centuries, instead of rejoicing that it is awaking from its lethargy and helping it to its feet, it is not generous, my dear," he would end, " and it is not English."

Mazzini at the Whittington Club (said this old friend of his and ours) made converts, quite as much by his winning persuasiveness, his intense earnestness, and evidently profound convictions, as by the force of his arguments and the soundness of his logic. It was almost comic to see his vexation when he lost at chess, a frequent occurrence when a tolerable player was his opponent ; he would replace the pieces to see where he began to lose, and one could imagine that he was rehearsing in his mind the whys, hows, and whens of other failures in other fields.

THE BIRTH OF MODERN ITALY

The state of Italy at the close of 1847, as compared with that at the commencement of 1846, justified Alfieri's saying that "the plant man is nowhere so sturdy and healthy as on Italian soil." Italians had proved that revolt, for the sake of revolt, was not in their nature, that they were willing, not to say anxious, to submit to just and enlightened authority, and were endowed with extraordinary faculties for intellectual and moral progress. They availed themselves to the utmost of the smallest opportunities for free discussion. Railroads, custom-house leagues, infant schools, agriculture, claimed their attention; scientific congresses proved that their thinkers and discoverers had not wasted their energies in moaning over political servitude. Each section grew rapidly in the recognition of Italian brotherhood, each yearned for and promoted intercourse with their neighbours; old time-honoured municipal jealousies and feuds disappeared: all felt that a step in advance gained by a section was a boon for the rest; all recognised that the one obstacle to progress—intellectual, social, material—was the presence of a foreign Power in the Peninsula, because that Power must, to preserve its dominion, hinder the other princes from granting such liberty and such institutions as Austria dared not grant to her own proper subjects. Despite Austria's threats, and her direct and indirect intervention, those princes, powerfully backed by England, had gone on steadily in the path of reform. Municipal institutions, civic guards, a free press, liberal ministers, gladdened the populations of Rome, of Tuscany, and, above all, of Piedmont. A commercial league also united the three States, while the people believed that their rulers, conscious that the one obstacle to the stability of those States was Austria, would find some means of crushing or of expelling her. Hence the prevailing sentiment was *Union*, a common bond of defensive alliance against the common enemy; *Union*, we say, not *Unity*, for neither the Romans, the Piedmontese, nor the Tuscans contemplated at that time the abandonment of their own rulers. They believed them to be at heart anti-Austrian, and because they accepted the idea that, although separate Governments, they would form one Italy, they still felt as Tuscans, as Romans, as Piedmontese; autonomy was still deeply rooted in their hearts.

The Pope and his ministers strongly shared this desire for political union between the States of the Peninsula, and their appeals to Charles Albert were both frequent and stringent. But neither he nor his ministers seem to have been at all anxious for the conclusion of a political league. At first they stated that the King of Naples must be included. He consented, with the proviso that the Pope should be the president of the Union and himself commander of all the land and sea forces, &c. Charles Albert seems to have preferred to keep his hands free, and for this he is much blamed by Mr. Bianchi,[1] but it seems to us natural, for it cannot now be denied that he had made up his mind to wage war against Austria, and he doubted exceedingly whether the other princes would really dare as much.

Cesare Cantù,[2] in his "Cronistoria," vol. ii. part ii., chapter xxxviii., page 124, gives us Mazzini's "Instructions and Methods" to his friends, probably found in the secret police archives of Milan, and which must have been issued late in 1846 or early in 1847. These coincide with his public writings and his letters to his mother, and are a fresh proof that all his thoughts were centred in the national idea pure and simple, without a care for the future form of government. In these he says:—

"So, the regeneration of Italy is to be initiated by princes. The Pope must enter on the path of reform by necessity; the King of Piedmont by the prospect of the crown of Italy; the Grand Duke from inclination,

---

[1] Bianchi, Nicomede (1818–1886), historian; was a member of the Provisional Government of Modena and Reggio during 1848.
[2] Cantù, Cesare (1804–1895), great historian, born in Lombardy; was imprisoned for an inscription to Ciro Menotti (*vide* note, p. 11). Later he did not take an active part in the movement for the Unification of Italy, and was a most ardent clerical and Catholic.

weakness, and spirit of imitation; the King of Naples by force. The people, when they shall obtain constitutions, and hence acquire the right to be exacting, may raise their voices and even threaten insurrection. Those who are still subject to (despotic) rulers must agitate for their rights, avail themselves of the slightest concessions to rally and arouse the masses. Expressions of gratitude for concessions, festivals, patriotic hymns, large gatherings, all tend to give wings to the idea, to inculcate in the people a desire for its attainment, a sense of their own strength.

"Associate! Associate! Associate! All is summed up in that word. Secret societies are a great force where they exist. Don't fear the divisions among them; the more they are divided, the better they succeed. All tend by different paths to the same goal."

This somewhat ambiguous sentence evidently alluded to the various ramifications of Young Italy's secret societies in the Neapolitan and Sicilian provinces; some affiliated with the old Carbonari, or the more recent Freemason Lodges, others to Niccola Fabrizi's "Legions," which in Sicily took the form of the famous "Squadre," which did yeoman's service in the Sicilian revolutions of 1848 and 1860 as scouts or rearguard to Garibaldi's band. The instructions go on thus:—

"Never mind either, if the secrets get divulged. Secrecy is necessary for the tranquillity of the members, but the transpiring of the fact that such societies exist arouses the slothful. When a goodly number of associates who have the password—to diffuse the *idea* and create public opinion in its favour—can succeed in concerting a movement, they will find the old fabric undermined and shaky, and it will fall in ruins at the first attack. Then they will themselves be surprised to see priests and kings, aristocracy and plutocracy, who now compose the old social edifice, capitulate and retreat before the sole supreme force of public opinion. Courage and Perseverance!"

It must be kept in mind that though the Pope, the King of Piedmont, and the Grand Duke of Tuscany had granted

1847] LORD PALMERSTON'S ATTITUDE

(generally under compulsion) important and extensive reforms, real constitutions were not wrung from them until in 1848.

In one of his letters to his mother Mazzini says, " Though the news seems too good to be true, it is confidently asserted that the English fleet is going to make a demonstration in the waters of Trieste." It was a fact that Lord Palmerston had decided on something of the sort, should Austria attempt to intervene, or even to interfere, in the affairs of Piedmont. However, such active measures were not required, and on October 29, 1847, the Foreign Secretary wrote to Lord Minto, who had just arrived in Rome from Turin : " As to the Austrians, they have been headed and will not break cover towards Italy. Many things have contributed towards this, but we have had our share in the merit, and were the first to set up the viewholloa which scared them. The Pope ought to be grateful to us for this, and if so he ought to give us some token of his thankfulness. The prohibition to assist the Irish Colleges " (which the Sacred Congregation, probably with the Pope's sanction, had forbidden the archbishops and bishops to establish) " is an unkind and most mischievous measure, which was little to be expected at the hands of the Pope at the very moment when we were stepping out of our way to be of use to him."

Mazzini's New Year's Day letter of 1848 to the dear ones at home, written on Christmas Day, 1847, shows the struggle he underwent during his tour in Switzerland, torn between the desire to once more clasp his loved ones in his arms and the fear that anxiety for him would outweigh their joy.

DEAR ONES MINE !—Would that I could enclose myself in this letter, and appear before you in person on New Year's Day. And I must tell you that when I was nearer to you than I am now, the longing to meet you once again took such strong hold of me, that I kept on hunting for a way to look in upon you if only for 24 hours, and I do believe that I could have done so without any danger. But the thought that your joy would have been frozen by terror, that to separate again after a few moments of reunion might have done you serious harm,

THE BIRTH OF MODERN ITALY

deterred me from making the attempt. So I resigned myself. If this paper could reflect the image of the writer, you would see me as in a mirror, such is the love that overflows in my heart for you. Will God never permit us to embrace each other here-down? I have hardly the courage to express my hopes—the hopes that I nourished for years—that—writing always on this date—I have ever felt that another twelve months could not pass without bringing our reunion in their wake. Yes! the hope abides with me, and increases, and, strange to say, I believe I shall owe its realisation to the Austrians. But if it is not to be, God's will be done, and let us still thank Him for two things: for our intense love, which sixteen years of absence has not weakened on either side, and our sure and certain faith that, if not here-down, we shall assuredly be reunited elsewhere. To this faith I cling; it has sustained me in suffering, it has also kept me faithful to the principles that I hold to be true. Mother, father mine, you have loved me though I believed in those certain principles, and do continue still to love me. I feel in the depths of my soul that they *are* truths, and that if I had betrayed them, I might have hastened the moment of our meeting here on earth, but that I should have postponed immeasurably the reunion of our immortal souls in a future life. These principles are the "talent" that God has confided to me, for which he will some day call me to account, that I cannot, without sin, hide or allow to rust uselessly. Love me then, just as I am! Your love has been a greater consolation to me than you can imagine. True it is that to-day in this country, I have men who love me as brothers, I might almost say disciples, women who love me as mothers and sisters love, but there have been moments in my life when I have felt alone in the world—alone, but for you—terrible moments when your love alone saved me from despair. And to-day also, nothing can take the place of your love for me, and in my moments of spleen my heart turns with tenderness to you—mother, father, sister—as to a trinity of affection which soars far above any other. And I unite in my thought of you, the two sisters who were mine, and who, I believe, still love me and inspire me with good thoughts.

He sends messages of affection to all relatives and friends by name, thanks his father for the cheque, his *perennial love gift*,[1] and leaves politics to another day.

That was the last New Year's Day letter that Mazzini's father was destined to receive. When 1849 dawned he who *did* care for " the material triumph of ideas here-down" had gone *elsewhere*, and the failures and disasters of 1848, the burning of his son's writings in the market-place of Genoa, were for him nothing but the records of that son's weary and unrecompensed pilgrimage.

[1] See note, p. 57.

X

THE GREAT REVOLUTION

1848

Milan's "Self-denying Ordinance"—Palermo's ultimatum—The Sicilian rising—Determination to regain the Constitution of 1812—Flight of the Governor—De Sauget abandons the Molo—Triumph of the revolution—Mazzini and Sicily—English interest—Louis Philippe's abdication—Mazzini in Paris—Lamartine's speech—Ledru-Rollin—Mazzini's influential position—Giovanni Ruffini—Mazzini's arrival in Milan—Cattaneo's efforts to form a Lombard army—Treatment of volunteers and of Garibaldi—Lack of military maps—Luciano Manara and Pietro Arcioni—Incapacity of the Provisional Government—False confidence—Pius IX.'s *volte face*—Its effect—Count Pompeo Litta's protest against the Government's intentions—The Plebiscite—Decree of the 12th of May—Disasters in the field.

THE year 1848 was inaugurated by the Milanese with the "Self-denying Ordinance." This was an idea probably suggested by Botta's graphic description of the "Boston Tea-Pot" in his recently published "History of the American Revolution," and it aimed at striking a blow at Austrian finance through tobacco and the State lottery. The tobacco monopoly brought in annually eight million liras; the lottery even more. No patriot was therefore to smoke or to take lottery tickets, and the order was implicitly obeyed—at what sacrifice to the cigar-loving Italians, inveterate smokers alone can appreciate. The infuriated authorities at once supplied the soldiery and many jail-birds, whom they purposely liberated, with cigars, and set them to parade the streets and puff

THE BIRTH OF MODERN ITALY

smoke into the faces of the ladies—a gentlemanly diversion indulged in even by the officers themselves. Feelings of bitter resentment were naturally aggravated by this ill-savoured joke, and Radetzky saw in the temper of the citizens a pretext for action. On January 2nd, cavalry brutally attacked the unarmed people, killing or wounding sixty-seven. Intense indignation was felt throughout Italy, and funeral services were held all over the country, the one at San Carlo dei Milanesi in Rome being attended by the civic authorities, the National Guard, and the students.

On the same date the citizens of Palermo sent their ultimatum to the King at Naples, demanding the restoration, by the 12th of the month, of the Constitution of 1812, which had been guaranteed by England. The Sicilians had never ceased their demand for this, and in 1817 Mackintosh and Bentinck had sustained their claims in the British Parliament. In 1820, 1824, 1827, 1828, 1830, and 1837, they had risen in arms for their rights, their insurrections being quenched in blood.

The servitude to which the Sicilians were condemned baffles all description. The poverty of the island was fearful; the people were overburdened by taxation, forced loans, and illegal exactions, the prisons and fortresses crowded with political prisoners and "suspects." King Ferdinand had himself watched the riveting of heavy chains on the arms and ankles of forty-seven patriots who had been condemned to death after the bloody suppression of the 1847 rising, but whom he had reprieved from execution only to consign for life to the fearful dungeons of Favignana and Nisida. The hatred for him in the hearts of the people was intense.

On January 12th, as arranged, the women of Palermo, clad in mourning, went to the Viceroy's palace to receive the answer to the popular ultimatum. That answer being in the negative, word for a general uprising throughout the island was circulated as if by magic. During the following night no one slept; men and women were busy arming or making tricoloured flags and cockades. The next day the guns at Castellamare, which boomed out a royal salute for the King's birthday, were instantly answered by the bells of St. Orsola, the Gancia Convent, and other churches ringing the tocsin; and the people, armed with little besides spits, hatchets, and stones, attacked and successfully disarmed the patrols all over the city. When night fell, the troops still retained most of their positions, but the insurgents occupied as their headquarters the famous Piazza dalla Fiera Vecchia, which the "Royals" hesitated to attack without the advantage of daylight. Next morning all the patriotic peasants poured into the town armed with implements of labour and whatever else had come to hand. A number of gensdarmes who were conveying the sum of 20,000 ducats—the troops' pay—were captured and the prize secured. Fierce fighting continued during nine days, and the insurgents formed four committees, several members of which afterwards fought under Garibaldi; for instance, Oddo, La Masa, Cianciolo, Rosalino Pilo, Orsini, and Francesco Crispi. The presidents of these committees were the Prince of Pantellaria, the Marquis di Rudini, the Judge of Palermo, and Ruggero Settimo; but later on the four bodies were combined under Settimo, a great patriot, who had taken part in the Sicilian revolution of 1821, and whose title was Prince of Fitalia.

On the third day of the fight the Neapolitan fleet, headed by the King's brother, and carrying 5,000 troops under General de Sauget, arrived in the port, landed the troops, and ruthlessly bombarded the city. So near to extinction came Palermo, that the foreign Consuls and the Minister of the United States protested indignantly against a bombardment which must produce a catastrophe that would stain the century; but nothing daunted the intrepid Palermitans. When an attempt was made by foreign sympathisers to induce the insurgents to give in for the sake of their city and trust to mediation, "Our rights! Our Constitution! Go and preach to the perjured Ferdinand!" was the unanimous reply. The bombs committed fearful havoc and the soldiery frightful excesses   Troops invaded the Benedictine Monastery, slaughtered two of the fathers, four of the servants, and eleven other persons who had taken refuge there, and, not content with murder, hacked the bodies of their victims with their bayonets, so infuriating the populace that Captain Lyons, an eye-witness of events, wrote to Lord Napier that "rich and poor, plebs and nobles, artisans and peasants, all declared that death was preferable to life under such a government, and even if Palermo should crumble to ruins they would rather be buried beneath them than yield."

Throughout the conflict the conduct of the women was extraordinarily heroic, both on the field and in the hospital. Among them, working unremittingly, the wife of the United States consul especially distinguished herself. General de Sauget, finding that he was gaining nothing, promised amnesty, reforms, asked the intervention of the commanders of the French and British fleets; but the insurgents declared that the only terms they would accept were the liberation of all political prisoners, the surrender of the forts and arsenal, with all artillery and ammunition, and the retreat of the troops. When news arrived that King Ferdinand had granted a constitution in Naples, the Sicilian patriots replied that "Sicily, represented by her General Parliament, will introduce the reforms needed by modern times into that Constitution (the Constitution of 1812) which she has never forfeited." This indicated that only war to the knife was possible. Finally, the Governor, De Majo, fled from the Royal palace, which the people promptly seized and despoiled, religiously consigning, however, to the general committee more than two million liras found in the vaults. All the sick and wounded deserted by De Majo were respected and cared for, and some detachments left behind were treated with chivalrous clemency, though spies and *sbirri* (the lowest riff-raff of the police) met with no consideration.

De Sauget, although occupying a strong position, entertained no real hope of victory, such was the temper of the people, and at last, on the night of the 27th, he abandoned the castle of the Molo, the arsenal, and the prison. In the final hope of stifling the revolution in anarchy, he liberated all the galley-slaves and criminals, numbering between five and six thousand, who had been starving in their cells for several days. It would be difficult to believe this were it not for the evidence of Captain Lyons, who wrote to Lord Minto on the 31st, " I confirm the fact; the general let all the galley-slaves loose upon Palermo." All the poor wretches asked for was bread, and as soon as this was given them they begged to be allowed to fight. Many fought well, and many expiated their past crimes by a noble death; but as soon as the fighting was over and their special enemies had passed away, many of them returned to their evil practices, and helped to bring about no small part of the troubles that subsequently racked the island.

After eighteen days' desperate struggle the Sicilian Revolution—the overture to the Liberation movement on the mainland—triumphed in six out of the seven districts of the island, and the only stain on the people's escutcheon was the shooting of twenty *sbirri* under the wall of the Pretorian Palace. This was the result of exasperation at the discovery of human remains and instruments of torture in the cellars of the police offices of San Celso and San Domenico, where some women were seeking vainly for husbands and sons who had been incarcerated there, and whom the revelation wrought up to madness. Ruggero Settimo, in the name of the general committee, issued a proclamation severely reprimanding the people for this act, while praising them for their otherwise magnanimous conduct, reminding them that " our Redeemer Jesus Christ and Pio Nono, his Vicar, enjoined on all and sanctified the forgiveness of offences."

The influence of Lord Palmerston's " hands off " to Austria had been undoubtedly great and beneficent in the affairs of the Peninsula; but in this crisis Palmerston would perhaps have been wiser to abstain from all intervention. Lord Minto, whom Palmerston had sent upon a sort of roving commission to Italy, and who had had an appreciable share in urging the sovereigns of Piedmont, Rome, and Naples to grant reforms, was now so beset on all sides that he went from Rome to Naples to see what intercession could do, although Lord Napier, our *chargé d'affaires* in Naples, had declined to attempt any mediation. Lord Palmerston only became aware of Lord Minto's decision after the latter's arrival in Naples, and his letter to Lord Minto affords complete refutation of the idea that Great Britain offered to the Sicilians in 1848 any sort of guarantee for the restoration of the Constitution of 1812. Lord Minto did his utmost to induce Ferdinand to renew and respect "rights" which the islanders felt had never been forfeited, and Ferdinand, in the hope that time would reintroduce a discord among the Sicilians which would give him his opportunity, allowed his minister, Bozzelli, to make some insincere acquiescence. The Sicilians, however, understanding better than Lord Minto the intentions of their perjured tyrant, convoked their island Parliament, and through it proclaimed the downfall of the Bourbon dynasty.

These tidings carried joy to every Italian heart; but Mazzini, while rejoicing in the prowess of the islanders, was filled with anxiety lest in their hour of triumph they should, through hatred of the Bourbon, forget their Italianhood and remember only that they were Sicilians. Strongly tempted to accede to urgent invitations, sent both to him and to Nicola Fabrizi by the Unitarian party, he constrained himself to keep away lest his presence should endanger the general harmony. He knew the British Government feared that Sicily might follow the example of France and proclaim a Republic, so he contented himself with indicting a letter to the Sicilians—in itself a chapter from the Unitarian gospel.

After congratulating them on the fact that they had, in a few days, done more for Italy than had been accomplished during years of continental agitation, because they had infused into the Italians a consciousness of their strength and inspired them with faith in themselves, he implored them to remember that they had rights and duties in common with the rest of Italy, and that, having shown themselves foremost in initiative and in bravery, they must in no degree separate their fate from that of their greater Fatherland; they had still, he said, to prove themselves great in a lofty conception of its future. On that future their conduct would have immense influence, for they formed a vital portion of the nation and had acquired the first possibilities towards the creation of a splendid navy and a national army. He then goes on to say: "You have taught us the power of will; teach us that union is strength; teach us the religion of unity which alone can restore to Italy her glory, her initiative, and her mission for the third time in Europe." After saying that he is of Genoa, a city with a wonderful history, but which, like Sicily, had been handed over to another Italian State, he explains that, though this handing over had once rankled bitterly in the hearts of the Genoese, yet the wisest citizens now looked upon it as a providential event, and he continues:—

"In the slow but constant evolutions of the populations, exhausted through centuries of oppression by foreign forces, by feudal aristocracies, by municipal discord and ambition —after the Italy of the Cæsars and the Italy of the Popes —the third Italy, the Italy of the People, is preparing. Every fraction of Italian soil united to another is a sign of triumph for us; one more obstacle pacifically removed; every detachment of one fraction is a backward step."

Through no fault of the Sicilians, but through that of circumstance, the hour for Unity could not sound yet. Mazzini's letter was hailed with enthusiasm, and his adherents kept the Unitarian flag aloft, sending their contingent to the Lombard war (which started in March) and during nineteen long months dauntlessly resisting the Bourbon. This vile tyrant, freeing himself by perjury and massacres from his oath to the Constitution, and by treachery and betrayal from participation in the War of Independence, was then able to concentrate the whole of his

THE BIRTH OF MODERN ITALY

land and sea forces upon the reduction of the heroic, ill-fated island, which succumbed, after repeated struggles, in May, 1849.

Meanwhile, in England, the interest in Italy and in the Italian Revolution steadily deepened. Mrs. Stansfeld, in a long letter to Shaen, gave the last details about Mazzini before he left to join the national crusade which had been so long yearned for. Among other things, she says: " On Sunday, with the exception of our Mazz, we were all alone at Muswell Hill. Mother had a fire lighted in the library for him to smoke, and when he coquetted about it she quite begged him to go. I believe she will soon allow him to smoke in the drawing-room." At that time Ralph Waldo Emerson must also have visited Muswell Hill, for Mazzini, in one of his letters to Lizzie Biggs, asks how she likes him.

The news of Guizot's dismissal seems to have aroused no suspicion of its probable consequences in the minds of foreign statesmen. Lord Palmerston was, of course, delighted, and hoped that his fall would prove a warning to Metternich and the princes of Italy, for he believed that Guizot had held that by a packed Parliament and a corruptly obtained majority he could control the will of the nation. This policy resulted, however, in " the will of the crown being controlled by an armed force." The surrender of Louis Philippe to the summons of the National Guard was, in Lord Palmerston's opinion, a " curious example of poetical and political justice." But when abdication and flight and the proclamation of the Republic followed so closely on the King's surrender, the " poetry " was less apparent, and the statesman's dislike to republics came at once to the fore. He was most thankful that Lord Minto " had urged the Italian sovereigns to move on the path of reforms, for if their impatient subjects had not been kept back, by this time there would have been nothing but republics from the Alps to Sicily."

Mazzini, who had formed an unfavourable opinion of French politicians and reformers during his visit to France in 1847, took immediate advantage of the proclamation of

1848] FRENCH ORATORICAL PROFESSIONS

the Republic to go openly to Paris and consult with the Italian exiles gathered there. He soon gained their adherence to the Italian "National Association" (of which he was President), explaining that while superseding "Young Italy" on the one hand and purely monarchical societies on the other, it offered a neutral camp to all who accepted the programme of Independence and Nationality. He was accompanied by Messrs. Stansfeld, Dobson-Collett, and W. J. Linton, these gentlemen being sent by the International League to present an address of sympathy to the French Government. Unfortunately no trace of this address remains, but the eloquent speech of Mazzini at the Hôtel de Ville and Lamartine's mellifluous reply have been preserved, and we here give some salient points of them, for it is well to remember promises made in the name of that French Republic which later became the destroyer of the Roman Republic and the reinstater of the Pope upon a throne sustained by corpses.

There had already commenced in the "Lombardo-Veneto" that revolution which was to result in the expulsion of the Austrians from Milan after the famous "Five Days." Mazzini pointed out that the one thought of all great Italians, from Arnold of Brescia to Macchiavelli, from Dante to Napoleon—"qui est à nous comme il est à vous"—had been the political unification of Italy. The establishment of a "compact nationality of twenty-four million brothers and freemen" ought to be assisted for the good of the world. He explained in detail how the formation of Italian nationality would benefit France, who, through it, would gain a sister—a faithful and powerful ally; and concluded, "So we feel we have a right to your sympathies, as you have a right to our admiration. Give them to us, gentlemen; they will not be wasted on the Italy of to-day, and still less on the Italy of to-morrow."

Lamartine, after a magniloquent declaration that he, if not by birth, was an Italian by adoption, hailed the coming union of the sister nations. He then went on to assure the delegates that their cause was that of France also, as France

THE BIRTH OF MODERN ITALY

bowed in respect before the names of those great geniuses who were the immortal glory of Italy. He, of course, could not enter into political questions reserved for the National Assembly, but he explicitly declared that the French Republic favoured the free choice of government for the whole world. He would not detain his audience long, as they were doubtless anxious to rush to the help of their heroic brothers in Italy, and he closed his oration with these words :

"Eh ! bien, puisque la France et l'Italie ne font qu'un seul nom dans nos sentiments communs, pour la régénération liberale, allez dire à l'Italie qu'elle a des enfants aussi de ce côté des Alpes (*Bravo*). Allez lui dire que si elle était attaquée dans son sol ou dans son âme, dans ses limites ou ses libertés, que si vos bras ne suffisaient pas à la défendre, ce ne sont plus des voeux ou des sentiments, c'est l'épée de la France que nous lui offririons pour la préserver de tout envahissement ! . . . (*Bravos unanimes*.)
    Notre amour pour l'Italie est désintéressé, et nous avons l'ambition de la voir aussi impérissable et aussi grande, que le sol dont elle a éternisé le nom ! . . . (*Grands applaudissements*)."

From his speech Lamartine had significantly excluded the name of Macchiavelli, thus indicating his intention to pursue a different policy from that of Guizot—who had been nicknamed " the Macchiavelli in-12° "—and the name of Napoleon. He replaced them with that of Washington, in token of his absolutely peaceful intentions. This appeased the fears of the European diplomats and satisfied Lord Palmerston, who had rightly disbelieved the rumour that France intended to invade Belgium, and was convinced that Lamartine meant " peace and no aggression."

Mazzini, while by no means desiring the intervention of even Republican France in Italy, assiduously cultivated the acquaintance of such Frenchmen as were, in his idea, favourable to her independence and unity. Foremost among these stood, he believed, Ledru-Rollin,[1] Minister for Home Affairs, who assured him that the 30,000 men despatched

---

[1] Ledru-Rollin, Alexandre Auguste (1807-1874), French politician and philosopher, a warm sustainer of universal suffrage, remained an exile in England from 1848 till after the fall of the French Empire in 1871.

by the Provisional Government to the Alpine frontier were sent merely as an army of observation to watch events, especially the movements of the Austrians. This, at least, was the ostensible object; the real aim, unsuspected as yet by Mazzini, was to profit by any indication that the long coveted province of Savoy was ripe for annexation to France. The idea of annexing Savoy was held to as tenaciously by Lamartine as it had been by Thiers, and it was nursed as carefully by Ledru-Rollin as by Louis Napoleon. But though Mazzini was not awake to it, Charles Albert and his ministers had taken alarm. On the 30th of March the Marchese Pareto informed Sir Ralph Abercromby that he had ordered the Sardinian minister in Paris to request the Provisional Government to keep its troops as far as possible from the frontier, lest the populations should imagine that France was going to interfere in their affairs, whereas " we intend every one to know that Italy means to act by herself—*farà da sè* "—a sentence which became celebrated.

Mazzini, always anxious that Italy should fight her own battles and achieve her own emancipation, regarded Charles Albert's diffidence as the result of his hatred of republics and his dread of republican propaganda in Italy, where the soil was naturally adapted to the seed. He reposed complete faith in Ledru-Rollin, whose political views seemed to coincide with his own, and who promised to prove a sincere and active friend to Italy, whose independence would result in benefit to France. This confidence of Mazzini's was so far justified that from his seat on the " Mountain," Ledru-Rollin headed the very small band of deputies who, from first to last, protested against the expedition to Rome.

During his sojourn in Paris, Mazzini was in constant intercourse with Giovanni Ruffini, who, in his letters to his brother Agostino—still a professor in Edinburgh—dilates on the wonderful and widely-increasing influence that Mazzini has obtained among the exiles not only in Paris but throughout Italy. In one letter Giovanni says :—

"His (Mazzini's) exposition of principles at the second meeting of the

THE BIRTH OF MODERN ITALY

Italian National Association was much admired (*molto gustato*) even by the Moderates. I must do him the justice to say that his speeches are most reasonable." But he adds, with his inevitable spice of malice, "the bone I pick with him is for what he does not say, and that I read in his heart"—this poor Giovanni was never able to do! "He is, alas! the head of the party, and extremely audacious, and if ever there was truth in the adage, 'Audaces . . . !' he is at that point. There is sulphur in the air one breathes, but, at the same time, there is in Italy a total absence of a centre of political opinions and creeds. All desire independence, and look no further ahead. Constitution or republic is all one to them, and Mazzini knows this, as everybody asks him instructions. 'What ought we to do?' they ask from Genoa, Tuscany, Rome, and the terrible cry that rises from the Lombard plains keeps up a strength of enthusiasm, a sort of anarchy in all. If Charles Albert does not decide on action—I dare not hope it—I foresee rocks ahead for him. You will understand the state of mind among the Genoese from our mother's enthusiastic tone. One of the chiefs of the popular party in correspondence with Mazzini is young Mameli" (Goffredo Mameli, the soldier-poet, who was killed in the defence of Rome).

In a subsequent letter, Giovanni sums up the European situation from his own point of view, which is important as showing how he, too, saw that republican unity was the desideratum. It is dated from Paris on the 22nd of March.

"We live in really stupendous times. I defy any one to be calm in the midst of a cataclysm of this sort. The Old World is falling to pieces, the rock of absolutism incarnate is shivered. The colossus with its feet of clay reels like a drunkard and threatens to fall. Students and men of the people are on guard at the palace of the Cæsars. Metternich, the great High Priest of Immobility, in flight! What lessons! . . . What retribution! . . . Good-night to the settlement of Europe in 1815. In the midst of crumbling Europe the fact of Italian Independence seems almost too easy of accomplishment. However, I foresee trouble for Charles Albert and Co. Yesterday's *National* saluted the 'great Italian Republic.' Balbo and Pareto" (Charles Albert's first constitutional ministers) "have seized the helm in an unlucky moment. Italian unity by means of a republic becomes a question of actuality. Who would have even dreamed a month ago of its possibility? By Jove! that would exceed even Mazzini's ideal! He is now at the summit of his glory; they clamour for him in Sicily, in Rome, in Genoa, and now in Milan. All Italy feels instinctively that its new destinies have dawned, and all Italy has its eyes fixed on him. What yesterday was exaggeration, a dream, a Utopia, to-day is foresight, wisdom. 'God and the People,' the programme of the most powerful nation of Europe. In the inevitable pressure that France is destined to exercise on Italy, Mazzini is called on to recite the first part, a part that no one in Italy or abroad disputes. As I separated myself from him in adverse fortune I shall not follow him in prosperity, out of pride, if for nothing else; besides, there are times for men of action, of energy, of enthusiasm, and I humbly confess that I do not feel that I was born for action. I am wanting in energy, in enthusiasm, and live only in my affections. On the other hand, I don't wish to seem to go to an excess by altogether changing my relations with him. I shall continue on the same footing as heretofore, so don't fear any precipitate action on my part."

In this letter we have Giovanni all of a piece : upright, gifted, but intensely selfish, so much so that in the same letter he confesses that "the amnesty will cost him ten years" of his life. He had made himself a delightful nest in Paris, where his friendship with "Cornelia" and her mother gave him all the joy that he was capable of feeling. An amnesty, "total and without condition," as it first appeared to be, left him no choice but to return to his mother and the hated village of Taggia, and to serve his country in some manner worthy of the martyred Jacopo. But his uprightness and patriotism ended by triumphing over his selfishness, for when elected deputy by his native town, he at once accepted, and prepared to be present at the opening of the Chamber. Following the example given even by such Moderates as Mamiani and Cerrutti, he refused the amnesty, because the Sardinian minister in Paris refused to give him a passport unless he signed an elaborate declaration to the effect that he would abide by the decision of the Chamber if it refused to ratify his election, and he decided to enter Italy without one.

But in those days the frontier officials, like most other persons, wore loose sleeves. Though the Marchese Brignole, ambassador in Paris, maintained the rigid red tapeism of the old *régime*, and when told by Giovanni that he was elected representative of the people, treated the matter "as if he had said that he was a cobbler," orders were given to let him pass unmolested. He spent a few days with his mother at Taggia, then went to Turin, and finally took the oath of fealty to the "inseparable welfare of the King and of the Country (al bene inseparabile del

Rè e della Patria)." But he became more discontented and exacting than he had even been with Mazzini. Visiting Mrs. Mazzini, he found her " politically reticent and the negation of all spontaneity "—the Genoese cold and standoffish; and in his letters he adds : " I, as you may imagine, gave them a Roland for an Oliver."

From Paris, Mazzini returned to London, to set his school in order and to leave his little house and belongings in the hands of Susannah Tancione, who always remained his housekeeper, and who brought up her two boys as he had taught her to do. On the 1st of April, he left for Paris again with the two brothers Achille and Massimiliano Menotti—sons of Ciro Menotti, victim of the Duke of Modena in 1821—and after a short sojourn in Switzerland he crossed the St. Gothard for the first time.

In a letter to the Ashurst family he gives vent to his unbounded admiration for that "sublime scene." He declares that no one knows " what poetry is like, who has not found himself there," and adds that "there is no atheism possible in the Alps."

On April 7th he arrived in Milan. The Milanese had during the "Five Days" (18th to 22nd of March), at first without arms and later on with those taken from the enemy, driven Radetzky and his 18,000 men, well furnished with artillery, from the streets, then from the palaces, the police offices, the roof of the Cathedral—occupied by the best sharpshooters of his Tyrolese battalions—and finally from the fortified castle. The Austrian general fled ignominiously, and but for the imbecility of the moderate, aristocratic Provisional Government, he and the disordered remnants of his army would never have reached the fortresses of Mantua and Verona. At Venice the Austrians had capitulated to unarmed citizens; all the Lombard and Venetian cities had followed the examples of their capitals, and this, before single " Royal soldier " had crossed the Ticino to their aid though on the 26th of March Charles Albert had issued the famous proclamation in which he offered the Lombards to " place himself and his sons at the head of their army and bring them such assistance as a brother offers to brother and friend to friend."

Mazzini's reception in Milan was far beyond his expectations, though not, we think, beyond his deserts. He was welcomed with wonder, reverence, and love. The *Gazetta di Milano*, organ of the Provisional Government, wrote : " This man, in whom you hardly know whether to admire most his lofty genius or the indomitable courage with which he has faced the vexations and incessant persecutions of the police and his changeless faith in the destinies of his country and of humanity, has spent eighteen years in exile, bearing public testimony before strangers to the life of Italian thought, which political atheism had declared extinct for ever, thus preparing with untiring energy, by words, by counsel, by action, these blessed days of our regeneration. In the days when selfishness prevailed in Europe, and the fear of prison and the scaffold hung over Italy, neither derision, nor treachery, nor the successful opposition of his enemies prevented him from proclaiming the inalienable rights of his country, and, wherever fate led him—amid inextinguishable hatred and unconquerable love—he lit the sacred torch of liberty and set it on high, to reanimate the courage of the combatants. We feel in our inmost soul the benefits conferred by this illustrious martyr of Italian Independence more deeply than words can express. Every Italian feels himself exalted and ennobled by the fact that such a man is his countryman."

Great crowds of citizens went out to meet him with lighted torches and bearing a tricolour banner, on which was inscribed : " The Nation to Giuseppe Mazzini." The civic guard escorted him along the Corso to the Hotel della Bella Venezia, and the houses on either side were illuminated in his honour. From the balcony of the hotel, Mazzini, bearing the banner aloft, addressed the people, extolling the prowess of the Sicilians, the Venetians, and the Lombards, but urging concordant action until the last foreigner should be driven across the Alps. The Provisional Government (the residence of which was opposite, in the

Palazzo Marino, now the seat of the Municipality) came to beg him to step over and address the populace from the palace balcony. Acquiescing, he gave a second address, in which he advised the people to reserve all discussion about the future form of government for the day when the whole of Italy, free to decide her own destinies, would send representatives to the National Assembly in Rome, the only true capital of United Italy.

On the morrow, Charles Albert, who had crossed the Ticino on March 29th, fought his first action at Monte Chiaro, routing the Austrians. Cattaneo, the soul and leader of the "Five Days," had insisted on the formation of a Lombard army, and Mazzini did all in his power to promote this powerful bulwark of Italian Independence; but the Milanese Provisional Government—composed with few exceptions of the old aristocratic faction who had welcomed so effusively the Austrians in 1814, and whom only Metternich's insane policy had been able to alienate from their allegiance to Austria—instead of using the volunteers, crowding enthusiastically to enlist in what ought to have been the Lombard army, retained them in Milan, saying that Charles Albert and his army were sufficient. The aristocratic faction evidently hungered after a new master, and feared the radical spirit of the volunteers. Mazzini, however, wisely considered that the need of the hour was experienced officers capable of ensuring discipline. His thoughts turned to the exiles who had gone to Spain and South America to fight the battles of liberty. So he wrote, on paper bearing the official seal of the Provisional Government, to Fanti, Cialdini, and others, pressing them to return at once.

Fanti came immediately, leaving his young wife and child, and abandoning a brilliant position. He was refused by the Provisional Government, and returned to his birthplace, Modena, "paid for his sacrifice by ingratitude and vexations of every sort." Cialdini met with the same fate, but telling the Piedmontese general Collegno that he had not come all the way for nothing, he determined to serve

ENRICO CIALDINI

as a private. In accordance with a plan arranged in 1847 through Medici, who had purposely gone out to Montevideo, Mazzini was expecting Garibaldi. When the latter arrived in June he too was treated cavalierly by the Piedmontese minister, and advised to go to Venice and ply his trade of " corsair " in the Laguna.

As the Provisional Government of Lombardy did little or nothing to organise the Lombard army, it was natural that the Piedmontese staff should profit by every occasion to concentrate things in their own hand. For instance, when the ill-health of Count Pompeo Litta—a veteran offiecr of Napoleon's artillery, loved by the Milanese not only for his family traditions, but for his high integrity and talents—rendered further assistance necessary for him in his post at the War Office, a Piedmontese general was appointed, and soon all idea of a Lombard army was definitely abandoned. Numbers of recruits were drafted into barracks in Piedmont to be incorporated in the Sardinian troops. The natural consequence of this policy of indicating that salvation lay with Piedmont, was to paralyse popular action. The Lombard Moderate party, more Royalist than the King, began to agitate in view of preparing an immediate annexation to Piedmont, notwithstanding the fact that the unaided valour of the people had achieved their liberation from Austria. As the British consul in Milan wrote to Lord Palmerston, the perfect accord hitherto reigning between all classes was broken " by the formation of two parties, one of the high aristocracy . . . who wished that Lombardy should be annexed to Piedmont ; . . . the other, of the middle classes, . . . favouring a Republic."

This letter bears date March 31st, and five days later the same consul wrote that the Lombards were greatly disappointed that Charles Albert had not cut off the retreat of the Austrians before they could reach their fortresses of Mantua and Verona. The obvious duty of the King was to turn Radetzky's line of retreat, but his staff did not possess a single military map of Lombardy,

THE BIRTH OF MODERN ITALY

nor could one be found even in Milan, for the Austrians had transferred to Vienna the splendid Topographical Institute founded in that city by Napoleon I. Unfortunately, in those days of slow communication, little was known in Turin of the events actually transpiring in Lombardy, save that Lombardy had risen and that fighting was going on.

The first line of the Piedmontese troops occupied Novara, Mortara, and Voghera; the second, Alessandria, Casale, and Vercelli. The reserves lay around Genoa and Turin. Through fear and jealousy of popular movements the Lombard volunteers had been refused arms, but they had plenty of their own, and only needed able, daring, yet prudent, chiefs. The few veterans of Napoleon I. who were still capable of bearing arms had forgotten their cunning during thirty-four years of peace and repression. General Lecchi, one of them, who had been appointed commander of the Lombard recruits on March 25th, wished to keep them in barracks and drill them; but Manara[1] and Arcioni[2] brought up their columns to give chase to the retreating Austrians, and harassed them first at Lodi, then at Cremona, and, turning northwards, at Iseo also. On the shores of Lake Garda they captured the steamers at Salò, and even seized the powder-magazine of the fortress of Peschiera. Elated by this success, they pushed on to Castelnuovo, where, halting for the night without the necessary precautions, they were surprised by 3,000 Austrians of the Verona garrison and overpowered, in spite of an heroic resistance. With unheard-of ferocity the Austrians fired the town, bayoneting indiscriminately men, women, and children, so that 400 inhabitants perished and only five houses remained standing. Pimodan

---

[1] Manara, Luciano (1825-1849), Lombard soldier and hero; distinguished himself during the Milanese Revolution of the "Five Days," and was killed at the siege of Rome. He is one of the most popular heroes of the time.

[2] Arcioni, Pietro, a popular leader during the Revolution of 1848; fell at Castelnuovo.

GOFFREDO MAMELI.

UGO BASSI.

LUCIANO MANARA.

himself, who belonged to Radetzky's staff, confesses to these brutal deeds, and draws a harrowing picture of the ill-fated town. Manara, who had been one of the heroes of the "Five Days" of Milan and who distinguished himself later in the siege of Rome, again almost met his fate, when, blindly rushing to attack the fortress of Sarnico, he fell into an ambush and barely escaped the general massacre. On that occasion twenty-seven prisoners were mutilated and shot by order of General Welden.

The same hesitating policy of the Provisional Government, which sought to believe that Charles Albert's army was quite sufficient, prevented the utilisation of between 10,000 and 20,000 Italian soldiers who had deserted from the Austrian army. Of these were 2,000 belonging to the Ceccopieri legion, who had deserted *en masse*, and they arrived in Milan the same day as Mazzini. Writing to the Ashurst family, the latter says: " My reception was such that I wished you all here, because I know that you would have felt happier than I did. *I* had experienced far more in the morning in seeing some 2,000 of our Italian soldiers . . . passing under my windows, in the midst of the people frantic with joy ; and they themselves looking intoxicated with the feeling of being, once in their life, loved by their countrymen. . . . I found myself crying like a child at the sight. . . ."

The error of the Provisional Government in disregarding the value of the Italian and popular elements was the more to be regretted inasmuch as all Austrian military authorities (Jellachich, Klapka, and others) had always declared that the Italians, when well drilled and well officered, formed the flower of their army. If the raw recruits, sent (under compulsion) by the King of Naples, by Tuscany, Parma, Modena, and the Pope, under Generals Pepe and Durando, had been incorporated with the disciplined Italian soldiers who had deserted from Austria, they would have proved a most precious reinforcement to the Piedmontese army, which was not more than 60,000 men strong. They became instead a crowd of " peasant soldiers," who gradually disbanded and melted away to till their fields or to protect their crops from eventual devastation.

Another proof of the incapacity of the Provisional Government was its utter inability to furnish rations to the Piedmontese troops, who were often starving in the midst of plenty, as they were strictly forbidden to touch anything or forage for themselves. This, of course, produced great dissatisfaction, and after the victories of Goito, Borghetto, and Monzambano (April 8th, 10th, and 11th) it brought about a disastrous pause in the operations.

The story of this campaign has been repeatedly written, so there is no necessity to repeat it here. Endless have been the criticisms on both sides, but it is generally forgotten that the Piedmontese army, from the King downwards, had gone through battles only on paper; while old Radetzky, their stern, silent opponent, had been, as it were, nurtured on battlefields. It is true that he was driven out of Milan by an unarmed populace, but, in the actual state of European feeling, he had not dared to bombard that town. Neither had he kept his hold on a single inch of Lombardo-Venetian soil, with the exception of the fortresses; but he was given Time, that great ally of the soldier, and his genius consisted in profiting by every second of it. Unable, however, to foresee the value of time to Radetzky, everybody in Turin, in London, and even in Lombardy, indulged in a most fatal confidence as to the approaching destruction of the Austrian army. Bixio, accredited minister to Turin by the French Republic, wrote on April 8th that " in the masses a most dangerous confidence unhappily prevails. . . . All speak of Italian Independence as a thing of history .
Austria as a phantom, and Radetzky's army a shadow. The King shares these opinions. . . ." Abercromby, the British ambassador, must not only have taken the same confident views, but have inadvertently misled Lord Palmerston, who, writing to Lord Normanby in Paris and to Lord Ponsonby in Vienna, speaks of "the establishment of a good State in Northern Italy" as an

1848] PIUS IX. DENOUNCES THE WAR

accomplished fact. He does not "regret the expulsion of poor Austria," as, to her, Italy was "the heel of Achilles and not the shield of Ajax"; and he concludes by expressing the opinion that a kingdom comprising Piedmont, Genoa, Lombardy, Venice, Parma, and Modena is inevitable, and much to be desired. Even Austrian statesmen accepted defeat as unavoidable, and asked the good offices of Lord Palmerston towards obtaining the best possible terms. It was clear that they would have yielded everything if the Italians had been willing to assume a very large portion of the Austrian debt.

But to the eye of the whilom exile, whose very excess of love for his country made him fear the inaction of the army, the defenceless condition of the Alps, and the junction effected by Radetzky with the forces of Generals d'Aspre and Nugent, clearly indicated the near approach of disaster. Then, at the end of April, a mortal blow was struck by Pius IX.'s Encyclica, which denounced the war against Austria and forbade his subjects to take part in it, although he well knew that the Papal troops, under Durando, had crossed the Po on the 21st of that month, and that the "Papal Keys" and the "White Cross of Savoy," both engrafted on the Italian *tricolore*, floated together over the Lombard battlefields. The reason of this sudden *volte-face* is still unknown, and has been attributed either to fears of a schism in Germany and Austria, or to previous accords with Austria ; its results were terribly momentous for the immediate future of Italy and for the destiny of the Temporal Power of the Church.

At the present day it is almost impossible to imagine the overpowering wave of enthusiasm which had carried away the Italians when Pius IX. had blessed Italy, and Italy alone. In Milan, the "Five Days" had been fought and won to the cry of "Viva Pio IX. e la libertà!" His bust was everywhere, and the Austrians considered him as the all-powerful ally of the insurgents, viciously telling the victims whom they robbed, tortured, or murdered, to look to him for redress. Victories were considered the consequence of

THE BIRTH OF MODERN ITALY

his prayers, and he himself was believed to be the mystical guide of the coming Italy. Charles Albert, in his first proclamation from Lodi, on March 31st, had invoked celestial inspiration, so that the angelic spirit of Pio IX. might descend upon the Italians, for then " Italy would be (l'Italia sarà) ! " ' It seemed to all that Gioberti's prophecies had been realised, and that God had performed a miracle by sending to Italy a liberal, Italian-hearted Pope. Even the most determined and convinced agnostics have told us with half-mournful, half-scornful emotion, that nobody escaped this wonderful dream.

The awakening was proportionately cruel. The Pope suddenly transferred his blessing to the Croats and Bavarians, who mutilated and massacred the Lombards! Rage and despair took the place of love and confidence, and timid souls faltered, fearing to fight in a war denounced by the Vicar of Christ. Mothers, wives, and sweethearts of the Papal soldiers under Durando, agonised with fear, begged the men to return home, that they might not, later, be pronounced outlaws and brigands by the authorities of the Church. The King of Naples found the moment propitious for renewed perjury and bloodshed. The Grand Duke of Tuscany opportunely cooled in his pretended sympathy for the cause of Independence. Henceforth, only those whose love of country had been their dominant passion continued to struggle ; but from that day religion and patriotism became antagonistic sentiments. The Italians had been cheated into a belief that the two feelings were synonymous ; now they reproached themselves for their gullibility and became wiser, if sadder men.

To the members of the Milan Provisional Government the Pope's defection added one more chance for the realisation of their scheme of immediately annexing Lombardy to Piedmont by a plebiscite, without summoning a legal assembly of representatives, as promised by themselves and by Charles Albert. Parma, Modena, Piacenza, and Reggio Emilia had proclaimed their annexation to Piedmont immediately after the flight of their reigning princelets ; and

POMPEO LITTA.

To face p. 159]

in Milan, Casati,[1] Durini,[2] and the other "fusionists," insisted that the same should be done in Lombardy. At the meeting of the Provisional Government summoned by them, the discussion was long and stormy, Anselmo Guerrieri, of Mantua, and the Abbate Luigi Anelli, representatives of Lodi and Crema, opposing the scheme and standing out vigorously for a Constituent Assembly. But the majority voted for the "fusion," so they drew up a document to which they even dared to attach the signature of Anelli, bringing down upon their heads his indignant protest. Count Pompeo Litta, absent through illness, also wrote an irate letter to his colleagues, saying that the document had been brought to him when he was seriously ill with fever, and after midnight, and that he had signed it when half-asleep, adding: " Ho fatto assai male (I have acted very wrongly). . The proclamation ought to have fixed the time for the Constituent Assembly   When will that be convoked? . . . This ought to be written in capital letters! . . . I beg the Government henceforward not to avail itself of my signature ! . . ."

When the Provisional Government's intentions became publicly known, a storm of protestation rose from all sides, as this decision was in strident contradiction even with Charles Albert's manifesto to the Lombards, in which he had solemnly stated that as "the people has freed itself from the foreign yoke by its own unaided valour, to the people belongs the sacred right of determining its form of government." Again, in a circular letter of the King's secretary to all Provisional Governments, it was stated that "His Majesty desires that at the earliest possible moment

---

[1] Casati, Conte Gabrio (1798–1873) was Podestà (Mayor) of Milan when the Revolution of 1848 broke out; he then assumed the Presidency of the Provisional Government. His conduct has been greatly discussed, but recent publications (notably those of Colonello Pagani) seem to exonerate him from the often repeated accusations of cowardice, ineptitude, and blind partizanship.

[2] Durini, Conte Giuseppe (1800–1850), one of the members of the Milanese Provisional Government; later Minister of Agriculture and Commerce in the Piedmontese Ministry of 1849.

the Provisional Government convoke a Constitutional Assembly which shall decide, with sovereign rights (*sovranamente*) on the future destinies of your province. . . . His Majesty further hopes . . . that the Assembly may emanate from a broad and liberal system . to be the sincere expression of the common will." In the same letter Milan was designated as the meeting-place of the Assembly, with the request that the letter itself should be suitably published.

But President Count Gabrio Casati and his aristocratic and timorous colleagues were well aware that " an assembly emanating from a broad and liberal system," would assuredly never confirm them in power. Hence their plot for a plebiscite of which they would be the omnipotent wire-pullers. On May 12th, the fatal and useless decree was issued, summoning the population to vote on the 29th. We say " useless," because once the foreign oppressors were expelled, annexation would have become certain, as the idea of unity predominated ; fatal, because hitherto all thoughts had been bent on war, and all had desired the postponement of domestic discussion until victory should leave time for calm deliberation. The violation of that programme naturally set all parties at variance and plunged them into strife. The fruits of this unfortunate policy were immediately felt. The princes and princelets who, under compulsion, had sent troops in aid of the Piedmontese army, eagerly seized upon the pretext to recall them, and dissension broke out, moreover, between Venice and the Venetian provinces of *terra firma*.

Disasters on the field quickly followed the proclamation. The Piedmontese, hoping to carry Verona by surprise, fought heroically at Sta. Lucia, but were forced to retreat and lay siege to Peschiera, instead of preventing Nugent's forces from arriving and taking part in the war. General Prince of Thurn and Taxis, acting for Nugent, with 16,000 men and 40 guns, attacked Vicenza, which was defended by the citizens, the Venetian volunteers, and the Papal contingent under Durando. His force was completely defeated, and fled, leaving him dead on the field; but Nugent operated his conjunction with Radetzky, and the reoccupation of the place was decided upon. The Piedmontese troops would have been surrounded had not the Tuscans (among whom the battalion of students of Pisa University were conspicuous), and the Neapolitans resisted for an entire day at Curtatone and Montanara. This gave Bava, the Piedmontese general, time to unite his forces, and he was able, on the 29th of May, to inflict a signal defeat upon the Austrians, compelling Radetzky to retreat once more. On the same day Peschiera capitulated; but that was the turning-point. After a furious battle lasting eighteen hours, the hills around Vicenza were taken by the enemy, and Vicenza capitulated with all the honours of war. Then Treviso fell, and later, Palmanuova. Charles Albert remained inactive on the right bank of the Adige, preparing for the siege of Mantua, while the only break in the cloud was the victory of Bava at Governolo, at the mouth of the Adige in the Po.

But the grief and rage at the loss of the Venetian cities, at the sacrifice of the heroic Tuscan band, and at the recall of the Neapolitan contingent after the 15th of May, had changed the entire military situation, and much for the worse; while the war of words raging in Milan between "fusionists" and "protestants" distracted the combatants from the main issue of the war. Colonel Forbes, an Englishman then travelling *en touriste* through Italy, and who afterwards served under Garibaldi, summed up the situation tersely when he wrote home that "while Radetzky was collecting bayonets, Charles Albert was collecting votes."

XI

THE GREAT REVOLUTION (*continued*)

1848

Count Casati—The question of the capital—Mazzini's neutrality—Protest against the decree of the 12th—Riotous demonstration—Democratic journals burnt — Question of the capital postponed—Appointment of a Lombard "Consulta"—Venice—"Fusion" voted—Garibaldi offers his sword to Charles Albert—Appointed head of the Volunteers in Milan—Ferrara occupied by the Austrians—Charles Albert willing to abandon Venice—Radetzky pushes his advantages — The alarmed "Consulta" summon Mazzini and Cattaneo—Defence Committee formed—Superseded by a military Commission—Mazzini joins Garibaldi's force as a foot soldier Charles Albert enters Milan—Secret terms with Radetzky—Fury of the populace—Escape of the King—The Austrians enter Milan Garibaldi's heroic efforts and defeat.

THERE is no proof, however, that Charles Albert took part in the indecorous manœuvre that violated his Royal pledges and gave the lie to his repeated promises. Count Casati, who had served Austria faithfully until her insane treatment even of her staunchest partisans compelled them all to abandon her cause, was the chief mover in the unworthy plot. His dread of popular government, his inordinate craving for rank and honours, and his keen remembrance of the agony of terror he had experienced during the "Five Days," spurred him on to be the first in the field with the future ruler of Lombardy, and he found many followers among certain members of the aristocratic classes.

In Turin, also, the ministry worked actively for the immediate union of Lombardy, *without conditions;* annexation pure and simple being their desire. Lombardy must accept Piedmont as it was. The very suggestion of a Constituent Assembly filled the Turinese with horror, and Count Camillo Cavour, who then was only considered a clever journalist, strongly opposed the idea. The fear that Milan might be chosen as the future capital of the Northern Kingdom aroused in Turin indignation and rage.

This new apple of discord—the question of the capital—was really launched by Gioberti, who left Paris at the beginning of May and visited Genoa. Finding that Mazzini, for whom, as chief of "Young Italy," he had been enthusiastic in 1833, was in the ascendant in his native city, he paid a visit of homage to Mrs. Mazzini. When she was afterwards asked by Giovanni Ruffini what she thought of him, she replied with her usual sarcasm : " He is a Jesuit perfumed *à la Parisienne.*" From Genoa, Gioberti went to Milan, visited Mazzini, and was invited by the Provisional Government to speak to the people from the palace balcony. In this speech, he acclaimed the new "Sub-Alpine Kingdom" and was applauded, but when he cried · "Viva Milan, capital of Northern Italy," silence fell on the crowd, silence broken by a few hisses, and all felt that the cry would arouse bitter dissension. This, in fact, happened at once.

The Torinese and their Parliament, either from prudence or from fear of being reduced to a mere province, had, until then, abstained from broaching the subject, but now they discussed it angrily. The Genoese were delighted to see the Torinese likely to be degraded to the same footing as themselves, and consequently fierce debates became the order of the day.

Mazzini so conscientiously maintained an attitude of perfect neutrality and abstinence from political disputes, that even Sirtori accused him of abandoning the republican flag. Furthermore, he had refused to found any paper, and the press was chiefly represented by the *XXII*

Marzo, organ of the Provisional Government; the *Lombardia* (*ex-Figaro*), edited by certain individuals who afterwards became partisans and even spies of Austria; *Il Republicano* (Sirtori), and the *Voce della Verita*, edited by Romolo Griffini and Pietro Maestri, the latter a distinguished economist. But when the decree of May 12th, deciding on the plebiscite appeared, Mazzini founded the *Italia del Popolo*, the forerunner of many papers destined to bear that name. The first number came out on May 20th, "under," as Mazzini said, "the saddest auspices." In it, an earnest, impassioned leader denounced the plebiscite as a violation of the trust placed by the people in the Provisional Government which they had elected from the barricades. Politics, declared the writer, were worse than useless at the moment; what the situation needed was military organisation and financial measures. Mazzini proved that from every point of view the haste manifested over the plebiscite had been indecorous, displeasing alike to the Republicans, who maintained that they would only bow to the will of the people legally expressed, and to the Constitutionalists, who said that after the close of a victorious war all parties would agree upon a programme. The article concluded thus: "Europe will say: 'The "Five Days" did not inspire the Lombards with a true sense of independence or dignity. The vote was taken under the sword-of-Damocles of fear. They do not care for liberty, but hasten to throw it under the feet of the nearest king!' . This decree of the 12th deserves the condemnation of all parties, and, alas, it brings no remedies to existing evils, does not further the war, nor promote the unification of the country! . " This is the sum and substance of the pronouncement which procured for Mazzini the title of "Betrayer of the Cause of Italian Unity," and the accusation of sacrificing "the cause of Independence to his republican Utopia." The article was followed by a formal protest, signed by a great many of the men who had led in the "Five Days," and who afterwards became generals and constitutional ministers—among whom

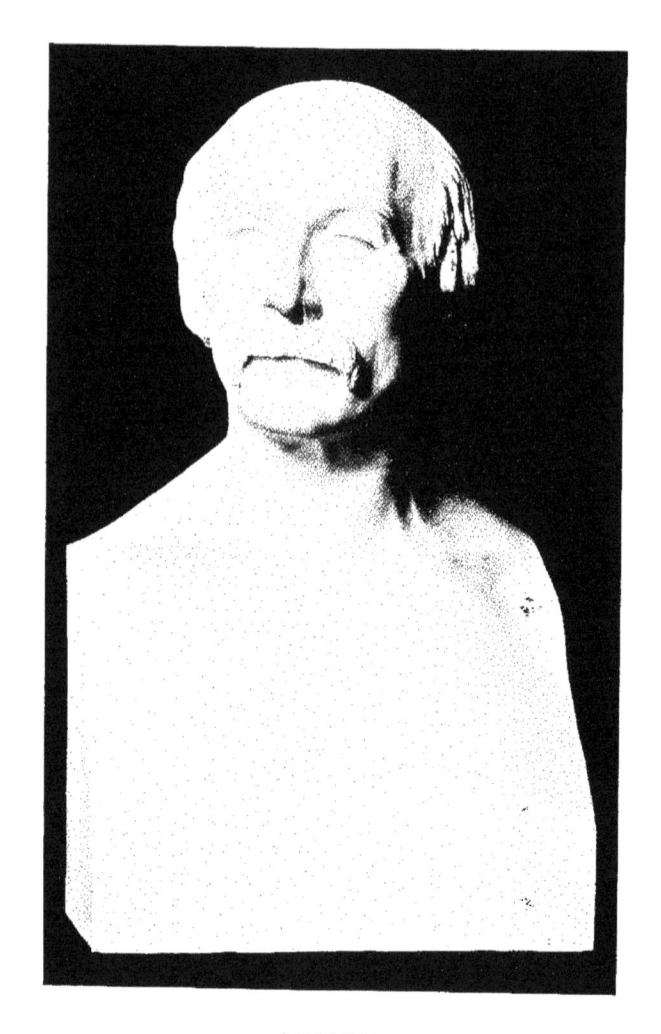

CATTANEO.

(Bust by Vela.)

To face p 165]

we especially note the name of Emilio Visconti-Venosta, the celebrated diplomat.

Towards the end of May a riotous demonstration occurred in Milan, promoted by individuals of doubtful private and political character, the leader of which, a certain Urbino, made a pretext of the atrocities committed by the King of Naples on the 15th of that month to declaim against all princes as traitors—Charles Albert included—and to call for the resignation of the Provisional Government. Pale and trembling, Count Casati, who tried to address the seething crowd, was carried fainting to his room, and Urbino had just begun proclaiming a new government, when suddenly a troop of students, who, though they disapproved the " fusion," objected still more vehemently to demagogues, collared Urbino and drove away the mob. Order was reestablished, and Casati, having collected his wits and got over his fright, addressed the population from a balcony. Of inciting to this ridiculous affair, the then Chief of Police, Fava (worthy successor of the Austrians Torresani and Bolza), accused Mazzini and Cattaneo. A warrant was even signed for their arrest, but it was indignantly torn up by Pompeo Litta, who, with Anelli, found himself implicated in the farce. Probably the whole thing had been arranged by those whose interest it was to rid themselves at one blow of those very inconvenient censors.

On June 8th the results of the plebiscite were finally known : 251,534 persons voted for immediate annexation ; only 272 for a postponement. Exulting in the triumph of his long meditated scheme, President Casati, with two colleagues, hurried to the camp of Charles Albert, near the lake of Garda, and presenting the results to the King, concluded his speech with these unctuous words, admirably portraying the man and the courtier : " Sire, I have not presented myself to your Majesty hitherto, not choosing to do so until I could call you *my King*."

Charles Albert received the vote and its bearer with his customary courtesy, and promised to transmit the " Act of Fusion " to his ministers for the necessary approval of the

THE BIRTH OF MODERN ITALY

Piedmontese Parliament. The news was hailed with delight by the Turinese, as the "fusion" had been effectively preached to them by Gioberti, Lorenzo Valerio,[1] the Ministers Ricci[2] and Pareto.[3] Brofferio[4] and the other democrats who ventured to dissent were outrageously mobbed, and their paper, the *Messaggiero*, burnt in the market-place of Turin. In Genoa Mazzini's *Italia del Popolo* received a similar honour, and this *auto-da-fè* of his son's writings was the last drop in the cup of bitterness that the exile's poor father was called upon to drink.

But when the Turinese learned that even the Minister Ricci inclined to acclaim Milan instead of Turin as capital of the "Sub-Alpine Kingdom" their enthusiasm fell to zero. Ricci was forced to amend his own decree to the effect that the seat of government should not be transferred without a special law passed by the Piedmontese Parliament. Violent discussions ensued, during which Giovanni Ruffini proposed "Union without conditions" as a first step towards Italian unity, and suggested that no permanent capital should be chosen until the whole of Italy should be reunited in Rome. Finally, it was decided that, provisionally, a Lombard "Consulta" should be endowed with sovereign power. The ministry then resigned, and in the new Cabinet Count Gabrio Casati became President of the Council, or Premier. To few mortals is granted the realisation of their highest personal ambition, but for this ex-devotee of Austria, decorated by Francis Joseph with the

---

[1] Valerio, Lorenzo (1810-1865), Piedmontese politician and journalist, founded the *Diritto* with Depretis, Correnti, and others. He was Extraordinary Commissioner in the Marche in 1860.

[2] Ricci, Marchese Vincenzo (1804-1868), statesman and lawyer, formed part of the Gioberti Cabinet in 1848.

[3] Pareto, Marchese Lorenzo (1800-1865), statesman, patriot, and geologist, born in Genoa, was Minister of Foreign Affairs in the Gioberti Ministry (1848).

[4] Brofferio, Angelo (1802-1866), Piedmontese historian, lawyer, and patriot, a staunch opponent of Cavour. He was one of the greatest orators of the Piedmontese Chamber.

Photo] [Broggi.
DANIELE MANIN.

Order of Iron Crown, Fate had reserved her choicest gifts, consigning to him, for the moment at least, both the destinies of Piedmont and those of Lombardy. But with his elevation to office came disastrous news from the field, and the first act of the new ministry was to implore assistance from the French Republic, whose offers they had hitherto contemptuously rejected.

Up to this moment Venice had kept her republican banner intact, but the "fusion" of her *terra-firma* provinces with Piedmont, the refusal of any assistance from the French Republic, and the manifest indifference of England to the fate of the "Queen of the Adriatic," alarmed many of the citizens, and an agitation for fusion with Piedmont commenced. Manin and Tommaseo, strong in the love and reverence of their citizens, declined to assume responsibility, still less to imitate the tortuous methods of the Milan Provisional Government. They convoked the Venetian Assembly for July 3rd, in order to set forth clearly the political situation and to formulate a policy. The population was taken somewhat by surprise, as it only knew of two forms of government—the old Republic and the rule of Austria. Charles Albert was to them a stranger, and replying to the "fusionist" agents who swarmed in the city, extolling him as "a republican prince, a second Enrico Dandolo," the people declared that they were quite satisfied with "their own Manin." However, such men as Restelli, General La Marmora, the poet Prati, and the great hydraulic engineer, blind Paleocapa, managed to persuade them that the only choice lay between Charles Albert and Austria. When the Venetian deputies met in the "Sala del Gran Consiglio" of the Ducal palace, Manin briefly explained the situation, saying that the Republic had been recognised by Switzerland and the United States, but that their possessions on *terra-firma* having joined with Lombardy and Piedmont, and their resources being at a very low ebb, they had pleaded for help from Tuscany, the Pope, and the King of Piedmont, but, up to that moment, without obtaining any response. Manin, though intensely opposed to the "fusion" because he did not believe in Charles Albert's sincerity in promising to defend Venice, spoke with absolute impartiality—"colourless and spiritless" the strong republicans called his address. The discussion was then suspended, and Count Enrico Martini, the famous intermeddler between Turin and Milan during the "Five Days," was allowed to present the decree of the Turinese Chamber for the union of the Lombard and Venetian provinces with Piedmont. He also presented a letter from the King's headquarters, dated Roverbella, June 30th, teeming with enthusiastic expressions of love for Venice and for the Italian cause, and promising in Charles Albert's name the expediting of 2,500 soldiers to the assistance of the city. Later, Tommaseo alone, the proud Dalmatian, spoke out resolutely against the proposed "fusion," expressing much the same ideas as those set forth by Mazzini. He closed his long and powerful discourse by thanking the Venetians for the confidence hitherto shown in him, but he resigned his position in the Government. Paleocapa urged upon his colleagues the necessity of "fusion" as the only means of uniting the country, and, finally, Manin adjured the deputies to forget party and only to remember that they were Italians, saying that all was provisional and that the permanent decision could only be taken by an Italian Diet in Rome. Eventually the "fusion" was voted by a great majority, and the members of the Provisional Government confirmed it, but as neither Manin nor Tommaseo accepted office, they were replaced by others. The Piedmontese soldiers arrived, but the King did not cross the Adige, and this, together with his letter of July 10th, of which we will speak further on, gave colour to the accusation that he meditated a second Campoformio.

Meanwhile Garibaldi, in accordance with an arrangement made between himself and Mazzini in 1847, arrived in Genoa, bringing about fifty soldiers and officers of his famous Legion. After placing his wife Anita and their three children in the care of his old mother at Nice, he went straight to Charles Albert's headquarters. This was not exactly in accordance with the first programme, but a letter from Garibaldi to his friend, Paolo Antonini, proves that he was ready to place his sword "at the service of whatsoever Italian prince would use it for Italy." It was only with the greatest difficulty that he had managed to leave Montevideo, as the people there had placed every possible obstacle in his way, and his impecuniosity had been so great that without the subsidies sent by Italian and English friends his departure would have been impossible.

Considering that Garibaldi had been condemned to death by Charles Albert's tribunals for high treason—*i.e.*, the attempt to suborn the officers and crew of the Royal frigate, *Eurydice*—and that he neither sought nor accepted amnesty, one can hardly be surprised that the King, while recognising the nobility of his conduct, received him coldly, if courteously—not cordially, as Vecchi and Guerzoni would have it believed. Garibaldi thus recounts the interview: "I saw him, saw the man who had executed Italy's noblest sons, who had condemned me and so many others to death, and I understood the coldness of his reception, and yet I would have served Italy under a king, as under a republic to free her from the accursed foreigner. . . . I will not now uplift the stone that covers a tomb, nor criticise conduct that must be judged by posterity . . . but called to head the war of Independence, he did not respond to the confidence reposed in him." Posterity has somewhat modified this judgment, but in those days it was endorsed by many Italians.

Being referred to the Minister of War in Turin, Garibaldi was, as already stated, told "to go and ply his trade of corsair" in the Adriatic. Medici, a silently ambitious, opinionated Lombard, who covered himself with glory in the defence of Rome and died a Senator, was highly offended that Garibaldi went to the King before conferring with him, and only pardoned him on account of the dying words of his friend Anzani, who said, "Garibaldi has received such gifts from Heaven that it is our duty to follow him. He is predestined, and I am convinced of his great mission." The young man who spoke thus was dear to every combatant of Montevideo and to every patriot. Already a prey, when sailing from South America, to a mortal malady brought on through the hardships of campaigning, he landed in Italy only to sink into the grave.

Repulsed by the Torinese War Office, Garibaldi accompanied Medici to Milan, where the provisional Government hesitated to confer any command upon him, but where Mazzini and Pompeo Litta retained sufficient influence to get him appointed head of the volunteers. In the *Italia del Popolo* of July 15th Mazzini glowingly narrated Garibaldi's exploits in South America, extolling his great military talents, and speaking of him as a chief endowed with swift vision and calm judgment.

Garibaldi, in his "Memoirs" written in America after 1848, speaks of "ostracism," of "the detention of youths in Milan," but assuredly Mazzini was not to blame, his one constant cry being "To arms! To arms! . . ." and when on the 10th of July Garibaldi was authorised to form a corps of volunteers at Bergamo, his every effort was directed to sending him all the youths capable of bearing arms.

But it was too late. Radetzky had become irresistible. On July 12th Prince Lichtenstein crossed the Po to attack and occupy Ferrara, driving the Papal troops out of the town, which, if necessary, was to be bombarded. The citizens surrendered at discretion, and this secured to the enemy the lower course of the Po and the chain of communication with Venice. Then, despite his formal acceptance of Venice and his promises for its defence, Charles Albert wrote an autograph letter, which is given by Abercromby to Lord Palmerston and published by N. Bianchi, in which he declared that "he would accept propositions which should give the Adige for the Eastern frontier of his dominions, and which should recognise the annexation of the Duchies of Parma and Modena with Lombardy." The King then proceeded to say that "if the Austrian Government would make such proposals directly to him, or through the British Government, he should not hesitate to accept them." The letter ended by stating that his Parliament and people, given the relative powers of Austria and Sardinia, would be easily induced to accept any terms which were both honourable and glorious.

Austria was inclined to accede to the proposition, but not so Radetzky, who strenuously opposed any such arrangement, insisting that he was in a position to regain the whole of Lombardy, and that his army and himself would feel dishonoured if prevented from doing so. On the other hand, the Piedmontese ministry hesitated, not daring to sanction a treaty of peace which, by handing back Venice to Austria, would indeed have been a "second Campoformio." A special envoy was despatched therefore to Paris to ascertain the intentions of the French Government in case a formal demand for armed assistance should be made. The Lombard "Consulta" also sent the Marquis Guerrieri-Gonzaga for the same purpose, with the result that the two envoys quarrelled over their respective rights, and their demands being "vague and indefinite," Cavaignac, who was then Dictator, absolved himself from giving a definite answer. His Minister of Foreign Affairs, Bastide, however, informed Lord Palmerston that they were willing to co-operate with England in negotiating peace on the basis already tacitly accepted by Austria, and which would grant to Venice a separate constitutional administration, headed by an archduke under the sovereignty of the Emperor.

But Radetzky's bulletins entirely altered the position of affairs in the eyes of the Austrian Government. On July 24th he was able to announce that "he occupied all the enemy's points of passage of the Mincio . and had complete possession of the south side of the mountain

... in a very strong flanking position. My communications with Tyrol are free, .. and this brave country where my Emperor reigns is thus freed from any danger." This bulletin, a real pæan of victory, was sent by Lord Ponsonby to Palmerston with the observation that "the line of the Adige would have been accepted . . but there may be, under present circumstances, further demands."

Alas! there were indeed further demands; it was not to be either the Adige or the Mincio; Radetzky would soon place himself in a position to insist on the Ticino. One more victorious stand was made at Somma-Campagna by three columns of Piedmontese troops commanded by the King, the Duke of Savoy, and the Duke of Genoa in person, but then the Austrians attacked in the rear, and a general retreat began.

These alarming tidings reached Milan and shook the "Consulta" from its inexplicable slumbers. Cattaneo and Mazzini were summoned to the council chamber, and by their advice a Triumvirate was named to organise a desperate defence. The men chosen were Maestri, Restelli, and Fanti, the best choice possible, as Cattaneo had refused to act. In three days more was done by this Committee of Defence than had been done before in as many months. The people became again the people of the "Five Days." The idea that Milan would fall back into the hands of Radetzky acted on them like an electric shock. Restelli and Fanti went to the King's headquarters at Lodi to ascertain his intentions. General Bava told them that the King would not give battle on the Po, but that he intended to come in person to defend Milan. On August 3rd a Military Commission arrived to supersede the Committee of Defence and take command of the city by virtue of the "Act of Fusion." The spirit of the projected resistance instantly suffered. The people, believing that they were to be saved by the proximate arrival of 40,000 soldiers, were, as Mazzini foresaw, "irrevocably lost" Seeing that he could effect nothing, Mazzini left the city to join Garibaldi, who, for the moment, was allowed to remain at Bergamo

1848] THE KING SECRETLY SURRENDERS MILAN

with his corps of 3,000 men, and there, "chosen by the affection of the young men" serving in the corps of Giacomo Medici, he was elected to carry their "modest banner," inscribed with the words "God and the People."

On the 5th Charles Albert entered Milan, and the last act of the tragedy began. The only method to honestly describe subsequent events would be to give side by side the narratives of the Triumvirate of Defence and that of the Royal Commissioners, together with the reports of the British consul, Campbell, to Lord Palmerston. That the King's intention was generous and sincere there can be no more doubt than there is that it was anti-military and fatal. It was, indeed, madness to shut himself up in an unfortified city, whence there was no issue save by cutting his way through Radetzky's victorious troops. The Piedmontese army, disheartened, wearied by continuous marches and counter-marches, almost starving, encumbered by ambulances full of wounded and fever-stricken soldiers, was unfit to fight, and its presence in the city could in no way encourage its citizens. They, however, directed by civil engineers, continued to erect strong barricades till the Piedmontese general Ulivieri told them to desist, saying that it was an insult to 45,000 brave soldiers with the King at their head.

Charles Albert, after spending the night in the camp outside the city, removed his headquarters to the Palazzo Greppi in the town. There had been a few unimportant skirmishes on the 4th, but at the dawn of the 5th the Austrian cannon was silent, and a sinister whisper spread like lightning that the King had capitulated, and that the surrender of Milan was to be the price paid for permission to the Piedmontese army to quit the city.

This incredible news was perfectly true. When the French and British consuls arrived at Radetzky's headquarters to demand an armistice of forty-eight hours in order to allow their countrymen to leave the city, and to request safe-conducts for them to the Swiss frontier, the Field-Marshal answered, "Why an armistice? They have capitulated." On their return to the city the consuls found it in a state of the wildest excitement; the King's carriages, already prepared for his departure, had been violently seized and transformed into barricades amid furious shouts of "We are betrayed! Death to Charles Albert!" The King, within whose hearing those threatening cries were uttered, summoned Litta and Anelli to ask them "what the Milanese desired?" Litta replied, "War or death," adding, "None of us can guarantee the life of your Majesty if you refuse to fight!" "But," replied the King, "the ammunition is exhausted. General Zucchi" (then already a traitor) "with the Military Commissioners assure me, and the mayor of the city confirms it, that surrender is the only alternative to bombardment by Radetzky, and that the people are resigned." "They lie!" thundered Litta and a soldier of the National Guard who was present. This soldier added: "The people *freme guerra* (thirsts for war), your Majesty. Remember 1821!" "Let it be war then," Charles Albert cried; "I am willing to shed my blood for you!" and he held out his hand to the soldier, who, shouting "War! war!" knelt down and kissed it.

The "Consulta" then announced the King's determination, and called on all to defend his life with their own. The King and the people were animated by a sublime madness, and while they thus proposed to do or die, the generals and the cowardly members of the "Consulta" were actually disposing everything for Charles Albert's departure. At two in the afternoon several pieces of artillery were brought up to act against the crowd which had collected, incensed by the news that the King was actually departing. Some shots were fired by the people at the balcony from which the Duke of Genoa endeavoured to harangue them, begging them to retire peacefully as the King was ill. "Better if he were dead!" was the stern and well-deserved reply. But the discharge of artillery, though made only with blank cartridges, dispersed the crowd, and the King was enabled to escape to his camp. At once the municipality informed the citizens that, " in consequence of the convention concluded between his Majesty Charles Albert and Field-Marshal Radetzky, the latter will occupy Porta Romana and enter the town at twelve."

The abject terms of the capitulation of Milan were probably never approved or even seen by Charles Albert; assuredly he never signed it, nor did any of his ministers, who afterwards repudiated it. It is likewise a fact that the King did refuse the first proposal for the evacuation and surrender of Milan, so that Radetzky informed the foreign consuls that he could not grant the armistice of forty-eight hours, as it would be altogether to the advantage of the enemy, but that if they could persuade the King to surrender the city on the 6th, he would, out of regard for them, postpone the bombardment, and that, in any case, safe-conducts for their countrymen would be given to all who asked for them. But assuredly the British consul had no share in persuading Charles Albert to escape from Milan, nor in the composition of the shameful convention.

By this act, signed in San Donato on August 5th by General Hess for Radetzky, by the Mayor of Milan, Paolo Bassi, and by the Piedmontese general Salasco, Milan was to be spared. Radetzky "promised, as far as it was in his power, to have that consideration for the past that equity may require," and granted twenty-four hours during which free egress from the city would be allowed to all who wished to leave it. And though this convention remained unsigned by the King and unrecognised by the Piedmontese ministers, Radetzky held the town in his iron grasp by virtue of it until liberation came in 1859.

The Austrian troops entered Milan to find it almost a desert. All the aristocratic and wealthy families had left in the wake of the Piedmontese army, and most of the youth had joined Garibaldi, who had been summoned by Fanti to attack the enemy surrounding the city. With 5,000 men, Garibaldi, following the river Adda, had reached Monza on the night of August 4th. There he received the news of the capitulation, and wrote to Durando and Griffini, suggesting that they should join forces, "as the evacuation of Milan by the Piedmontese does not concern us." Radetzky at once sent his cavalry in pursuit of the volunteer general, but the latter, marching rapidly to Varese, and thence to Sesto-Calende, gained Castelletto on the Piedmontese frontier, and there issued his famous proclamation: "Elected at Milan by the representatives of the People to lead men fighting for Italian Independence, I cannot conform to the humiliating convention ratified by the King of Sardinia with the hated foreigner. If he chooses to preserve his crown by dint of crime and cowardice, we will not abandon our sacred soil to the profanation of usurpers." Then, recrossing the frontier, he seized two steamers and eight barges on Lago Maggiore and landed at Luino, where he completely routed 1,200 Croats. But presently, attacked by General d'Aspre, he resisted victoriously for a whole day, in spite of the overwhelming numbers of the enemy, and in the night, after disbanding his soldiers and appointing them to meet him in Lugano (where Mazzini, Bertani, and other Lombards were organising armed bands), he crossed into Switzerland, leaving his opponent entirely mystified as to his whereabouts.

Garibaldi, however, being a prey to fever, returned to his home in Nice, and went thence to Genoa, where he was offered the command of a division in the regular army, which he peremptorily refused, as he "had other plans in his head."

XII

VENICE, ROME AND SISTER CITIES

1848-1849

Radetzky—Cattaneo—Venice—Manin keeps the Austrians at bay—Palmerston and France—Kossuth supports Radetzky—Palmerston deaf to Venice's plea—Radetzky ravages Lombardy—The Pope summons Rossi to form a Ministry—Sicily appoints Settimo head of an independent Government—Death of Mazzini's father—Rossi stabbed—Pius IX. flies to Gaeta—Mazzini and Saffi—The Chartists in England—Registration of Aliens Bill—Cavaignac dispatches Oudinot to receive the Pope—Garibaldi cries "Vive la Republica"—Mameli summons Mazzini to Rome—First Triumvirate—Carlo Pisacane—The Republic decides to aid Piedmont—Charles Albert's abdication—Mazzini and Garibaldi in Rome—Second Triumvirate—Garibaldi's desire to invade the Kingdom of Naples—Oudinot advances on Rome—Roman victory of April 30th—Armistice—De Lesseps—King of Naples driven to retreat—Ancona and Perugia—De Lesseps recalled to Paris—Oudinot announces that he will attack on June 4th.

THROUGHOUT September and October, 1848, flying bands of volunteers crossed from Switzerland into Lombardy. There were many skirmishes with the Austrians, and this so incensed Radetzky that he expelled all the Swiss from Lombardy and threatened the Canton of Tessin with extermination because the authorities there were compelled by the Federal Government to send away their Italian refugees. Mazzini, who had despatched Cattaneo to Paris to see what Bastide, then Minister of Foreign Affairs, and other Republicans, were inclined to do for Italy, or at least for Venice, remained in hiding, watching the things that

THE BIRTH OF MODERN ITALY

were going on in Rome and in Tuscany, and awaiting the issue of events in Venice. In the last-named city there had indeed returned "an hour of blind old Dandolo," for when the people realised that the Royal Commissioners had only taken possession of the town and forts to hand them back to the Austrians, and that, in accordance with Article IV. of the Milan Convention, the Sardinian sea and land forces were to leave the city, they fetched Manin from his study and conducted him to the balcony of the Ducal palace, where Sirtori [1] and Dall'Ongaro [2] were protecting the Piedmontese Commissioners from the anger of the populace.

After a brief consultation with these perplexed representatives of royalty (who had received no definite instructions, but merely an intimation from General Welden that he would take over Venice), Manin announced that "the Royal Commissioners had resigned; that in two days the Assembly of the city and province would meet and nominate a new government, and that for the next forty-eight hours" he himself would govern. Not for forty-eight hours only, but for an entire year did the "Lion of St. Mark" float from the city and the forts, and Manin govern righteously and victoriously, holding the Austrians at bay both on land and at sea. Abandoned, with the exception of a handful of noble souls, by the Roman and Neapolitan contingents, refused even moral help by England, kept in suspense, and without assistance from republican France, he was yet only conquered when at length cholera and famine enabled the besiegers to take possession of the starving, plague-stricken city.

Lord Palmerston, even while straining every nerve and, in fact, overstepping the limits of diplomatic etiquette to

[1] Sirtori, Giuseppe (1813–1874), Lombard patriot and soldier; he took orders, but unfrocked himself in the revolutionary movement. He was chief of Garibaldi's staff during the expedition of the "Thousand," and decided the success of the battle of the Volturno in 1860. His stern austerity of life has remained proverbial in the Italian army.

[2] Dall'Ongaro, Francesco (1808–1873), Venetian poet and patriot, took part in the defence of Rome and Venice, then lived in exile. His popular "Stornelli" on patriotic subjects were powerful means of propaganda during the fight for liberty.

favour Piedmont and the formation of a strong monarchy in the North of Italy, never seems to have contemplated any better fate for Venice than government by an Austrian Archduke, under the sovereignty of the Emperor. But at least he held out no delusive hopes; on the contrary, he went out of his way to prevent France from affording Venice any material assistance.

As soon as the Piedmontese entered Lombardy, Palmerston had made overtures to France in view of a joint mediation. Lamartine naturally pointed out that the Government had been expressly requested by Charles Albert to refrain from interfering, but added that France "had no desire to see a strong North-Italian monarchy on her frontiers," and he could not perceive any reason why Venice, merely because she had restored her old republican government, should not be abandoned to Austria. Soon Paris and the French were in the throes of the terrible July revolution, which was only quieted, after frightful bloodshed, by Cavaignac, who was confirmed "Delegated Dictator" by the National Assembly.

The Lombard and Piedmontese envoys, Guerrieri-Gonzaga[1] and Ricci, were in Paris when the news of the evacuation of Milan arrived (August 6th). After consultation with Lord Normanby concerning the proposals made on May 24th by the Austrian ambassador in London for the territorial arrangement between Austria and Sardinia (which had been rejected by Charles Albert and his ministry), they drew up a modified draft, guaranteeing to Venice a separate administration similar to that of Hungary. But "to-day was not yesterday"; Radetzky was master of the whole of Lombardy, the Diet of Frankfurt had formally supported the rights of Austria to retain *all* her Italian possessions, and even Kossuth had voted the despatch of Hungarian troops to assist Austria in the war against Charles Albert! Also, after the French Revolution of July, Austria knew that Cavaignac dared not deprive himself of troops for the pur-

[1] Guerrieri-Gonzaga, Marchese Anselmo (1819–1879), Mantuan patriot and poet, was a member of the Provisional Government of Lombardy.

pose of intervening in Italian affairs. It is true that General Oudinot, who from the first seems to have aspired to interfere in Italy, told Cavaignac that "if he was not allowed to lead his army to the assistance of the Italians, his army would go without him." But that was mere *blague*, as the sequel proved.

Lord Palmerston, however, did not relinquish his hopes, as we see from a letter of August 31st to Lord Ponsonby, in which he says: "The real fact is that the Austrians have no business in Italy at all, and have no real right to be there. The right they claim is founded upon force of arms and the treaty of Vienna." Palmerston then details the reasons for which the Austrian Government "cannot when it suits their purpose" alternately "claim the treaty and reject it." By the occupation of Cracow and their refusal to give national institutions to their Polish subjects "they have themselves set the treaty at naught." As to Austria's title founded on force, "force may be employed to defeat it, with just as much right." He plainly demonstrates that "if Austria is stubborn" France will intervene, and then the Austrians "will be driven, not to the Mincio, or the Adige, or the Piave, but clean over the Alps." He does not relish seeing the French in Italy "for many strong and weighty reasons," but he would rather "that they should go in, than that the Austrians should retain Lombardy," and if "the people in Vienna" continue to be obdurate, "the French will enter Italy with England's consent." Then, after demonstrating that Providence has divided mankind into different nations and races, separated by natural barriers, he says that "there is no case in the globe in which this intention is more manifest than in that of Germany and Italy," which "are kept apart by the Alps and as unlike in everything as two races can be." Historically, Italy was never part of the Austrian Empire, "but was always held as a conquered territory. There has been no mixture of races," the only Austrians living there being soldiers and officials, and "her rule has always been hateful." This remarkable letter ends with the declaration that it is the duty of a friend to tell the truth, and "the truth is that Austria *must not*, and *cannot* retain Lombardy, while she ought to think herself 'well enough off' by retaining Venetia, if indeed, that province is really advantageous to her."

But, on the other hand, when Manin addressed to Lord Palmerston a succinct *résumé* of Venetian history since the treaty of Campoformio, pleading that Venice should enjoy the benefit of the armistice, that Austria should not be allowed to descend with all her forces against her, and that in future arrangements of Italian territory England should prevent the Venetians from falling again under the abhorred Austrian yoke, Palmerston coldly replied that "it formed no part of the proposals made by the British Government to Austria for the pacification of Italy that Venice should cease to be under the Imperial crown, hence it would be wise for the people of Venice to come to an understanding with the Austrian Government."

Manin and his colleagues applied also to Abercromby, who, though more in sympathy with Venice than his chief, was compelled to reply that "according to the Milan Convention, Venice was one of the territories to be evacuated, and that he could take no step which might have the effect of establishing a difference in its application."

While Radetzky was ravaging Lombardy, laying forced loans on the absent Milanese and quartering his Croats in their palaces, his lieutenant, Welden, was ordered by him to occupy the Legations, on the plea of putting down anarchy and preventing incursions into Parma and Modena, where the Austrian forces had already reinstated the fugitive princelets. The Bolognese defended their unfortified city with magnificent valour, driving away Welden and his Croats, though not without heavy loss. The Pope protested to Austria *pro forma*, but there is every reason to believe that he secretly connived at the occupation of Bologna, so Austria took no notice of Lord Palmerston's recommendation "that her troops should withdraw within the Lombard frontier"; neither did Radetzky cease his reprisals upon the Canton Tessin.

THE BIRTH OF MODERN ITALY

Tuscany was now in full revolt. The Pope had summoned Rossi, who, under Louis Philippe, had been French ambassador in Rome, to form a new ministry, much against the inclination of the Romans, who hated him as a representative of Guizot's and Metternich's policy. The King of Naples was at open war with the deputies of his suspended Parliament, and Sicily, after the Duke of Genoa had refused her proffered crown, had named Ruggero Settimo head of an independent Government, and was manning her cities and seaboard to resist the Neapolitan troops.

In Turin, a new ministry passed a Bill for the levy of 13,000 conscripts, and some French officers who visited the headquarters reported that no troops could be finer than the Piedmontese infantry and artillery, while the cavalry was quite good, but that the weak points were the command and the commissariat. Very little progress was made in the negotiations for peace, as Charles Albert evidently intended to renew the war, which was clamoured for rebelliously, and demanded not only by the Genoese, but by the great majority of the Chamber in Turin.

Garibaldi, while in Genoa, chartered a vessel with the intention of going to Sicily with a band of volunteers, as his assistance there had been entreated by Ruggero Settimo; but events in Tuscany and Rome induced him to land at Leghorn. Mazzini, invited by the Florentines, was hesitating, for he meant to make one more attempt to visit Genoa and see his father, whose dangerous illness had not been concealed from him, owing to a solemn promise given him by his mother. But Signora Mazzini peremptorily forbade the attempt, telling him that alarm and anxiety would only hasten his father's end. She had good reason for this, as the head of the police, by order of the Commissary Extraordinary, had been to her home and demanded to see her son, "who had, he knew, arrived in that city." She replied that her son was not there, that she had received a letter from him promising her not to come, and she offered to show it to the Commissary, but her word sufficed. On

1848] DEATH OF MAZZINI'S FATHER

December 13th she had to write to Mazzini that all was over, and that he would never again embrace his father here below. His grief was profound and not unmixed with remorse, because from the time when he had found himself unable to follow his profession it had never been in his power to gratify a single wish of, or to give a single satisfaction to that father whose whole life had been, as he believed, devoted to him. To the Ashurst family he wrote that he was "resigned. But though a believer, I am a man. I wanted to see him before his going away. I was dreaming from time to time that I would still be able to give him joy —one single joy—before, for I have given him none in life, . . . to realise in part the idea through which I have been an exile, and to go to him and say : We have been separated, but our sufferings have achieved some good for our country, for our fellow-creatures. To me success in life is nothing, to him it would have been a supreme, all-compensating joy. . . . I think of my mother, too—of her loneliness—and dream of joining her somewhere—but where and when ? "

In the meanwhile, grave events were occurring in Rome. After the entry of Radetzky into Milan, Pius IX. dismissed his Prime Minister, Mamiani,[1] and, as above stated, called the ex-ambassador of France, Count Pellegrino Rossi,[2] to take his place. The hatred of the populace for this man was kept alive by the newspapers. On November 15th, as

---

[1] Mamiani Della Rovere, Conte Terenzio (1799–1885), Italian philosopher, poet, and statesman ; took part in the revolutionary movement of 1831 in Bologna ; was exiled in Paris ; later became Pius IX.'s Prime Minister in his Liberal Ministry. In after years he was Minister of Public Instruction in the kingdom of Italy, and brought wise and useful improvements into the education of the nation.

[2] Rossi, Conte Pellegrino (1787–1848), born at Carrara, in Italy ; passed his youth in France, where he rose to the highest honours. Was member of the Académie, Pair, Minister of Home Affairs, and then ambassador to Rome. A man of high culture and elevated feelings, he was chosen by Pope Pius IX. as Prime Minister after Mamiani's dismissal. He, however, could not stem the current of hatred by which the Roman people surrounded him on account of his reactionary policy, and was murdered while entering the Roman Assembly. His death decided the Pope's flight from Rome.

he was alighting from his carriage at the steps of the House of Assembly, an unknown man stabbed him, and he died immediately. This assassination has been alternately attributed to the Republican party, to the Jesuits, and to the "Albertists": and a son of Ciceruacchio, the leader of the populace, has also been designated as the man who struck the blow. Garibaldi, in his "Memoirs" (vol. i. p. 298), unfortunate, as usual, with his pen, says: "As a follower of Beccaria, I am opposed to capital punishment, and therefore I blame the dagger of Brutus. . . . Be that as it may" (he was then at Ravenna, and had been refused access to Rome) ". our affairs were . . . in a deplorable condition, and a Roman dagger made us worthy no longer of proscription, but of belonging to the Roman army. The ancient metropolis of the world, worthy once more of her former glory, freed herself on that day from the most formidable satellite of tyranny, and bathed the marble steps of the Capitol with his blood. A young Roman had recovered the steel of Marcus Brutus." There was then, however, no "Republican party" in Rome, and the populace, headed by Ciceruacchio,[1] still deluded themselves with the belief that Pius IX. was really the angelic being whom they had made an object of worship, that he loved Italy and his own people, and that he had been absolutely coerced into a reactionary policy by the enemies of Italy. Rossi, when ambassador of Louis Philippe, had opposed the Pope's reforms, had manifested his hostility to Charles Albert as the "Sword of Italy," had opposed the dispatch of Roman soldiers to the Lombard War, and had applauded their recall. That was his deadly sin in the eyes of the Romans, and when Pius IX. chose Rossi as his Prime Minister, he practically signed his death-warrant. The opposition to him had been violent and general. On the day of his murder, which was also that of the opening of the Roman Parliament, the *Contem-*

---

[1] Ciceruacchio, the surname of Angelo Brunetti (1802–1849), Roman agitator, popular leader of the Trastevere; was with Garibaldi during his retreat from Rome, was caught with Father Ugo Bassi by the Austrians and shot with him.

AURELIO SAFFI.

To face p 185.]

1848] ROSSI'S MURDER : THE POPE'S FLIGHT

poraneo published a most violent article against him as a
" traitor to the Italian cause, a traitor to the Prince who
called him to his exalted position." When he fell under
the dagger of the populace, the Assembly continued its
sitting as though nothing had happened ; no arrests were
made ; the troops and National Guard did nothing to
disperse the shouting, tumultuous crowd. The ministry
resigned, and no new ministry could be formed ; the Swiss
Guard alone defended the Pope, closing the gates of the
Vatican and firing on the people.

Subsequent to these events, Pius IX., after refusing the
mediation proffered by Piedmont, and the offer of an asylum
in France, escaped to Gaeta on November 24th disguised as
a dependant of Count Spaur, the Bavarian minister ; and
from thence he concerted plans with Austria, Spain, and the
King of Naples for wreaking vengeance on his rebellious
subjects.

It was at this moment that Mazzini entered into correspondence with Aurelio Saffi, and strenuously advocated the
convocation of a Constituent Assembly in Rome. He
wrote : " Pius IX. has fled ; his flight is an abdication.
An elective Prince leaves no dynasty behind him, you are
therefore a Republic *de facto* because, except in the people,
you have no source of authority. Once that people shall
have formed a Government, the Italians, not yet free, would
gather there, initiators and precursors of the future Italian
Constituent. Some write to me that the dread of invasion
deters them from action. Will you not be invaded in any
case ? What will you gain by leaving the initiative to the
invaders ? You will fall dishonoured and derided. As a
Constitutional Government you will not be left unaided."

At that time Mazzini still hoped for the co-operation of
Guerrazzi—then the virtual Dictator of Tuscany—in an
alliance with France and Venice, and he never lost sight of
the probable renewal by Piedmont of the war against Austria,
which would once more bring the whole of Italy to the
Lombard plains. And so the eventful year of 1848 drew
to a close.

THE BIRTH OF MODERN ITALY

No country in Europe had been untouched by the earthquake that shook Europe to its very centre. Even England had felt its reverberation, for the Chartists, under O'Connor, were at the height of their success. One of them, Julian Harney, gained the show of hands against Lord Palmerston at Tiverton, and O'Connor was returned for Nottingham with a considerable majority over Sir J. Cane, a member of Lord John Russell's administration. The cry of the Chartists—"A Charter or a Republic!"—resounded in many places, and it was resolved to hold a monster meeting of 500,000 persons on Kennington Common to carry the great Chartist petition to the House of Commons. Terror and excitement in London reached almost comic proportions, heightened as it was through the precautions taken by the Government for the maintenance of order. A great number of special constables were sworn in, and we well remember the high and angry words that passed in our school between the music and the French masters, the latter calling the former a "sneak" for enrolling himself against the defenders of liberty. With consummate hypocrisy, which amounted almost to genius, Louis Napoleon Buonaparte was sworn in amongst the 170,000 special constables, thus offering a pledge of his love for law and order, and of his attachment to British institutions. Extraordinary military precautions were taken, the "Iron Duke" being in command of all the forces in London. One hardly knows which became most ludicrous, the Government in its exaggerated precautions against the prohibited procession, or the miserable figure cut by the Chartists on Kennington Common, where not more than 30,000 manifestants appeared. The monster petition proved to be filled with spurious signatures and joking allusions, and thus Chartism sank into ridicule.

But the awful distress that prevailed in the country, added to events on the Continent, served as warnings to statesmen of the fate incurred by rulers who despise the complaints of their subjects. Carlyle's earnest advice awakened the public conscience, and that conscience has never since slept in

1849] FRANCE ESPOUSES THE POPE'S CAUSE

England. The Christian Socialists on the one side, and the system of co-operation commenced at Rochdale in 1844, afterwards nursed into power by Holyoake on the other, helped on work of social and material improvement, while educational schemes, initiated and supported by many of the friends of Italy, did much for the moral and intellectual advancement of the English masses.

How anxiously friends of the inner circle watched for news from Italy, for letters from " the Angel " can well be imagined, and the sad ending of a year which had dawned so hopefully cast a gloom over many a Christmas party, even when no member of the actual family had left a vacant chair.

The Bill for the Registration of Aliens, passed in the last Session of 1848, came into operation with the first days of 1849, causing some anxiety to the friends of the exiles, and it is difficult to see why Lord John Russell, whose maiden speech had been a protest against a Bill almost the facsimile of his own, should have been so eager to secure it. It seemed to dim the radiancy of our hospitable traditions, at a time, too, when we were loyally acting up to them, treating Mazzini, Louis Napoleon, the Orleans, and Metternich with large-minded generosity.

Cavaignac, notwithstanding the protests of Louis Blanc (who a few weeks later left France as the scapegoat of the terrible June uprising, and remained an exile in England until 1870), sent 3,000 men to Civitavecchia under Oudinot to receive the fugitive Pope. Oudinot's landing with the Italian and French tricolors intertwined bewildered every one, including Palmerston and the Roman Assembly, so that it is possible to account for the permission given to the dastard to land. It was fortunate indeed that in that moment the Romans had in their midst men inspired by a profound sense of their Italianhood. Garibaldi, who had gathered together a good number of volunteers, had been elected deputy for Rieti, and was the first to cry " Viva la Republica!" Mazzini, who was in Florence trying vainly to induce Guerrazzi to unite Tuscany to Rome, received the news from Goffredo Mameli in the three words : " Rome, Republic, Come " ; and having been acclaimed a Roman citizen was also elected a member of the Assembly. During this visit to Tuscany Mazzini went to Modena and, after fourteen years' separation, once again saw " Giuditta," who entrusted to him her only and beloved son Achille. The young man accompanied Mazzini to Rome, and fought bravely at the Vascello, and throughout the siege, under General Giacomo Medici.

On March 16th Mazzini proposed to the First Triumvirate, Armellini, Saliceti, and Montecchi, the nomination of a " War Committee " to organise the army. Carlo Pisacane (afterwards the martyr of Sapri) became the soul of this Committee, which fixed the number of troops at 45,000, and it was decided that if Piedmont renewed the war, 10,000 men should be sent to its aid under Colonel Mezzacapo. This was decreed notwithstanding Charles Albert's refusal to recognise the Roman Republic, and although Gioberti, his Prime Minister, had stigmatised the partisans of Unity as a " horde of audacious, evil-minded madcaps " (*audaci, malvagi sconsigliati*). But Zucchi had abandoned Palmanova without a shot ; in Lombardy the fates were adverse, and the Piedmontese army, under the leadership of a Pole, Krzanowsky, imposed on the King by his ministers, was first beaten at Mortara, and then decisively at Novara. The King vainly sought death upon the battle-field, and, refusing to sue for an armistice, abdicated in favour of his eldest son, Victor Emanuel, crossed the Alps under the name of Count of Bard, and went to Oporto to expiate his early faults and his later noble, though abortive, attempts at reparation. In abdicating he knew that his son would obtain better terms than he himself would have done, as all the hate and spite of Radetzky was concentrated upon his head. The fact that he had willed the renewal of the war saved the honour of his house and the future of his dynasty.

Palmerston did not abandon Piedmont in the bitter hour of her defeat, and would have done more, and remonstrated

VICTOR EMMANUEL II

even more severely with Austria, had it not been for Lord John Russell, the violent opposition of the Tories, and the strong feeling of the Catholic Peers who were devoted to Austria and to the restoration of the Pope. At any rate, he said in the House that "Mazzini's government of Rome was far better than any the Romans had had for centuries," and in reply to a violent attack on Garibaldi, he gave a glowing account of his prowess in Montevideo.

The greatest misfortune which befell the Roman Republic was that Garibaldi and Mazzini, the arm and head of the defence, did not always see eye to eye, but far too much has been made of their differences, which were never on vital, but always on secondary points. Avezzana, a Genoese, in exile since 1821 and who had greatly distinguished himself in the United States, was named Minister of War; Rosselli, a Roman, a brave, conscientious soldier who could fight and win any number of pitched battles on paper, but who lost his head even in the mildest emergency, was Commander-in-Chief; and these two, together with Pisacane—educated in the Military College of Naples and ex-officer of the French Légion Etrangère — stood out for the rules of regular warfare. So it became impossible for the new Triumvirate, elected on April 1st, and consisting of Mazzini, Saffi, and Armellini, to make Garibaldi Commander-in-Chief of the Roman forces, still less Military Dictator, as Sterbini,[1] Mameli and even Avezzana[2] desired. Again, despite the real discipline reigning in Garibaldi's legion, now over 1,500 men strong, their aspect and methods alarmed the population, which, from October 25th till December 21, 1848, had been called upon to provision the force; and Garibaldi's fixed idea to invade the Kingdom of Naples and there proclaim the Republic did not find favour in the eyes of the Triumvirate, as Austria, with 150,000

---

[1] Sterbini, Pietro, patriot and member of the Roman Giunta in 1849.
[2] Avezzana, Giuseppe (1789-1879), Italian soldier and patriot; took part in almost all the wars of the Risorgimento; had served under Napoleon I., and fought for the Independence of Spain; also in Mexico against the Spaniards.

victorious troops, commanded the line of the Po and could rapidly march down to help the King of Naples, whose army had been fully reorganised and was staunch to the Bourbons.

With Mazzini, personally, Garibaldi's relations were most cordial, and on April 8th he wrote from Rieti thus :—

"Brother Mazzini : These lines bring you salutations which I like to send you with mine own hand. May Providence sustain you in your brilliant but arduous career, and may you be enabled to carry out all the noble designs which you meditate for the welfare of our country! Remember that Rieti is full of your brethren in the Faith, and that immutably yours is G. Garibaldi."

With this letter Garibaldi sent a plan for marching by the Via Æmilia, calling to arms the Romagnols and the inhabitants of the Duchies, and attacking the Austrians.

But, as stated before, Oudinot, with his troops, had landed at Civitavecchia and announced his intention "of effectuating a reconciliation between the Pope and his subjects," who had not only abolished the temporal sovereignty of the Papacy *de facto et de jure*, but had resolved to defend their rights and their Republic against whomsoever should attack them. The understanding between Government and people was perfect : no police force was ever needed to keep order, as is testified by the private letters of French, English and American residents, and by the reports of the foreign consuls. Oudinot had been informed by his consul of the state of things, and told that he would not only not be welcomed, but that force would be repelled by force. With the usual French impertinence, he had replied : "*Les Italiens ne se battent pas,*" and on the dawn of April 30th, 10,000 French soldiers, their officers with white gloves and sheathed swords, marched upon the Eternal City. As soon as their extreme vanguard was seen, Avezzana gave a signal from St. Peter, and the bells of the city pealed forth the terrifying notes of the tocsin. A battery from the walls opened a fire, which was immediately returned with terrible accuracy by the Chasseurs de Vincennes, and by guns posted in a convenient situation. No confusion ensued : the dead and wounded were carried away at once, and Oudinot was about to press his attack, when Garibaldi, who, though only two days in Rome, had, with his " eye for possession," occupied the villas, palaces, woods, and vineyards outside Porta San Pancrazio, flung his men upon the French, falling back from the first assault, like stones from a sling. A furious *mêlée* at the bayonet's point ensued, Garibaldi personally leading the students who had never seen fire, with the result that Oudinot was forced to retreat, leaving, by his own account, on the field, 400 killed, 530 wounded, and 460 prisoners, while the Roman losses amounted to 214 killed and wounded, 25 being officers. The sole trophy of the French was Father Ugo Bassi,[1] the beloved chaplain of the army, whom they took prisoner while he was comforting a dying soldier.

Garibaldi would have pursued the fugitives to Castelguido, Palo, and Civitavecchia, " to drive them back to their ships or into the sea," but the War Committee, Mazzini not excepted, objected for many cogent reasons ; hence the only serious difference between Garibaldi and the Triumvirate. Mazzini believed that it would be sufficient for republican France to know that Rome would not receive back the Pope, and at the same time he feared the on-come of night, and the absence from the city of her best defenders. Garibaldi obeyed, as was his wont, but he bitterly resented, and never forgave, this refusal. A complete defeat of the French troops could not have been hidden from the French Assembly and nation, Oudinot would, he believed, have been recalled, and Louis Napoleon's position endangered ; whereas if French troops were allowed to remain on the Roman soil the necessary time would be gained in which to concert and carry out France's treacherous schemes.

---

[1] Bassi, Padre Ugo (1800–1849), Barnabite monk, and one of the purest patriots of the Italian Revolution. He was chaplain to Garibaldi's forces. Was taken prisoner by the Austrians near Bologna and shot. The last sacraments were denied to him by Pope Pius IX.

THE BIRTH OF MODERN ITALY

An armistice was concluded, and Lesseps,[1] then in the French Diplomatic Service, began negotiating a Convention with the Triumvirate, while Oudinot was secretly preparing to renew the attack. Thus passed the entire month of May.

In the meanwhile, the King of Naples with a large army crossed the frontier. Rosselli and Garibaldi were sent against him, and, but for that divided command, he would have been taken prisoner. Unfortunately, between Garibaldi attacking too soon, and Rosselli, as usual, arriving too late, Ferdinand and his army got warning in time, and decamped. Rosselli was ordered to continue the pursuit over the Neapolitan frontier, but he objected, as he had only 10,000 men, and no artillery or cavalry, and the region to be traversed was defended by two great fortresses, Capua and Gaeta. He was therefore recalled to Rome, Garibaldi being left with only 2,500 men to harass the enemy. The Neapolitans withdrew with so much dispatch that in two days they reached Naples. Garibaldi, after beating a horde of brigands led by Zucchi,[2] passed the frontier, and occupied Arce on May 26th. With prophetic vision he remarked to Sacchi, one of his companions of Montevideo who afterwards became an Italian general: "Here the destinies of Italy might be decided. A battle won under Capua would give Italy into our hands."

Ancona had been invested by General Wimpffen with 16,000 men, while Lichtenstein with another corps occupied Perugia. Livio Zambeccari,[3] "a jewel of a patriot," who commanded the fortress, refused indignantly to surrender. Later, when the French fleet appeared and its admiral offered to occupy the city and defend it against the Austrians, Zambeccari told him "that he saw no difference

---

[1] Lesseps, Ferdinand de (1805–1894), the famous constructor of the Suez Canal; was a diplomat in his youth, and was *chargé d'affaires* in Rome before and during the siege of 1848.

[2] Zucchi, Carlo, General of the Bourbons, and organiser of a brigandage during 1848.

[3] Zambeccari, Livio, Bolognese patriot and soldier.

1849] NEGOTIATIONS WITH DE LESSEPS

between the Austrians and the French, save the impudence of the latter." Then the Austrian fleet also appeared, and Austrian troops occupied the hills around the town. Avezzana left the Ministry of War in Rome and reached Ancona in time to concert for its defence.

At Arce Garibaldi received orders from the Triumvirate to return, as, in view of the favourable progress made in the negotiations with Lesseps, it had been decided to reunite all available forces against the Austrians. Garibaldi at once wrote to "the Citizen Triumvir Mazzini" (on May 27th) that "he would obey, but thus lose all the advantages of the expedition." He asked to be allowed at least to march by Sora and Aquila, to Terni, so as to be placed on the left flank of the Austrians, or in their rear, if they should march upon Rome. But this demand was also refused, some doubts having evidently at last arisen in the minds of the Triumvirs as to the good faith of the French commander.

On his return to Rome, Garibaldi was immediately asked by Mazzini to give his candid opinion on the situation. On June 1st he replied · "With the same confidence that your letter breathes, let me command the 1st Division, send me against the Austrians, with unlimited power to unite all armed corps . . to be found north of Rome, to organise them all . . . on the same footing, and to use them in the most profitable way . . . Dispense me from proving the necessity of my assertions. Be persuaded that the troops round Ancona cannot be placed under a different command from those operating in Tuscany." The Triumvirate would certainly have accepted the above suggestions, had they not been called upon to cope with a more terrible enemy, whose chief weapons were treachery and falsehood.

During the whole of May, under cover of Lesseps' industrious negotiations for a convention, Oudinot had been preparing for a siege. On May 31st the convention was signed by the Triumvirate and Lesseps, with the proviso that it should be approved by the French Government, but the President's private instructions to Oudinot were to let Lesseps parley until the moment should arrive to throw away the mask. Oudinot therefore summoned a council of war, to which Lesseps was invited, and in which all present voted for the immediate renewal of hostilities, notwithstanding the protests of the diplomat. Oudinot thereupon wrote to the Triumvirate that he considered Lesseps' authority null and void; hence the aggrieved "Ministre Plenipotentiaire en Mission" started at once for Paris, where he arrived on June 5th, after having received, already open, through Oudinot's hands, a humiliating dispatch putting an end to his mission. In the French Assembly the Foreign Minister, de Tocqueville, and Odillon Barrot[1] violently attacked Lesseps for "wishing to make French troops the laughing-stock of the civilised world" by keeping them outside of Rome at the beck and call of a "so-called Assembly" when "every European nation sent forces to help his Holiness the Pope." These words were covered with applause, and the voices of a small band of real patriots were silenced by the hisses and shouts of a majority ripe for Empire.

It was a bitter awakening for the Roman Triumvirate, confident to the last in the assurances of the French Republic; but they had to face the terrible fact that Oudinot now declared the armistice ended and intimated his intention to attack "*on June 4th.*"

[1] Barrot, Odillon (1791–1873), eminent French statesman, under Louis Philippe; was Minister and then chief of the "Constitutional" Opposition. He at first sustained the policy of Louis Napoleon.

XIII

THE DEFENCE OF ROME

1849

Mazzini's opinion—Oudinot's treachery—The night surprise of the 2nd and 3rd—Goffredo Mameli—Heroism of men and women—Pisacane's tribute to the Government—Garibaldi deprecates further "useless butchery"—His difference with Mazzini—Manara's influence—His death—Garibaldi's last effort—Death of Aguyar—The three alternatives—Garibaldi summoned to the Assembly—Cernuschi's resolution—Mazzini's protest—Carlyle's diary—Garibaldi, Anita, and about four thousand march out by the Porta San Giovanni—The Tuscans refuse them hospitality—San Marino—Garibaldi disbands his followers—Attempts to reach Venice—Betrayed by the moon—Gorzkowsky's ferocity—Death of Anita—Dom Giovanni Verità—Garibaldi imprisoned in Genoa—Mazzini's journey from Rome—Reaction general—Napoleon's dupes—Thiers—Victor Hugo—Arago—Frenchmen decree the death of the Roman Republic.

BEFORE the end came, Mazzini made yet another appeal to Garibaldi. He asked him, now that his departure from Rome was impossible, how matters could be adjusted to his satisfaction, without wounding the susceptibilities of the other military chiefs. Garibaldi, on the morning of June 2nd, replied with equal frankness:—

"MAZZINI: Since you ask me what I think, I will tell you. Here I cannot avail anything for the good of the Republic, except in two ways: as unlimited Dictator, or as a simple soldier. Choose.—Immutably yours, G. GARIBALDI."

This was Garibaldi's first expression of his profound conviction that in times of great danger the only way of salvation is to confer on a Dictator unlimited powers for a limited time.

Garibaldi's proposal was not even discussed. Oudinot, adding perjury to treachery, attacked suddenly on the night of the 2nd to the 3rd, and Garibaldi, who was being attended to for injuries incurred in the Velletri[1] expedition, only received the tidings just in time to summon his men, who were resting after their long, forced march from Arce to Rome. To his horror he found that the excellent positions from which he had successfully driven the French on April 31st, had been left undefended, so that, in the night, the Villas and vineyards had been again occupied by the enemy, with the exception of Villa Corsini, the Church of San Pancrazio, and the Vascello. Garibaldi for fourteen hours carried on a terrible struggle, repeatedly driving the French from the Villas Pamfili and Valentini, but reinforcements continually poured in, and finally the French retained all the positions with the exception of the Vascello.[2] This terrible fight cost the Republic many of its bravest defenders, among them Goffredo Mameli, the young soldier-poet, beloved by all Italy and specially dear to Mazzini and Garibaldi, between whom he formed a *trait d'union*. He was carried to the Hospital dei Pelligrini, where, several days later, Dr. Bertani amputated his thigh, still entertaining good hope of his recovery. He lay apparently undisturbed by the shells falling all around the building, even when one burst through the roof. This hospital suffered severely, and a heart-breaking entry in Bertani's diary records his own anguish when three bombs pierced the walls, destroying a floor and a ceiling and causing the death of forty of his cherished wounded ; for in the terrible scene which ensued, hæmorrhage undid the effects of all his loving care and skill. Mameli reawakened to consciousness of the surrounding horrors ; gangrene set in and nothing could save him.

[1] For a full description of the Velletri expedition see Trevelyan's "Garibaldi's Defence of the Roman Republic."

[2] The "Vascello," a villa just outside Rome, so called from its resemblance to the prow of a ship.

GIULIA CALAME MODENA.

To face p 197]

Garibaldi, after his letter to Mazzini, simply obeyed orders; but he could not even comfort himself with that spark of hope which, for a moment, buoyed up Mazzini. During a brief hour the Triumvirate imagined that the change in France from a Constituent to a Legislative Assembly might entail a change of policy, but the illusion did not last, as it was soon evident that the Prince-President and Odillon Barrot and his followers had a freer hand than before. Nothing remained but to save the honour of Rome. From the members of the Assembly to the last Transteverien, from the flower of Italian womanhood—among whom may be mentioned the Milanese Principessa Cristina Belgiojoso, Giulia Modena, the wife of Italy's greatest tragedian, and Margaret Fuller, the American—to the old crones of the Ghetto who lovingly assisted the wounded, this was an accepted fact. Not a murmur, not a wish for capitulation was expressed. Enemies have spoken of Mazzini's " Dictatorship," but in what did his supreme power consist? In his having, from the first, understood the noble and profound heroism and constancy of which the Romans and their Italian brethren were capable.

No better proof of the devotion of the people is needed than the following tribute from Carlo Pisacane—a man utterly opposed to Mazzini on religious and social questions, and who, together with Garibaldi, disapproved absolutely of all the religious ceremonies that were sanctioned and countenanced by the attendance of the Triumvirate and of the Assembly. " The Roman Republic," Pisacane said, " was governed by a Triumvirate, invested with supreme power, elected by the Assembly at the moment when the defeat of Novara proved that they would be left single-handed to cope with the Austrians. For the first time in history modern Rome offered an example of perfect harmony between the people and their rulers. The Triumvirate assumed power at a moment when the want of coin rendered the issue of paper-money necessary, and it could obtain no credit owing to the numerous enemies who menaced the Republic. The six ministerial departments had been left by

THE BIRTH OF MODERN ITALY

the late Papal administration in such disorder as to render evident that absence of all understanding of social interests which is peculiar to the sacerdotal caste. Austria, France, Naples, Spain threatened the Republic. The armed forces were few and scattered—not men, but arms were wanting. In this state of things there were but two ways in which to organise the Government. The first was to ignore all popular prejudices, trample on individual susceptibilities, assign to each the part for which his intelligence fitted him, and rule the Republic with an iron hand. The other was to take individuals whose prestige with the people might be superior to their merits, so as to enlist the popular sympathies, and govern by mildness, obtaining by love the sacrifices necessary for the salvation of the country. To obtain great things the first course must be adopted. The Triumvirate chose the other, with the result that such perfect harmony reigned that it never needed the slightest coercion to enforce its decrees. The people were convinced of the rectitude of the Government, and the Government, endowed with unlimited personal abnegation, with the single aim of the public weal, was true to its motto, 'God and the People.' That was the mainspring which constantly directed the Triumvirate. Of these three men, Carlo Armellimi dedicated himself exclusively to the judicial department, taking no part in the actual government. Giuseppe Mazzini is too well known to the world to need any word of mine. He soared above the other two on the wings of genius, and his opinion prevailed in every department : his intelligence shone resplendent, an absolute element, this, of grand conceptions. No one contested his superiority, he was the giant among comparative pigmies. Aurelio Saffi, bound to Mazzini by fraternal friendship, seconded him, sharing all his painful work (*travagli*) ; there was perfect accord between these two beings whom Nature had utterly deprived of personal ambition and interest, substituting for these an excessive patriotism and the desire of sacrificing themselves to the Universal Good."

This tribute from an agnostic and a socialist who, with

1849] RESPECT FOR THE PEOPLE'S RELIGION

Garibaldi, considered the guaranteeing of the spiritual independence of the Pope as a suicidal act for the Republic, needs no comment. We may add here, as regards the position taken by Mazzini and the Triumvirate in relation to the Roman Church, that while Pisacane and Garibaldi wished to close what the latter called the " Holy Shop" (*Sacra Bottega*), considering religious ceremonies as "useless symbols of a decrepit institution which fostered in the people their tendencies to bigotry and superstition," Mazzini not only wished to prove to the world that his Government would do nothing to offend the susceptibilities of Catholics in Rome or abroad, but, in his profound wisdom, recognised the fact that the spiritual power of the Roman hierarchy can be extinguished only when men shall have ceased to accept any intermediary between their own conscience and the Invisible—between " God and the People," as he would have said.

The situation of the besieged city now grew more precarious day by day. Oudinot, though he had a strong force, did not dare to attack ; so the hopes of the Triumvirate that the siege might be transformed into a battle were thwarted. The French opened their trenches, and it was decided to attack Villa Pamfili at night, in the hope of destroying the enemy's works. But the night attack failed owing to a sudden panic, and Garibaldi was compelled to re-enter the town. On the 12th of June Oudinot again demanded surrender, which the city having refused, he unmasked six batteries. The conflict lasted throughout the 13th, 14th, and 15th, until, on the 20th—the breaches being practicable—Oudinot prepared three columns of assault. Garibaldi would have harassed the enemy with continual sorties, but Rosselli each time countermanded his orders as " contrary to military rules." However, Garibaldi manned the breaches with his troops, and by his terrible fire prevented an attack until the French had erected new batteries and bombarded the bastions and the city. Garibaldi from that moment saw that any further effort would prove " useless butchery," and he was loath to sacrifice the

THE BIRTH OF MODERN ITALY

"youths whom he loved as if they were his sons." This he openly states in his Memoirs and other writings. How, then, was it possible for Mazzini to retard the catastrophe indefinitely, and reserve to Rome the "glory of falling last," *i.e.*, after Venice and Hungary?

In this terrible plight the population, all in arms, crowded around the Triumvirs, the Minister of War, Rosselli, Garibaldi, and all the staff on the Janiculum at nightfall, asking to be allowed to unite with the troops in a last desperate sortie The Minister of War and Rosselli seemed to approve this plan, which accorded well with Mazzini's own views, but Garibaldi tells us that he himself opposed the proposal on the ground that a panic—more disastrous than ever in such an emergency—would certainly ensue. Mazzini, beside himself with grief, wrote a reproachful letter to Manara, then chief of Garibaldi's staff, but Manara must have smoothed out the difference between his commander and the great Triumvir, because, on the 26th, at 8 a.m., Garibaldi sent a friendly letter to the Triumvirate, in which he proposed to leave Manara in Rome and to himself issue secretly from one of the gates with a considerable force to go and take up a position between the French and Civitavecchia and harass the enemy in the rear. The idea was bold, but came to nothing, as it proved impossible for a force to issue secretly from any gate; and in a note written by Manara on the same day, at 1 p.m., from Villa Spada, we see that he "had begged Garibaldi to return to San Pancranzio, not to deprive that post at this moment of his legion and his efficacious power."

This was Manara's last letter: he—the hero of the "Five Days" and of the Lombard plains, the commander of the Lombard Bersaglieri (Sharpshooters), "the most beautiful and fearless"—fell, pierced through the heart by "the long-yearned-for bullet." An entry in Dr. Bertani's diary runs: "29th–30th June.—The very devil of a night till 2 a.m. Bombs and cannonades, then silence. Then ever fresh wounded brought in. I heard a horse galloping furiously, then a voice—'Manara mortally wounded: he calls you; come!'"

AGOSTINO BERTANI.

Manara died as the barbarians entered Rome.

Garibaldi, with Medici, then made a last attempt. Sword in hand, at the head of their men, they furiously charged the enemy, twice driving back the serried ranks to the second line of attack. Thrice the French returned in overpowering numbers, but as they gained the gate of Porta San Pancrazio they were received by murderous volleys of musketry from the barricades of Villas Spada and Savorelli. There fell the flower of the Lombard boys of the "Band of Hope," and with them Garibaldi's giant negro—faithful, brave Aguyar; six hundred were added to the 3,400 corpses upon which the soldiers of the "grande Nation" were to reconstruct the gory throne of the Supreme Pontiff, Vicar of Christ on earth, and guard it with their bayonets until the sword of their self-elected master should fall from his trembling hand at Sédan.

What remained for the heroic survivors to do or to attempt? Three ways were opened: to surrender, to quit Rome with the army and the Assembly, or to remove all the population from the Trastevere, cut the bridges and barricade the streets, there to continue the struggle. Of the first alternative no one thought; the second was suggested by Mazzini (and Pisacane, speaking of it later, said that, though audacious, it was feasible, as in the Romagna they might have fallen on the flank of the Austrians, roused the inhabitants to insurrection and reinstated the Republic); the third required the will of the people. Mazzini's idea was not entertained by the Assembly, and resistance on the other side of the Tiber was likewise deemed impossible because the 30,000 Trasteverini, though willing to defend their homes inch by inch, would not consent to abandon them. Garibaldi was summoned. He came in, dripping with blood and sweat, and said that the only chance of keeping up the struggle lay in ordering an instant exodus from the Trastevere—then the defence might be prolonged *for a few days*. The Assembly at once voted for a resolution moved by Cernuschi, formulating their decision to desist from further resistance and charging the Triumvirate with the execution of their decree. But this the Triumvirate would not undertake. They resigned rather than sanction what seemed to them sacrilege, and Mazzini wrote a protest, of which, in a letter to us, written in 1856, he said he "did not yet repent. To continue the war to extermination was to me the elementary duty of the Republicans in power, hence I had never even discussed it with the members of the Assembly. A capital error ! . I found them utterly changed, panic-stricken, and disanimated. My proposal was followed by a long silence, broken at last by Cernuschi,[1] who, livid, his voice broken by emotion, protested against the departure of the Assembly and army from Rome; other speakers followed—their arguments were puerile, the discussion grew bitter. For the first time in Rome I lost my calm, became unparliamentary, and then I left the Assembly."

During those last days of the siege Mazzini tasted, indeed, the bitterness of death—death that seemed to him dissevered from honour. He could not realise it for a time, and he could not submit. He wandered about the Trastevere, where the people, sad and silent, thronged around him to touch his hand, bringing their children that he might bless them, and exhibiting the bombs and the devastation they had wrought. He sat among the ruins of the Janiculum, or watched the sunset from the Pincio, feeling that Rome's glory too had set.

In a letter to his mother, written on the day following the decision of the Assembly, he scarcely gives a clue to his real feelings : " Two lines to keep you tranquil. I am well in health. Of the French I care not to speak : they are far worse than the Croats; state of siege, military commissions, arrests ; no honest man will serve them. Our officers have all resigned. The troops are disbanded. The civil servants also quit their posts and the French are surrounded by spies and thieves, old agents of Gregory XVI.

---

[1] Cernuschi, Enrico (1821–1896), politician and economist, born in Milan ; was, with Cattaneo and others, the soul of the Revolution of 1848 in Milan. A staunch and uncompromising republican, he preferred to take the French citizenship rather than live under a monarchy in Italy.

Give the enclosed protest to our friends to read. I have not published it, because these are no times for public divisions among us, but I wish you all, my men and women friends, to know that the surrender lies not upon my soul. Poor Goffredo (Mameli) is dead; even amputation could not save him. *Ahi* . for his poor mother !"

For few acts of his life has Mazzini been criticised and blamed so much as for this protest; it was not even inserted in the reports of the Assembly, but Carlyle, while differing from many of Mazzini's methods, recorded what he considered to be the duty and the only possible course for the man he loved and respected.

In his diary there occurs the following : "Mazzini is busy at Rome resisting the French, resisting all people that attack his *Republica Romana*, standing on his guard against all the world. Poor Mazzini ! . . . if he *could* stand there in Rome, in sight of all Italy, and practically defy the whole world for awhile and fight till Rome was ashes and ruin, and end by blowing himself and his assailants up in the last strong post, and so yield only with life, he might rouse the whole Italian nation into such a rage as it has not known for many centuries, and this might be the means of shaking out of the Italian mind a very foul precipitate indeed. Perhaps that is what he really was worth in this world. Strange, providential-looking, and leading to many thoughts . . . Mazzini came much about us here for many years . . . patronised by my wife . . . a beautiful little man, full of sensibilities, of melodies, of clear intelligence and noble virtues. . After many sad adventures, he is *there!* . . . What will become of him ? we ask daily with a real interest. A small, square-headed, bright-eyed, swift, yet still Ligurian figure, beautiful and merciful and fierce, as grand a little man, when I saw him first—eight or nine years ago—as has ever come before me. True as steel, the word, the thought of him pure and limpid as water, by nature a little lyrical poet, with plenty of quiet fun in him, too, and wild emotion Shall we ever see him more !"

Garibaldi, on his part, would not submit to the decree of the Assembly. He collected his men, and offering them " hunger, thirst, forced marches and constant combats " commenced that marvellous retreat from Rome which by some of the highest authorities is considered one of the most wonderful military feats on record. Anita, his wife, who had accompanied him throughout his extraordinary South American exploits, had, in spite of his prayers and commands, come to him in Rome, after leaving their children in Nice, and she arrived at the Villa Savarelli as the bombs came hurtling through the roof. Despite her delicate condition, she insisted upon accompanying her husband to what was to be her doom. She cut off her magnificent hair and was the first person to mount a horse on Piazza di San Giovanni. The audacious band marched towards the sources of the Tiber, and at Terni joined Colonel Forbes with 900 other volunteers. But the reaction of hopelessness had succeeded to the enthusiasm of faith. The Tuscans would not listen to the veteran leader; Arezzo, by order of the poet Guadagnoli, closed its gates in his face. Soon Garibaldi was hemmed in on all sides by the Austrians; by his genius he always evaded them, but at the same time death, want, and desertions were thinning his ranks, and he was obliged to seek refuge in the little independent Republic of San Marino, on the summit of Mount Titano. Though threatened by the Austrians, the sturdy Republicans would not surrender their guests. Garibaldi, however, did not wish to expose San Marino to reprisals, so it was arranged that his men should lay down their arms and disband. In his last order of the day he took leave of his men, reminding them that Italy ought not to rest in ignominy, and that it was better to die than to be the slave of the foreigner. Garibaldi, observing that Venice was still left to die for, again, by a wonderful march, slipped through the enemy's lines with the 200 men who would not leave him, and, crossing almost impassable ravines, arrived at Cesenatico, on the Adriatic, after twenty-two hours' exhausting tramp.

ANITA GARIBALDI.

ANITA'S DEATH

Chartering thirteen fishing-boats, he no longer doubted being able to reach Venice, but the wind dropped just as he rounded Punta di Maestra, and the moon suddenly shone out, betraying him to the Austrian blockading squadron, who at once attacked his little fleet. The fishermen manning the boats, paralysed with fear, scattered at the first broadside from the brig *Oreste*; eight of the boats were captured, and five, piloted by Garibaldi himself, made the shore of Mesola. The Austrian general, Gorzkowsky, was so furious at Garibaldi's escape from San Marino, that all the volunteers he could capture were either shot, ferociously bastinadoed, or condemned to irons and hard labour in the worst dungeons of Mantua. Of the few who landed at Mesola the soldiers murdered eight in cold blood, and a proclamation was issued warning the inhabitants that " whosoever should shelter, feed, or assist Garibaldi would be hanged, drawn, and quartered." Garibaldi alone remained with Anita and his faithful, one-armed friend Leggiero (surname of a Captain Culiolo). Anita, exhausted by privations, fatigue, and the delicate condition in which she found herself, began rapidly to sink. Through almost incredible difficulties, and in constant fear of capture, the two managed to carry her to a farm belonging to the Guiccioli family, where, fortunately, they found a doctor. But it was too late ; life was ebbing fast. One draught of water from the beloved hand, one look of anguished passion, but no word ; then, folded on his breast, Anita passed away from him to whom for ten years she had been lover and wife, nurse and comrade.

Garibaldi became for the time indifferent to his own fate, but others watched over him for the sake of Italy. Devoted hearts, among whom was a priest whose name should ever be held sacred, Don Giovanni Verità,[1] managed

---

[1] Verità, Don Giovanni (1807-1885), a noble and patriotic Roman Catholic priest ; was later chaplain in the Italian army. He saved at his own peril Garibaldi's life in 1849, when pursued by the Austrian and Papal troops. The Pope when he died denied him the Extreme Unction.

to smuggle him through unfrequented paths of the Apennines into Tuscany, and, still accompanied by Leggiero, he gained Prato, then Poggibonsi, where he was hidden by a friend, and, passing through San Dalmazio and Massa, reached Follonica on the Mediterranean, where brave fishermen took him in their *paranza* to Vado, and thence, disguised as a fisherman, he reached Chiavari. But the Intendant of Chiavari, hearing of his arrival, requested a passport *viséed* by some Sardinian consul. Garibaldi answered that "not having had the honour of meeting a Sardinian consul among the rocks, ravines, valleys, and rivers through which he had journeyed," he could not satisfy the Intendant. So, escorted by *carabinieri*, he was taken to the prison of the Palazzo Ducale in Genoa, and incarcerated under the same tower where Jacopo Rufini had died by his own hand.

Mazzini's fate was very different. His friends, the Modenas, feared for his safety, yet dared not urge his departure. Giulia Modena, the wife of the great tragedian, whom we have already mentioned as helping in the hospitals, used to say that Mazzini in those days "neither slept nor ate. He could neither be consoled nor induced to depart." But on the 11th of July he must have made up his mind, as he warned his mother that he was on the move. His faithful friend Scipione Pistrucci afterwards wrote to Signora Mazzini that "Pippo meant to make every effort to get a sight of her in Genoa," but it was evident that he could not succeed. The American consul, Cass, had given him a United States passport, he also furnished Garibaldi, Saffi, and in the same way others, but it was useless without the French *visa*, for which naturally Mazzini would not ask. He went, therefore, to Civitavecchia, and there finding a ship bound for Marseilles walked on board and said abruptly to the captain, "I am Mazzini; I have no passport; do you dare to give me a passage?" The captain consented, and so Mazzini was carried from the Roman shores. At Leghorn the Austrian officials came on board and made a rigorous search. "Do not be frightened," said Mazzini to the captain, " they will not take me, and you will not be compromised." He borrowed the steward's cap, and pulling it over his magnificent brow, which, with his wonderful eyes, distinguished him from other men, he set to work to wash up the glasses, and the Austrians returned on shore, little suspecting what a dangerous enemy had escaped their vigilance.

Arrived in Marseilles, he wrote to his mother on the 20th : " I am here, and in half an hour start for Geneva where, I think I shall certainly arrive safely. . When you receive this I shall be there and will write at once. I was anchored off Genoa, and did not let you know ; you may imagine my state, but I thought it best for you."

He reached Geneva in safety, and on the 23rd wrote : " You thought me at Malta, and so did every one. . . . I do not yet know what I shall do. I have kept on travelling, and now, with little tidings, and my friends all dispersed, I must take time to look round. Then one must ascertain to what point European reaction will attain. It is a mortal duel between us and them, and from that duel I do not intend to retire."

The convulsion which shook Europe to its centre in 1848-1849 occasioned international diplomacy many serious forebodings, especially after the fall of Rome. The free and unconditional restoration of the Pope by France, who, instead of imposing terms on him, was compelled to act for him as jailer and hangman, constituted the sole " glory " won by the Republican " grande Nation," who rewarded the real engineer of this " triumph " by acclaiming him President, Dictator, and Emperor.

With the reinstalment of the Pope reaction also became reinstated on the Continent, and even in England Liberty had a hard fight to hold her own. Throughout 1849 the Liberals had manfully endeavoured to support the people in their struggle, but Lord Palmerston, always in the van, was sorely handicapped by the conduct of Louis-Napoleon and of the French troops in Rome, which was wholly incomprehensible to him. In a letter to Lord Normanby dated

THE BIRTH OF MODERN ITALY

July 16, 1849, he admirably depicts the situation: "The debate on Brougham's motion will turn chiefly on Italian affairs. . . . Lombardy, Sicily, and Rome will, of course, be the main topics on which Brougham, Stanley, and Aberdeen, the three witches who have filled the caldron, will dilate." . . . The Government will have no difficulty in answering about Lombardy and Sicily, "but the Roman affair is not so clear, and it would be very useful not only for us . . . but also for the French Government, if . . . from the Ministerial Bench . . . we were able to say something positive and definite as to the intentions of the French Government." The question which would certainly be asked was, "Were the French in Rome as friends of the Pope or as friends of the people?" He continues: "The question is hard to answer, and for us, unaided by the French Government, impossible." He then explains at great length how France ought to act so as to secure the maintenance of a constitution in the Papal States. "If the French, who are in possession of Rome, make the Pope and his Cardinals and Austria clearly understand that the Pope cannot return except on these conditions, the Pope will put his allocution of April 20th in a drawer and will accept all." If the Pope should refuse, Palmerston will advise France to retire and let the Pope and the people settle their differences as best they can, with the proviso "that no foreigner whatsoever should be suffered by France to intervene; foreigners, that is to say, no persons not Italians, for it is pedantry to call men belonging to other parts of Italy 'foreigners' in Rome."

If Louis Napoleon had one thing on which to pride himself in his first year of perfidy and crime, it was the quality of his dupes. Lesseps, Mazzini, Palmerston, three of the most honest and honourable men in Europe, and possessing, it will be generally admitted, an average amount of brains, yet wholly failed to sound the depths of depravity to which human nature in his person could descend.

Public opinion in England did not take any great interest in the Roman question. Only a sudden, unanimous, strong outburst of Protestant, anti-papal feeling would have rendered possible a movement in favour of the Roman Republic ; but though various attempts were made to induce a widespread agitation in favour of " Rome against the Pope," they evoked no response. The friends of Italy could do no more than welcome all exiles and friends who landed on our shores, or, by means of subscriptions, send back to their native country such Italians as chose to return there.

In France itself the settling of the Roman question gave rise to much discussion and fierce debates in the Assembly. Ledru-Rollin and a few, very few, brave spirits tried from the " Mountain " to recall France to a sense of her dishonour—France, who was willing to become the "gendarme of absolutism and theocracy." The battle was waged with special virulence in October on the occasion of the vote for Supplementary Estimates necessitated by the expedition to Rome. Fifteen Commissioners were elected to examine into the proposition, among whom were Montalembert, Victor Hugo, General Oudinot, and Thiers. The last was chosen as *rapporteur* of the commission, and was, on October 13th, requested to openly read his report, instead of handing it in as usual. In his speech, which was often violently interrupted by the members of the " Mountain," he gave his version of Roman history since the election of Pius IX. to the Papacy, and the "shameless little Jesuit " not only recognised the right of Austria " to reconquer those provinces which were incontrovertibly hers," but insisted upon the duty of France to sustain the temporal power of his Holiness the Pope, without which the majestic monument of the Catholic Church must fall asunder. The Pope ought to be so placed that neither prince nor people could dictate to him. France could not remain behind the other Catholic Powers in this work, for which the "glorious soldiers of France had renewed the exploits of Lodi and Arcole." The " Mountain " greeted this pompous nonsense with derisive cheers, but, unmoved, Thiers went on to express the opinion that France could

THE BIRTH OF MODERN ITALY

not attempt to enforce any orders on the Pope ; she could but humbly supplicate the Holy Father to deign to satisfy the just aspirations of his subjects. This he had done by a recent *motu proprio*, and France must stand by him as long as it should be necessary to guarantee the integrity of his domains and the safety of his person.

A great number of orators continued the debate. Of those in favour of the occupation, only Montalembert was listened to with respect, as all knew he was profoundly sincere in his convictions. He maintained the requisiteness of the Papacy as the basis of the Catholic religion and of political and religious order, therefore, as absolute authority was indispensable to the Papacy, the Roman States must be subjected to pontifical autocracy by force if necessary. The liberty of the Roman people was contrary to the liberty of the Roman Pontiff, therefore the former should be enslaved; this was required by the Catholic faith. What is just in France is iniquitous in Italy.

Victor Hugo, not yet the Apostle of Liberty, showed that the first intention of France after Novara had been to prevent Austria from restoring despotism in Italy, and to defend the Roman Republic against all foes. This intention had been repudiated by the bombardment and conquest of Rome, and the destruction of the Republic. As the French army was in Rome it must now remain there until the Pope had been induced to sanction secularisation of the Government and a general amnesty. "The power," he concluded, "which has by its act restored the temporal power, has a right to impose its terms, otherwise the presence in Rome of the Republican banner of France, dishonours her and places her on the same level as Austria."

It was reserved for Emanuel Arago [1] to deliver the greatest speech of the debate—an impassioned appeal to the Government to retrace its steps. He seemed inspired by a prophetic spirit, for he cried : " But be assured, the end of the temporal power of the Papacy is at hand, and you

[1] Arago, Emanuel (1812–1896), French statesman and writer, died ambassador of the present French Republic in Bern.

render a poor service to the Pope's spiritual authority by binding it to that crumbling little throne ! . . . Beware lest the fall of that throne bury one day in its ruins the name and the glory of France !" Arago closed his indictment by hurling at the ministry the following words :—
" But you care not for the honour and name of France ! You will continue on the path marked out to you by hypocrisy, by Catholic fanaticism—the path that leads to the abyss. Ah ! . . . but you will be punished ! History, posterity, will glorify the heroes you calumniate and avenge the insults that you pour upon them, while your names, oh ! ministers of the French Republic, will be written on that dark page of its annals headed 'Treachery,' (*trahison*) !"

Odillon Barrot, President of the Council, summed up the discussion and recalled the Assembly to the main question. It was either to be war against all Catholic nations and even against their own Catholic countrymen, or they must remain in Rome for the protection of the Pope and of his absolute sovereignty ; but he asked the Assembly to trust in the power of diplomacy and in the well-deserved French influence, to secure gradually for the Romans amnesty, secularisation, and a liberal government, although not, of course, a parliamentary government, that being absolutely incompatible with the sovereignty of the Pope and his independence. These words were crowned by success, even Victor Hugo and others of the " Left " withdrawing their orders of the day to unite in one proposed by Savoye, Joly, Lamennais, and many others, in which the action of the Government was sanctioned, with the proviso that no efforts should be spared to protect the just aspirations of the Roman people, while the motion refusing supplies was only put amid a storm of insults. Out of 649, 469 voted for, and only 180 against, the treacherous murder of the Roman Republic. A bare 180 for honour and justice and the fair name of France, while nearly three times that number raised their voices to perpetuate slavery in Rome, and so, unwittingly, to introduce the thraldom of France herself.

This happened on October 20, 1849.

XIV

THE WEARY INTERVAL

1849–1851

Ledru-Rollin and Barbès—Letters from Georges Sand to Mazzini—*L'Italia del Popolo*—Mazzini's letter to Tocqueville and Falloux Georges Sand's estimate of the French spirit—Her adhesion to Communism—Mrs. Stansfeld visits her—Law restricting suffrage in France—Mazzini's foresight—His return to England—Hartmann's description of Mazzini—"Italian National Committee"—"European Democratic Committee"—Death of Mme. Ashurst Bardon.

AFTER this decisive vote the French Republicans seemed to lose all heart, and the socialists to become demoralised through the enforced absence of Louis Blanc. The trials of Ledru-Rollin and his friends and the imprisonment of Barbès, for their attempting on June 13th to force the Assembly to recall the expeditionary corps from Rome, appeared to strike terror into the Democrats.

Georges Sand's letters to Mazzini insist that French Liberals must rest on their oars, at least for the moment, for the masses will neither follow nor listen to them, the incidence of the taxes being the only thing which arouses the interest of the people. She confesses that her compatriots are not ripe for liberty, and tells him that she has abstained from politics since the days of June, taking refuge in her art, endeavouring to depict her fellow-creatures as she would have them, and as she firmly believes they will yet shine forth in the future.

Her grief for the fate of Rome was poignant. On June 23rd she wrote to Mazzini:—

"Ah! mon ami, mon frère, quels événements, et comment vous peindre la profonde anxiété, la profonde admiration et l'indignation amère qui remplissent nos cœurs ? Vous avez sauvé l'honneur de votre cause ; mais, hélas ! le nôtre est perdu en tant que nation ! . . . Chaque jour nous nous attendons à quelque nouveau désastre . . . Aujourd'hui nous savons que l'attaque est acharnée, que Rome est admirable, et vous aussi. Qu'apprenderons nous demain ? Dieu récompensera-t-il tant de courage et de dévoument ? livrera-t-il les siens ? Ou bien protègera-t-il la trahison et la folie la plus criminelle que l'humanité ait jamais soufferte ? Il semble . . . qu'il veuille . . laisser cette génération comme un example d'infamie, d'une part, et d'expiation, de l'autre ! Quoi qu'il arrive, mon cœur désolé est avec vous. Si vous triomphez, il ne me restera pas moins une mortelle douleur de cette lutte impie de la France contre vous. Si vous succombez, vous ne serez pas moins grand, et votre infortune vous rends plus cher, s'il est possible, à votre sœur."

To a friend in Toulon she writes in July : ". . . Rome espérait et combattait. Hélas ! . . . nous l'avons tuée ! . . . Nous sommes des assassins ! et on parle de gloire à nos soldats ! . . . Mon Dieu, mon Dieu ! . . . ne nous laissez plus longtemps douter de vous ! Il ne nous reste qu'un peu de foi, si nous perdons celà nous n'aurons plus rien." In this letter Georges Sand goes on to say that she hopes that Mazzini personally is safe, but fears greatly that his soul will not be able to withstand the terrible disasters which have assailed him. She fears for his life too, " car l'Europe est livrée aux assassins." She has received from him " une lettre admirable," but will not give any particulars of his plans as she fears the curiosity of the police.

On July 24th, Georges Sand again addresses to Mazzini, who she thinks is at Malta, a most eloquent and tender letter, confessing that in the tragic end of Rome her first thought was for his personal safety, and adding · " Que Dieu me le pardonne, et vous aussi, qui êtes un saint ! " A friend in Toulon has reassured her as to Mazzini's safe departure from Italy, but now her heart is agonised by " une sorte d'intime solidarité qui fait passer dans notre propre cœur le remords que devraient avoir les autres." Yes! her heart is torn by shame and remorse; she who was so proud of being French, "durant les glorieuses journées de Février," feels the crime that her country has committed. And in fear of future retribution she exclaims: "Quelle expiation nous réserve la Justice Divine avant de nous permettre de nous relever?" But he (Mazzini) must be, in spite of defeat, persecution, and exile, much happier than she is, because he is a Roman, more Roman than any born on the banks of the Tiber. He and Kossuth are the two men in Europe who have done their duty to the bitter end, and she brackets with them those who have fought and suffered in their company, for "les plus obscurs dévouements sont aussi chers à Dieu que les plus illustres." She is certain that he (Mazzini) has "des jours résignés et des nuits tranquilles. Je suis certaine que vous êtes calme et goutez les joies austères de la Foi." She closes her letter by expressing to him all her love and admiration, and offering him her purse, as a sister, for in such a time as patriots are passing through he may be in want.

Two days later she hears from her friend in Toulon that Mazzini is in Geneva, and she writes to him at once. This letter of July 26th is almost a duplicate of the preceding, though the wording is entirely different, proving, once more, if proof were needed, the extraordinary flow of language with which Georges Sand was gifted. She repeats her cordial offer of financial aid and expresses her pleasure in knowing that he is in Switzerland, so much nearer to her than in Malta. After expressing her conviction that he certainly is calm, resigned, and serene, because he has done "tout votre devoir," she says: "Si vous avez échoué politiquement, c'est que la Providence voulait s'arrêter là, et que ce grand fait doit mûrir dans la pensée des hommes avant qu'ils en produisent de nouveaux." She urges him not to despair, as nationalities cannot die, and will rise surely again from their ruins. "Ne pleurez pas ceux qui sont morts, ne plaignez pas ceux qui vont mourir. Ils payent leur dette: ils valent mieux que ceux qui les égorgent, donc ils sont plus heureux. Et pourtant, malgré soi, on pleure et on plaint. Ah ! ce n'est pas sur les martyrs qu'il faudrait pleurer, c'est sur les bourreaux."

Meanwhile Mazzini had started his new review, *L'Italia del Popolo*, at Lausanne, and he sent a copy of it, containing his admirable letter to Tocqueville and Falloux, to Madame Sand. On October 10th she replies, drawing a most vivid picture of the political state of France. After thanking him she expresses her enthusiastic admiration for his letter to Tocqueville and Falloux, telling him that she has already read it in the French newspapers. It is for her an historic document which will remain indissolubly bound with the history of Rome and of all republics. It has, she believes, made a profound impression in France, " même dans ce peuple humilié et avili." No one has been, or will be, able to refute it, as it is " le cri du droit, de l' honneur, de la vérité qui devrait tuer de honte et de remords la tourbe jésuitique." But the fault of all the backsliding lies in the people themselves. " La grande majorité des Français est surtout malade d'ignorance et d'incertitude . c'est effrayant comme on hésite avant de se réunir sous une bannière." The French are tormented by a surfeit of " ideas," and it is on account of this that their Republic was seen to falter and then halt, as if suffocated " par ses palpitations secrètes." It is for this "qu'elle laisse une immonde *camarilla* prendre le gouvernail et commettre en son nom des iniquités impunies." In Italy, in Poland, in Hungary, and perhaps also in Germany, one single "idea" occupies and absorbs the people, the " idea " of liberty. The French have Liberty, they are seeking Equality, " et pendant que nous la cherchons, la Libérté nous est volée par des larrons . . . qui ne se préoccupent que des faits."

In a subsequent letter she expresses her prophetic belief that only one remedy can avail to save France and place her on her true road : " Il lui faudrait des invasions et de grands maux extérieurs pour la réveiller. . . . S'il plait à Dieu de nous secouer ainsi, que sa volonté s'accomplisse ! Nous irons plus douloureusement mais plus vite au but." Yet she avows that she has still some faint hope for France, as the melodrama which represents the entry of the French troops into Rome was hissed every night by the rabble. This, however, is but a very faint glimmer of light, and she tells Mazzini that he must not count upon it. The republican party is, she feels, gradually sinking into its grave.

But the amicable and cordial relations between Georges Sand and Mazzini were destined to be troubled, and later on interrupted, by a difference of opinion concerning the social question, and we find the first traces of this discord in a letter from Georges Sand dated the 13th of November. After thanking Mazzini for all the numbers of the *Italia del Popolo*, which the police have not yet thought of suppressing, she says: " Vos articles sont excellents et admirables. Je ne vous dirai pas comme Kléber à Napoléon : 'Mon Général, vous êtes grand comme le Monde !' Je vous dirai mieux : 'Mon ami, vous êtes bon comme la Vérité !' Non, je ne suis pas d'un avis différent du vôtre sur ce qu'il faut faire. . . . Vous vous trompez absolument quand vous me dites que ma persistence dans l'idée communiste est au nombre des choses qui ont fait du mal. Je ne le crois pas pour mon compte, parceque je n'ai jamais marché, ni pensé, ni agi avec ceux qui s'intitulent 'l'Ecole Communiste.' Le Communisme est ma doctrine personnelle : mais je ne l'ai jamais prêchée dans les temps d'orage, et je n'en ai parlé alors que pour dire que son règne était loin, et qu'il ne fallait pas se préoccuper de son application." The doctrine of Communism possesses, however, according to her, rules immediately applicable, which go under all sorts of other names, and are accepted because immediately possible. They are the first steps towards her ideal, and she never was among those who, unable to establish the preponderance of their entire faith, reject " l'ètat intermédiaire, les transitions *nécessaires, inévitables, justes et bonnes par conséquent.*" But she fears that her explanation is poor, and hopes that Mazzini will understand her better than she herself is capable of explaining. She closes her letter thus: "Je vous dirai où est notre mal en France: trop de foi dans l'idèe personnelle chez quelques uns, trop de scepticisme chez la plupart. L'orgueil chez les premiers, le manque de dignité chez les autres. Je constate un mal, et ne fais rien de plus. Je sais, je vois qu'on ne peut pas faire *agir* des gens qui ne *pensent* pas encore et qui ne croient à rien, tandis que ceux qui agissent un peux chez nous, n'ont en vue qu'eux mèmes, leur gloire ou leur vanité, leur ambition ou leur profit."

Mazzini, however, not being convinced that all was over for the time being, determined to remain in Switzerland, preaching and preparing for action. Not even the pleasure of spending Christmas in England allured him to her shores; therefore many of his English friends visited him in Lausanne, among them Emilie Ashurst Hawkes. He must also have met Mr. and Mrs. Stansfeld in Paris with Eliza Ashurst, who, in 1848, had married a Monsieur Bardon, a French gentleman whose acquaintance she and her father had made during the "Journées de Juin." Mrs. Stansfeld visited Georges Sand in the "Vallée Noire" in July or August, 1850, for the latter wrote to Mazzini on August 4th that she had been entertaining "votre jeune et jolie amie, Caroline." She knows that Caroline's sister is, or has been, with him, and exclaims: " Qu'elles sont heureuses, ces Anglaises, de pouvoir courir où leur cœur les pousse!" She is happy to hear that he has seen them, as it will have afforded him a certain consolation and pleasure, and she needs not to tell him how much he is "aimé, estimé, vènère" by all. She knows how much Mazzini is touched by affection, as his nature is a most loving one. She finds Caroline "charmante," and hears that Eliza is very happy, and that they frequently see Louis Blanc in London and esteem him highly. His (Mazzini's) young friend has asked her, in his name, to contribute something to a paper, but she fears it is impossible, because she lives entirely in the past. She finishes her letter as follows: "Aujourd'hui on ne vit plus en France, on est comme frappé de stupeur au bord d'un abime, sans pouvoir faire un mouvement pour le fuir. Heureusement, cette stupeur même empêchera peut-être qu'on ne fasse un mouvement pour s'y jeter : mais que la vie qui s'écoule ainsi est lente et triste ! "

This despondency was relieved for a brief season in March, as she wrote : " You are satisfied for the moment, are you not ? Our elections are good, and all my friends are full of joy and hope. They say, and I think they are right, that we shall go on without shocks until the next general election, and that then the majority will be Republican. I also believe this." But alas ! the Assembly was called upon to pass a law restricting the suffrage in open violation of Article II. of the Constitution. At that moment his friends begged Mazzini to come to Paris to concert measures for the revival of the Roman Question. He acceded to the request, and at once suggested the necessity of all true Frenchmen joining to protest against the " suicidal law " just proposed ; but although he remained three weeks in Paris he found it impossible to unite any of the contending factions. There was no understanding between Paris and the Departments : the chiefs of the different schools were so hostile to each other that they would not settle on a list of members to form a new Provisional Government in case of success.

So while Montalembert proposed " une expédition à l'intérieur," Thiers quietly insulted " la vile multitude." The law passed triumphantly, and reaction instantly commenced. Clubs were closed, the press gagged ; among other papers suppressed was *Le Travailleur*, supported by Georges Sand and her friends, and its editor was arrested and imprisoned. Hundreds of individuals were deported to the islands, yet no one seemed to suspect the imminent danger hanging over France. No one took Louis Napoleon *au sérieux*. When Mazzini pointed out facts that betrayed his guilty designs, they answered that " if the ridiculous imbecile should attempt a *coup d'état*, he would be quietly removed to Charenton (Bedlam)." To Mazzini it appeared as clear as daylight that while the Monarchists, Odillon Barrot, Thiers, Changarnier, &c., were plotting against the Republic with the Orleanists for the restoration of Henry V. under the regency of the Duchesse de Berry, the Bonapartist party was plotting against both.

In April, 1850, Mazzini wrote to Mr. Ashurst that "Eliza is well and coming, it appears, with me to London." This in fact she did, and Mazzini remained in London a few months, shocked and grieved at the misery of the Italian exiles, who, expelled from every spot in Italy, and now also from France, resorted to their one asylum. The Friends of Italy taxed themselves to the limits of possibility to assist them, either finding work for them or helping them to emigrate to the United States. Warm was the welcome given to Mazzini by his "own family" at Muswell Hill, and one not less hearty awaited him at Cheyne Row.

His first visit to the Carlyles after his long absence is described by the German patriot and poet, Moritz Hartmann, who happened to be present, as follows : "We were all sitting by the fire in the drawing-room, . . . and after some talk about the German Parliament Carlyle fell into one of his monologues, full of wit and feeling ; to listen to him was like sitting by a rushing torrent and watching the waves roll one after the other. Suddenly Mrs. Carlyle started : a voice in the hall had reached her ear, stirring her like an electric shock. Her eyes sparkled, and opening the door she grasped the hands of the visitor in such a transport of joy that it seemed almost an embrace. Carlyle ceased talking, and with his stork-like legs in one long stride reached his guest, who was not less moved than those who had welcomed him with so much delight. I, who did not know him, shared the sentiments so vividly depicted on the faces of all three. The few words spoken by the unknown, the ineffable harmony of his voice, would have moved the hardest heart. It was Joseph Mazzini, and his friends had not seen him since he had left them in 1848. Mrs. Carlyle, caressing his beard with her hand, exclaimed with tears in her eyes: '*Ahi!* . . . how white it has grown! . . .' The woman's faltering voice showed that she realised at that moment all the toil and travail, the sorrow and suffering, that had blanched the hair of the Roman Triumvir. For those who know Carlyle and his opinions, this welcome to the great agitator and liberator who returned vanquished, this warm friendship for the man at whose sole name millions of 'Philistines' made the sign of the cross, may seem surprising. At that time Carlyle was writing his 'Past and Present,' where he derides liberty and the efforts to achieve it. Yet, this formidable Carlyle was profoundly moved at the sight of his friend, and at the thought of the perils and pains he had gone through during these two years of separation. The truth is that great men are attracted to and understand each other. Then I must add that Mazzini was a man whom the hardest heart could not have repelled, and a man such as Carlyle could not but love. At that time he was forty-five, but his beard, once very black, was white; he was thin and pale, his complexion olive-tinted, of middle stature, well knit, delicately framed, and dressed with extreme simplicity; beautiful indeed was his majestic forehead and the form of his head. If you had met him in the street with his brow concealed, you would hardly have noticed him, but when you saw his eyes a sense of pleasure mixed with veneration possessed you; when he spoke, the harmony of his voice conquered you. But then! Mazzini! his eyes, his smile, his voice, no one can describe."

Availing himself of the authority conferred on him by sixty of the representatives of the Roman Parliament, Mazzini organised the Italian National Committee, and issued a national loan for ten million Italian liras. The sums subscribed were deposited with Messrs. Martin, Stone & Martin, bankers, 65, Lombard Street, and James Stansfeld consented to be their London agent, giving his address 2, Sydney Place, Brompton. His father seems to have cast doubts on the propriety and even on the legality

Prestito NAZIONALE ITALIANO (Italia e Roma)

Diritto unicamente ad affrattarr l'indipendenza e la libertà d'Italia.

V1985

Franchi 100

Ricevuto da FR.I.VVHI CENTO dei Capitale cet. mercantile
dei use de mezzi pronto 1 mese a datare da questo giorno
25 febbrajo 1850

PEL COMITATO NAZIONALE.

Gius. Mazzini   Aurelio Saffi
Giuseppe Sirtori   Mattia Montecchi

La Cedola N.1, contenente le basi e i particolari
di Impresto si distribuisce colle cedole.

(seal: COMITATO NAZIONALE ITALIANO)

(seal: REPUBBLICA ROMANA 9 FEBBRAJO 1849)

LONDON AGENT, JAMES STANSFELD, 2, SYDNEY PLACE, BROMPTON.

NOTE OF ITALIAN NATIONAL COMMITTEE.

of this step, and he must have withdrawn his name almost at once, for in 1864, when he was badgered by Sir H. Tracy for having been "the banker of the conspirators," he replied, "I have taken the opinion of a very old friend of mine, a most eminent member of the legal profession, and acting upon that opinion . . . I requested . . . that my name should be withdrawn from those notes. These are the simple facts."

In September, 1850, there appeared the first proclamation of the Italian National Committee. It raised a hornets' nest about the ears of the signers, among whom were Saliceti, Sirtori, and Agostini. The Committee, intended to be a rallying point for all patriots, had for its central idea unification, to be attained by means of war and a Constituent Assembly. But the Lombard "fusionists" and the Piedmontese "municipalists" would not hear of any Constituent Assembly. The republican "puritans" repudiated Piedmontesism ; Montanelli objected because "a door was left open for the House of Savoy"; Cernuschi reacted because he was certain that republican Paris would triumph over reactionary Rome, and declared it high time "to republicanise Mazzini" ; Ferrari wrote a pamphlet to demonstrate that Italian Unity was a mere Utopia, and that a federal republic alone could suit Italy—and then solely by the aid of republican France ; Carlo Cattaneo, who had approved of the authority delegated by the sixty deputies, and who had himself prepared the plan of the republican loan, objected to the proclamation because it called on Piedmont to prepare for the renewal of war against Austria. The fact was that almost all the Italian exiles congregated in Paris counted on a fresh revolution, which, through the return to power of the republican party, would lend a hand to Italy by recalling the French troops from Rome, and thus stem the tide of reaction in Europe.

In Italy itself, on the other hand, the National Committee was looked up to with hope and confidence. "The loan notes passed like current coin among patriots in Mantua," wrote a man who, though escaping the gallows, spent many years in an Austrian dungeon after his companions had been shot.

At this period Mazzini, with Ledru-Rollin and Arnold Ruge, also set on foot the "European Democratic Committee," and to this committee Kossuth—still confined in honourable captivity at Katahia—adhered through Adriano Lemmi, the head of a powerful commercial firm in Constantinople. Lemmi had spent large sums during the existence of the Roman Republic for the transport of arms, and for Manara and his "Bersaglieri Lombardi," and had remained in the city throughout the siege.

Mazzini stayed only three months in England. He was shocked and surprised to note the change that had supervened in public opinion—the torpor, the indifference exhibited towards European affairs. He had to return to his hiding-place in Switzerland, using the utmost precaution, for France, Piedmont, and Austria had again jointly demanded his expulsion. Meanwhile, Emilie Hawkes, and Matilda Biggs with her children, went to winter in Genoa, and were in daily communication with the Signora Mazzini, who repaid their enthusiasm for her son with unremitting kindness and solicitude. While they were there it fell to Mazzini to communicate to them, and to the parents in England, the sad intelligence that Eliza Bardon, who in September had returned from Muswell Hill to her husband in France, had died, giving birth to a child which only survived a few hours.

To the sisters in Genoa he wrote : "Eliza is lost to us. It is strange that it is from me that you are to receive the sad news, but I would have claimed the mournful task had I been with you. . . . I have lost two sisters during my exile, and I know that such a loss puts into one's life a shadow never to be removed, a blank never to be filled. I cast my arms and my soul around you and ask you to be strong for your mother's and Caroline's and my own sake. I could say, for Eliza's sake, for I do not believe in such a thing as death. It is for me the cradle of a new existence." On November 29, 1850, he wrote to

ADRIANO LEMMI.

To face p. 222.]

MAZZINI'S FAITH IN IMMORTALITY

Mrs. Ashurst : ". . . draw nearer all of you who remain ; love each other more dearly ; see, help, advise one another more than ever ; commune with her who has loved and loves you all by communing more intimately with one another ; and remember, for God's sake, that there is no such thing as death for all that is best in us ; that what people call death is only a transformation and a step onward in life. . . . And this faith of mine which I would gladly give all my actual life for feeling able to infuse into you all . . . and my loving you all more dearly than before—that is all the consolation I can give to you, dearest friends."

XV

EUROPEAN POLITICS

1850–1852

Lord Palmerston's courageous policy—The Porte and the Hungarian and Polish Exiles—Palmerston's action—Kossuth, Mazzini, and Ledru-Rollin—" The judicious Bottle-holder "—Lord Stanley's attack on Palmerston—Death of Sir Robert Peel—General Haynau and Barclay's draymen—" The Friends of Italy "—Louis Napoleon's Coup d'État—Palmerston's dismissal.

WE must now return to Lord Palmerston's courageous foreign policy. He stood alone in Europe, defying Austria and Russia, this time determined even to follow up, if necessary, words by deeds. The British ambassador in Vienna, Lord Ponsonby, must have had a hard time of it in obeying instructions. It is worth while to give the gist of one of Palmerston's typical letters. On September 9, 1849, he wrote from Penshanger : " My dear Ponsonby—The Austrians are really the greatest brutes that ever called themselves by the undeserved name of civilised men. Their atrocities in Galicia, in Italy, in Hungary, in Transylvania are only to be equalled by the proceedings of the negro races in Africa and Haiti. Their last exploit of flogging forty odd people, including two women, at Milan, is really a too blackguardly and disgusting proceeding. As to working upon their feelings of generosity and gentlemanliness, that is out of the question. But I do hope that *you* will not fail constantly to bear in mind the country and the Government you represent, and that you will maintain the dignity and honour of England by expressing *openly and decidedly* the disgust which such proceedings excite in the public mind of this country; and that you will not allow the Austrians to imagine that the public opinion of England is to be gathered from articles put in the *Times* by Austrian agents in London, nor from the purchased support of the *Chronicle*, nor from the servile language of the Tory lords and ladies in London, nor from the courtly notions of royal dukes and duchesses. I have no great opinion of Schwartzenberg's statesmanlike qualities unless he is very much altered from what he was when I knew him; but at least he has lived in England and must know something of English feelings and ideas, and he must be capable of understanding the kind of injury which all their barbarities must do to the character of Austria in public opinion here; and I think that in spite of his great reliance upon and fondness for Russia, he must see that the good opinion of England is of some value to Austria, if for nothing else, at least to act as a check upon the ill-will towards Austria which he supposes, or affects to suppose, is the great actuating motive of the revolutionary firebrand who now presides at the Foreign Office in Downing Street. You might surely find an opportunity of drawing Schwartzenberg's attention to these matters, which may be made intelligible to him, and which a British ambassador has the right to submit to his consideration. There is another view of the matter which Schwartzenberg, with his personal hatred of the Italians, would not choose to comprehend, but which nevertheless is well deserving of attention, and that is the obvious tendency of these barbarous proceedings to perpetuate in the minds of the Italians indelible hatred of Austria, and as the Austrian Government cannot hope to govern Italy always by the sword, such inextinguishable hatred is not an evil to be altogether despised. The rulers of Austria (I call them not statesmen or stateswomen) have now brought their country to this strange condition, that the Emperor holds his various territories at the goodwill and pleasure of three external Powers. He holds Italy just as long as, and no longer than, France chooses to let him have it. The first quarrel between Austria and France, the latter will drive the Austrians out of Lombardy and Venetia. He holds Hungary and Galicia just as long as, and no longer than, Russia chooses to let him have them. He holds his German provinces by a tenure dependent, in a great degree, upon feelings and opinions which it will be very difficult for him and his ministers either to combine with or to stand against. The remedy against these various dangers which are rapidly undermining the Austrian Empire would be generous conciliation, but instead of that, the Austrian Government know no method of administration but what consists of flogging, imprisoning, and shooting. The Austrians know of no argument but Force."

Animated by such sentiments and motives, it was natural that Lord Palmerston should oppose with the utmost energy the demands made by Russia and Austria that the Sublime Porte should deliver up the Hungarian and Polish refugees in Turkey, and, above all, Kossuth and Zamoyski. After the staunch refusal of the Sultan, and the suspension of all diplomatic intercourse between the two Imperial Powers, Lord Palmerston, notwithstanding the fierce opposition of the Tories, was upheld by his colleagues, and the British fleet was ordered to proceed higher up towards the Dardanelles. Upon this, Russia and Austria declared that England had infringed the Act of July 9, 1841, which forbade foreign warships to enter the Dardanelles; but Palmerston pointed out that this Act only applied to times of peace, and that the Austrian and Russian Governments had declared it would be tantamount to a declaration of war if the Sultan allowed a single refugee to escape. And in a private letter to Ponsonby, Palmerston said, "Hence it behoves us to lose no time in preparing to defend Turkey against the two Imperial and imperious bullies." Fortunately, France, though reluctant, sustained England, and sent a fleet to Turkey; the Imperial " bullies " were baffled, and after some further laborious negotiations Palmerston, now powerfully backed by English public opinion, obtained the liberation of the refugees who had been in honourable detention in Turkey, and by thus sturdily asserting the noble policy of the Liberals earned the gratitude of all Hungarian and Polish patriots. Kossuth, arriving at Marseilles, pronounced an out-and-out republican speech, and when he reached London, previous to his departure for the United States, he, Mazzini and Ledru-Rollin came to a complete understanding, and were for a time regarded as the Triumvirs of the European republican party.

Great indignation presently prevailed in the Tory and "Philistine" circles over Lord Palmerston's reception of a deputation from Islington which went to the Foreign Office to congratulate him on his long perseverance and complete success, and over his observation, that to gain the day much generalship and judgment had been required, and "a good deal of judicious bottle-holding was obliged to be brought into play." *Punch* represented "Plucky Pam" as "The Judicious Bottle-Holder" of the prize-ring, with a sprig of myrtle in his mouth.

The French and British Governments had disagreed rather sharply about the affairs of Greece, and the fashion in which Lord Palmerston had sustained the claims of a Gibraltar Jew, Don Pacifico, living in Athens. This caused the French ambassador, Drouhyn de Lhuis, to be recalled in May, 1850. Lord Stanley fiercely attacked the Foreign Secretary, but in the Commons Mr. Roebuck's resolution, forcibly endorsing the whole of the Government's foreign policy, was passed by a majority of forty-six votes after a debate lasting five days. During this debate, and after Palmerston had defended all his actions, Sir Robert Peel, though voting against the Cabinet, exclaimed, referring to the Foreign Secretary, "It has made us all proud of him!" The sitting was the last in which Sir Robert Peel took part, for on the 2nd of June he was thrown from his horse and died from the consequences. It was an immense loss to England and the cause of peaceful progress, and Sir Robert was profoundly mourned by friend and foe alike.

About this time the Austrian general Haynau, notorious

all over Europe as the "woman beater" and "the butcher," because of his atrocious cruelties in Hungary, as well as in Brescia and other Italian cities, visited London. Being recognised by the draymen of Barclay's brewery, he was mobbed and so severely drubbed that he had to fly for his life, till rescued by the police, who, to safeguard him, locked him up in a cell at the police-station [September, 1850]. Of course, Lord Palmerston diplomatically deplored the untoward incident, but the old Adam comes out in a letter to Lord Grey, in which he says "that the draymen were wrong in the particular course they adopted, as they ought to have tossed him in a blanket, rolled him in the kennel, and then sent him home in a cab, paying the fare to the hotel."

Gradually other Englishmen began to admit the impossibility of the Italians remaining under the infamous governments imposed upon them, and Mr. Gladstone's famous letters on the Neapolitan Government, which he qualified as "the negation of God" and as "infernal," created a great sensation. Papal aggression also began to awaken remorse in the hearts of the Protestants, who had done nothing towards assisting the Italians to destroy that temporal power which was now striving to gain a renewed footing in England.

Around Mazzini, who had returned to England in 1851 (longer residence in Switzerland having been rendered impossible), there gathered an ever-increasing number of sympathisers. A society of "The Friends of Italy" became founded, and in the list of the 120 members of its council we find, besides all his old adherents, several clergymen, and such names as G. H. Lewes, Macready, Edward Miall, Professors Newman and Nichol, Lord D. C. Stuart, D. Lonsdale of Carlisle, Arthur Trevelyan, W. Scholefield, Sir John Fife of Newcastle, &c. Peter Taylor undertook the treasurership, and David Masson was the first secretary. The members pledged themselves "by public meetings, lectures, and the press, and especially by affording opportunities to the most competent authorities for the publication of works on the History of the Italian National Movement : To promote a correct appreciation of the Italian Question in this country ; to use every available constitutional means of furthering the cause of Italian National Independence in Parliament ; and generally to aid, in this country, the cause of Independence, and of political and religious liberty, of the Italian people."

The Society published many important papers, one of the principal being a complete history of the Roman Republic, with a documentary refutation of the charge of terrorism in Rome. They also published an account of the revolution in Sicily, which brought home to the Britons a sense of their shortcomings towards that unfortunate island, a feeling strengthened by the insolence of the King of Naples, to whom Lord Palmerston forwarded the information that " he had sent a copy of Mr. Gladstone's letter to all his diplomatic agents in Europe."

It seems almost inexplicable that so keen-sighted a statesman as Lord Palmerston should have been bamboozled by so treacherous an adventurer as Louis Napoleon, and inveigled into countenancing the *coup d'état* and its massacres. The only explanation is that Palmerston profoundly disliked and distrusted both the Bourbons and Orleanists, whom he knew to be industriously plotting and scheming for a restoration; and being aware that the internal condition of France was most unsatisfactory, and that no party was strong enough to insure a stable monarchy or a stable republic, it seemed to him that the rule of a Bonaparte afforded the only possible bulwark against anarchy and civil war. He took Lord Normanby to task for consorting exclusively with the partisans of Orleanism, and for being " systematically hostile " to the President. So when news came that in the early morning of December 2, 1851, Changarnier, Tocqueville, Thiers, Odillon Barrot, and other " Burgraves,"[1] had been suddenly arrested while engaged in

[1] " Burgraves," name ironically given by the Parisians to the chiefs of the Liberal *doctrinaires*, from the tragedy of Victor Hugo, which appeared at that moment.

a secret council, Palmerston concluded that these men had meant to strike a sudden blow, and that the President had simply "knocked them down first." He reproved Normanby for the character of his despatches, which gave little or no information, though hostile to Napoleon, one of them having consisted of a dissertation about Kossuth "which would have made a good article for the *Times* a fortnight ago." Though Palmerston's official instructions were all that they should have been, he was, perhaps, less circumspect in private conversation, and it transpired that in an interview with Count Walewski, the French ambassador, who had informed him of what was going on in Paris, he expressed approval of what the President had done.

So it appears to have been destined that the *coup d'état* in Paris, which wounded France to the heart with the same sword that she had sharpened for the murder of the Roman Republic, was also to cut short the career as Foreign Minister of one of England's sincerest champions of liberty and of nationality. The Queen, her private "Prime Minister," Prince Albert, and his confidential adviser, Baron Stockmar, were decidedly adverse to Palmerston's policy, so when despatches from Paris, reporting the confidential words of the Foreign Secretary, were laid before her Majesty, she was exceeding wroth. Lord John Russell, who had previously expressed his opinion about French affairs quite as freely as Palmerston, was forced to call the latter to account. Palmerston, while affirming that Walewsky had given a high colouring to the remarks he had uttered in their private conversation, frankly confessed that in the actual condition of affairs in France "he was not surprised at the President's speedy action, though there can be but one feeling as to the wanton destruction of life in Paris."

The extent of the December massacres has never yet been ascertained, though it seems as if the numbers given by the much abused Kinglake come nearest to a truthful estimate. But as by degrees the truth became partially known in England, the abhorrence inspired by such measures caused the nation to ratify the action of the Premier in asking her

Majesty to appoint a successor to Lord Palmerston. To this the Queen graciously consented, doubtless with cordial gratitude to Lord John Russell, but the Premier gave the odd trick to "Pam," by offering him the Viceroyalty of Ireland, which was at once declined with the remark that "this very offer refutes the charge of violation of judgment and decorum, as for the due performance of the duties of Lord Lieutenant of Ireland, judgment and decorum cannot well be dispensed with."

Great was the joy and triumph in the realms of absolutism; Schwartzenberg gave a ball to celebrate "the victory of Austrian policy" and the fall of "the Devil's son"; equal was the grief and consternation of the Liberals everywhere, but especially in Italy and Spain. And Lord Howden at once sent in his resignation as ambassador in Madrid, "feeling that Lord Palmerston's dismissal was a direct concession to the reactionary spirit which is riding roughshod over the world at present."

XVI

SORROW AND GRIEF

1852–1854

Death and the galleys—Mazzini and the Socialists—Georges Sand stands by the Socialists—Mazzini's last letter to his mother—Her sudden death—Emilie Ashurst Hawkes breaks the news—Signora Mazzini's wise legacies.

AT the close of 1851, and throughout 1852 and 1853, the Italians subject to Austria openly defied her. Though during the first six months of 1851 exactly 2,552 condemnations to death or to perpetual hard labour had been passed for political offences, besides 115 sentences pronounced by the military court-martial in Este, conspiracy continued rife in Lombardy. At Mantua sixteen patriots were summarily shot for posting up revolutionary proclamations issued by a committee of eighteen who called upon their fellow-townsmen to "wipe out the shame of Mantua in 1848." This conspiracy came as near to success as any conspiracy ever did in Italy until the triumph of Palermo in 1860; but, betrayed by a tortured suspect who was subjected for three consecutive days to the lash, five of the flower of the patriots perished on the scaffold (December 7, 1852). Their names were Don Enrico Tazzoli, a saintly priest, Dr. Carlo Poma, a celebrated physician, Tito Speri, Guido Montanara, and Grazioli, now venerated in Italy as "the Martyrs of Belfiore."

Mazzini, horrified by the massacres of December in Paris, was profoundly surprised at the stolid indifference of

1852] DIVISIONS AMONG FRENCH LIBERALS

France. He could not explain the success of Louis Napoleon, who "has no party; the National Guard, the middle classes, the people, part of the army are against him, and yet the idea of resistance is confined to a small minority"; so he writes to his mother on December 10th. He finds that "all moral sense is dead in France," and it is the "furious and useless propaganda of the Socialists that, frightening the *bourgeois*, has produced this lethargy." In this same letter he goes on to say that "Louis Blanc, Proudhon, Courbet and a hundred other idiots (*stolidi*) who believe themselves the saviours of the world, have filled the heads of the people with wild hopes of fairy-land (*paesi di cuccagna*), and until the people see the means of realising these dreams, they will not stir." As usual, this letter closes with a reflection about the position of Italy. He says: "For us nothing is changed, and the Italians might understand this and redouble their activity, and prepare to profit by any opportunity that presents itself—to create one, if none offers, *per Dio!*"

Mazzini was perfectly right in considering that the dissensions of the Socialist leaders among themselves, and the opposition to their doctrines by the radical Republicans, divided the French Liberal camp into two warring factions, but he forgot that the great mass in the provinces knew little or nothing of these theories. The chief mover of public opinion was the gaunt misery which reigned throughout the land, the stagnation of commerce and industry, the desertion of a large number of wealthy foreigners, Russian, English, and American, and the consequences of the gigantic system of corruption, bribery, and mad speculation which had fallen to pieces with the throne of Louis Philippe. A one-man rule was therefore believed by many to offer a chance of safety from constantly recurring revolution; and, again, with the people, the name of Napoleon stood as a synonym for "Glory," and this is the *ne plus ultra* of a Frenchman, even when starving and in rags. The great Catholic majority soon became aware that a restoration of either the Bourbons or the Orleans was entirely out of the question, and so they preferred the despotism of a man who, after all, by his sole will maintained the Pope on his temporal throne. The sudden and immense rise in French consols and other investments, immediately after the *coup d'état* proved that "Property" and that wealthy classes approved of the crime; hence it was scarcely fair to make socialism the scapegoat for the multitudinous sins of France.

Mazzini set forth his opinions forcibly and calmly in his writings on "The Systems of Democracy," commenced in 1847 in the *People's Journal*, and terminated in 1849. In 1851 there appeared a new paper, entitled *Le Proscrit*, written in French and co-edited by Mazzini and Ledru-Rollin: it contained a terrible indictment of socialistic teaching from Mazzini's pen. This formidable "J'accuse," assailing the Socialists in their hour of exile and defeat, excited their wrath and indignation, as it was an attack upon doctrines which for some—for Louis Blanc assuredly—were sacred truths for which they lived and were willing to die. Many years later, when he was really striving to find a common standpoint from which all the forces of democracy might unite and fight the common foe, Blanc wrote: "Mazzini made upon the Socialists, their ideas and influence . . . the most violent attack ever made. Mazzini has been unjust to the Socialists; they will not now descend to be unjust to him. By devoting all his life to the independence of republican Rome, by serving the sacred cause of Italy with indomitable courage . . . he has conquered a title which neither his prejudices nor his errors can obliterate; he may therefore, as far as the independence of Italy is concerned, count entirely upon our hearty support."

But in the first moment after the publication of Mazzini's virulent accusation it was impossible to expect this generosity of sentiment from men smarting under the bitter sense of defeat, and Louis Blanc, Courbet, and others—among whom it is not easy to explain the presence of Pierre Leroux—bitterly refuted the accusation in a collective answer. This attack was thoroughly personal; Mazzini's conduct in Milan and Rome was severely criticised, and himself taken to task for aiming at dictatorship, *tout bonnement* like Louis Napoleon. Mazzini deeply resented this personal accusation—but had his own been impersonal?

He sent his letters and articles to Georges Sand, almost as if he expected that she would act as umpire in the quarrel. He, however, counted without his host, for Georges Sand resented the articles of Ledru-Rollin in *Le Proscrit*, and besides being a disciple of Louis Blanc, she knew of the writer's inimical feelings for the latter. In her answers, therefore, to Mazzini she staunchly denied that Louis Blanc's doctrines were materialistic; at any rate she declared him to be profoundly convinced of their truth and justice, and asserted that though she might admire Ledru-Rollin as a man, she certainly did not approve of him as a politician or a statesman. Accordingly she declined to write for *Le Proscrit*, or to induce others to contribute to it.

Some later letters of Mazzini, of which we have no trace, seem to have irritated Georges Sand afresh. In one of her replies she explains her reasons, and though rendering absolute justice to the purity and disinterestedness of Mazzini's motives and actions, " of which one cannot doubt, save in a moment of delirium," she contends that "it is a fault, a grave fault, to provoke such an access of delirium in a fellow-man." Mazzini must understand that what has been written in answer to his own intolerant attack is "an outburst of bleeding patriotism," that "he has committed the sin of pride," and that as another Pope he has cried, " There are no saints outside my Church." She goes on to say that for some time she has seen ideas developing in him, which may be necessary to Italy (and in this respect she does not think herself a competent judge), but in defeat he ought to have been more circumspect and scrupulous, as he was speaking not to a nation, but to a party vanquished " under circumstances which cannot be compared to Italy under the yoke of the foreigner "; and she adds : " What you would do as the Pope of Roman

THE BIRTH OF MODERN ITALY

Liberty has no sense for French ears stunned and deafened by the cannon of civil war." Then she writes of the internal conditions of her country and explains very lucidly why and how it has come to pass that Louis Napoleon has not only been able to assume absolute power, but that the nation continues to sustain him by its votes; for he has guaranteed a sort of universal suffrage, delightful " to the ignorance of the workman and the peasant, who in their *bêtise*, in their *naïveté*, imagine it is they who have created an emperor." The people have not voted "under the influence of fear and calumnies," as Mazzini has been told, for they would in any case have voted for Napoleon. At the close of this letter she accuses Mazzini of knowing little or nothing about France, "not as much as he knows about China," and says, "You have sown the wind and will reap the whirlwind."

For the strictures on himself Mazzini cared very little, but from Georges Sand's last letter to him (May 23, 1853) it may be argued that he reproached her for withdrawing from political life, for having resigned herself to become the artist pure and simple, as she tells him that " un véritable artiste est aussi utile que le prêtre et le guerrier," and protests that she is unchanged for him and for everything. But alas! henceforth there was between them, now and then,

> ". . . a glimmer of twilight,
> But never glad, confident morning again!"

The break between the Republicans and Socialists, though not as damaging as in France, did not advance the cause of democracy in Italy.

For the New Year's Day of 1852 Mazzini writes hopelessly to his mother, speaking of reaction triumphant, of the military despotism in France, and of the cowardly desire of peace in England which had led to the dismissal of Lord Palmerston, who was hated, and with good reason, by the despots. He told her of the letters he had received from the prisoners in Rome, condemned to ten and fifteen years in irons—letters which contain "words of love and enthusiasm for me that make me weep." Later, on March 30th, he told her of a grand meeting of the "Friends of Italy" in London, of a speech which he had been compelled to deliver, and of an article of his about to appear in the *Westminster Review*. In England, his separation from the Socialists had done him anything but harm with the general public, though his rupture with Louis Blanc had been extremely painful to some of his friends, and above all to the Stansfelds, who were sincerely attached to Blanc and received him as an honoured guest. He referred to his article on the Socialists in the *Italia del Popolo*, "which has raised another great tempest." Louis Blanc, Leroux, Courbet, and three or four others, again replied in a letter full of acrid personalities, and "repeating the stupid accusation that Mazzini wanted to become the Cæsar of democracy, comparing him to Louis Napoleon." Ledru-Rollin answered this attack, without consulting him, and claimed that the initiative for all reforms must rest with France. "But in the work against the common enemy," Mazzini goes on to say, "Ledru is entirely in accord with me, and you must let our friends know this, as they might imagine from this, his last article, that our political alliance is dissolved."

Again, in another letter, begun on July 30th and finished on August 2nd, Mazzini tells his mother "not to worry about his war with the Socialists," as he "foresaw and almost desired it." Alluding to Louis Napoleon, he says · "The Prince is making for Empire; then will come the Tarpeian rock, a parody of the Emperor who died at St. Helena." In a postscript he adds: "Mother mine, I have your lines of the 21st of July. I reply briefly, as your letter too is short. The storm will soon pass over. The essential is that we are both well in health, and that we love each other. I will write to Nina (Isabella Zerbini) as soon as I have time. Take care of yourself, mother, and love the son who loves you."

This letter reached Genoa on August 8th, and while, on her

THE BIRTH OF MODERN ITALY

return from Mass, his mother was reading it to her friend "Nina," she was seized with dizziness. She cried out twice "Mio figgieu! . . . Mio figgieu!" (in Genoese patois "My son!") and her sight and consciousness both suddenly failed. A doctor was summoned at once, who bled her, but in vain. Her daughter and her friends, Napoleone Ferrari, Cosenza, and Alberto Mario, came to the house and never left her for a moment. Her daughter was in despair, because la Signora Mazzini could neither confess nor receive the Sacrament. On this occasion the priests did their best to obtain possession of her son's letters, but Napoleone Ferrari, the executor of her will, had already secured them.

The particulars which follow concerning the general grief of Genoa and the funeral of the mother of the greatest of its citizens were given me by Alberto Mario, who was one of "Scia Maria's"[1] Benjamins. The English and American steamers in the harbour set their flags at half-mast. Some of the American officers joined the funeral procession, and on being thanked for their gracious act by the president of the Genoese Working-men's Association, replied by an admirable and sympathetic letter dated August 13, 1852, signed by Richard Pick, John Wilmer, John Davis, James Nickerson, Henry Purchase, and Thomas Patterson, which is now sacredly treasured by the same association. The concourse of the population at the funeral was truly enormous: all the associations were represented, and the coffin, carried by forty-two relays of eight working men, was covered with flowers. Even the *Corriere Mercantile*, which had waged furious war against Mazzini, even the clerical paper *Il Cattolico*, rendered homage to the feelings of the citizens of Genoa, and it was reserved for the Turinese *Opinione* alone to insult the memory of the dead woman by stigmatising her as a bigot and a nullity, thus commencing that ignominious warfare, the weapons of which were falsehood and calumny, and which descended later even to forgery.

An intimate friend of Mrs. Hawkes and Mrs. Biggs sent the news to England, to be communicated to the son.

---

[1] "Scia" is the Genoese dialect word for signora (pronounced *shah*).

EMILIE, YOUNGEST DAUGHTER OF W. H.
ASHURST, MARRIED TO SIDNEY HAWKES,
AFTERWARDS TO CARLO VENTURI

1852] MAZZINI'S GREAT BEREAVEMENT

Homage or insult were alike powerless to alleviate or augment the agony inflicted upon him by the stunning, unexpected blow. It fell to Emilie Ashurst Hawkes to be the bearer of the dread tidings, which seemed at first to petrify Mazzini. Mrs. Carlyle went at once to his tiny lodgings, but he could not see her. The following note addressed to Caroline Stansfeld seems intended for the entire family : " I am strong, and I have nerved myself to this blow these last six months. Do not distress yourselves too much. My mother is too much a sacred thing for me not to be strong. Do not come. I want to be alone for one day. But write, each, one word of blessing ; it will do me good. And you, Emilie, write what particulars you have. God bless you ! Your Joseph." The next day, Sunday, he wrote : " I trust you all go to Muswell Hill. One day lost for your mother would be a sin. But if she is ill, and you think your news can do her harm, do not say the whole. . . . The blow is hard to bear, now especially that I had a hope to repay, within the year, her long years of loneliness with a moment of joy. Now, even if I reach that moment, I shall be an exile in my own land. Perhaps it is better so. Who knows what can happen ? I feel as if they had taken from me some essential part of myself ; but I am calm and firm. She has not lost me ; and I deeply believe that I have not entirely lost her and her holy influence. Tell James (Stansfeld) that I know all that he feels. Your notes have done me good, and I feel your presence and love around me."

Later, on August 28th, he writes to Mathilda Biggs : " I am sadly well. My heart is full of grateful love for you and for all the members of your family—I may call it mine. I wish that I could do you all   half the good that you have done to me. I am at work, as before, though only from a sense of duty."

When Mazzini had time and courage to look into his mother's affairs he found that about 52,000 lire (about £2,080) would come into his hands at once, and that, with loving care, she had secured two annuities to her son, bringing in about 4,000 lire (£180) per annum. She had made the trustees, Ferrari and Bettini, swear never to allow him " to turn them into a sum down," knowing well what would have been the fate of the capital. The two thousand pounds were soon lost in the vortex of his work, and he often led the poor trustees an awful life, trying to wring from them the principal of the annuities. Of the annual income of £180, he gave half to his old housekeeper Susanna until her sons should be able to support her, and even of the £80 remaining, little enough went towards his own personal expenses.

XVII

THE RISE OF THE HOUSE OF SAVOY

1853

Abortive insurrectionary attempt in Milan, February 6, 1853—Kossuth's Manifesto—Monarchical influence ascendant—Cavour becomes Premier—His hostility to the Mazzinian party—Garibaldi in England—The Crimean War—Piedmont a party to the peace negotiations—Garibaldi challenges Rosselli—A duel averted—Miss White accompanies Garibaldi's betrothed to Italy and Sardinia.

ON February 6, 1853, the revolt which the Milanese had prepared so carefully broke out and failed completely. Mazzini could not have prevented it if he had tried, so he assisted it with advice and money. Aurelio Saffi, Picozzi, and Piolti were the recognised leaders. It was on this occasion that the extraordinary incident of Kossuth's manifesto to the Hungarian soldiers of the Austrian army—urging them not to fire on the Italian patriots—occurred, and this affair has never yet been clearly explained. The original of the manifesto was undoubtedly given by Kossuth to a certain individual who, in America, had acted as his private secretary, and had never been cancelled. If the revolution in Milan had been successful, there is also no doubt that Kossuth would have admitted the authorship; but it failed, and first Captain Mayne Reid, then Kossuth in person, repudiated it. In the general *débacle* ensuing, it was perhaps considered best that Kossuth's fame should remain undimmed by failure, but for Mazzini that denial added one more feather to the burden of calumny and reproach heaped on his shoulders.

Alluding to the tempest which broke over his head after this insurrectionary attempt, Mazzini himself says:[1] ". . . When Louis Kossuth was about to make a journey of indefinite duration through the United States of America, it was agreed upon between us that he should sign and leave with me a proclamation to the Hungarian regiments serving in Italy, calling upon them to support any national movement that might take place there, and that I should sign and give to him a proclamation to the Italian regiments serving in Hungary for the same purpose. And we did this . . . each of us, therefore, was to have full authority to affix a date to the proclamation in his hands, and to make use of it when he should think fit. I availed myself of the authority thus given. . . . The first news of the insurrection that reached London brought no details, and Kossuth was so roused that he applied to my friend Stansfeld for pecuniary aid in order to join me, which was given. But when the news of our defeat arrived, next day, Kossuth . . . hastened to declare through the English press that the proclamation to the Hungarians was purely and simply an invention of my own. . . . I wrote to the *Daily News* simply saying that the original proclamation was still in my hands and might be seen by any one desirous of doing so. This was enough for the English public. . . . When I returned to London . . . he (Kossuth) came to me, embraced me with the air of one deeply moved, and uttered not a syllable with regard to the proclamation. The alliance between us—unstable as it was—might yet prove useful to our cause; I shrugged my shoulders and held my peace."

Mazzini's grief was not alone for the failure itself, for the sixteen noble patriots executed by Radetzky in Milan, for the hundreds and thousands condemned to prison in the fortresses and dungeons of Austria; it was also for the discredit into which the republican party of action had fallen

[1] From the "Scritti Editi ed Inediti di Gius. Mazzini," vol. viii. p. 229.

CAMILLO CAVOUR.

from the zenith of its glory in Rome and Venice. This date, February 6, 1853, marks the decline of the republican and the rise of the monarchical star.

The rise of monarchical ascendancy in Italian affairs had, however, in reality begun somewhat sooner. For many months after the disaster of Novara, Piedmont was in a state of agitation bordering upon revolt. The liberals demanded a renewal of the war, while the absolutists and clericals clamoured for the abolition of the Constitution (Statuto), and for alliance with Austria. D'Azeglio at the helm, with the help of England, steered carefully and wisely between the rocks, and King Victor Emmanuel, by his famous proclamation of Moncalieri, warned the electors that if they did not send deputies to the new Parliament willing to ratify the treaty of peace with Austria, measures would have to be taken to effect that necessary sacrifice without them. The nation understood; the Parliament ratified the treaty, and thus the *tricolore* and the "Statuto" were saved. Many Lombard, Venetian, and other Italian refugees in Piedmont became naturalised; the Siccardi law, abolishing the "Foro Ecclesiastico," or special tribunals for the clergy, and thus emancipating Piedmont from Rome, was passed, notwithstanding the violent opposition of the clericals. This gave Cavour the first opportunity, in his memorable speech of March, 1850, to ventilate his famous theory of "a free Church in a free State." Then, when the Sovereigns of Austria and Prussia jointly advised the King of Piedmont to "set his house in order" and harmonise his system of government with that of the other States of Italy, covertly hinting at reprisals if he neglected their advice, he politely answered, requesting them to mind their own business, as D'Azeglio's long despatch to the Piedmontese ministers in London and Paris clearly proves.

It was evident that neither the young King Victor Emmanuel nor the Tory Government in England—whose advent had been hailed by Austria with exultation—was going to be cajoled into joining a new "Holy Alliance." When "Bully Buol," the Austrian ambassador in London,

THE BIRTH OF MODERN ITALY

presented notes from Rome and Modena demanding the extradition of their refugees by England, Lord Granville "threw them after him as he left the room"; and Lord Malmesbury, to whom the same Buol behaved in a coarse and insolent manner, also refused to receive the said notes, telling the ambassador that "English ministers were not accustomed to his 'style.'"

In November, 1852, Cavour, who with extraordinary ability had successively held the portfolios, first of Agriculture and Commerce, then of Finance, was, by the advice of D'Azeglio, called to the premiership, although King Victor had always resented his "masterfulness," and had told D'Azeglio, in his usual bluff language, that "the fellow would kick them all to the devil." By his famous *ripudio* (*i.e.*, abandonment of his old alliance with the Right) and his *connubio* (union) with Rattazzi and the Left Centre, Cavour gave proof of his intention of marching with the times. But after February 6, 1853, he began his life-long policy of hostility towards the republican, and especially the Mazzinian party. The exiles suspected of complicity in the Milanese plot were relegated to the island of Sardinia; the republican papers were pursued implacably, and although the juries almost always absolved the incriminated editors, the papers themselves were ruined, with the one exception of the *Italia del Popolo*, which was saved by the perseverance of its editor Savi and of its chief writers, Maurizio Quadrio and Alberto Mario.[1] Saffi, who had barely escaped capture by the Austrians in Romagna, where he had attempted to renew the revolution, and Francesco Crispi, were expelled and forced to seek refuge in England and Paris.

But Cavour, though showing his determination to keep

---

[1] The *Italia del Popolo* was sequestrated fifty times between February and September, and four of its editors were imprisoned. Once when a journalist, who had suffered two months' *preventive* imprisonment, had been acquitted, the advocate for the crown consoled himself by the reflection, angrily expressed in the court, that, anyway, "God Himself could not undo" those two months' incarceration.—E. F. R.

down the revolutionists, was in no way working in the interests of Austria, and when Radetzky, amazed and infuriated by the discovery of vast ramifications of rebellion, despite death-sentences, imprisonments, and court-martials, issued an ordinance for the sequestration even of the properties of those Lombards who had been naturalised Piedmontese, he firmly protested, and, the Austrian Government remaining obdurate, he broke off all diplomatic relations with Vienna. But on the other hand Cavour insisted, with the Swiss authorities, on the expulsion from the Confederation of all exiles. So England became once more the refuge of hundreds of homeless, hunted patriots. Their poverty was appalling, and many must have perished from sheer starvation had it not been for the unexampled generosity of the "Friends of Italy" and of a very few well-to-do Italians. Mazzini, still in hiding in Switzerland, after spending the last sous of the capital inherited from his mother, wrote to Saffi to stir up the wealthy Italians to a sense of their duty, but told him "to ask nothing more of our friends (the Ashursts, Stansfelds, Shaens, Taylors, Crawfords, &c.), as they have done, and are doing, more than their own circumstances justify . . our rich and selfish merchants and bankers ought to blush . . . seeing their own poor countrymen dependent on the generosity of Englishmen."

In the following year, Garibaldi, "Europe's rejected guest," returned from his four years' wanderings, during which he had even worked for his living in a tallow-chandler's store, and had occasionally taken charge of vessels bound for China. In March, 1854, he arrived in Newcastle in command of the *Commonwealth*, a ship belonging to a wealthy Italian merchant of Boston. The death of his old mother during his absence made his return to Nice an absolute necessity, as his orphaned children had no one to care for them. The only difficulty in the way was to know if the Piedmontese Government would allow him to re-enter and sojourn in the country.

"Cannie Newcastle" gave Garibaldi one of her special welcomes. Joseph Cowen, the champion of every forlorn hope, presented him, on behalf of the citizens, with a splendid telescope and a gold-hilted sword, inscribed : " To General Garibaldi, by the People of Tyneside, friends of European Freedom." On board the *Commonwealth*, Julian Harney proposed the toast of " Mazzini, the illustrious compatriot of Garibaldi," which was drunk with great enthusiasm. Garibaldi, after handing over the command of his ship to an American skipper, went by rail to London, where he remained some time, during which he was in frequent contact with Mazzini. On this occasion he made the acquaintance of an English lady of considerable fortune, who, falling in love with him " at first sight," was for the next two years formally engaged to him, and it would indeed have been fortunate for him and his children if his scruples, when he ascertained the extent of her fortune and the disdainful attitude assumed by her eldest son, had not decided him to give her back her freedom and retain his own.

According to his habit of the last four years, he refused all demonstrations in London, but Mazzini introduced him to his circle of friends, and on his last day in England asked them all to go with him to speed the parting guest, as his letter to Mrs. Nathan proves : " *Amica*, will you tomorrow, Thursday, at 12.30, be at Blackwall Station, Fenchurch Street, where I and our mutual friends will be, so that we all may go together to greet Garibaldi on his ship ? . . . We will fix also a second meeting at the home of one of our friends." This " second meeting " took place at the house of James Stansfeld, and Garibaldi and Stansfeld made an impression upon each other which by and by ripened into warm friendship.

The relations between Garibaldi and Mazzini were therefore then most friendly, and the former listened to all the plans and projects of the latter, especially to his animadversions on the fast approaching Crimean War, into which he feared Piedmont might be drawn. This would be a great misfortune, as, according to him, Piedmont would be wise to keep itself prepared to attack Austria, since Austria would have her hands full if she joined in the fray, or would be neglected and deserted by England and France if she kept neutral. Garibaldi, however, pledged himself to no definite action, saying that he would consult all their common friends in Italy; then he left in the *Commonwealth* for Genoa, where in due time he arrived, to find those friends divided into two distinct parties, *pro* and *contra* Piedmont and Cavour. The Piedmontese authorities did nothing to prevent or disturb his return home, so he went to Nice and resumed his old coasting trade.

But from the moment that the question of Piedmont's participation in the Crimean War was mooted, Garibaldi sided with the partisans of Cavour who vehemently supported it, notwithstanding that most of the radicals, including Kossuth and Manin, opposed it as pledging Piedmont to an alliance with Louis Napoleon, the murderer of the Roman Republic. The Crimean War might have been delayed if Palmerston had been at the head of the English Foreign Office, but sooner or later it must inevitably have burst forth, as its causes would not have ceased to exist. It was undoubtedly a most lucky event for Italy—if the existence of a monarchy is to be considered a blessing to her population—that it took place when it did, and on this question Garibaldi was in the right, while Mazzini proved to be wrong. At the helm of little Piedmont, now just beginning to recover from her calamities, Fortune had placed a man greater and more hard-headed than Bismarck, as unscrupulous as Metternich, and as high-handed as Palmerston, who resolved with an unflinching will that his master's dominions should extend from the Alps to the sea, and who set to work to find allies by whose aid he could oust Austria from Italy, shrewdly guessing that this great step once made, the rest of Italy would unite with Piedmont.

The history of the events which led to the Crimean War has been elsewhere amply discussed and narrated; it is therefore useless to again cover that ground. The Piedmontese troops arrived in time to distinguish themselves, and Cavour was enabled to realise his determination to take part in the peace negotiations, and to make the occasion an opportunity for discussing the condition of Italy. There occurred, however, one curious incident which has been generally overlooked or forgotten, and that was the appearance in London of a remarkable document, which, though believed to have issued from " very high quarters," received the approbation of many of the strongest Radicals of the day. In this document it was said, among other things, that " the exclusion of the Turks from Europe and the establishment of a Greek Empire in the present European Turkey " was highly desirable. Now, curiously enough, this had been one of Mazzini's ideals, concerning which he had written many years before in his articles about " The Slavonian Nationalities," and which he now again upheld, the more steadfastly because he could not tolerate the alliance of England with the " Man of the 2nd of December."

During these months Mazzini was busy reorganising the " Party of Action," and Kossuth was again entirely at one with him, issuing fresh manifestoes to the Hungarian soldiers in Italy, appearing with Mazzini on public platforms in England, and writing letters for the distinct purpose of publication. But in spite of all these efforts, none of the attempts at insurrection in Italy succeeded.

Garibaldi continued to live quietly in the Sardinian States, but his mere presence served to raise the hope that he would consent to head some uprising. When Felice Orsini urged the people of Massa and Carrara to rise against the Duke of Modena—an insane idea, as the Duke was protected by the Austrian and Tuscan troops—their answer was : " Let Garibaldi call us, and we are ready." Garibaldi had not approved of this or of any other attempt, so to cut short all doubts he published in the *Italia del Popolo* a notice warning " our young men who are always ready to affront danger " not to allow themselves to be drawn into insurrectionary movements, which he disapproved, or to be deluded by the " insinuations of men who are either deceived or deceivers " (" dalle fallaci insinuazioni di uomini ingannati od ingannatori "). This communication gave rise to endless replies and recriminations, as it was easy to demonstrate that no unlawful use had been made of his name, and that only his great popularity was to be blamed if the people looked up to him as their natural chief. But, unexpectedly, Rosselli, Garibaldi's ex-commanding officer and colleague during the siege of Rome, thought fit to publish a long indictment of Garibaldi's military conduct in the same *Italia del Popolo*, saying that Garibaldi's action at the battle of Velletri [May 19, 1849], victorious though it had been, was "more criminal than that for which General Ramorino had been shot for bringing about the defeat of Novara." Garibaldi sent his seconds to Rosselli and to the editor of the *Italia del Popolo*, poor, peaceable, devoted Savi, but mutual friends intervened, and the incident left no trace, save an ineradicable impression in Garibaldi's mind that Mazzini was the instigator of Rosselli's publication.

In the autumn of 1854 I accepted an invitation from the lady who was betrothed to Garibaldi to accompany her and her daughter on an Italian tour. This was the realisation of a life-dream, and I not only made the acquaintance of the great General, but saw face to face many of the noble patriots whose names, since 1848, had been household words to me. I had read most of Mazzini's works, and in Paris I had known many Liberals—especially Cousin, the devoted friend of Santorre Santarosa, the Italian hero of Greek independence—who had imbued me with their reverence for Mazzini and their sense of shame at the part played by France in the destruction of the Roman Republic. These men were Constitutionalists, and expected more from the plucky little kingdom of Piedmont than from any popular uprising having for aim the proclamation of an Italian republic. It is worthy of note that this view was rapidly becoming general, even Daniele Manin, who lived in Paris in extreme, though honoured, poverty, subscribing to it. In Nice, also, we found that the refugees from Naples, Modena, and Sicily, with the sole exception of Dr. Paolo Fabrizi, brother of Niccola, declared that nothing could be attempted in the way of insurrection until the part that Austria intended playing in the Oriental drama should be known. But in Sardinia, where we went with Garibaldi for a month, the young men thronging round him did not seem to share his opinions about the advisability of abstaining from action till they should see which way the wind blew. These young men—almost all ex-officers who had served under him in Rome—were also worshippers of Mazzini, whom they considered their spiritual father, and, moreover, with few exceptions, they were all in banishment from the mainland States of Piedmont, sent to Sardinia by the inexorable Cavour, who had taken no pains to ascertain whether they had, or had not, been accomplices of the Milanese revolutionists, but who had expelled them as Republicans, as writers in the *Italia del Popolo*, or as individuals who, not having demanded Piedmontese citizenship, possessed absolutely no rights.

Sardinia is a delightful resort for a month's shooting, especially when the grandees of the island organise boar-hunts, as they did for Garibaldi, with their retainers all in native costume ; but as an all-the-year-round residence the prevalence of malarial fever gives it another character and none but those utterly destitute or compelled by the pressure of insurmountable circumstances would think of remaining there.

From Nice we went to Florence and Rome, where, of course, Garibaldi could not escort us, but he gave us letters of introduction to many of his friends. Everywhere the attitude of the people was strikingly sullen, or, after they felt that they could trust us, passionately hostile to Austria the Pope, the Cardinals, France, and their Dukes. In Florence we had the joy of a cordial welcome from Robert and Elizabeth Browning. All the people that we met—chiefly at their house—were admirers of Piedmont, believing that the young King would yet wipe out the stain of Novara they thought that, once the Austrians should be turned out of Lombardy, the Tuscans would easily " settle things with their Grand Duke," but till then they must be prudent and silent. Of Orsini's attempt in the Lunigiana they spoke with pity, as it was simply ridiculous to expect any success while the Duke of Modena was powerfully backed by Austria and Tuscany. As to the Brownings personally, Elizabeth had already become half "Cavourian," though D'Azeglio was then her hero. Robert was sceptical of things in general, and indignant at the "muddleheadedness" of men in high places in his own dear England, away from which—but for the health of the frail being for whom he lived—he could never have schooled himself to remain so long. Their little boy, Bertino, was a fierce Republican, an Austrian-and-French-hater, trained by Ferdinand, their manservant—a sometime Garibaldian soldier—to cry *sotto voce*, "Viva la Republica!" and, withal, the brightest, daintiest, loveliest child imaginable. Mrs. Browning had much to tell us about Margaret Fuller, Contessa d'Ossoli, relating how, on the eve of her departure, she had said, as if struck by a presentiment, that her one prayer was that Ossoli, Angelo (their child), and she, might die together, and that the struggle might be brief, and Browning added: "Her prayer was answered, but oh! that her story of the Roman Republic had been saved!"

In Rome, where we arrived for the Easter ceremonies, we had but few occasions for free intercourse with individual Italians. Barbara Leigh Smith, who was staying there, introduced us to Hatty Hosman and the artistic circle, who, perfectly indifferent to political aspects, regarded Rome as their personal property, the exclusive heritage of art and artists. However, under the guidance of one true Roman, for whom Garibaldi had given us a letter, we went over all the theatre of the siege, the ruins of the Vascello—where the bones of the defenders remained unburied until 1870—and the Villa Panfili, where "the sod was green over many a grave." So we mentally re-enacted the entire tragedy in reverence and awe for that heroic defence. Our guide was known and trusted by the Trasteverini, who showed us the traces of the bombs, though without uttering words, as they understood we were English; only one woman brought out a coarse print of Garibaldi in his red shirt and poncho, whispering:

"He will return . . . he must return to free us from the assassins. . . . Bid him come quickly ! . . . we are weary so weary ! "

And we faithfully delivered this message on our return to Nice, where we found him enchanted by news of the arrival of the Piedmontese Expeditionary Corps at Balaclava, in February. He used to live literally in the newspapers, expressing his confidence that the Piedmontese army, the *enfant* as he called it, would, if only well officered, gloriously win its spurs.

XVIII

MISS WHITE MAKES THE ACQUAINTANCE OF STANSFELD
AND MAZZINI

1855–1856

Ricciotti Garibaldi—Mr. Stansfeld—Pietro Fortunato Calvi—Garibaldi at Portsmouth—English Ambassadors and "Bomba's" prisoners—Felice Orsini—His escape from prison—Acclamations for Cavour—The words "British subject" held to refer to males only—Mazzini at Cedar Road.

WE returned to England in May, 1855, and the lady to whom Garibaldi was betrothed took with her his son, Ricciotti—then suffering from a serious affection of his leg. The boy was placed under the care of the most noted English specialists, especially Dr. Little, and to this gentleman is due the almost complete cure which enabled Ricciotti to render sterling service to the cause of Italian liberty in 1866–67, and, in 1870, to command the troops who captured the only Prussian flag (of the 62nd Pomeranians) taken during the Franco-German war, and afterwards to become leader of the Italian contingent in Greece.

Certain of being summoned to fight against the Austrians or lead the Italians in revolution, Garibaldi had obtained my promise to be the nurse of his wounded, so, to fit myself for the task, I now resolved to secure the best medical education possible, Dr. Little and other eminent surgeons warmly encouraging and assisting me to carry out my plan.

In July, 1855, I first made the acquaintance of Mr.

THE BIRTH OF MODERN ITALY

Stansfeld, to whom I was directed when wishing to ascertain whether an Italian patriot, named Calvi—just reported to have been hanged in Mantua by the Austrians—was the ardent and generous young Lombard whom we had met in Sardinia. Mr. Stansfeld eventually found out that the martyr who had been executed at Mantua was not that Calvi, but a greater hero from Cadore—Pietro Fortunato Calvi, who had, in 1848, thrown up his officer's brevet in the Austrian army and headed the fierce insurrection of his fellow mountaineers. Later, he commanded the *Cacciatori delle Alpi* during the siege of Venice. After the fall of that city, he had taken part in every forlorn hope, aiding the plans set on foot by Mazzini and Kossuth during the year 1853. He was expelled from Piedmont for participation in the unsuccessful attempt of February in Milan, but ventured to return to his native valleys to continue organising. Arrested on September 17, 1853, he was confined in the dungeons of Mantua, where, after repeated and shocking tortures, he was condemned to be hanged, his prayer that he might be shot instead being brutally refused.

In 1856 Garibaldi again visited England, and became the honoured guest of my father at Portsmouth, and of myself in London. We had many long and earnest talks about Italian affairs. I asked him whether, now that the Crimean struggle was over, without bringing any benefit to Italy, he still believed in the King of Sardinia's intention and capacity to wage war against Austria, and whether he did not think that a general rising in the subject provinces would put him on his mettle. I had, throughout 1855 and the commencement of 1856, received cuttings from newspapers with articles by Mazzini and speeches by friends of Italy, and daily and hourly the longing grew in me to be up and doing for them. Garibaldi answered me thus: "If a general rising of the people of Italy could be ensured, there would be no necessity to wait for kings or diplomacy, but, at this moment especially, no one will stir hand or foot: the bravery and patience under hardships of the Sardinian contingent in the Crimea has awakened the pride of our people. You know how unpopular the war was, how only the King and Cavour carried the day in the teeth of the opposition and the resignation of the Minister of War, Dabormidax! . . . Well, they are all expecting great things from the Conference. [Peace Congress in Paris.] Believe me, there could be no greater mistake than to choose this moment for a rising. We must wait. If nothing comes of the Conference, and I, personally, expect but very little, then, bad as things are in Lombardy and Venice, they are worse, as far as actual suffering and oppression go, in Sicily and Naples, and there some conflagration is bound to burst out soon. We shall see if we can succeed this time in liberating the Neapolitan prisoners, as you know I tried to do with Ripari, last year."

This was one of the objects that had brought Garibaldi to England, besides the desire to visit his betrothed. His brother, Felice, had, at his death, left him a sum of money with which he had bought a portion of the island of Caprera, and now he wished to purchase a cutter in England, to ply to and from Genoa for the building of the house he desired "on his own rock," where, in the intervals of war and revolution, he intended to take up his abode with his children. Yet this prospect of peace and rest, which appealed to him for the first time in his life, did not deter him from throwing himself heartily into the scheme planned between Sir William Temple, the English ambassador at Naples, Sir James Hudson, English minister at Turin, and Anthony Panizzi, of the British Museum, for securing the escape of the political galley-slaves of King "Bomba." For this purpose, Sir James Hudson had consulted his friend, Dr. Agostino Bertani, well knowing that for such a risky affair he must apply to the "Party of Action," and Bertani had lost no time in securing Garibaldi's consent. Medici, the defender of the Vascello in the siege of Rome, came to England and purchased a vessel—the *Isle of Thanet*—but it got wrecked

THE BIRTH OF MODERN ITALY

off Yarmouth, and a considerable time was lost. Garibaldi saw Panizzi in London, and then went to Portsmouth as the revered guest of my father, adored by every man, woman, and child in the house and shipyard, where he delighted the shipwrights by the knowledge he displayed of the smallest detail of their craft.

In order to attempt the liberation of the Neapolitan prisoners, Bertani, Rosalino Pilo, the Sicilian, and Carlo Pisacane, were to accompany Garibaldi. The English subscribers to the funds, among whom were Mrs. Gladstone, Lord and Lady Holland, Lord Overden, and others, openly signed their names and willingly consented to a second attempt. We have reason to believe that Lord and Lady Palmerston subscribed anonymously. The prisoners had steadfastly refused to demand or even accept an amnesty, and were daily, almost hourly, expecting the signal for their deliverance, and, though the delay caused by the wreck of the *Isle of Thanet* rendered the attempt more and more dangerous, the secret never transpired. Finally, Panizzi telegraphed to Bertani: " Our commercial speculations must be suspended," which meant that Sir William Temple had sent instructions from Naples countermanding the attempt at rescue, as he thought himself certain to secure an amnesty, on the sole condition that the released prisoners should be deported to the United States. Sir William Temple, however, was at that period so seriously ill that, in August, 1857, he returned to England and died. The prisoners were released in 1859, when, though despatched to America, they were liberated on the high seas by Settembrini's son,[1] and brought to England to be *fêted* and applauded, for they were "constitutionalists." This episode, in which two English ambassadors took so leading a part, must be recorded

---

[1] Settembrini, Luigi (1818–1876), patriot, historian, and literary critic, born in Naples; was imprisoned together with Poerio, Imbriana, Spaventa, and others, by the Bourbons. Wrote the celebrated "Protest of the People of the Two-Sicilies." His son, hereafter mentioned, Raffaele (1837–1903), was, later, rear-admiral in the Italian Navy.

among the many friendly deeds of England to Italy, in the bad and sad old days of despotism—though, doubtless, it will make diplomats shudder.

Shortly after his return to Genoa in 1856, Garibaldi and Dr. Paolo Fabrizi gave Felice Orsini—who had just escaped from the dungeons of Mantua—letters of introduction to me, and I helped him to put together his book entitled "Austrian Dungeons," published by Routledge at 1s., which became extremely popular. The author got £60 for the copyright—a windfall, as he was penniless and in absolute want. Orsini was, at that time, apparently devoted to Mazzini, and fully admitted that even if Piedmont were anxious to drive the foreign oppressors out of Italy, only a rising of the populations could afford an excuse for attacking Austria. His own account of his three failures in Lunigiana, Massa, and Lombardy substantially differed from those afterwards given by his fellow conspirators, Campanella[1] and Maurizio Quadrio.[2] It is, however, certain, that his imprudence in losing a most compromising letter of Mazzini's, of September 15, 1854, and in communicating plans and details to persons who were not in the plot and who could not assist in its development, greatly contributed to the failure.

Rightly or wrongly, I still believe that success would have been impossible in any circumstances, because, as Garibaldi said, Italy would not stir. Orsini's mad idea of taking service in the Austrian army as a Swiss who had served in the Papal troops, was entirely his own, and it is a matter for wonder that, though more than once recognised, the authorities did not arrest him either at Vienna or at Arad. But at Hermanstadt he was apprehended on telegraphic orders from Vienna. When interrogated, he at once admitted his name and owned that his passport was false. He was transferred *via* Laybach, Treviso, and Verona to the Gonzaga Castle in Mantua, to await his fate in the same

---

[1] Campanella, Federico. See p. 11, note 2.
[2] Quadrio, Maurizio (1801–1876), born in Valtellina; agitator, patriot, and journalist, ever the faithful and devoted friend of Mazzini.

dungeons where so many martyrs—Tazzoli,[1] Poma,[2] Tito Speri,[3] Grazioli, and Guido Montanara, to name a few among the hundreds—had languished till led forth to the gibbet. With a prisoner's true instinct, no sooner did he find himself caged than he set his wits to work to discover some means of escaping. He succeeded in transmitting letters to his friends, chiefly to Pietro Cironi in Switzerland and to the Herwigs in Germany; and money and six tiny saws were successfully smuggled into his cell. Then the execution of Pietro Fortunato Calvi, so long delayed that a commutation to the galleys had seemed possible, warned him that whatever it was possible to do must be done quickly. Fortunately for Orsini, in September, the astute vigilant, incorruptible, though not too brutal Cassati Governor of the Castle, was superseded, and his successo happened to be less conversant with the manners and customs of caged birds. Even the jailors were changed Orsini appeared invariably docile and cheerful, so tha one turnkey reported that "the gentleman in No. 3 wa so resigned that if even the door had been left open h would not have escaped." The guardians were, howevei all scrupulously staunch to their orders. His removal t a fresh cell, in company with seven other prisoners, dis concerted him for a while, but, nothing daunted, h persevered, and succeeded in sawing through certain bars though badly lamed by a fall, he managed to let himse. down into the fosse, and, being assisted by some casua passers-by, was smuggled from hand to hand throug Lombardy to Genoa, thence to Switzerland, and, finall

---

[1] Tazzoli, Enrico (1812–1851), Roman Catholic priest and patric hanged in Mantua. The Pope, Pius IX., ordered that the last rites the Church should be denied him.

[2] Poma, Carlo (1823–1852), young patriot and artist, hanged by tl Austrians at Mantua after severe tortures.

[3] Tito Speri (1825–1853), born in Brescia, patriot and martyr, foug during the revolution of 1848, and during the heroic defence of Bresc against Haynau was the soul of the resistance. Implicated in lat conspiracies, he was strangled by the Austrians with the Spanish *garr* on the bastions of Mantua, together with Grazioli and Guido Montana

he arrived in London, where he was received with open arms by Mazzini.

At the close of the Crimean War, the "Friends of Italy" resumed their activity, and their fly-sheets and publications were regularly sent to me by Mr. Stansfeld.

Though Cavour returned from the Paris Conference without any definite prospect even of moral assistance from the Allies, he had been able, as he had planned, to expound Italy's grievances, and to point to the frequently recurring revolts, which prevailed all over the Peninsula, as a proof that there could be neither peace nor progress as long as the Austrian system continued in force. In Turin he was received with the wildest demonstrations of gratitude, admiration, and enthusiasm, addresses were showered upon him, and King Victor Emmanuel came in for a share of his popularity. Even the *Times* wrote that "the populations and rulers of Lombardy, Venice, Tuscany, Rome, and Naples, the first with hope and admiration, the second with terror and hatred, agree in regarding the King of Sardinia as the personification of Italian independence." In one of the fly-sheets of the "Friends of Italy," Mr. Stansfeld, alluding to certain speeches delivered by Lord John Russell when England and France had lost all patience with Austria's tergiversations, urged that now was the time, in concluding peace with Russia, to compel Austria to restore the estates and properties unjustly confiscated, to insist upon the withdrawal of her troops from Tuscany and Central Italy, and, at the same time, to give the King of Naples to understand that his tyranny could no longer be tolerated, and that if he wished for a continuation of diplomatic relations he must radically alter his methods of government.

Encouraged by Dr. Little, Sir Benjamin Brodie, Sir Bence Jones, and other physicians, I had continued my study of medicine at University College, in the hope of being able to qualify for the full degree ; but votes being numbered and not weighed, the authorities decided that the words " British subject " referred to males only, and I was

THE BIRTH OF MODERN ITALY

debarred from obtaining equality of treatment. This, together with other circumstances—the decision that Ricciotti Garibaldi should go to school in Liverpool, the marriage of one sister, and the engagement of another—set me at liberty, with my father's hearty consent and blessing, to dedicate myself to the cause of Italy, fully conscious that it was a question of "all in all or not at all." I therefore decided to put myself under the guidance of its chief apostle, Mazzini.

My first visit to his tiny room in Cedar Road remains ever present to my heart and vision. Birds were flying about the apartment, a few lilies of the valley stood in a vase on the mantelpiece, books and papers were scattered everywhere, and there, writing on his knee on the smallest fragment of the thinnest imaginable paper, sat Mazzini. He rose at once: his hand-grasp and luminous eyes fascinated and encouraged you, yet filled you with momentary awe. But the simple greeting, the gladness shown in welcoming "one more volunteer to the noble band of English workers and lovers of Italy," put all fears to flight, and soon he was talking, and I was listening as a student to a master anxious to convince, but not in the least desirous of *imposing* his convictions.

From notes made directly I left Cedar Road, I quote some of his words : " It was a mistake to suppose that the ' Party of Action ' was opposed to the intervention of Piedmont in the liberation of Italy : Piedmont's assistance was necessary, but it could not initiate ; revolts, revolutions were inevitable, the people suffered too terribly to be silent and submit ; all that their leaders could do was to direct and combine their efforts ; failures were inevitable, and enormous sacrifices must be made before a people, enslaved for over three hundred years, then bartered and sold to suit the convenience of despotic powers, could achieve their end and conquer their liberty, and, still more, their unity. But 1848 and 1849 had proved that the will to achieve this existed in all the populations, and that the courage to do, to dare and die, was not lacking. Since the failure of those two years, due to many causes—chiefly to the unhindered intervention of Austria and France, the help given by England to monarchical Piedmont exclusively, and to the lack of organisation among the Italians themselves—an entire change had been wrought. The conviction that only the expulsion of all foreigners, the abolition of the temporal power of the Popes, the fusion of all the provinces into one, could effect the real emancipation of the country, had taken root in the nation; they did not trouble themselves about the future form of government, and, once free, they would decide on that according to circumstance."

"You are therefore prepared," I questioned, "if a revolution brings Piedmont into the field, and it should fight resolutely and successfully, to let its King have the crown of United Italy?"

"I am prepared to acknowledge the sovereignty of the people, whether they decide on a United Republic or on a United Monarchy; if the latter, we Republicans shall carry on our republican propaganda, but without attempting to overthrow the government of the people's choice."

"But can a great general revolution be organised and carried on with two foreign armies in occupation, with the determined efforts of Cavour to keep down revolutions, and with most of the old leaders apparently willing to leave all initiative in his hands?" I interposed.

"Lombardy will go on attempting; you see, she gives no quarter even to Maximilian, though he is doing all he can to win the Lombards over: the restoration of the sequestered property, the amnesty granted, have no effect. Sooner or later the revolution will be successful in Milan, then Piedmont will step in and annex Lombardy and Venice. But the rest of Italy will not remain quiescent. Look at Naples and the monthly, almost daily, revolts that happen there; look at Sicily, deploring her error in remaining isolated in 1848-49. See how even your Government recognises the impossibility of the continuance of the present state of affairs."

"But," I remarked, "the King of Naples laughs at moral

suasion; he has Austria, and apparently Russia, on his side, and England will not wage war against him!"

"The 'Friends of Nationalities' can work on public opinion, for the English are disgusted with the termination of the Crimean War, as they see they went to work on a wrong basis; that if they had helped the Poles, Hungarians, and other oppressed nationalities to rise against Austria and Russia, they would have formed the best barrier against the Turks."

After this Mazzini spoke of Garibaldi, deploring that he had not seen him during his last visit to England, and admitting that much would depend upon his actions; but "for sure, when he saw that nothing came of Cavour's intervention at the Congress, he would return to his *rôle* of revolutionary leader," and thus ensure the union of the "Party of Action."

XIX

THE MARTYRS OF SAPRI

1857–1858

Mazzini in Genoa—Attempts in 1856—Letter from Garibaldi—Pisacane and Pilo—Pisacane's first venture—He goes to Sicily—Second expedition—Three days of suspense—Terrible news—Pisacane's fate—Nicotera—Miss White imprisoned—Attempts to prove her insane—Cavour appeals for an expert French *agent* to unearth Mazzini—Mazzini eludes the police—Reaches Hastings.

SHORTLY after the conversation related in the preceding chapter, Mazzini left secretly for Genoa, and I, having been prevailed upon to give lectures on the "Italian Question," followed him there to obtain certain particulars I needed. There I saw him among "his own people," who literally worshipped him, "hiding him in their hearts and houses," passing him from one workingman's home to another, keeping sentinels on the watch against any surprise, so that he saw all the people he desired to meet, and laid his plans with Pisacane for an expedition to Naples, which, however, was postponed to the following year. Mazzini was also hidden in Pisacane's house, where he enjoyed the society of Silvia, Pisacane's adored daughter, and Enrichetta, her mother. Garibaldi was then staying at Caprera, but his *alter ego*, Medici, came daily to see me. Medici was a splendid fellow, full of ardour, and quite convinced that if Piedmont could not or would not stir, the "Party of Action" must be up and doing. However, he was opposed to any action in the North, as there Piedmont must be left alone, for she would certainly follow, even if she refused to lead.

Several attempts were made in that year (1856) in the South, one of which Garibaldi decidedly approved, and General Cosenz wrote to the Marchese Pallavicino, a wealthy Lombard who had been fourteen years a prisoner of Austria in the Spielberg, and who now contributed largely to the cause: " The South is ready for rising, but arms are wanted; Garibaldi is among the warmest supporters, . . . but again, arms and money are indispensable." This attempt at revolution in Sicily had been admirably organised by Rosalino Pilo and Fabrizi; but the leader, heroic Baron Francesco Bentivegna, was surprised, disarmed, and shot summarily at Mezzoiuso, on December 23, 1856, just when a reprieve had arrived, his death-sentence having been recognised as illegal. On the 8th of December Agesilao Milano, one of the most audacious of the Neapolitan conspirators, finding himself in a review face to face with the abhorred "King Bomba," suddenly sprang upon him with his bayonet; but it broke against the mail-shirt worn by the tyrant, or was, as another version has it, turned aside by the horse of the King. Then the steam frigate, *Carlo III.*, laden with arms and soldiers for the suppression of the Sicilian insurrection, blew up; fifty soldiers perished, and many more were wounded; the gas was extinguished throughout the city, the Royal family was paralysed with fear, but even then the population did not stir. On this account most of the leaders, Medici, Cosenz, even Bertani, grew discouraged; but not so Carlo Pisacane and Rosalino Pilo, who insisted that success was certain if an expedition were led by Garibaldi. However, when they applied to him he refused point-blank.

Surprised to hear of this refusal, I wrote to Garibaldi, who answered in the language he adopted with his " sisters in the faith," and which some of them, mistaking his patriotic outpourings for personal affection for themselves, received as love-letters—one, indeed, insisting that they entitled her to marriage, as she knew that his other engagement had been broken off :—

"Sister beloved," he wrote, "whatever happens, I never meant to vex you, and should be grieved at heart if I have done so. You certainly have no need of tenderness, and I am far from wasting it on you; but what you cannot hinder me from saying is the truth. Well, I love you, which matters very little to you; I love you for myself and for my boy, and for Italy, which I idolise and venerate above all earthly things. As to principles, Jessie, I know that your opinion of your brother is even too high. Well, I can assure you that if Garibaldi was sure to be followed by a goodly number on presenting himself, with a flag, on the field of action, to his country, with even a slight probability of success, Jessie mine, can you doubt that I should rush forward with feverish joy, to realise the ideal of my whole life, even knowing that the reward awaiting me should be the most atrocious martyrdom? If you doubt me, you must know me but ill, after all. Sister, I say with pride that I dare take rank with the most staunch of Italian patriots, and in writing this my conscience tells me that I am not making a vain boast. My life, all spent for Italy, is my witness; to unsheath a sword for her is the paradise of my belief: my wife, my children, the desire for rest, nothing has ever been able to restrain me from fighting for the holy cause. I will say one thing more, that all and any of the movements directed by your friend [Mazzini] although disapproved of by me, would have had one follower more if I had found myself on the spot. If I do not offer myself as chief of an attempt, it is because I see no probability of success; and you know enough of my past life to admit that I do understand something of daring enterprises. One word about Piedmont. In Piedmont there is an army of 45,000 men and an ambitious king; these are elements for an initiative, and for success, in which the majority of the Italians believe to-day. Let your friend furnish similar elements, and show a little more practicability than he has done hitherto, and we will bless him also and follow him with fervour. On the other hand, if Piedmont hesitates and proves itself unequal to the mission which we believe it is called upon to fulfil, we shall repudiate it. Let any one, in short, commence the 'Holy War' with temerity even, and you will see your brother first on the battlefield. Fight, I say, and I am with the fighter; but, sister mine, I will not say to the Italians: 'Arise,' just to give the curs (*canaglia*) food for laughter. This is frank speaking, is it not? I shall remain at Genoa for a few days, then I will return to Nice, and go to Sardinia towards the end of the month. There and elsewhere, command your brother,
"G. GARIBALDI."

Aurelio Saffi and I went through Scotland lecturing in many cities, notably in Edinburgh, Glasgow, Paisley, and Dumfries, where leading citizens took the chair for us, and where subscriptions liberally flowed in, some merely for "benevolent purposes," others for the "Fund of the 10,000 muskets" which were to be offered to the first Italian city that should rise successfully, others, again, to be given to "the Apostle of Italian Unity," and to "be used as he thought fit."

Pisacane and Pilo having decided to persist in their enterprise, with or without Garibaldi, in April, 1857, Mazzini returned to Genoa; and as I had been offered the post of special correspondent by several English newspapers, it was decided that my presence in Genoa might be useful. I obtained the position on these papers through the influence of Mr. Stansfeld, who was now honorary secretary of the "Italian Committee," and with the Taylors, the Shaens, and the Cowens, wholly devoted to the insurrectionary projects, for which they were busily engaged in securing the sinews of war. It can, without exaggeration, be said that, with the exception of the large sums of money contributed by Adriano Lemmi, and some minor ones by other Italians, the funds for the Pisacane expedition were exclusively contributed by England and Scotland. As I have already stated, Garibaldi refused all participation, even sending Medici to implore me to abstain; but if ever I was convinced of the righteousness of any action, I was convinced of the righteousness of this crusade against the fiendish despotism of "King Bomba." By the hundreds of Italians with whom I became intimate the scheme was approved: by Alberto Mario, to whom I was betrothed, and who was determined to accompany Pisacane; by Mosto, by Stallo, and by other Genoese merchants, and by all the working-men, fourteen of whom composed the rank and file of the expedition.

The expedition of Pisacane, and the preparations made in Genoa to second his efforts for the liberation of the Neopolitan Provinces, was the prelude to Garibaldi's famous "Expedition of the Thousand," undertaken for the same end, and by almost identical methods. The latter succeeded, while the former failed; and though Victor Hugo's saying that " Pisacane was greater than Garibaldi " may seem exaggerated, justice demands due tribute to the " pioneers " who dared to fight and who fell in a magnanimous undertaking, and to the noble Genoese who, in both cases, seconded these patriotic efforts. But, in spite of the later declarations of Cavour and the efforts of his judges to prove it, in neither case was there any desire or intention to overthrow the Piedmontese monarchy. On the contrary, there was the obvious design to use Piedmont as the lever of emancipation, to open out for King Victor Emmanuel, who had, on the very battlefield of Novara, so nobly nailed the Italian *tricolore* to the mast, an opportunity for carrying that flag into the still enslaved provinces. Fettered as he was by diplomacy and by treaties, the King could not do so on his own initiative. In the case of Pisacane, the movement was doubly justified by the alarming increase in the ranks of the " Muratists " (the supporters of Prince Murat, heir to Joachim, the late Napoleonic King of Naples, shot at Pizzo), who, though originally very few, had grown in numbers through the powerful help secured to them by the agents of Louis-Napoleon. Many even of the Neapolitan Moderates, in despair of obtaining anything from the Bourbons, which would save the country from their degrading despotism, were willing to accept a foreigner, who, it was hoped, would grant them free institutions, and, in good time, favour the cause of Independence and back up Piedmont in a war against Austria. Even the "Italianissimo " Cavour, as his letters published by Edmondo Mayor amply demonstrated, so far from opposing the " adventurer," was willing to co-operate in his success, although at that time Mazzini was accused of calumniating him when he charged him with this sin against unity. But from the fearful dungeons of " King Bomba " the imprisoned patriots had protested, saying " that they would rather die in prison than grasp in their pure hands those of a foreign adventurer."

There was, however, division of opinion as to the wisdom of seizing arms and ammunition in the arsenal and fortresses of Genoa, but if the first expedition was to be followed by other volunteers, arms and ammunition would become vitally indispensable, and the only means of procuring them was to take by force all that was necessary. The 10th of June was the day fixed for the departure of Pisacane, Nicotera, and Rosalino Pilo, with their twenty followers, among whom figured an expert "skipper," who, after the seizure of the postal steamer, was to take command of it. But, just as afterwards happened to Garibaldi with his " Thousand," the schooner laden with arms and ammunition was overtaken by a storm, and the crew were compelled to jetison the cargo. Pisacane then returned to Genoa, and, with Mazzini, decided to begin again. Accordingly he went to Naples to make fresh arrangements. Yet, with so many in the secret, not a whisper nor a sign transpired, though Louis Napoleon, having discovered, by intercepting letters between England and Genoa, that something serious was brewing, warned Cavour. The latter, however, was sceptical of any insurrection being hatched in Genoa, and wrote to the Marchese di Villamarina, Sardinian minister in Paris, that " as the news came from the Emperor himself, one must appear very grateful, although he was certain that the aforesaid news were devoid of all foundation."

Pisacane returned from Naples radiant and full of hope. He had found the Secret Committee in Naples working admirably, with Dragone and Fanelli at its head, and he felt both astonished and delighted that everything seemed ready for a second attempt. The postal steamer chosen was the *Cagliari*. On June 26th we saw Pisacane for the last time, and I wrote under his dictation a note for the two engineers of the steamer—discovered at the last moment to be English —in explanation of what was going to happen. These two men, Wate and Parks by name, were afterwards imprisoned for seven months in the Neapolitan dungeons, in consequence of which one lost his mind and the other became permanently afflicted with epileptic convulsions. An indemnity of £3,000 was finally secured to them by English diplomacy.

Pisacane gave me his political testament and other papers

to be published in England, together with a magnificent letter of Cattaneo, which appeared, translated, in the *Daily News*, but the originals in my possession were sequestrated by the Piedmontese police.

At 7 p.m. of the 26th, from the heights of Carignano, Alberto Mario and I watched the vessel steam out of harbour, and then began for Mazzini that most terrible of all trials, suspense. For the next three nights he slept in Alberto Mario's modest apartment, and, from hour to hour, sent us little notes. Once more, by a strange fatality, as Mazzini had feared, the boats which carried the arms and ammunition, with Rosalino Pilo and his nineteen men, did not find the steamer, although they cruised about for thirty-six hours, sending up rockets constantly. However, Pisacane successfully captured the *Cagliari*, steamed to the island of Ponza, and on the 27th, having easily disarmed the garrison and liberated the political prisoners, re-embarked with four little cannon, two hundred muskets, and sufficient ammunition. He proceeded to the Bay of Policastro, and landed at the little village of Sapri. Then terrible news reached us rapidly. Pisacane had set the *Cagliari* free, with a certificate to its legitimate captain stating that he had been compelled by violence to lend his ship. In Sapri, Pisacane and his companions awaited the arrival of Albini, Pisani, and Mattina with their well-organised men; but instead, the Bourbon troops, advised by a man who had managed to escape from Ponza in a boat, appeared upon the scene, seconded by the deluded population, whom they assured that the band who had landed were escaped bandits and murderers. Seeing massacre imminent and that resistance would be impossible, Pisacane and his followers took the road to Padula, hoping to get into the mountains, but, assailed by over three thousand men, sixty-five of his companions fell killed or wounded. As long as ammunition lasted and their bare arms held out, the remaining heroes stood their ground; then Pisacane ordered the survivors to make one last attempt to gain the mountains. One hundred and eleven fell under fire of the troops or were done to death by

THE BIRTH OF MODERN ITALY

the misguided populace, armed with pitchforks, spits and hatchets; among these, Pisacane himself and Falcone were so mutilated and disfigured that none of the survivors could distinguish the fair-haired, fair-featured Sicilian noble from the black-haired, bronzed Calabrese Falcone. Colonel Ghio, who was in command of the Bourbon *Cacciatori*, took thirty-five prisoners and had them shot on the spot. Nicotera, equally dear to Garibaldi and to Mazzini, who called him his "Leoncino" (Little Lion), shot in the head and with his right wrist broken, was left for dead on the field and then taken to Sanza. As he showed some signs of life a compassionate guard attended to him, and at his request returned to the field of slaughter to see if any papers were left upon the corpses. This guard found a few, and notably one which, deciphered "in a *free* translation" by the wounded prisoner when the latter was brought before his judges, saved all the accomplices in Naples and the provinces.

Harry Wreford, the only honest Italian correspondent that wrote for the *Times* in those dark days, gives a glowing account of Nicotera's conduct during the trial that ensued, denouncing the scandalous system employed by the judges, and the illegal acts of the Government in loading prisoners with chains and dragging them bound and bleeding through the streets from their prisons to the shore.

Of the survivors of this ghastly business six were condemned to death, but their sentences commuted to the galleys for life; sixty-five were taken to the island of Favignana and imprisoned in the fortress of San Giacomo; and Nicotera, by the King's personal order, was transported to the fortress of Santa Caterina and thrown into a cell over a ditch full of putrid water, where he had a stone bench for bed. There, fed upon black bread only, he remained for five long months, despite the reports of the commanding officer and of the doctor, who testified to his continued fever and to hæmorrhage of the lungs. At last a thunderbolt smashed in the roof of his cell, water flooded the pestilential hole, and the sentinel, on his own responsibility, carried the prisoner out in his arms. Entreated by the commandant

GIOVANNI NICOTERA

CARLO PISACANE

To face p. 270.

to sign a petition already drawn up and addressed to " His Sacred Royal Majesty, Ferdinand, King of the Two Sicilies," Nicotera with his left hand wrote across it : " To the Wild Beast (*Belva*) Ferdinand, not yet satiated with the blood of the human race." To the last he was dauntless and heroic, and in 1860 Garibaldi welcomed him and the other survivors of Sapri as the "light-bearers and path-finders of the Liberation."

From Leghorn, where it had been arranged that an insurrection should break out simultaneously with Pisacane's attempt in the Neapolitan provinces, good news came at first. The insurgents, commanded by Maurizio Quadrio, Civinini, and Simeoni, attacked the patrols, some of whom even seemed inclined to fraternise with the people. But the principal attack failed, many were killed and wounded, and the chiefs had barely time to escape.

In Genoa, where the organisation to seize the arms was perfect, up to the evening of the 29th there was not the slightest sign of alarm. But shortly before midnight Mazzini received warning that the Government had been advised of the contemplated rising. The authorities being on the alert, the attack on the arsenal became impossible. In a moment messengers were despatched with orders to suspend all operations, and, save for one mishap, all would have gone off quietly. At the Fort Diamante, where the order did not arrive in time, the troop of young men who were spending the evening with the soldiers had succeeded in shutting up the entire garrison in a *casemate*, when a soldier discharged his musket at the insurgents, and one of them returning fire, killed a sergeant of the 7th Regiment of Infantry. That was the only blood shed in Genoa.

Once assured of the failure of Pisacane's expedition, the Piedmontese authorities set no limit to their calumnies, asserting—as in the reign of King Charles Albert—that Genoa was undermined in different places, that pillage had been promised to the rabble, and that the convicts were to have been let loose, though the contrary had been carefully guaranteed by the formation of a special squad under the orders of Mosto. But lies have short legs, and despite the superhuman efforts of the police and the judicial authorities, no one could substantiate any count against the patriots, save the clear fact that they had intended seizing arms and ammunition to be sent in aid of the insurrection in the southern provinces. I was arrested on July 4th, and although Cavour assured D'Azeglio, the Sardinian ambassador in London, that "the arrest, which he regretted, was necessary, because Miss White was one of the persons most deeply compromised, as the magistrates charged with the 'instruction' had found upon her person a correspondence which left no doubt as to her participation in the most violent acts of the conspirators," nothing was discovered in my possession with the exception, as already stated, of Pisacane's political testament and Cattaneo's letter. The persistence of the interrogating magistrate during five months' imprisonment was so great concerning the details which preceded the Pisacane expedition that I was compelled to ask him "whether he acted for the King of Sardinia or King Bomba." Both the British consul in Genoa, Brown, and the British minister in Turin, Sir James Hudson, washed their hands of me, for Cavour had assured them that the evidence in his possession was more than sufficient to condemn me either to death or the galleys. The consternation of the two diplomats was therefore great when they became aware of the fact that there was no evidence whatever against me, and that I should have to be liberated without even being sent to the assizes, as no true bill could be found for the prosecution. They knew that they would have to answer for their lack of protection of a British subject, who had been kept so uselessly and so unjustly in prison, without any energetic action, or even remonstrance, on their part. They were therefore willing to help Cavour in his attempt to have me proved insane, in which case no trial would be needed, insanity arguing irresponsible guilt; but my counsel, the ever-watchful and devoted Carcassi, got hold of the plot, and, by an article in the *Italia del Popolo*, warned the doctors, who were

JESSIE WHITE MARIO IN THE YEAR OF HER MARRIAGE

To face p 272]

1857] CAVOUR'S SEARCH FOR MAZZINI

induced to lend themselves to the "pious fraud" in the honest belief that a certificate of insanity would save me from the galleys. Thus informed of the true state of the case, the medical men refused even to visit me in my prison, while the commander of the fort, who behaved most nobly to his prisoners, and the male and female warders, called upon to depose by the magistrates, declared unanimously that "Scià (The lady) Jessie was quite other than demented," one even saying to the judge: "*Scià Jessie à sà più lunga de lei*" (The lady Jessie is more wideawake than you are). The order of release had accordingly to be signed, to the dismay of Sir James Hudson; and he would have been called to account by a number of members of Parliament, headed by Roebuck, had it not been for the downfall of the Palmerston Cabinet in February, 1858. This was well, for Italy never had a more devoted or enthusiastic friend than Sir James Hudson, whose only fault was a blind faith in Cavour. The latter, however, never hesitated to deceive him, or even directly to lie to him—as over the subsequent cession of Nice and Savoy—to Sir James's endless vexation and trouble.

My personal tribulations, and those of the hundreds arrested with me, were to some extent soothed by the knowledge of Cavour's frenzied rage at the failure of his agents to discover the whereabouts of Mazzini, who, according to the information sent by Louis Napoleon, had been in Genoa and was still there. This was perfectly true, for with the exception of a few flying visits to Turin, he stayed in Genoa from the end of April till the 10th of August, 1857. Notwithstanding that the French Emperor sent special agents to aid the Sardinian police, it proved impossible for any of the spies to discover his hiding-place. On July 8th Cavour wrote to Villamarina, the Sardinian minister in Paris: " J'ai répondu sur le champ à votre depêche télégraphique de hier au soir, en vous chargeant d'engager le gouvernement français de nous expédier sans delai, l'agent qu'il croit capable d'arrêter Mazzini. S'il réussit, il peut compter sur une belle récompense, car,

> Mazzini is everywhere where tyrants tremble
> That the supreme hour may reach the traitors.
> Mazzini is everywhere where the hope doth blossom
> To shed our blood for the whole of Italy."

Mazzini was then staying in the house of the Marchese Ernesto Pareto and his wife, Constance Beart. During a preliminary search by the police Pareto was arrested; Mazzini then warned Constance that if she opposed his plan he would surrender himself to the authorities, as he could not permit Pareto to suffer imprisonment for his sake. Next time the search was renewed he quietly went downstairs, opened the door, let all the agents in, and stopping to ask a policeman for a light for his cigar, walked out unmolested, and after proceeding a few yards on foot, took a carriage and drove to Quarto. Thence he succeeded in reaching Lugano without difficulty, and by way of the Rhine and Ostend he arrived in due course at Dover. He went to pass a few days at Hastings with the Stansfelds, and Mr. Stansfeld wrote to me: "Pippo has returned in a pitiable state. He has aged terribly; he is ill, unconsolable on account of the death of Pisacane, whom we all loved. He cannot find peace thinking of his 'Leoncino' (Nicotera) . . ."

The following year (1858) was a sad one for the friends of Italy, but it proved to be "the dark hour before the dawn," for the period of liberation was fast approaching.

XX

THE SHADOW OF COMING EVENTS

1858-1860

Change of Ministry in England—Orsini's attack on Louis Napoleon—Cavour at Plombières—Cavour and Garibaldi—Piedmontese-French alliance—Exiles return to be enrolled in the Piedmontese regular army—Louis Napoleon vacillates—Cavour's determination to declare war—Austria invades the Sardinian States—French army corps crosses the Alps—Mazzini morally triumphant—Napoleon suddenly resolves to end the war—He writes to the Emperor Francis Joseph—Palmerston's foresight—Diplomacy—Napoleon and Francis Joseph at Villafranca—Humiliating position of Victor Emmanuel—Cavour's fury—His resignation—Desire of the Italians for unity—Army of Central Italy—Military League to be commanded by Garibaldi and General Fanti—Both deprived of their commands—Garibaldi determines to resume revolutionary methods—Cavour again Premier—Cession of Nice and Savoy—Mazzini discovers the secret—Formal act of cession.

ALBERTO MARIO and I were married in England immediately after release from our imprisonment in Genoa, and we sailed for the United States, where we gave a series of lectures on the "Italian Question" in New York, Philadelphia, Washington, and Boston. When we returned to England in June, we found a new ministry installed, the elections having returned 350 Liberals and 302 Conservatives. A vote of want of confidence, proposed by Lord Hartington, had been carried by a majority of 13; Lord Derby had resigned, and Lord Palmerston had succeeded in forming a strong Cabinet, including the chief leaders of the Whigs, the old Peelites, with the Duke of Somerset and

ALBERTO MARIO.

To face p. 276.]

Milner Gibson of the advanced party. "Four outright *Italians*," said Mr. Stansfeld, M.P.; "lucky for Italy that the Tories are 'out,' for between their Austrian proclivities and the German sympathies of the Court, England's weight would have gone into the wrong scale."

In January, 1858, Louis Napoleon was terrified by the formidable attempt on his life committed by Orsini, which spread horror and death in the streets of Paris. It caused the Emperor to go in continual fear of the poignard of some Italian conspirator, and he could not forget the words which Orsini addressed to him in a letter dated from the Mazas prison, February 11, 1858: "   . que votre Majesté se rapelle . . . que tant que l'Italie ne sera pas indèpendente, la tranquilité de l'Europe et celle de votre Majesté ne sont qu'une chimère." Cavour, delighted with this letter because it presented arguments which he himself intended to advance, caused it to be reproduced in the Piedmontese *Official Gazette* together with a suitable notice.

Cavour could not but be aware that the failure of the Pisacane expedition and the resentment of a large portion of the Party of Action over the abortive attempt in Genoa had gone far to quell any remnant of hope in the possibility of a popular uprising ousting Austria or dethroning the Bourbons. His opportunity came at Plombières, in a meeting arranged (July 20, 1858) between himself and Louis Napoleon. There, unknown to all, he framed an alliance between France and Piedmont, whereby Victor Emmanuel was to give his daughter Clothilde, aged sixteen, to Prince Napoleon, a middle-aged rake, and Piedmont was to cede Savoy, and perhaps Nice, to France. Cavour, even after gaining his Sovereign's consent to these arrangements, knew that his difficulties could never be more than half vanquished till the great Party of Action was won over to his policy. He was too great a statesman to repeat the error of 1849, when the popular element had been repelled, and the volunteers excluded from their rightful share of the field. Knowing that the Party of Action would follow Garibaldi's lead, he sent in December for that popular hero, and confided to him that it was almost certain Piedmont would declare war against Austria in the coming year. In that event he would, of course, call upon all Italians for their help, enroll Lombard and Venetian exiles in the regulars, form a corps of volunteer auxiliaries, and entrust Medici with the organisation of companies of sharpshooters (*bersaglieri*) in the National Guard.

This was the greatest proof of statesmanship Cavour ever gave. The pivot of all popular movements and insurrections had been the general belief that Piedmont neither would nor could take the initiative, though she might be counted on to second a revolution. Now, not only was she resolved to initiate a war of liberation, but she actually intended looking to the Italian people as natural allies.

On January 1, 1859, the Emperor Louis Napoleon pronounced, perhaps without fully appreciating the meaning conveyed by his words, the famous apostrophe to the Austrian ambassador, which was instantly seized and commented upon as the prelude to a declaration of war. On the 10th, at the opening of the Piedmontese Parliament, Victor Emmanuel uttered the sentence which has become historic, and which rang as a signal throughout the country: "We are not insensible to the cry of woe which has reached us from so many parts of Italy." Then the French alliance became a certainty; there was no dissension, and the idea that the ally would be able to dictate peace to the King and to the people in arms, should he presently consider it necessary for his own ends, was scoffed at. Mazzini, however, from the very beginning, warned the Italians not to trust him, for, as Mr. Stansfeld told us, " Pippo adheres to his first strong conviction that Venice will not be liberated and peace concluded on the Mincio." Mazzini once more proved a true prophet. But at that moment Cavour was considered more than a match for Louis Napoleon as a diplomat, and every one seemed convinced that the King would never repeat his father's error of 1848, and sacrifice Venice a second time. So Prince Napoleon and Maréchal Niel were *fêted* at Turin, where the formal treaty of offensive and

1859] CAVOUR AND THE VOLUNTEERS

defensive alliance between France and Piedmont was signed on January 16, 1859, including the secret clauses for the cession of Savoy and Nice. On the 30th followed the wedding of Princess Clotilde with Prince Napoleon ; later, the passionate welcome given to the King and Cavour by the Genoese. The loan of fifty million francs—notwithstanding the refusal of all foreign bankers to launch it—was subscribed twice over by the people of Italy, thus refuting Lord Malmesbury's assertion that " not a thousand liras " would be subscribed in the Peninsula.

Over snow-clad mountains and by rain-swollen rivers exiles and deserters from the Austrian army poured into Piedmont, where they were enrolled in the regular army, this fact of itself giving Austria a grievance which justified her in proclaiming war against Piedmont. Despite the opposition of La Marmora, Minister of War, who protested, in obedience to the formal pledge given to the French Emperor, that only regular troops should be employed in the war, Cavour opened a depôt at Cuneo for the volunteers, and on March 17th the King signed the decree which named Garibaldi commander of the " Cacciatori delle Alpi " (Sharpshooters of the Alps), a troop to be organised by Cialdini, Cosenz, Medici, and others who had served in Rome and Venice. This audacious act, which absorbed the revolutionary element, was decisive for the future of Italy, and created in England an enthusiasm for the King and his omnipotent minister which a merely dynastic war would never have called forth.

Louis Napoleon in the meanwhile grew irresolute and greatly perturbed. He was violently opposed in his Italian plans by Walewski and by the Empress Eugènie. It was difficult to withstand the strong pressure brought to bear on him by the English Court and Government, and he was rendered still more anxious through the defiant aspect assumed by Prussia and Germany ; moreover, he felt in no way supported by the French people. But, as Mazzini had said, he knew that his throne would totter and his end come near, unless he could give *de la gloire* to the French nation. So he strove to induce Cavour to temporise, to delay, even to disarm and consent to a Congress. But Cavour, who now held him in the palm of his hand, stood firm. When in Paris, he threatened to return immediately to Turin, resign his premiership, advise the King to abdicate, and then publish the whole story, which would prove that the Emperor, and not he, had proposed the war, and had, moreover, received his first payment on account in the marriage of Prince Napoleon. And he peremptorily refused to disarm. Lord Cowley, on his side, endeavoured to persuade Cavour to accept the policy of a disarmament of France, Austria, and Piedmont to a peace footing, but it was of no avail. Cavour said to Lord Odo Russell, " Congress or no Congress, I shall force Austria to declare war."

Austria well knew that a duel to the death was inevitable, but, in the hope of paralysing the Piedmontese before their French allies could arrive, the Emperor Francis Joseph sent Baron von Kellesberg to Turin with an ultimatum demanding immediate disarmament, the dissolution of the volunteer corps, and, within three days, a " YES " or a " No."

Cavour's mighty will prevailed. The Baron took back " No."

" Alea jacta est " was Cavour's quiet announcement of his triumph, which Mazzini declared to be " a master-stroke."

On April 27th the Austrian vanguard passed the Ticino, and on the 29th the King issued his eloquent appeal " to the people of Italy." The Piedmontese army, echeloned between Casale and Alessandria, behind the Po and the Tanaro, prevented the Austrians entering Pavia. Fifty thousand Italians thus confronted 150,000 Austrians. To Garibaldi and his volunteers belongs the honour of being the first to cross the Ticino and enter Lombard territory, still dominated by Austria.

Austria had declared war, Austria had invaded the Sardinian States, Louis Napoleon was therefore "justified " in going to the assistance of his ally. His 1st Army Corps crossed the Alps on April 29th, and on May 12th he himself arrived at Genoa, welcomed by Cavour, whom he greeted with the words: "Vous devez être content, vos plans se réalisent." Assuredly Cavour was "content," but it became almost immediately evident that the plans of the allies were not identical. Napoleon in his proclamation had said "qu'il faut . que l'Italie soit libre jusqu'à l'Adriatique," but had been carefully silent regarding the rest of the Peninsula.

He had not reckoned with his host. The Italians had now something to say for themselves, and soon performed deeds which testified that the ideal of Italy "not only independent but united" had sunk into the very depths of their beings, dominated the intellects of her statesmen, and entranced the hearts of the masses. Mazzini was morally triumphant, though willing to stand apart, almost forgotten, in the rush of the moment. Cavour, the omnipotent factor in forcing on the War of Independence, now realised with astonishment that Italian Unity was no Utopia, that the thirty years of agitation, rebellion, and revolution—failures all—were but so many attempts on the part of the people of Italy to become a nation, to create a visible country for themselves.

Massa and Carrara were the first two cities to rise (April 28th), tear down the ensigns of the Duke of Modena, and proclaim the dictatorship of King Victor Emmanuel: Parma followed suit. In Tuscany, the Grand Duke had offended his people by visiting "King Bomba"—execrated more than ever for the recent sentences on Nicotera and the other martyrs of Sapri—but he remained blind to the many proofs indicating that the passion of his subjects for autonomy was fast disappearing. The Tuscans clamoured for alliance with Piedmont and war against Austria; hundreds of youths left Tuscany to join the Sardinian forces, and at last, on April 27th, the Duke finally comprehended that nothing was left for him but to decamp. Thus the dynasty of Lorraine ceased to exist. On May 12th the Tuscan Provisional Government, with Baron Bettino Ricasoli at its head, sent Don Neri Corsini to entreat King Victor Emmanuel to accept the sovereignty of the Grand-

THE BIRTH OF MODERN ITALY

Duchy. Cavour recommended acceptance, and proposed that the King's cousin, the Prince of Savoy Carignano, should at once go to Tuscany in the King's name. However, the Emperor Napoleon not only objected, but ordered Prince Napoleon, then at Genoa, to embark with the 5th French Army Corps for Leghorn. Cavour sped to Alessandria to remonstrate, on the ground that the presence of Prince Napoleon with a French army in Tuscany would awaken suspicion and jealousy in all the Courts of Europe. Failing to alter the Emperor's decision, he, with admirable promptness, advised King Victor Emmanuel to himself appoint the Prince by an order of the day, in the following terms: " Holding you worthy to fight side by side with the victorious soldiers of France, I place you under the orders of my well-beloved son-in-law, Prince Napoleon, to whom the Emperor of the French has entrusted important military operations. Obey him as you would obey myself." Baron Ricasoli welcomed the Prince with all due honour, but his ideals and intentions are admirably summed up in a letter to his brother Vincenzo, who was serving as an officer in the Piedmontese army: " We shall soon proclaim Victor Emmanuel King of Italy here in Tuscany, with hereditary rights : the Romagna will not delay to follow : Italy will be one up to the Garigliano, and before long up to the Faro (Straits of Messina)."

This was a stride beyond Cavour assuredly, but as a Unitarian, Ricasoli could even vie with Mazzini, for though his conversion had come late his conviction was deep. The Emperor Napoleon thought himself omnipotent, so he resented Cavour's opposition and the order of the day by which Victor Emmanuel boldly spoke to the Tuscans as if they were already his subjects. This was the first rift within the lute of the Franco-Piedmontese alliance. But presently the Duke of Modena joined the Duchess of Parma and the Grand Duke of Tuscany in Mantua, and the successive victories of the Franco-Piedmontese armies compelled Austria to evacuate the Legations. Ancona, Bologna, Ferrara tore down the Papal emblems, and proclaimed

BETTINO RICASOLI

Victor Emmanuel Dictator, an example followed at once by Forli, Ravenna, Fano, Sinigaglia, Jesi, Fossombrone, Città di Castello, Perugia, and Orvieto. The King named Massimo d'Azeglio his lieutenant in the Legations, with plenipotentiary powers, but the French Emperor put his veto upon the nomination, and rudely repulsed a deputation from Bologna, which came to his headquarters of Montechiaro on the eve of the battle of Solferino. He abruptly asked the deputation · " Why did you revolt against the Papal authorities as soon as the Austrians had left the Legations ? Revolted against whom ? Against the Pope ? But the French did not come over to Italy to deprive the Pope of his possessions ! "

Eventually, however, Napoleon consented to the mission of D'Azeglio as Military Commissioner ; but the cruel and bloody massacre of the people of Perugia, sanctioned by Cardinal Pecci (the future Leo XIII.), and the reoccupation of Ancona and the Marches by the foreign mercenaries of Pius IX. was due to this delay.

It is not our task to follow the victories of the allies, though historians in general seem to remember only those of the French, whereas Victor Emmanuel and his regulars came in for even more than their share of gains and losses, while Garibaldi won the admiration of Victor Emmanuel, of his generals, and of Cavour, who stood by him staunchly to the last, and, what was still more to the purpose, of the volunteers themselves and of the populations with whom they mixed. These were soon to rally around his standard to fight without foreign allies till Unity should become an accomplished fact.

It seems to us unprofitable to discuss the motives which led to the French Emperor's apparently sudden resolve to end the war. The growing hostility of Prussia and of the German Confederation, the agitation of the ultramontanes in France, the harrowing spectacle of the battlefields, have been all, and severally, put forward as conjectural reasons. May not the stubborn, unexpected manifestations of popular resolve to make Italy ONE, which greeted him at

THE BIRTH OF MODERN ITALY

every step, the evident intentions of the King, Cavour, Ricasoli, and D'Azeglio to encourage and accede to the popular demands, even though they listened courteously, nay deferentially, to his arguments, be included in the speculation? Prince Napoleon was with him, it must be remembered, and he had done nothing but abuse the Tuscans' laxity in enlisting under his command. The dream about a possible kingdom of Etruria had vanished, and there was the threatening spectre of Italian Unity staring him in the face. How render this impossible? Clearly by the retention in Italy of the Austrians, who would at any rate preserve to the Pope such remnants of the temporal power as were not yet reft from him. But his solemn pledge, his promise that " Italy should be free from the Alps to the Adriatic," what of that? What, however, could the breaking of a promise to Italy mean to the perjurer who had violated his presidential oath to France? Certain it is that his offer of peace to Austria was neither sudden nor unpremeditated.

On July 6th, without warning any one, he sent General Fleury, his Master of the Horse, to Verona with an autograph letter to the Emperor Francis Joseph, but already on the 2nd he had telegraphed to Persigny (French minister in London) to ascertain whether the new English Cabinet, with Palmerston at its head, which, as stated above, had just assumed office, would take the initiative and propose an armistice, on the following terms: Italy to be "Italian"; Venice and Modena to be consigned to an Austrian Archduke as independent sovereign; Lombardy and the duchy of Parma to be handed to Piedmont, Tuscany to be restored to the Grand Duke; the Legations separated from the Papal States and governed by a lieutenant of Victor Emanuel under the suzerainty of the Pope; these Italian States to be all united in a Confederation, with the Pope for President. Persigny declared to Palmerston that this idea was his own, but the Premier ironically asked him whether Austria, the King of Sardinia, and Cavour were parties to the proposals? Persigny could but answer negatively, and Palmerston, with his keen foresight, had been so well aware of the fact that he had already written to Lord John Russell that "a proposal that Italy should be left to the Italians would not be accepted by Austria, nor are we told whether the Piedmontese and the Italians would accept the proposed federation. It could never answer. The Venetians would revolt, Austria would intervene, and, with a footing in Modena, she would take the opportunity of intermeddling in Central Italy. If the project is the Emperor's, he can only be influenced by jealousy of Piedmont or deference to the Pope ; in any case, it would never prevent the Italians from realising their aspirations, and why should we propose to carve out the people of Italy into morsels, as if we had the right to dispose of them? No, I cannot back up Persigny's plan!"

So Palmerston not only returned a clear and uncompromising "No" to the French proposal, but he called upon D'Azeglio,[1] the Piedmontese minister, who had already heard rumours that King Leopold of Belgium was actively working to save Venetia for the Austrian Archduke Maximilian, and told him that both Lord John Russell and himself were of opinion that "no proposals by third parties should be proffered." D'Azeglio, in his letter to Cavour of July 4th, describes in detail his interview with the Premier, and tells of the decision arrived at by the British Government, adding, "mais qu'en tous cas ils étaient également convaincus que ce qu'il pourrait y avoir de plus utile pour les Italiens serait de constituer un royaume de la Haute-Italie, dont Lord Palmerston nommât, une à une et sans que je les lui suggère, toutes les parties. . . . Il s'agit de joindre à nos États, non seulement le Lombardo-Vénitien, mais Parme, Modène, la Toscane et les Legations. Lord Palmerston revint également sur ce qu'il m'avait déjà dit, que dans les idées des hommes principaux du Ministère actuel, il n'y avait aucun danger

---

[1] D'Azeglio, Marchese Emanuele, nephew of Massimo d'Azeglio, not to be mistaken for him. Was for a long time Minister, then Ambassador, in London.

pour les intérets Anglais à ce qu'un Etat, fort comme celui-là, possède Venise en même temps que Gênes."

But the Emperor Napoleon, as Palmerston had tersely expressed in his letter to Lord John Russell, "was tired of *his* war, and found the job tougher than he expected," so, as soon as he received Persigny's telegram stating that England had refused to interfere, he, as we stated above, sent Fleury to the Emperor of Austria with proposals for a truce. Then he immediately telegraphed to the Empress what had taken place, and this the official *Moniteur* published to astounded Europe. To King Victor Emmanuel the Emperor simply communicated the fact that he had agreed to a suspension of hostilities, but added that he intended, during the armistice, to bring his army up to 200,000 men, and advised his ally to augment his own contingent to at least 100,000 men, as, though he had thoughts of proposing a peace, the terms he would offer could never be accepted by Austria. King Victor Emmanuel, though deeply offended at the discourtesy, sent General della Rocca as his plenipotentiary for the truce, which was signed on July 8th by Maréchal Vaillant for the Emperor Napoleon, Field-Marshal Hess for the Emperor Francis Joseph, and General della Rocca.

On July 11th, Napoleon having sought and obtained a personal interview with the Emperor Francis Joseph, they met at Villafranca, and then and there they agreed upon the general terms of peace. These were as follows: The creation of an Italian Confederation under the presidency of the Pope, who should be asked to grant to his subjects "des réformes indispensables"; the cession of Lombardy (with the exception of the fortresses of Mantua and Peschiera) to the French Emperor, who would remit it to the King of Sardinia; Venetia was to remain under the domination of Austria but to form part of the Italian Confederation; the Grand Duke of Tuscany and the Duke of Modena were to reacquire their States. But of the duchy of Parma nothing was said.

When King Victor Emmanuel was informed by his faith-

URBANO RATTAZZI.

1859] CAVOUR'S WRATHFUL RESIGNATION

less ally of the terms he had arranged with the enemy, he must have protested with all his energy, and it is known that he immediately spoke of carrying on the war singlehanded, to which threat it was reported that the Emperor had cynically replied, "A votre aise, mais au lieu d'un ennemi, vous pourriez bien en trouver deux." In these terrible conditions, what could the King do but append his signature to the shameful treaty? This he did, but with the reservation, which, later, proved most useful, "Approuvé, pour ce qui me concerne."

Humiliated and resentful, he returned to his headquarters at Monzambano, to confront a fury which surpassed even his own, an exasperation that he was powerless to calm. Cavour, who had learned the news only from the Emperor's telegram to the Empress, published in the *Moniteur*, arrived at Monzambano like a thunderbolt, and openly denounced the treachery of the Emperor. The account of the ensuing interview between the King and his Prime Minister, as it is given by Chiala, shows that it must have been more than stormy. Cavour implored the King to withdraw his army from Lombardy, leaving " his perfidious ally to carry out his nefarious schemes alone." "Abdicate, as did your father," he is reported to have said; then, beside himself with grief and rage, he cried to his sovereign that he, Cavour, alone knew the Italians, and that he, he alone, was their true King. Victor Emmanuel, utterly furious, is said to have replied in his native Piedmontese dialect, "*Chiel a l'è 'l Re? Chiel a l'è un birichin!*" (So, you are the King, are you? You are an impudent puppy!). Cavour tendered his resignation on the spot, which was as immediately accepted, and the King designated Rattazzi his successor.

"Evil does not always harm," says the Italian proverb, and in this case it proved true. Cavour's despairing outburst showed him to be intensely human; it told the Italians that he, at least, was not untrue to them, and it gave them still a ray of hope in the immense consternation and fury by which the country was overcome when the treaty of

THE BIRTH OF MODERN ITALY

Villafranca became publicly known. Had Cavour quietly acquiesced in the ignominious terms proposed, the revolted provinces and the volunteers would have felt themselves deliberately betrayed, and would have probably resolved on some desperate attempt which, considering that the French Emperor had nearly 200,000 men in Lombardy, and that Austria was now free-handed, could only have ended disastrously. Now, Prime Minister or not, the people of Tuscany and of the Legations, with their leaders, all looked to him, and to him alone, for the watchword of every succeeding hour; and while as a minister he had been bound by many considerations, as a private citizen he was free to advise the Royal Commissioners resident in Modena, Bologna, and Florence concerning the line of least resistance to be pursued. And so, to Farini he whispered, "Arms and money"; he advised Massimo d'Azeglio to hold on his way rejoicing, and counselled the Tuscan Provisional Government to yield not one iota to diplomatic pressure, but to stick to their faith in Piedmont and keep their powder dry. One consolation was, however, vouchsafed to Cavour, for the Emperor Napoleon, on leaving Turin, had said to Victor Emmanuel, "Your Government will pay me the expenses of the war, and we will say no more about Nice and Savoy."

Napoleon did not suspect for a moment that the overwhelming passion for unity, which had silently and wonderfully welded together the hearts of the Italians, would frustrate his best-laid plans. "We desire our annexation to the constitutional kingdom of Piedmont : we will neither receive back our renegade princes nor permit the formation of a separate kingdom in central Italy," came as a unanimous, formidable rejoinder to the French Emperor's machinations. The British Government, admirably informed by Sir James Hudson, decided that no intervention of any kind should be permitted, and Palmerston wrote that "the people must be allowed to elect their representatives to a National Assembly, empowered to decide on their future destinies, of which the people are, undoubtedly, the only arbiters."

Thus, the Assemblies were convened, and each unanimously pronounced for "annexation immediate and unconditional" to Piedmont under King Victor Emmanuel; and to prove that the people intended to support their votes by force if necessary, the formation of an army of Central Italy was resolved upon, and Baron Ricasoli, head of Tuscany's Provisional Government, invited Garibaldi, who was still in command of the "Cacciatori delle Alpi," to assume the lead of the Tuscan contingent. Garibaldi at once sent his resignation to the King, who accepted it, and he went to assume the new command with the utmost alacrity, followed by all his officers and most of his volunteers. So, with such men as Fanti, Farini, and Ricasoli resolutely united, no doubt as to ultimate success could be entertained.

Mazzini, intent only on Unity, and, as ever, indifferent to personal success, together with the few exiles who had refrained from taking part in the war with Napoleon, recognised the wonderful strides made by the Unitarian principle, and never looked above or beyond the question of national sovereignty. For Mazzini, the one thing needful was to urge on the annexation of Central Italy, and from thence carry the Unitarian flag into the Neapolitan provinces and Sicily, where a network of associations, Unitarian pure and simple, already existed. Mazzini arrived safely in Florence, and remained there for three months, his presence being well known to Ricasoli, with whom he often communicated through the popular tribune, Beppe Dolfi. From Florence he wrote his famous letter to King Victor Emmanuel, urging him to make Italy One, and become King, Dictator, or President—a letter which, though Mazzini never believed much in its effect, powerfully influenced the King.

My husband and I came to Milan, having accepted Garibaldi's invitation to join him; Mario was to be in his corps of "Guides," and I was to fulfil my old promise by becoming the "nurse of his wounded." In Milan, Mario, acting under Mazzini's advice, wrote in the *Pensiero e Azione*, which had reappeared on July 10th, an article on

THE BIRTH OF MODERN ITALY

"The Duty of Republicans," in which, after pointing out that Unity was the corner-stone of their creed, he concluded: "My brother Republicans, while maintaining our political faith intact, we respect the freely expressed wish of the nation, and now, one and all, loyally and openly let us arm and fight under the leadership (*duce*) of Victor Emmanuel. This is our duty." Mr. Stansfeld—who kept us posted concerning public opinion in England and sent us the papers, which were unanimous in affirming the right of Italy to decide on its own destinies and in stigmatising the French Emperor in unsparing terms, as well as in declaring that after the massacre of Perugia the Pope's temporal power must cease—fully approved of this article, adding that "Palmerston and Russell are, of course, for Italy, but none is more ardent than Mr. Gladstone, who is now an enthusiast for Italian Unity under Piedmont, and would rejoice if 'Bomba' were sent to the right about."

We were accordingly as much "astounded and disgusted" as Mr. Stansfeld was, when we were arrested, by order of Leone Cipriani, Governor of Bologna (but really agent of Napoleon III.), as "Austrian spies," and imprisoned in the castle of Ferrara—the very same prison in which Tasso had been incarcerated. Avvocato Brofferio, sent by Garibaldi to obtain our release, was threatened by the populace with their vengeance and unable to do anything for us, so we were transported as felons across Lombardy to the Swiss frontier.

The following months, from August, 1859, to March, 1860, were dreary indeed; but the conduct of the Italians deservedly won the praise of Europe, and especially the enthusiastic approval of the English people. The unanimous votes of the separate Assemblies of Tuscany, the Duchies and the Legations, enthusiastically reaffirming their desire for annexation to Piedmont, were presented to King Victor Emmanuel by their deputations; but Rattazzi, entirely dominated by Louis Napoleon, dissuaded the King from accepting them. He could only "receive" these votes. But the tergiversations of the Rattazzi Cabinet so wore out the patience of the people that the clamour for the return to power of Cavour became continually more pressing, and finally the King most unwillingly recalled him from his retreat at Lerici (January 16, 1860).

In the meanwhile each of the four States—Tuscany, Romagna, Parma, and Modena—gathered its little army of regulars and volunteers, and now agreed to form a military League, while Ricasoli, who, lest such a step should lead to the formation of a separate " kingdom of Etruria " for Prince Napoleon, had refused to unite the States under one government, now spurred on the armaments energetically, and, as already stated, offered to Garibaldi the command of the Tuscan contingent. General Fanti, of 1848 fame, and now of the Piedmontese regular army, was summoned to head the League. King Victor Emmanuel not only accepted the resignation, which he was, of course, bound to tender, but assured him that he should be at any time readmitted to his military rank and rights. Between the King and Garibaldi a real friendship, founded on mutual esteem, had grown up, for both had formed one common resolve—to promote the interests of Italy at all hazards and against all adversaries. Fanti possessed the same absolute confidence in Garibaldi's patriotism and loyalty, and accordingly named him his second in command of the League; and these two warriors, both glorious sons of the Revolution, decided, with the assent of Ricasoli and Farini, to support the populations of the Marches and Umbria in their efforts to throw off the abhorred Papal yoke and proclaim their annexation to Piedmont. The Tuscan and Modenese divisions were united under Garibaldi's command, and Fanti gave him the following instructions in writing:— To defend the frontier, if attacked by the Papal troops; if an entire province, or even a single city, should rise, to at once declare its annexation to Romagna, sending immediate assistance to prevent a repetition of the Perugian massacres; and if the Papal troops attempted to reoccupy the risen territories, to demand the aid of the entire League.

THE BIRTH OF MODERN ITALY

Of course, the populations were ready to revolt, and, of course, Garibaldi was quite as prepared to go to their rescue; but Cipriani, Napoleon's agent, got scent of the affair and informed his master, who at once threatened the trembling ministers in Turin with intervention. Cavour himself deemed the plan too risky, as did Ricasoli; but Fanti and Garibaldi both persisting, it was arranged between the ministers that they should be deprived of their commands. It is clear that King Victor Emmanuel got wind of this, for he wrote to Fanti, on October 29, 1859, as follows: " My dear General, I fear that you and Garibaldi are to be deprived of your commands. I advise you to resign and return here. Suggest to Garibaldi to do the same, and in case he should refuse, leave to him the responsibility of whatever may happen." Clearly, if Garibaldi succeeded, all would be well; if he failed, the King knew that he would take the entire blame on to his own shoulders.

Cavour, on his arrival at Turin, induced La Marmora to prevent Fanti by telegram from resigning, and with Ricasoli and Farini he believed that they would thus persuade Garibaldi also to abandon his designs. But Cavour, after a brief interview with the King, hearing that the people in the Marches had risen and that Garibaldi was on the point of crossing the frontier, caused Fanti to stop him with all his troops at Cattolica, and then the King, acting under the advice of La Marmora, vehemently urged by Cavour, summoned Garibaldi to Turin, where the hero at once flung up his commission, respectfully declining to enter the regular army, and immediately afterwards launched his celebrated proclamation to the Italians.

A momentous fact this, as it indicated the popular leader's intention to return to revolutionary methods for the attainment of the noble goal of Unity. In this proclamation Garibaldi, after alluding to the subtle and perfidious artifices which rendered his presence in Central Italy useless for the furtherance of the common cause, went on to say that " the day in which Victor Emmanuel should again summon my warriors for the redemption of the Fatherland I shall be found armed, side by side with my brave companions. The miserable feline policy which retards the majestic march of Italian affairs ought to make us rally, more than ever, round the brave and loyal soldier of Italian Independence, who is incapable of receding from his sublime and generous purpose, and to prepare money and arms to withstand whomsoever shall attempt to throw us back again into our ancient miseries."

When Mario and I, after our detention in Ferrara, reached Lugano, all hope of fighting for Italy seemed at an end, for, as Mr. Stansfeld wrote, "things seem to get no 'forrarder.'" Our friend wanted to know "what they are waiting for and what are they afraid of? Why does not the King accept at once all the populations that demand annexation? If he cannot go himself, why not send his uncle? He must recall Cavour, convoke the new Parliament with members elected from all the States, and proclaim the new kingdom. The British Government would recognise it immediately."

These questions, simple and logical as they were, remained unanswered for a long time, one dilatory step following another, such as the proposal of a new Congress, with Cavour as Italian plenipotentiary, then no Congress and Cavour recalled to Turin, and so on, although the provinces of Central Italy had now, by universal suffrage, voted once more for union with Piedmont. At last the enigma was solved.

Cavour, on January 20, 1860, assumed the premiership, and the King warned him at once that, in order to obtain the consent of the French Emperor to the annexation of Tuscany and Central Italy, Savoy and Nice would have to be sacrificed. Cavour made no demur, inexplicably, for had the King and his minister refused to surrender them and meanwhile annexed the other States, no one could have prevented his taking that decisive step, as England would have awakened in time. On his return to power Cavour found that the dream of Unity was less than ever a " Mazzinian Utopia ; " he saw that it was deeply rooted in the hearts of the Italian masses ; so he now accepted the idea in its entireness, determined to utilise it for the benefit of the House of Savoy, thus crushing any lingering tendencies towards a republic which still lurked in the hearts of those who had loyally lowered their flag on the sacred altar of Unity. The cession of Nice and Savoy—two small provinces with at most 800,000 inhabitants—in exchange for the Duchies, Tuscany, and the Legations—four provinces with eight million inhabitants—he considered an excellent bargain; but he foresaw rocks ahead. Garibaldi, whose goodwill he was anxious to retain, would certainly be up in arms; the English Government would prohibit the barter —probably with more than words; hence, for the moment, he kept the affair a profound secret even from that faithful henchman of his, Sir James Hudson, who had made himself conspicuous in paving the way for Cavour's return to power.

But the secret was an open one for Mazzini, who, on his way to England to spend New Year's Day with the Stansfelds, passed through Lugano, and gave the warning to Mario for the *Pensiero e Azione*, which he was then editing from his hiding-place, and he informed Mr. Stansfeld of the whole affair for future discussion in the House of Commons. And as soon as the House met Mr. Stansfeld asked the Foreign Secretary whether it was, or was not, true that at the end of the preceding December the formation of a new association, entitled " La Nazione Armata," having as its object the arming and organising of large numbers of the population in the new kingdom of Piedmont, at the instance of the King and under the direction of General Garibaldi, had been set aside, and that the nomination by Royal decree of the same Garibaldi to be Inspector-General of the National Guard had been withdrawn, on account of the opposition of Sir James Hudson, under instructions from the British Government? He further wished to know if Sir James Hudson had acted in conjunction with the French ambassador in protesting against the measures cited—measures which would undoubtedly have been adopted had it not been for a threat that the good offices of Great

Britain in regard to Italian affairs would be withdrawn if they were persisted in?

Lord John Russell replied that in consequence of Sir James Hudson having privately expressed an opinion adverse to this armed association in the Sardinian States, Garibaldi had resigned the presidency of the aforesaid association. Stansfeld could not have been satisfied with this incomplete answer had not Lord John also given him private information. Light is thrown into this imbroglio by the following letter of Garibaldi to Medici—which the latter sent to Panizzi—dated January 5, 1860:—

> MY DEAR MEDICI,—Once again I have preached to the desert. I believed that I had obtained permission to organise the National Guard in Lombardy. This very day I awaited the nomination, instructions, &c. Instead of this the foreign diplomats, incited by Cavour, Dabormida, La Marmora, who have tendered their resignation, have signified to the King that they do not understand that there could exist in the State any other force or power or armed persons except the King and his army. You will be stupefied to hear that Hudson, whom I consulted, gave me the identical answer, which proves that he, with the other members of the diplomatical family, has imposed on the King the conditions which result in preventing me from composing the differences which divide the liberal party, which, as you know, was my object in going to Turin.

The efforts of the Cavourians, among whom were most of Garibaldi's chief officers and friends—Medici, Bertani, and Bixio, &c.—having at last succeeded, and Cavour having formed his new Cabinet, satisfaction became general, although his policy eventuated in the sacrifice of Savoy and Nice, which Rattazzi had refused to surrender, but over which Cavour never in reality hesitated. To the last, however, he denied the facts.

Lord John Russell was enchanted at Cavour's return to power, not foreseeing the consequences, and writing to Sir James Hudson he said: "The critical moment has arrived, and I am delighted to have Cavour's sense and ability to conduct matters at Turin, instead of the late incapables." Sir James Hudson, in sending an account of affairs to Lord John Russell, observed: "I was not a little astonished to learn that I am accused of having exercised an undue pressure upon the Ratazzi Cabinet (if I had had the power it would have been by the application of hemp to its wind pipe, and not by sending a scrap of paper), which had forced its chief to send his resignation to the King. I cannot say that I was particularly affected by the intelligence, but I deemed it advisable to enter a protest against the truth of that assertion."

Privately Mr. Stansfeld was able to warn Lord John that Savoy and Nice were to be ceded, and that the Emperor's reason for dispersing the dream of a Congress was that at a Congress it would have been impossible to moot that subject. He was also able to state that the Emperor and Cavour were positively agreed on the cession of those two provinces, provided Louis Napoleon abstained from opposing the annexation of Tuscany to Piedmont. Of course, Stansfeld had his information from Mazzini, while Hudson, who believed all that Cavour told him, or at least held as right all that Cavour did or attempted to do, sought to convince Lord John that no territorial cession was contemplated.

So January and February passed in a delusive uncertainty, and not until March 1st, when the Emperor at the opening of his Parliament declared that a vital necessity existed for France "de réclamer les versants Français des montagnes," was anxiety reawakened. But the time had passed for preventing the cession of the two provinces. That Hudson had been a dupe and not a passive instrument in the hands of Cavour it is impossible to believe, for the King himself, interrogated by Garibaldi through the Hungarian Turr, replied in so many words that "as he, for the good of Italy, had consented to sacrifice the cradle of his race, so Garibaldi must make an equal sacrifice of his own birthplace."

A perusal of the correspondence between Thouvenel (successor of Walewski at the French Foreign Office) and the Duc de Grammont, French ambassador at Rome, leaves no doubt as to the formal engagements of Cavour for this cession; and so convinced was the Piedmontese statesman that by it he would commit Napoleon to "becoming his accomplice," and would probably gain his assistance in a war against Austria for the liberation of Venice, that he cut himself off deliberately from all offers of support, rejecting tentatives that might have saved one, if not both, of the imperilled provinces. Immediately after the Emperor's speech Lord John Russell impressed upon Sir James Hudson the necessity of preventing " any revendication of natural frontiers," and urged that even if Savoy had been promised at the commencement of the war, since Venice had been left to Austria the agreement was null and void, adding : " If the King sells his inheritance of Savoy to obtain Tuscany, he will be disgraced in the eyes of Europe, and we shall not hesitate to affix to his conduct the fitting epithets." But Sir James Hudson replied that he had read his despatches to Cavour, and that Cavour had emphatically replied : " I declare to you that at this moment no engagements exist between us and France for the cession of Savoy. If the Savoyards, by a great numerical majority, petition Parliament for separation, the question will be treated parliamentarily. But I tell you frankly that the best way to meet this question is openly and sincerely, and that in no other way will I ever consent to meet it. I agree with Lord John 'that the King would be disgraced were he to *céder, troquer ou vendre la Savoie.*'"

Now, the Savoyards did not desire union with France ; they were, instead, loyally attached to their Royal house. The inhabitants of the county of Nice were Italians to the backbone, but, nevertheless, a month after Cavour's return to power, in spite of Rattazzi's entreaties to be allowed to make one last attempt to save Nice at least, a secret treaty concerning the cession of the two provinces was signed on March 12, 1860, before even the annexation of Central Italy to Piedmont had been officially sanctioned. This, in spite of the protests of the Savoyards, of the touching petition addressed to the King by a great majority of the inhabitants of Nice, and of the fact that the new Parliament had not yet been convoked.

The French Foreign Secretary, Thouvenel, fearing that

the prey might yet escape by a hostile vote in the Piedmontese Parliament, sent Benedetti, "Directeur des Affaires Politiques" in the French Foreign Office, to Turin, who told Cavour that "*l'Empereur veut absolument Nice et la Savoie, lors même qu'il aurait contre lui l'Europe entière.*" And a private letter to Lord John Russell from Hudson narrates that when Benedetti told Cavour that if the treaty were not signed the French troops, on their withdrawal from Milan, would be ordered to occupy Bologna and Florence, he at last consented to affix his signature to the treaty.

The formal "Act of Cession" was published in the *Moniteur* on the morrow of this interview, the 25th of March. The ratification of the treaty by the Piedmontese Parliament and the plebiscite of the populations were mere farces, as the immense majority of the former were the instruments of Cavour and the provinces were occupied by French troops and inundated by French agents. Affairs in Nice would, however, not have gone forward so quietly to the end had Garibaldi been allowed to go there to head an armed protest, as he intended, and, if we may credit Laurence Oliphant, who was to have accompanied him, "to smash up the ballot-boxes."

But other great events were maturing, and these prevented Garibaldi from carrying this plan into execution.

FRANCESCO CRISPI.

XXI

THE "THOUSAND"

1860–1861

Crispi's work in Sicily—Rosalino Pilo—Parts played by the King and Cavour—Cavour's embarrassment—Garibaldi fixes the number of volunteers at a thousand—He starts for Sicily—His intention to invade Naples—Five days of suspense—Pilo's death after six weeks of heroic struggle which kept the way open for Garibaldi—Castelfidardo—Volturno—Garibaldi hands over eleven millions of Italians to King Victor Emmanuel.

EVER since the tragedy of Sapri, where Pisacane and most of his followers were massacred, Nicotera and his few fellow-survivors being immured in the frightful dungeons of Favignana, the Neapolitan and Sicilian patriots had been unremitting in their efforts to bring about a combined revolution, while Rosalino Pilo, Crispi, and other exiles laboured with Mazzini to second their plans. Twice, at the risk of liberty and life, Crispi had gone through the island in different disguises to organise committees in the chief cities, to introduce arms and instruct conspirators in the secrets of bomb-making. Rattazzi and Farini had been willing to help the Sicilians, but Cavour, not desirous of keeping so many irons in the fire, had discountenanced any movement in the South, and his *alter ego*, La Farina, an ex-Republican, had successfully prevented more than one rising from taking place in the island.

Rosalino Pilo, in February, 1860, interrogated Garibaldi concerning his views on the subject, and the general, while impressing upon him the absolute necessity of avoiding any unsuccessful revolt, gave him letters for Bertani and the president of the Committee for the "Million of Muskets" requesting them to furnish Pilo with money and arms, and he added: "In case of action, remember that the programme is '*Italy and Victor Emmanuel.*'" Garibaldi then promised to lead or to second any movement, however hazardous, that offered a chance of success, but he deemed the moment unfavourable, because "the fate of the Central Provinces was being weighed in the scales of the diplomats." This was a natural, straightforward course, and proves the falsehood of Garibaldi's calumniators, who affirmed that, in the beginning at least, he opposed the Sicilian revolutionists because they were Mazzinians. The truth is that it was Cavour and his agents who prevented Pilo from obtaining either arms or money.

Meanwhile an insurrection broke out in Palermo, and Rosalino Pilo started from Genoa for his native island in a tiny pilot-boat with a single companion, hoping to encourage the Sicilians to hold out, as Garibaldi would be coming.

At that very moment Garibaldi arrived in Genoa from Caprera, bent upon rushing to Nice to prevent its annexation to France at any cost. But Bertani, Medici, Bixio, all his friends and generals, were unanimous in wishing to assist the Sicilians, and determined to go to Sicily with or without him. The return of Rosalino Pilo's pilot with excellent news proved to be the proverbial feather in the balance. He reported the island to be actually in full revolution—the insurgents, though defeated at Palermo, triumphant in the mountains; and Pilo wrote in the highest spirits that nothing was needed save Garibaldi's presence to ensure success.

The part played in regard to the Sicilian expedition by the King and by Cavour has been repeatedly and most passionately discussed, the latter's adversaries maintaining that he opposed it vehemently, though forbidden by the King to take steps for its prevention. According to them,

Cavour was glad to be rid of the popular idol, who was holding him responsible for the sale of his birthplace, and who, therefore, hated him as a traitor to the cause of Italian Unity. They maintained that the Premier even went so far as to deprive Garibaldi of the sinews of war indispensable to success, and accused him of suborning the boatmen who were to have carried the arms and ammunition on board the steamers.

But the letters of Cavour himself, published after his death, together with those of Massimo d'Azeglio, La Farina, Admiral Persano, and others, place Cavour's conduct in its true light. He had just induced Victor Emmanuel to write a letter to the young King of Naples, successor of "Bomba," inviting him to grant reforms, to show himself a true Italian, break with Austria, and join in a war for Italian Independence. Furthermore, the Prime Minister desired time and calm to properly organise the newly acquired provinces; he knew that, in case of Garibaldi's success, all Europe would accuse him of connivance, while in case of failure he would be reproached by Italy for allowing precious lives to be sacrificed in an enterprise as desperately hopeless as those in which the brothers Bandiera and Pisacane had perished.

As regards the King, it is true that Cavour, although not at the moment minister, had induced him to recall Garibaldi from Cattolica when he had been about to cross into the Papal States and liberate the Marches and Umbria, so that the general, ever docile to the voice of Victor Emmanuel, had then thrown up his commission and retired in dudgeon to Caprera. But in the present case the King saw differently; Garibaldi, before pledging his word to go to the assistance of the Sicilians, had informed him of his project, requesting to be allowed to take the Reggio Brigade, chiefly composed of his old volunteers, and of which one regiment was commanded by Sacchi, his faithful comrade since Montevidian days. The King, it appears, neither assented nor dissented, so that Garibaldi summoned Sacchi and bade him hold himself ready. But in the meanwhile Cavour convinced the King of the unwisdom of such a step, and Garibaldi received a direct prohibition, upon which he immediately informed Sacchi that he must not only remain at his post, but prevent any of the soldiers from deserting. It has even been stated that Cavour insisted, in a long and heated discussion with the King, that Garibaldi should be at once arrested. This Victor Emmanuel refused to allow, asking, " Who would dare to do it ? " and, according to the French diplomat, d'Haussonville, Cavour replied, "I will ! I, Cavour, in person ! "

Nevertheless, what appears certain is that Cavour refrained from taking any active measures to prevent the enlistments that went on openly in Genoa, and that he connived at the loading and departure of the two steamers in which the expedition embarked, and which belonged to Rubattino, a patriotic shipowner. Cavour also secretly arranged for them to escape the capture which would otherwise have been their fate, and he took no steps to prevent the utilisation of the military stores purchased by the committee of the " Million Muskets," and deposited in the barracks of the *Carabinieri* in Milan. Massimo d'Azeglio, however, then Governor of Lombardy, put his veto upon this proceeding, deeming it highly incorrect to allow arms to be furnished to Sicilian revolutionists while Piedmont still had a representative at the Court of Naples. So 12,000 Enfield rifles and a quantity of ammunition were left idle in the barracks of Milan until Cavour ordered their transfer to serve for the second expedition, commanded by Medici.

Cavour's embarrassment must have been a most serious one. He, better than any man in Italy, understood the difficulties surrounding the country. The French Emperor had assured him and Ricasoli that if Austria intervened to prevent the annexation of Tuscany to Piedmont France would remain neutral. He also knew that Russia, Prussia, and of course Austria, were opposed to any attack on the dominions of the King of Naples—that Napoleon III., satisfied with the acquisition of Savoy and Nice, was anxious to withdraw his troops from Rome and leave the

Pope to the guardianship of Neapolitan troops and the mercenaries recruited from all quarters by devout Catholics. He was not unmindful that the Emperor had requested him not to oppose the occupation of the Marches by these motley soldiers, for when he had replied, "In that case Piedmontese troops will occupy Ancona," Napoleon at once manifested considerable ill-humour. He knew that the Neapolitan troops were concentrated in the Abruzzi, that the son of the King of Wurtemberg had been invited to assume the command of the Papal forces, that Spain had offered assistance, that the Dukes of Modena and Parma had sent cannon and had promised large sums of money, and, finally, that both the King of Naples and the Pope, aided by the Government of Austria, were busy recruiting soldiers in that country. It can scarcely be wondered at if this audacious but prudent statesman declined to put his hand into such a hornets' nest.

But how could Cavour prevent others from doing so? The immense ascendancy which he had obtained over Garibaldi and his followers in 1859 had been forfeited by their recall from the Cattolica, for which he was held responsible, while the cession of Savoy and Nice had alienated from him the entire "Party of Action." Clearly it would have been impossible for the Premier to prevent the expedition by moral suasion, and force was out of the question. His instinct told him that, after all, success might crown the enterprise, however risky and rash it looked; so, hour by hour, the anxious and perturbed minister received news of the preparations.

Garibaldi refused to accede to the entreaties of a band of Republicans to lead them under a "neutral flag," and fixed the number of volunteers to accompany him at 1,000. Bixio was commissioned to secure the steamers *Piemonte* and *Lombardo* from the willing Rubattino, and departure was arranged for the 5th of May from Quarto, near Genoa. Cavour ordered Admiral Persano to cruise in the waters of the island of Sardinia and arrest Garibaldi's two vessels "if they entered any port," but he was not to interfere with them if he happened to meet them on the high seas. One point Cavour made unmistakably clear: he told Sirtori that, however much the Government might choose to ignore the departure of volunteers for Sicily, they would hinder, at any cost, an invasion of the Papal States. But it happened that this invasion formed part of Garibaldi's original plan, and he had left Medici behind in Genoa expressly to organise it. Exactly as in Pisacane's case, the schooners bearing the ammunition, missed the steamers, owing to a treachery never decisively brought home, and Garibaldi decided to land at Talamone, near Orbetello. He succeeded in persuading the grim old disciplinarian who commanded the Orbetello fortress to deliver up to him a quantity of ammunition, of which he stood in sore need. Then he left a small detachment under the command of Colonel Zambianchi, with instructions, written in his own hand, to invade the Papal territory, attack the foreign mercenaries hired by the Pope's Government, foment popular insurrection, enlist all Italian deserters from the Papal forces, and avoid infringing the territories belonging to King Victor Emmanuel, whose name must be the battle-cry of every true Italian. Should other Italian troops arrive with Medici or Cosenz at their head, Zambianchi was to place himself under their orders. These instructions were signed "Giuseppe Garibaldi, General of the Roman Government elected by universal suffrage and with extraordinary powers."

For five days it can be truly said that the whole of Italy held, as it were, its breath, dreading, hoping, trembling, praying for the best and yet fearing the worst. Vague, contradictory telegrams only rendered the suspense harder to bear, until there came the following, dated from Salemi, the 14th of May: "DEAR BERTANI,—We landed safely at Marsala the day before yesterday. The populations receive us with enthusiasm and join us in crowds. We shall reach the capital by short marches." Three days later the victory of Calatafimini was won by the sheer impetuosity and rush of the "Thousand," and on the 31st Garibaldi entered Palermo, in spite of 20,000 Bourbon soldiers, admirably armed and provisioned, who flung more than 1,500 bombs upon the defenceless city, an act which Lord Palmerston stigmatised in the House as "unworthy of our time and of our civilisation."

In about four weeks 24,000 regulars had been conquered by 1,000, and an island won that possessed a population of two millions.

"Miracles have not ceased!" cried astonished Europe. "Italy will be One and Free," said Mazzini, who was again secretly in Genoa, organising fresh reinforcements for Sicily. And as a proof of how that noble heart ever sacrificed personal aspiration to the accomplishment of a great mission, let it be remembered that he wrote to Crispi, who was then at the head of political affairs at Palermo: "Hold Sicily if you can, till Garibaldi sets foot on *terra firma*, but if the separatists agitate, precipitate annexation to Piedmont."

Mr. Stansfeld's letters to us bear witness to the immense interest that was felt throughout England in Garibaldi and the brave Sicilians, whose dauntless initiative, daring courage and devotion to the leader and his "Thousand," alone produced the wonderful exploits which gave liberty to the South. The letters were brief, almost telegraphic, and full of notes of interrogation. In one he said :—

"The death of Rosalino Pilo was a bitter drop in our cup of delight. He left us so full of hope and trust, and wrote a beautiful letter of gratitude to his English friends from Genoa. After his risky voyage in a cockleshell, his success in landing and getting together such a number of volunteers, fate was cruel indeed to strike him down without letting him welcome Garibaldi to his beloved island, but his lot was less bitter than Pisacane's. He had, at least, a Pisgah view of the Promised Land."

A young Sicilian nobleman, Rosalino Pilo had been the Benjamin of the exiles in the circle of the "Friends of Italy." As a mere lad, he had conspired, been exiled, fought through-

THE BIRTH OF MODERN ITALY

out 1848-49 in Sicily, and continued to conspire until 1857, when, an accident preventing him from joining Pisacane's expedition, he almost died of despair in his London refuge. Later, he threw himself into Crispi's conspiracy, and after a most adventurous journey, during which he twice narrowly escaped shipwreck, he arrived in Sicily just in time to revive the drooping spirits of the insurgents with the magic words: "Garibaldi is coming!" He collected a splendid band of followers and kept the Bourbon forces at bay for six weeks, under incredible difficulties, until Garibaldi landed and defeated General Lanza at Calatafimini.

"To-morrow," Rosalino wrote to the woman of his heart, "I shall join Garibaldi at Alcamo, if the bullets respect me." But, alas! while he was penning his last bulletin to Garibaldi a bullet pierced his brain and killed him on the spot.

Rosalino Pilo had rendered it possible for Garibaldi and his Thousand to win their immortal fame in this marvellous campaign.

We are here under the necessity of once more contradicting the calumny that Mazzini and Bertani, in open defiance of Garibaldi's instructions, attempted to utilise on their own account the forces destined for Sicily, in order to undertake a revolution in the Papal States. From the very initial stages of the enterprise Garibaldi had designed to send an expedition to Rome, and had given details to Zambianchi and his hundred men, whom he had purposely landed at Talamone. Medici, who organised the second expedition to Sicily, had received orders and was fully disposed to follow up Zambianchi, but the latter having deplorably mismanaged everything, it was deemed preferable that the force should go at once to Garibaldi in the island. It was only when Garibaldi found that the splendid expeditionary corps, under the command of Pianciani, had been compelled by the orders of Cavour to sail from the Golfo degli Aranei to Sicily that he, with a wonderful stroke of audacity and genius, decided upon the apparently impossible enterprise of crossing from Sicily to the Continent, with the small army under his orders, and assailing the Bourbon forces, 100,000 strong.

It was this movement of Garibaldi that gave Cavour the strength to induce the French Emperor to permit, or at least not to oppose, the advance of the Piedmontese army in the Marches and Umbria ; it was necessary for Cavour's policy that the glory of the volunteers, mostly men of the " Party of Action," and of their leader should be counterbalanced by the regular army and the purely monarchical party. Furthermore, if nothing had been done, Garibaldi would have found no obstacle to his march upon Rome from the south, and the safeguarding of the Pope was Napoleon's condition *sine qua non* for his neutrality.

On September 11th the Piedmontese troops, 33,000 strong, entered Umbria and the Marches, while the fleet sailed up the Adriatic to attack Ancona. On the 18th, Lamoricière, who commanded the Papal mercenaries, was defeated at Castelfidardo by Fanti, and while the Franco-Belgian soldiers fought well, leaving on the field twenty-five killed and 120 wounded out of a force of 300 men, the Swiss and Austrian troops fled in the greatest disorder over the Mugnone to Loreto, where they capitulated on the morrow. Ancona and its fortress was the only point on which the Papal flag still flew, and there Lamoricière attempted a last resistance, in the hope, ay, in the certainty, that the French Army of Occupation would come at once to his relief, or that the Archduke Maximilian, who commanded the Austrian fleet stationed in Trieste, would appear in the offing. He was doomed to disappointment. Attacked by land and sea, Lamoricière, after the Piedmontese troops had successfully carried the suburbs of the town and Porta Pia at the bayonet's point, capitulated on the 29th, and General Cadorna, commanding the Piedmontese troops, allowed him the honours of war, the officers being sent to Genoa and the men to Alessandria, from whence they were at liberty to return to their homes, upon the sole condition that they should not take up arms against Piedmont for a year.

On October 1st the great battle of the Volturno was fought and won by Garibaldi, under the fortress of Capua, which now alone with Gaeta remained to the Bourbon king.

THE BIRTH OF MODERN ITALY

About 400 men only, of the regular Piedmontese army, took part in the fight; but Garibaldi seized the occasion to compliment them warmly upon the part they had played in the combat.

Garibaldi, who had entered the city of Naples with eleven followers, much in advance of his forces, and had received the voluntary surrender of the whole Neapolitan fleet (with the exception of one frigate, the *Partenope*), had only maintained his dictatorship in Sicily and Naples as the basis for a projected march on Rome. This he now saw to be impossible for the moment, so, unswervingly true to his pledges, he called upon the populations of the island and the continental provinces to record their votes by plebiscite, and, with the unassuming simplicity of the true hero, he handed over eleven millions of Italians to their King-elect, asking nothing for himself, save that the King should protect his volunteers, "who had deserved well of their country." Then, bidding them farewell with the words "to meet again on the road to Venice and Rome," he took ship on November 9th for Caprera with his two war-horses "Calatafimini" and "Milazzo" and a bag of dried beans—the sole trophy of his great campaign. History will hesitate to decide which of the two was the more admirable: the Liberator, triumphant from Marsala to the Volturno, or the Dictator, who departed thus in poverty and obscurity.

XXII

THE KINGDOM OF ITALY

The Moderates and Mazzini in Naples—Garibaldi's indignation—
Napoleon's petty revenges—Garibaldi elected to Parliament—
February 6, 1861—Cavour's death—Rumours as to the cession of
Sardinia—Lord John Russell warned—Baron Ricasoli succeeds Cavour
—Lord John Russell deprecates the habit of looking upon Italy as
the mere vassal of France—"Emancipation Committees."

TOWARDS the middle of September Mazzini arrived in Naples and had been warmly welcomed by Garibaldi, but the apostle of Unity at once became the target for Cavour's envenomed darts. The Moderates, who had kept quiescent and out of the way as long as fighting was going on, invaded the city and soon raised a mob to cry tumultuously, "Death to Mazzini! Death to Crispi!" while the Vice-dictator, Giorgio Pallavicino, invited Mazzini to leave the city. Garibaldi's indignation knew no bounds. He fiercely rebuked "the misguided populace for crying death to its best friend—to the apostle of Italian Unity," and upbraided Pallavicino for his unpardonable conduct. To Mazzini, however, he wrote the following letter:—

CASERTA, *October* 18, 1860.

DEAR MAZZINI,—When one must yield, it is better to yield with good grace. As to you, I flatter myself that you will not bow to the intimidations of any one while I am at the helm.

Ever yours,
G. GARIBALDI.

THE BIRTH OF MODERN ITALY

The conduct of Napoleon III. seemed a petty reve: discomfiture. He never ceased, until resolutely cau to encourage the hopes of the reactionary partisans ex-King of Naples, who fomented brigandage, revol general disorders in the Neapolitan provinces, abet a fanatical clergy, who shamelessly promised a martyr's to any who fell in attempting to murder the " sacri Piedmontese." But there was a deep-laid scheme apparent aberration ; all that could prevent or reta consolidation of the " kingdom of Italy " came as g his mill. Hence, when Francis II. finally took ref Rome, Bourbon brigands, and men placed in the field the blessing of Pius IX., crossed and recrossed the 1 border, encouraged by the French, two of the most fer being diplomatically placed under the protection French flag.

Garibaldi, after his retirement to Caprera, refused come a candidate in the General Election for the first Parliament. But when he witnessed the unjust and sive treatment meted out to his volunteers, treatment he attributed entirely to the ill-will and hatred of Cav(himself and his followers, he suddenly changed his mi: accepted the offer of one of the constituencies of the Naples, where, in a by-election on March 30, 1861, returned almost without opposition.

In the meanwhile, a solemn, memorable scene tool in Turin, where the new Parliament unanimously con the result of the plebiscites of Umbria, the March Neapolitan provinces and Sicily, and, on February 6, proclaimed Victor Emmanuel II. King of Italy. WI so long looked like an impossible Utopia was now tra into actual fact ; and the heart of Mazzini must have high in his lonely exile, for although not under the R(to which he remained unswervingly attached, yet the for which he had striven and suffered for so many had none the less arrived.

But, with cruel suddenness, death followed up(important development. On May 6th, after a short undoubtedly brought about by the tremendous and prolonged strain to which the Prime Minister's passionate nature had been subjected, Cavour died, leaving Italy bereft of her one great statesman. Had he lived, he would undoubtedly have piloted the fragile barque of Italian Independence safely into port, avoiding the numberless shoals and quicksands, rocks, and treacherous under-currents amid which his successors floundered. Had Cavour lived there would have been no Aspromonte and no Mentana, nor would he have signed that fatal " Convention of September " which perpetuated the occupation of Rome by the French troops, and deprived Italy of its capital until the day when the throne of Louis Napoleon crumbled down into the dust of Sèdan. Cavour had been resolutely bent on claiming Rome as the natural capital of United Italy, but he would never have attempted to take violent possession of it while the French troops remained there. He had, nevertheless, so far emancipated himself from subservience to Napoleon that he had actually brought the latter to see the " sweet reasonableness " of withdrawal.

His cession of Nice and Savoy, with all the duplicity that characterised the transaction, remained a very sore point with the English Government, and as vague rumours were afloat concerning a proposed cession of the island of Sardinia to France, a keen watch upon Italian policy was kept in English diplomatic circles. Cavour's opposition, however, to any " march on Rome " had been approved, and the annexation of Sicily and the Neapolitan provinces cordially recognised, so that harmonious relations were resumed between the two Governments. The interest felt by the English in the fate of Italy never abated; subscriptions were set on foot for the liberation of Venice, and petitions to Parliament for the withdrawal of the French troops from Rome were signed by thousands. The " Friends of Italy " became more active than ever, James Stansfeld being, perhaps, the most active of them all.

As early as July, 1860, Mr. Elliott had sent from Naples to Lord John Russell a document purporting to be the copy of a secret treaty existing between Piedmont and France, by which the Emperor agreed to the annexation by Piedmont of the Two Sicilies, the Marches and Umbria, on condition that Liguria and the island of Sardinia should be ceded to France. Lord John believed the document to be a forgery, but Mr. Stansfeld, informed by Mazzini, also warned him that a private document existed in which the cession of Sardinia was marked as the price for the annexation of Sicily. So the motion of Mr. Kinglake for further information on the matter did not find Lord John unprepared. He had previously made clear, both to Lord Cowley in Paris and to Sir James Hudson in Turin, that any change in the balance of power in the Mediterranean would be considered by England as most serious and would entail grave consequences.

Baron Ricasoli, who succeeded Cavour as Premier, was by no means disposed to accept unreservedly the inheritance of Cavour's relationship with Louis Napoleon. The new Prime Minister announced in his first speech in Parliament that "the King's Government declares once and for all that it does not know of a plan of territory to be ceded, that it will never cede a span—absolutely not a single span." He went on to insist in unmistakable terms that Italy had "not only a national territory to defend, but other portions to be claimed," and pronounced the names of Venice and of Rome amid a great storm of applause. He closed his speech by declaring that to arm for these two purposes was the paramount aim of his administration.

Lord John Russell's capital speech in reply to Mr. Kinglake and to Mr. Stansfeld, who—the latter especially—had dwelt at considerable length on the aspirations and rights of the Italians, completely cleared the situation. Without giving an opinion as to past negotiations between Cavour and the French Emperor, he said that he had in his despatches repeatedly and most emphatically explained to all parties concerned that the cession of the island of Sardinia could not remain a simple transaction between France and Piedmont, but would decidedly put an end to the alliance of

Pensiero ed azione

GARIBALDI AND MAZZINI.

(Taken for the Emancipation Committee.)

France and England and thus endanger the peace of Europe. Referring to the remark that perhaps Ricasoli did not consider the island of Sardinia as Italian soil, he professed full faith in the honour and integrity of the Piedmontese Prime Minister, who would, he knew, never condescend to equivocate. He added that the habit of looking upon Italy as a mere vassal of France was much too prevalent and very pernicious, since, though Italy owed much to France for the assistance given during the Lombard War, she must henceforth count on her own resources and look to her own sons to secure her final independence. This debate, of course, gave great offence in France, but was hailed with deep-felt joy in Italy, where Ricasoli's opening declaration had rallied all patriots to his flag, while his openly expressed resolution to secure full liberty ot speech and association was the signal for fresh activity among the "Emancipation Committees"[1] sitting in Genoa with Mazzini and Garibaldi as honorary presidents.

Ricasoli in the meanwhile continued manifesting proofs of his intention to promote national armament and to encourage the "Emancipation Committees"[1] in holding public meetings; he made no objection, also, to the signing of petitions for the withdrawal of the French troops from Rome and for the recall of the great exile, Mazzini. Taking advantage of this temporary liberty, the Central Emancipation Committee of Genoa invited delegates from all the sister associations of the Peninsula, together with the Liberal members of Parliament, to form a vast Federation of Emancipation Associations, Garibaldi and Mazzini to be joint honorary presidents. Ricasoli was unaware that his colleague, Minghetti, was sending private circulars to the prefects, instructing them to prevent these manifestations of the national will.

[1] Committees founded to further the national purposes and especially the union of Venice and Rome.

XXIII

ROYALTY AND THE PEOPLE'S HERO

Garibaldi presides at the Plenary Assembly—Campanella voice
aspirations of the Democracy—The Moderates overthrow Rica
Garibaldi arranges a "Dalmatian" scheme with the Kin
Rattazzi—He enrols volunteers—A stormy meeting at Tra
—Arrest of certain volunteers—The people attack their pr
Garibaldi returns to Caprera—The condition of the So
Provinces—"The eagle flies southward"—Garibaldi in Pale
Louis Napoleon threatens to march on Rome—Victor Emr
orders Garibaldi's movement to be suppressed—General beli
secret understanding between Garibaldi and the King—Ga
evades the Government troops and crosses into Calabria—A t
march—A royal bullet strikes Garibaldi to the ground at Aspro
—Mazzini and Cattaneo—Hopeless misery—Subscription in E
—Dr. Parkins—Professor Zanetti extracts the bullet—Lady P
ston's gift—Mazzini, the Greco plot, and the Moderates—M;
correspondence with Victor Emmanuel only interrupted.

IN 1862 a deputation composed of Crispi, Mo
Musolino, and Miceli, deputies, and the T
popular tribune, Beppe Dolfi, went to Caprera.
succeeded in convincing Garibaldi that Mazzini an
entire democracy were united with him in aiming a
liberation of Venice and Rome, and that, as only
national armed movement could this aim be realise
presence on the Continent was indispensable. They
succeeded in securing Garibaldi's promise to preside ov
Plenary Assembly, convoked for March 9th.

emissaries were sent into Rome to prepare the people for action, subscriptions for funds to procure arms and ammunition were freely circulated throughout the land, as well as petitions for the withdrawal of the French troops from Rome and for the recall of Mazzini.

Garibaldi came to the meeting and made an admirable speech to the very flower of Italian patriotism. Campanella, also, that most uncompromising and stern of Republicans, clearly expressed the political ideal of his companions: "What is the aim of General Garibaldi? What was the aim of our Assembly of December 15, 1861? That is the aim of the present one, namely, to further the execution of the plebiscite of October 21, 1860. We are all determined to complete Italy, to make her One and Indivisible under Victor Emmanuel, our constitutional King. We aim at the fuller development of our institutions, at universal suffrage, at liberty of conscience and of the press, at freedom for public meetings and associations, at inviolability of the domicile, at national armament; and we desire that all these things shall be secured by guarantees which modern civilisation necessitates. In accepting the plebiscite we rendered homage to the great principle of national sovereignty, which we have always held sacred, and to which every good citizen must adhere."

Such concord, such explicit declarations of the acceptance of constitutional monarchy, were the result of Ricasoli's national policy, of his faith in liberal principles, and of the belief he had instilled into the whole nation that he would admit no impediment to the national enterprise—the liberation of Venice and Rome.

But while Italian democracy proposed, the Moderates and their leaders disposed. The old Cavourian party, divided by personal jealousies and ambitions, united as one man for the overthrow of Ricasoli, whose rigid and independent character had not ingratiated him with the King, the proposed morganatic union of whom with Rosina, Contessa di Mirafiori (already mother of two illegitimate children), the Prime Minister had respectfully but firmly opposed. On

THE BIRTH OF MODERN ITALY

his side, Louis Napoleon detested the "Iron Baron"[1] for his scornful treatment of "Plon-Plon's"[2] pretensions in Tuscany, for his "no cession" speech, and for his obstinate insistence upon the withdrawal of the French troops from Rome, to say nothing of his intention to wage war against Austria with purely national forces. Moreover, Bonaparte was violently opposed to the free return of Mazzini to Italy, where, in conjunction with Garibaldi and the whole democracy, his influence would strengthen the hands of Victor Emmanuel and his Premier against the intermeddling of France.

It is certain that Ricasoli had pledged himself to obtain the recall of Mazzini, the only exile excluded by Cavour in the amnesty of 1859, and that he was bent upon obtaining this great act of justice. He fully appreciated Mazzini's character and his patriotic abnegation during the annexation struggles in Tuscany, and recognised him as the apostle of that Italian Unity to which, though late, he had become a fervent convert. His real difficulty lay in finding a formula for the repeal of the death-sentences passed in 1833 and 1858, and in couching the invitation to him to return in such terms as should neither offend the prerogatives of the crown nor hurt the dignity of the man who could accept no pardon, no amnesty, for sacrificing his whole life to Italy's redemption.

In this noble and wise purpose Ricasoli succeeded: he had just induced the King—who never shared Cavour's hatred and distrust of Mazzini—simply to cancel the two death-sentences by Royal decree, when, unhappily, Court intrigues, the underhanded antagonism of some of his colleagues, and his own opposition to "certain schemes brewing on the Danube," forced him to send in his resigna-

---

[1] The name bestowed upon Ricasoli, and which he fully deserved for the unswerving directness and staunchness of his principles.

[2] "Plon-Plon" was Prince Napoleon's derisive nickname, given to him on account of his large bulk and very unmilitary bearing. It was first used during the Crimean war, when he appeared at a review in full uniform and, as it was raining, with a huge umbrella.

tion, which was at once accepted by the King, who made no effort to retain his services.

The dismay caused by this news in the democratic camp was as intense as it was justified. Campanella, who had had several interviews with the Prime Minister, wrote after his resignation : " Ricasoli, for whose exquisite tact Italian democracy feels intense gratitude, had excogitated a formula which, maintaining intact the rights of the crown, at the same time guaranteed the dignity of the great exile. If Ricasoli had remained but one week longer in power, the question would have been solved, and we should all be now rejoicing with exceeding joy in this grand act of national justice."

Garibaldi alone seemed satisfied with the advent to power of Rattazzi, for he had always nourished a certain grudge against Ricasoli, believing that his recall from Cattolica had been due to the latter's influence as much as to Cavour's. Garibaldi went to Turin and obtained an interview with the King and his new Prime Minister, but nothing has ever transpired of the terms upon which they agreed, though it is generally believed that they discussed a project for attacking Austria on the Danube. Kossuth was to head an insurrection in Hungary, and Garibaldi, with a corps of volunteers, was to effect a landing on the coast of Dalmatia.

But Mazzini, who entertained no illusions on this subject, had already, with his wonderful foresight, written while Ricasoli was still in power : " Rattazzi has been to Paris with an autograph letter from the King to the Emperor, proposing the withdrawal of the French troops from Rome and moral co-operation for the liberation of Venice, in exchange for a defensive and offensive alliance on the Rhine. Louis Napoleon gave no decisive answer. Ricasoli knows of this and is opposed to the scheme. If it should be accepted, Ricasoli will be deposed and Rattazzi return to power."

In the light of recent publications, no doubt can longer exist that the principal cause of Napoleon III.'s downfall was

THE BIRTH OF MODERN ITALY

his obstinate attachment to the temporal power of the Pope. Had he acquiesced in the complete unity of Italy his fate might have been very different; but it seemed a fitting retribution that the perjured assassin of the Roman Republic should have perished through his crime against it *Qui de gladio ferit, de gladio perit.*

Garibaldi, after his visit to Turin, made a sort of tour through Lombardy, calling on the populations to collect money and arms and to prepare for taking up the cross afresh in a coming crusade. The enrolment of volunteers began without any specific aim being assigned, the masses believing that they were destined for the liberation of Venice: only to his immediate followers did Garibaldi impart their actual destination. He found all his friends decidedly hostile to the idea of his quitting Italy under any pretext whatever. When, or if ever, he resolved to throw over the Dalmatian scheme, has never been made clear, still less whether he really meditated an invasion of Venetia. If he did so, he evidently never communicated his intentions to Victor Emmanuel, who, knowing that Napoleon was absolutely opposed to such projects, would never have consented. Moreover, his own friends, with the exception of a few of his old officers who would have followed him blindly anywhere, considered such an attempt sheer madness, and told him so plainly, dwelling upon the certainty that the volunteers would be arrested before they could reach the Venetian frontier, and pointing out that there was no organisation in those provinces, and that, above all, the Moderates would gain an excellent pretext for dissolving the Emancipation Committees, the rifle-clubs, the shooting matches, &c., which were becoming widespread. A general *débacle* would be the fatal consequence of any premature, ill-concerted, rash expedition.

Mazzini took the same view, though actively carrying on a propaganda in the Trentino, where arms and ammunition were accumulating. "For any movement to be successful, it must commence from within" was the belief he firmly held in regard to Venice. Garibaldi, however, seemed fully convinced that the Government would shut its eyes and allow him a free hand, only disowning him in case of failure. So, in order to come to an understanding with the dissentients, he invited his friends, his officers, and the delegates of the Emancipation Committees to meet him on the 5th of May at the Baths of Trescorre, near Brescia, whither he had gone for his health.

The meeting was a most stormy one. Bertani, Mosto, and Mario openly opposed the general's plans on the grounds already stated, and he, extremely wroth, accused them of abetting Mazzini in thwarting his schemes, so that Bertani and Mosto indignantly left the assembly. Mario, who yielded implicit obedience to his adored chief on the battlefield, could never tolerate dictatorship elsewhere. He had already written a long letter from London to the general, showing how unfounded were his suspicions as to Mazzini contravening his plans, for, as a matter of fact, all the exile's efforts were concentrated on preparing a fresh field for action, in which he (Garibaldi), at the head of his volunteers, should be able to complete the programme—one Italy with Rome for her capital. Mario had likewise explained how the English Government and nation were, in heart, for the Italians, though they would deplore any rash attempt not openly sanctioned by King Victor Emmanuel; and that it was generally believed that the French Emperor and Rattazzi wished only to get Garibaldi and his volunteers out of Italy, in order to prevent their making any attempt on Venice—an attempt which could not succeed, because the Venetians were unarmed, unorganised, and their young men capable of bearing arms nearly all in exile, existing, for the most part, on pittances doled out by the Government. He reminded the general that the real enthusiasm of the Italians was for Rome, where the populations were daily evincing their resolution to revolt, and that, should the Government arrest him and such volunteers as might follow him, before action could commence, he must not count upon an uprising of the free

THE BIRTH OF MODERN ITALY

northern populations against the Government, for he (Garibaldi) himself had imbued them with "devotion and obedience to King Victor Emmanuel."

The General, who had listened impatiently to Mario's short and tranquil exposition of facts, cried out, "Mario, you are a Mazzinian!" to which Mario, always fearless, replied, "Neither a Mazzinian nor a Garibaldian! . . . I think with my own head!" "That's the worst of it!" retorted Garibaldi. But on looking round the room he understood from the silence of the assembly that Mario had voiced a general opinion, and so, faithful to his proverb, "If you must yield, better to yield gracefully," he adjourned the meeting, and on the following day issued a most sybilline manifesto, which, for the members of the assembly, signified that for once in his life the General had yielded to the unanimous advice of his friends—that he had given up his designs on Venice, and would think twice before quitting Italy with his volunteers.

The general public, however, who knew nothing of this stormy meeting, took the proclamation as one of the habitual *fervorini* (bursts of eloquence) written to keep alive the hope and enthusiasm of the Italians and centre their eyes on their "Warrior-King."

Personally I did not then, nor do I now, believe that Garibaldi had abandoned his designs, unless, indeed, in the brief interval he received a communication from the King, which seems scarcely probable.

Rattazzi, possibly warned by some spy in the Garibaldian ranks, discovering that the enlistments going on were destined, not for Hungary, but for Venice, instead of advising the King to summon the General and tell him clearly that no attempt upon Venice would be countenanced—in which case Garibaldi would, as usual, have obeyed the voice of his charmer—suddenly, without any warning, arrested Nullo[1]

---

[1] Nullo, Francesco (1826–1863), patriot and soldier, born in Lombardy, fought with Garibaldi at Rome in 1848, later at the Volturno in 1860, and was killed at Aspromonte.

1862] GARIBALDI RETURNS TO CAPRERA

and Ambiveri [1] among many other volunteers at Sarnico, and took possession of their arms. But the people of Brescia surrounded the prison in which Nullo was incarcerated, and attempted to break open its gates, whereupon the soldiers, in obedience to orders, fired upon the crowd, killing four men and wounding a number of others.

Garibaldi, justly exasperated, informed the Prefect of Brescia that the volunteers were enrolled by himself, and that he alone was responsible and deserving of arrest. But he was left unmolested at Trescorre, where, as a protest, he started a subscription for presenting a sword to Papoff, a Russian officer who had broken his own at Warsaw rather than use it against an unarmed populace. This *boutade*, and still more the letter he wrote to the *Gazzetta di Milano* saying that "Italian soldiers ought to fight against the enemies of their country and their King, not to kill and wound unarmed citizens . . . their place being at the frontier and on the battlefield, not elsewhere in Italy," grieved his friends and irritated his old officers, Bixio, Medici, Cosenz, Sirtori, Sacchi, who were now Generals in the regular army. And, looking back dispassionately at the incident, it must be admitted that the great man would have been more logical had he openly broken with the Rattazzi Government and sought an interview with the King to ascertain the limits of his liberty of action. Instead of this he resigned the presidency of the Emancipation Committees and returned to Caprera, apparently to lead a private life.

The state of the Southern Provinces had meanwhile been going from bad to worse. Brigandage was rampant. General Pinelli's proclamation,[2] tremendous and far-reaching

---

[1] Ambiveri, Luigi (1847–1895), patriot, and later historian, born in Piacenza.

[2] General Pinelli's proclamation was issued to the populations of the Neapolitan provinces in view of a radical destruction of brigandage. By this proclamation the mere fact of bringing food or supplies of any kind to such persons as were declared outlaws was punished by execution on the spot after a drum-head trial, and without appeal.

though it was, could scarcely cope with the enormous difficulties, especially as the ex-King of Naples, now in Rome protected by the French troops, sent leaders, arms, and money to this horde of assassins.

Suddenly, old Dr. Ripari, who never left his worshipped chief, Garibaldi, warned one of his friends in Genoa by the ominous words: "The eagle flies southward." A few days later Garibaldi, who had gone to Sicily without giving notice to any except a few of his most faithful followers, raised from the balcony of the Royal palace in Palermo, where the prefect, Giorgio Pallavicino, once a prisoner in the Spielberg, had invited him to stay, the cry of "To Rome! to Rome!" Haranguing the massed crowds, he cried: "Rome or death, people of the Vespers! people of '48! people of '60! . . . Napoleon, the man of the Second of December, the assassin of the Roman Republic and of France, must decamp from Rome, and if fresh Vespers are needed, fresh Vespers let there be!"

Instantly volunteers flocked to the camp which he proceeded to establish at Ficuzza, the Sicilian women, without distinction of rank, labouring to prepare red shirts for the soldiers; and all over Italy ardent youths responded to the inflamed summons of their idolised chief. But the evil genius of Louis Napoleon, the Spanish Eugenia, said, "Death if they like, but Rome—never!" and the Emperor gave King Victor Emmanuel to understand that, unless he prevented Garibaldi from marching on Rome, he would do so himself, and that speedily. The Government issued hasty orders for the suppression of the movement, but no doubt existed in the minds of the masses that Garibaldi and the King were tacitly agreed, and the King's manifesto, in which he warned the Italians "to be on their guard against blameworthy impatience and hazardous agitations," and promising that "when the hour for the completion of their grand task should arrive, their King's voice would proclaim it," came too late. The people remembered well that in 1860 the King had likewise ordered Garibaldi not to cross the Straits of Messina, yet, nevertheless, he had accepted from his victorious hands the kingdom of Naples. De Ferrari was at once sent to Sicily to replace Giorgio Pallavicino, who indignantly resigned rather than obey the order to arrest Garibaldi; and General Cugia, Military Dictator, placed the island under martial law, sending various columns of troops to arrest the triumphant march of the popular hero. But Garibaldi, with his usual wonderful ability, avoided them, marching through Castrogiovanni to Catania, where he was received enthusiastically by the population, and even by the Royal troops themselves, to whom he proclaimed the duty of remaining faithful to their King; then, unhindered by the three men-of-war which had been stationed to watch the harbour, he embarked with about half his legion on two steamers, the *General Abbattucci* and the *Dispaccio*. Though loaded to their utmost capacity, these vessels could not carry the whole of his men. The unfortunate little band was wretchedly armed and almost destitute of provisions, nor could their commander procure any further supplies, either at Melito or at Reggio, on the Calabrian coast, where they landed.

Cialdini, who had neither forgiven nor forgotten Garibaldi's demands on behalf of his victorious but shabby-looking followers after the King's entry into Naples—his own insulting letter to the General and the latter's crushingly noble and dignified reply—saw that the hour of his revenge had come. His orders to Colonel Pallavicini, who commanded the flying column sent against Garibaldi, were therefore peremptory and explicit: he was, at all hazards, to pursue, crush (*schiacciare*), capture him. So, after a terrible march of forty miles over the precipitous hills of Aspromonte, Garibaldi and his starving, exhausted followers were assailed by the Colonel's *bersaglieri* on August the 29th, and though, unwilling to shed Italian blood, he repeatedly ordered his men not to shoot, the *bersaglieri* fired a volley into them, and a bullet striking the General himself in the ankle, brought him to the ground. The great crime, the great sacrilege, had been committed.

THE BIRTH OF MODERN ITALY

Firing ceased almost at once, and Colonel Pallavicini hastened, with head uncovered, to kneel beside the wounded hero and beseech him to surrender, for he had no power to offer terms, simply orders to fight. Garibaldi handed him his sword, recommended the wounded and the deserters to his care, and allowed himself to be carried to a peasant's cottage, from whence on the morrow, laid upon a rude stretcher which the Aspromontini still cherish as a relic, he was carried to the shore and placed on board the steamer *Duca di Genova*. Cialdini, from the bridge of the *Stella d'Italia*, stood with covered head and folded arms, exultingly watching the departure of his hated rival, defeated, wounded, and a prisoner.

Garibaldi never forgot the courtesy and kindness of Colonel Pallavicini, with whom to his dying day he maintained friendly relations, nor the good offices of Commander Wright, of the *Duca di Genova*; but the passage from Calabria to Spezia was one long agony. On board there were neither ice nor remedies, and the foot and leg became so swollen and inflamed that for many days it was impossible to verify whether the bullet was still in the wound or not.

There is grief that excites energy and spurs men to action, and there is grief that stuns, seeming to stifle every faculty of body and mind. The news that Garibaldi lay, " wounded and a prisoner," in the fortress of Varignano, by Spezia, seemed to strike the Italians with paralysis. The cruel reaction which ensued, the persecution, the imprisonment, even the shooting of volunteers, roused no protest in the masses. One question alone was put with bated breath: " Will he live ? " The first news wildly telegraphed to the provinces even exaggerated the patient's state, serious as it was. Bertani was summoned by wire, but the Government prohibited his access to the prisoner, nor, so long as the General remained at Varignano, was he permitted to visit him.

I happened to be in Milan, collecting money and gifts, which the patriotic Milanese furnished generously, when the friendly mayor, Beretta, gave me the fatal intelligence, urging my immediate departure, in a closed carriage, for Monza, as the prefect, Pasolini, had received strict orders to arrest me. I fled in great haste to Como, where the prefect, Lorenzo Valerio, gave me a passport for the frontier, and I finally reached Lugano, to find Mazzini and Cattaneo together there, eagerly discussing the chances of a renewal of the miracles of 1860. Mazzini was even ready to start with an expedition which was preparing in Genoa. The last tidings they had had told them of the successful passage of the straits, qualified, however, by a rumour of some collision with the Royal troops.

When I told them what had really happened, such a cry burst from Mazzini's lips as " erst from David of his son bereaved." Cattaneo wept, hard, dry sobs choking his utterance. But the first paroxysm of their grief over, Mazzini did not doubt for a moment that the Italians would rise as one man to avenge their outraged chief. He had disapproved of the expedition, but, once commenced, had urged all his friends to second it ; now, no doubt was left in his mind as to their duty, and he would have started for Milan then and there had I not dissuaded him, insisting upon the certainty of his arrest, and the equal certainty that if the Italians rose to action it would be on the spur of the moment, on an impulse which would need no incitement.

Then Mario arrived, half mad with grief, exasperated by the apathy of the populations, who, he said, seemed reduced to a state of idiocy, and he at once scouted the idea of any attempt " to galvanize a corpse." For Mario, " the catastrophe was the logical consequence of the programme, and the only logical action at that moment would have been its reversal " ; but he was likewise convinced that any attempt at this would be instantly disowned by Garibaldi himself, who would, with his dying breath, acclaim the " Rè Galantuomo," Victor Emmanuel. This view was absolutely correct, and was fully confirmed by the fugitives who now came flocking to Lugano.

THE BIRTH OF MODERN ITALY

Such a time of hopeless misery I never remember to have spent. All hope for the liberation of Venice had vanished, and the chains of Rome seemed only riveted the closer by the abortive effort to break them. Mazzini's state was heart-breaking to witness. After the first fiery protest, written as soon as he could hold a pen, his whole soul appeared centred in Garibaldi: he recalled their first interview at Marseilles, dwelling on the stalwart beauty of the fair, bronzed Ligurian, with his sunny, flowing hair; then, following with fatherly pride the meteoric career of the hero, he recalled the tragic days of Rome, where, but for the unsurmountable opposition of the professional military element, he certainly would have named him military dictator; the victories of 1859, the miracles of 1860 . . . and now ? he lay wounded, dying perhaps !

I can still see his passionate gesture of despair, and hear the agonised exclamation: " Christ ! . . . spare him to Italy ! Take me instead ! "

If the days were gloomy, the nights were worse. Mazzini could neither eat nor sleep. From the tiny room that opened into ours I could hear the sound of his feverish pacing up and down, and one night the old terrible paroxysm of 1836 returned. He kept groaning : " Jacopo Jacopo ! I did not betray ! " Then, when he had regained control over himself, he called Mario to him, and said : " Bear witness that this blood of Garibaldi is not upon my head."

A visit, welcome as unexpected, first roused us from the stupefaction of misery. William and Bessie Ashurst, with James Stansfeld, stopped in Lugano on their way to Turin, "from whence," said William, "James meant to enter Varignano, at the cost even of remaining there a prisoner." He told us that indignation was the only sentiment yet evinced in England, where nothing was understood save that a "Royal bullet" had struck down the "Liberator" on the road to Rome : the people had subscribed £1,000 to send out a surgeon, and the committee formed for the purpose wished me to go to the victim as nurse. " Coals to Newcastle to send a surgeon to Italy," was my comment; and as for a nurse, Garibaldi had his own daughter, three surgeons, and his sons. If only the £1,000 might be spent for the wounded of Aspromonte, starving in prisons and fortresses, Garibaldi would be far more pleased, and cared for none the worse. But William, like a true Briton, sided with the Britons, and insisted that a British surgeon must be sent, although he admitted that Bertani would be the next best substitute, " only he can't get in."

William Ashurst, who could always win a laugh from Mazzini, even in his saddest moods, succeeded once more in rousing his spirits, declaring that when the official news reached England the hatred of Louis Napoleon would be increased tenfold; that he would be known as the true, responsible culprit for the crime committed. " Decamp he must! He will decamp from Rome thus!" cried William, and with a dance on the door-mat, he so comically depicted the manner of Louis Napoleon's expulsion that Mazzini could not help laughing heartily; and so the cloud began to lift.

With Carlo Cattaneo, Mr. Stansfeld was enchanted. He knew the great thinker's wonderful essay on Ireland, written in 1833, and they had also another subject in common—their love and admiration for Richard Cobden, whom Cattaneo had met in Milan in 1848. The commercial treaty negotiated between France and Great Britain by Cobden had won Cattaneo's unbounded admiration, and he said these memorable words to Stansfeld: " Napoleon will pass away, but commercial relations between France and England will pave the way for a political understanding between the two countries, whose union must promote the liberty and progress of the world."

The news sent to us from Varignano by William Ashurst, who went on there, was far from reassuring, and his anxiety for the arrival of the English surgeon became almost comic. That surgeon arrived in the person of a Dr. Parkins, unknown to fame, who left no trace of his presence save the receipt for £1,000 sterling, to which handsome sum he insisted should be added £176 for travelling expenses. Mr. Stansfeld went to Spezia some days later, and found Garibaldi better than he had expected. He received a most loving welcome, and made such an impression upon Garibaldi that the General afterwards told me himself that he conceived the greatest admiration " for this true Englishman, this typical representative of a free and freedom-loving nation." Mr. Stansfeld, in a letter from Spezia, dated September 21st, described this visit to his father : " We have seen G. this morning, the most exquisite and touching sight I ever saw : thin, feeble, with a smiling, grateful, almost prayerful look as he looked up from his bed and took my hand in his ; half child, half martyr was what he seemed."

Mr. Stansfeld then returned to Lugano, and Mazzini consented to go back with him to England, for, as he wrote from Turin, " there is nothing to be done or attempted in Italy or Switzerland, and he would only wear out his heart and health by remaining in inaction."

The Italian Government was all along terribly embarrassed to know what to do with their great prisoner. Accordingly, at the first favourable moment which presented itself, they released him by a decree of general amnesty, dated October 5, 1862, the occasion being the marriage of the Princess Maria Pia, daughter of Victor Emmanuel, with the King of Portugal ; and the General was transferred from the fortress of Varignano to the town of Spezia. Once there he was free to receive his friends, and our anxiety being too great to be allayed by reports at second hand, we journeyed thither, arriving the same day as Bertani, who fully agreed with Dr. Basile that the bullet was still in the wound, and that it alone was keeping up the inflammation, the patient's sufferings being complicated by a return of the arthritic affection to which he had been subject from his youth. Nelaton, the great French surgeon, confirmed this diagnosis, and all agreed as to the climate of Spezia being unfitted for the invalid. His daughter Teresita was compelled to return to Genoa for the birth of her third child, so with Mario's approval I remained to nurse Garibaldi, and to supervise his journey to Pisa, where the climate happily tended to restore his general health.

One day Garibaldi suddenly said to me : " I have decided to tell the whole story of the last three months. Can you find me an English publisher who will take it ? " I thought this, of course, most probable, and, through Mr. Stansfeld, I opened negotiations with Mr. George Smith, who, provided "that the whole story would be told and guaranteed by the General himself," made no difficulties about emolument, as "he thought nothing of four figures." Mr. Stansfeld was most anxious that this publication should take place, saying it would " be an immense relief to the English people and to the ' Party of Action ' to have this incident placed in its true light." But, as I had feared from the beginning, the General, on mature reflection, came to the conclusion that though speech might be silver, silence was golden, and the memoir remained unwritten. Words now might, he feared, prevent action in the future : he would be compelled to divulge what had been his real agreement with the King, both as regarded the Dalmatian[1] scheme and the rest. Was this wise ? Had he a right to do it ? At any rate, he decided on silence, and silence seals the secret yet—perhaps for ever. Rattazzi's papers were sequestrated as soon as his widow, Letizia Wyss Bonaparte, had published the first volume of her late husband's memoirs ; nor have King Victor Emmanuel's biographers thrown any light on the subject.

Meanwhile the General's health improved visibly, the inflammation and the swelling abated, although the agony, borne with a fortitude and serenity never surpassed, was sometimes terrible to behold. At last Professor Zanetti, the great Tuscan surgeon, enlarging the orifice of the wound by inserting cotton-wool steeped in gum, felt prepared to

[1] The " Dalmatian scheme " is an allusion to a plan which had been secretly arranged between King Victor Emmanuel and Garibaldi to land a corps of volunteers under the command of the latter on the Dalmatian coast. It was hoped to foment thus an insurrection of the Hungarians and other races subject to Austria as a diversion to the main attack on the Venetian frontier. It was abandoned for many reasons, never clearly explained.

make an attempt to extract the ball. Garibaldi held my hand during the whole of the operation, and as soon as the forceps entered the aperture he exclaimed : "*Per Dio! c'e!*" (By God, it's there). A few seconds later Zanetti produced the sharpshooter's bullet, which, striking first against a boulder, thence rebounding into the ankle, had assumed the perfect form of a cap of liberty, the point, deflected by concussion with the rock, forming the tassel.

It was a supreme moment of emotion when Zanetti held it up to view. Garibaldi embraced the surgeon, then all of us : the news spread—spread like magic, and rejoicing was universal. Sheets and bandages, stained with the blood of the martyr of Aspromonte, were eagerly sought for, and torn to ribbons for distribution, to be treasured as sacred relics. Menotti, the General's son, kept the bullet, refusing to part with it, though an Englishman offered a fabulous sum for its possession. Never did I pen such a joyful telegram as the one announcing to England that the ball had been at last extracted and that the General was " doing well."

Lady Palmerston sent him a perfect invalid bed, which could be placed at any angle for the patient's comfort, and on it Garibaldi slept ; on it he was moved from Pisa to Leghorn, and thence by steamer to Caprera. Never was a gift so welcome, or so much appreciated ; never was a gift so conducive to repose and the alleviation of pain. Though all danger had passed, excruciating pain was still suffered by the hero, every movement being agony because of the arthritic complications ; and never was suffering borne with such angelic patience, such care to avoid giving trouble, and such gratitude for the services that all were proud and thankful to render.

When Mr. Stansfeld replied to the letter in which I gave him detailed news of Garibaldi's condition, the idea of a visit to England was first mooted. But this visit was, of course, put off until the complete healing of the wound, and, as we shall see, it only took place in April, 1864.

In 1863 nothing of importance happened in Italy. Early

in 1864 a new and determined attempt was made to implicate Mazzini in a pretended plot, hatched by Italians, to assassinate Louis Napoleon. A certain Greco, one of Garibaldi's volunteers at Aspromonte, was arrested in Paris, and confessed to having come there with the intention of committing this murder under the instructions of Mazzini, with whom he was in correspondence, addressing his communications to No. 35, Thurlow Square, which was Mr. Stansfeld's house. That Greco was a spy, and had been paid by the police of Louis Napoleon to launch this accusation, there can now be no doubt, especially since the publication of the secret Tuileries papers in 1873. But at that moment the whole affair roused doubt, besides immense interest, and it had a memorable repercussion in the English Parliament. Mr. Stansfeld, who had accepted office in the Liberal Cabinet as Junior Lord of the Admiralty, was violently attacked by the Opposition, and with indignant eloquence defended both himself and Mazzini from the not always straightforward aspersions of his adversaries. Finally, not to be a cause of embarrassment to the Cabinet, he resigned, and Lord Palmerston ended by accepting the resignation, although at first he had refused. The evident purpose of the whole cowardly plot was to prevent further communications between Victor Emmanuel and Mazzini; for the King, unknown to his ministers, had been carrying on a private correspondence with the great exile, and this having come to the ears of Louis Napoleon, he decided to cut it short at any cost. After the publication of " Politica Segreta Italiana (1863-70)," no doubt can be entertained that Victor Emmanuel was disposed to conspire on his own account, and it is a fact that with the aid of Mazzini he was really preparing a general rising in Transylvania and Galicia, in order to attack Austria and liberate Venice. When the great scandal of the Greco affair broke out, he simply procured exact information, proved to himself that Mazzini was not only innocent but most infamously defamed, and continued his correspondence with him. So the plan of Louis Napoleon and his confederates, the Italian Moderates, signally failed.

XXIV

GARIBALDI IN ENGLAND

1864

Extraordinary reception—Stay in the Isle of Wight—Entry into London—Dinner-party at Stafford House—Lord Palmerston gives an official dinner—Visit to Mazzini—Banquet of Revolutionaries—The Duke of Sutherland opportunely concerned for Garibaldi's health—Provincial tour given up—The Prince of Wales visits the General—Departure—Mazzini warns Menotti of a "friendly" scheme which Garibaldi thwarts.

GARIBALDI'S visit to England in March of that year somewhat complicated matters. He had been erroneously led to believe that he was invited by the British Government, but this was certainly not the case. The Government knew full well that his reception would be enthusiastic, and that this would give the very greatest umbrage to the French Emperor. To leave Garibaldi in the hands of the British democracy, to allow what they could not prevent — a triumphant tour through the provinces—did not exactly suit the views of the English aristocracy, who, wise in their generation, therefore took the matter in their own hands.

Garibaldi, reaching Southampton on board the *Ripon*, found everything prepared for his arrival. All was settled; an official reception, a residence in the Isle of Wight, then a stay in London as the guest of the Duke of Sutherland, who came to Southampton to receive him, together with many other aristocrats, also delegates from municipalities, working men's associations, &c.; in short, there was awaiting him such a welcome as had never before been offered to a triumphant warrior.

The Moderate portion of the Italian residents in London, however, took their cue from the Italian Embassy, where the honours awarded to Garibaldi gave extreme umbrage. The ambassador, D'Azeglio, nephew of Massimo d'Azeglio, openly avowed his surprise and disgust that England should thus applaud a rebel to his King; and for once there was a "touching similarity of views" between the Italian and Austrian diplomats, and they both peevishly remained *perdus* in their respective residences.

As arranged, Garibaldi went to the Isle of Wight, and for eight consecutive days was there visited by "illustrious personages." Tennyson invited him to plant a tree in his garden, recited to him some of his own poetry, and listened, without understanding a word, to Garibaldi's recitation of Foscolo's "I Sepolcri." Then, at an urgent request, Mazzini went to the Isle of Wight, as Garibaldi was anxious to hear his views concerning the contemplated English trip. Mazzini reminded him that it was the Liberals, the *people* of England, who really loved him and Italy, and who had given such substantial proofs of their interest in the cause of Italian Independence; he must therefore visit Newcastle, Edinburgh, Glasgow, Liverpool, and other great towns, or else he would disappoint them and seem most ungrateful. Garibaldi replied that, of course, such was his intention, but he added that the English Government—Lord John Russell, Lord Palmerston, and Mr. Gladstone especially—had likewise given practical and steadfast proof of their goodwill to Italy, so that to them also he owed a debt of gratitude and courtesy. He never dreamed that his presence was occasioning them serious embarrassment.

The Duke of Somerset, First Lord of the Admiralty, placed a steam yacht at the General's disposition, and the first use he made of it was to go and visit my father's

THE BIRTH OF MODERN ITALY

widow at Sherbourne Cottage, Portsmouth, a graceful act, for which I thanked him heartily; but I felt compelled to suggest to him that during his intercourse with the British aristocracy he must not forget the French proverb, "Je t'embrasse pour t'étouffer."

At first he seemed inclined to accept the invitations made to him by deputations from all the great English cities, and wished to arrange a prolonged tour in the provinces, to be finished off in London. But he was over-ruled by the announcement that all the preparations for his reception in London had been completed, and that his visit there could not be postponed.

On the 11th of April, therefore, he made his solemn entry into the metropolis. Nine Elms Station was transformed into a reception hall, where members of Parliament, aldermen, working men, exiles of all nations, together with an enormous crowd, awaited his coming, and an address from the City of London eloquently expressed the sentiments of the whole nation. Finally, after a six hours' drive in a carriage drawn by four horses, and acclaimed by the thousands who assembled in such a throng as had scarcely before been seen in London, he arrived at Stafford House, where the *fine fleur* of English and Scotch nobility visited him, the ladies vying with each other in paying him homage.

On the 13th of April the Earl of Malmesbury wrote: "We dined at Stafford House to meet Garibaldi; the party consisted of the Russells, Palmerstons, Argylls, Shaftesbury, Dufferins, Gladstones, &c., the Derbys and ourselves being the only Conservatives, so I greatly fear we have made a mistake and that our party will be disgusted at our going. Lady Shaftesbury told me after dinner, in a *méchante* manner, that we had fallen into a trap, to which I answered that I was very much obliged to those who had laid it, as I should be very sorry not to have seen Garibaldi. The Dowager Duchess of Sutherland walked off with him to her boudoir, where he smoked. This created great astonishment and amusement, as this particular boudoir, which is fitted up most magnificently with hangings of velvet and everything that is most costly, has been considered such a sacred spot that few favoured mortals have ever been admitted in its precincts, and as to allowing anyone to smoke in it, it is most astounding to all who know the Duchess."

Then Lord Palmerston gave an official dinner, at which all the State dignitaries were present. These official functions were a severe trial to the patience of a man whose habits had always been simplicity and frugality itself—who preferred a dish of beans to a *salmi* of partridges; nor was he pleased that his modest suite were not included in the invitations.

His first private visit was to Mr. Stansfeld, *l'amico d'Italia e non della ventura* (the friend of Italy and not of her good fortunes), who had just then resigned office, and who, knowing how the land lay, advised him to set out at once on his provincial tour. On the same day he visited Mazzini in his tiny one-room lodging in Cedar Road, Fulham, and there the same advice was pressed upon him, so he agreed, deciding to commence the tour at Newcastle as the guest of Joseph Cowen, of whose welcome in 1853, when he was an exile uncertain even of being allowed to land in Italy, he retained a grateful remembrance. But before his departure from London he was pledged to assist at the banquet given in his honour by Herzen, the great Russian revolutionary leader, and at which Mazzini, Saffi, Mordini, Ogareff, and Stansfeld, with a few others, were present.

This banquet, the arrival in London of all the most celebrated agitators of Europe, together with Garibaldi's visits to Louis Blanc and Ledru-Rollin, gave great umbrage to Louis Napoleon and his partisans in England, and became a new source of embarrassment to the Government. So the Duke of Sutherland conveniently became most "seriously concerned for Garibaldi's health" (which had never been so flourishing since Aspromonte), and he summoned the famous surgeon Fergusson, who gravely opined that

THE BIRTH OF MODERN ITALY

"the fatigue and excitement of the proposed tour would be fraught with danger" to the General, an opinion which Dr. Basile, the surgeon who, since Aspromonte, had never left Garibaldi for an hour, scouted disdainfully. Garibaldi, therefore, was still preparing to depart when a long interview which he had with Mr. Gladstone revealed to him that in spite of so many official receptions, dinners, and addresses, his presence was really an embarrassment to the Government. This interview greatly troubled and grieved the simple-minded General. Again he consulted Mr. Stansfeld, who, though certainly most unwilling to annoy the Premier, by whom he had been so considerately treated, felt that it would be a great injustice if the British people were deprived of the hero's promised appearance, and feared that disappointment might diminish their future enthusiasm for the Italian cause. He accordingly advised him to start at once for Newcastle, in spite of all representations, and there to decide whether his health and strength would suffice for the other visits.

But the pressure brought to bear on Garibaldi at Stafford House was too pointed for him to remain blind to the fact that he had outstayed his welcome. He abruptly refused the offer of a pension for himself and family, for which over £2,000 had been subscribed in a few hours; then, after visiting Foscolo's grave at Chiswick, where he deposed a laurel wreath of bronze, with the inscription "Ai generosi giusta di gloria dispensiera è Morte" (Death is a just dispenser of glory to the great-hearted), he suddenly announced to the Duke of Sutherland his intention of returning to Italy. Sending for Mr. Stansfeld, he set forth his position, explaining how he could not remain even if the embarrassment felt by the Government were merely imaginary, and requested his friend to write a few lines of explanation to the organisers of the provincial tour, which Mr. Stansfeld did in the following terms :—

LONDON, *April* 21.

DEAR FRIENDS,—Accept my heartfelt thanks for your sympathy and your affection. I shall be happy to meet you under more favourable circumstances, and when I can enjoy at ease the hospitality of your country. For the moment I am obliged to leave England. Once more accept my ever-abiding gratitude.

Yours,
G. GARIBALDI.

The Duke of Sutherland, who had kept his yacht under steam in anticipation of this solution, placed it at the General's service, offering to accompany him. The Prince of Wales, who had not been permitted to attend any public reception, came to visit the General on the eve of his departure without a " by your leave " to any one, and was warmly welcomed. On April 22nd Garibaldi, with the Duke of Sutherland and Dr. Basile, went on board the *Ondine*, and started immediately, while the rest of the general's suite, including his son Menotti, were dexterously left behind. The Duke had arranged a plan with the Italian ambassador whereby he was to take Garibaldi on a yachting tour in the East, and Maffei, the secretary of the Legation, joyfully wired the good news to Turin ; but Mazzini had also been informed of the project, and he made it known to Menotti, who wired at once to Malta warning his father. Garibaldi, on becoming aware of the project, insisted on proceeding at once from Malta to Caprera, thus, in spite of party intrigues, cutting short the intended voyage.

He never referred to his famous English journey. The Liberal press in England declaimed against "the smuggling out of England of Garibaldi," but on calm reflection it can be seen that something of the kind was inevitable. As Mr. Stansfeld had feared, however, a real, though almost imperceptible, "damper" was cast by the circumstance over British enthusiasm for Italy.

EPILOGUE

THE notes of Jessie White Mario at this point terminate rather abruptly, and in the very bewildering mass of papers entrusted to our care, in spite of the most minute research, we have been unable to discover any account of later events in Italy. Feeling that this conclusion of the story of the Italian " Risorgimento " must prove unsatisfactory to the ordinary reader, and especially to those of the younger generation, who, as a rule, are woefully ignorant of European events and personages of thirty years ago, we will here attempt to recall, as compendiously as possible, what happened in Italy from 1864 to the fulfilment of Italian Unity, and how and when the great national heroes disappeared from the scene of their glorious achievements.

In 1864 the aggressive policy of Austria and Prussia towards Denmark had its natural sequence in the annexation of Schleswig-Holstein: this fact clearly demonstrated to Europe that new forces were at work within the Germanic Confederation, which would, sooner or later, bring about the disruption of that antiquated organisation. From the Revolution of '49 we date the resurrection of Pan-Germanism and Prussia's silent but unceasing efforts to perfect a military organism which, later on, caused her army to be considered one of the most formidable war-machines of modern times. From the beginning of the Danish War, Bismark, whose domineering statesmanship made itself felt in all the branches of Prussian administration, the oft-recalcitrant King not excepted, eagerly sought for an occasion to bring the inevitable Austro-Prussian conflict to an immediate and decisive termination; but his efforts

EPILOGUE

to irritate Austria failed, as King William would not be persuaded to adopt his views. The Danish War came to an end, only to be followed by other and more momentous events.

Bismarck, in prevision of the future, sought for allies, and, above all, for the assurance that in the coming conflict France would remain neutral. The French Emperor, with his vague dream of a reorganisation of Europe, was unquestionably no match for the Prussian Foreign Secretary. Bismarck persuaded Napoleon that he had everything to gain by allowing Austria's exclusion from the Germanic Confederation : he went so far as to indicate Belgium and the right bank of the Rhine, as in 1814, as the territorial compensations to which France would be entitled in the case of a Prussian victory. This was the capital and fatal error of Napoleon III.'s policy, as French interests could never have been advanced by the establishment on its western frontier of a powerful and united Germany. It was therefore undoubtedly with Napoleon's permission that the Italian Cabinet negotiated an offensive and defensive alliance with Prussia.

In 1866 war was finally declared, and remembering '59' the Italian Government entrusted the command of the volunteers to Garibaldi, although the customary jealousy and prejudice of the professional military element prevented their being furnished with the proper armament and *impedimenta* and the volunteers being almost four times as numerous as in '59' it was impossible to keep the men up to the high standard they had previously attained. Garibaldi, though much handicapped by his rheumatic complaint, which forced that ever active and omnipresent leader to head his troops in a carriage, succeeded in beating his opponent, General Kuhn, who was perhaps the highest exponent of mountain warfare, in the only two actions fought during this campaign, the battles of Bezzecca and Condino. These victories practically determined the conquest of the Italian Tyrol (Trentino), as Medici was less than a day's march from the city of Trento and on the eve of joining hands with his old chief. But on the Mincio and in the Adriatic ineptitude and treachery did their shameful work. The defeats of Custozza and Lissa were the result : the Trentino had to be abandoned, and the Italian army and navy unjustly suffered for the faults of those who led them.

Prussia triumphed at Sadowa, and Napoleon III. finally perceived that he had committed a serious error in permitting the humiliation of Austria, so he hurriedly endeavoured to detach Italy from the Prussian alliance. He persuaded Austria to cede Venetia to him, with the understanding that Italy should receive from him this much longed-for province. Austria, aware that the Italian army was still most threatening, and needing all her forces for the defence of Vienna, towards which the victorious Prussians were moving, acquiesced, and the Italian Cabinet submitted to the humiliation of receiving Venetia as a gift, thereby acting disloyally to their ally.

Garibaldi now concentrated his efforts on the liberation of Rome, and in 1867, after evading the Italian cruisers patrolling round Caprera, he took command of the volunteers gathered on the pontifical frontier, probably through the tacit connivance of the Italian Government, and at their head moved towards Rome, where he had been led to believe an insurrection was going to take place. But the Romans did not stir, and Garibaldi found himself confronted by the French " Corps d'Occupation." The disaster of Mentana ensued, and the *chassepots* of General Failly *firent des merveilles*. At Villa Glori, near Rome, the heroic brothers Cairoli fell, overpowered, under the historic fig-tree, while hopelessly striving to rouse the Romans. Then Napoleon imposed the Convention of September, by which the Italian Government was bound to respect the territorial possessions of the Pope. In those dark and troubled days patriots must indeed have despaired of the future of Italy.

The Franco-Prussian War of 1870 annulled the Convention of September, and Italy reacquired, at last, her long-lost

EPILOGUE

capital. The dream of centuries was fulfilled, but the great man who, from the beginning, had impressed upon the Italians that absolute Union of the country must be their goal was not present. Ricasoli's plan for worthily recalling the exile had never again been broached by the Italian ministers, who, representing only the narrowest section of the Moderates, hated and feared Mazzini, who now, enfeebled by age and illness and the unceasing labour to which for so many years he had devoted his strength, was no longer able to sustain the unequal combat. The monarchical idea had triumphed in Italy, and he saw that, during his own life at least, there was no chance of success for his own cherished ideal. Yet he made a last effort, and for this purpose came secretly to Italy, hoping to foster a republican movement in Sicily. But as he landed at Palermo he was arrested and subsequently imprisoned in the fortress of Gaeta, having been betrayed by an agent (Wollf) who had long ago traitorously won his confidence.

A few weeks later Rome was liberated and the prison doors were opened to him, but he once more refused amnesty. How was it possible for Mazzini to accept a " pardon " for the immense services he had rendered to his country ? How could he consistently submit to such an insult ? The Resurrection of Italy was mainly due to the education of the moral and intellectual capabilities of the nation, and to this great work he had sacrificed his whole existence. Not to have understood this, not to have felt that Mazzini soared high above the petty rules of political " opportunism," was the criminal mistake of those surrounding King Victor Emmanuel.

Thus the Italian Government presented to the world the ludicrous and despicable farce of pretending to ignore the fact that the unpardoned exile was living in the kingdom, concealed under a false name. Worse than a stranger in his own land, he died on March 10, 1872, at Pisa, pillowed in the loving arms of Janet Nathan Rosselli, the daughter and wife of his best and most devoted Italian friends. No death could have been sadder and more

THE BIRTH OF MODERN ITALY

profoundly pathetic than this of Italy's greatest and purest hero, who breathed his last unhonoured by the nation he had redeemed. Italians should bear in mind that the most magnificent monument they could ever erect to him will fail to cancel this indelible stain on the nation's honour.

On February 9, 1878, United Italy lost her first king, Victor Emmanuel II., who had steadfastly and faithfully maintained his unconquerable faith in the destinies of his country, even during those dark days of Novara, when he had ascended his father's throne in the presence of the victorious Austrians. Four years later, on June 2, 1882, Garibaldi expired, the last of the great men who accomplished the mighty work of the Italian "Risorgimento."

Mazzini, Cavour, Garibaldi and Victor Emmanuel are the four colossal figures in the most extraordinary event the history of the world has known : the indissoluble welding together of a race for centuries divided against itself, the victorious birth of a great nation from out of that which Metternich had scornfully called " a mere geographical expression." And the most powerful factor in this wonderful redemption, the factor without which it never could have been achieved, was the Italian People.

MAZZINI ON HIS DEATH-BED.

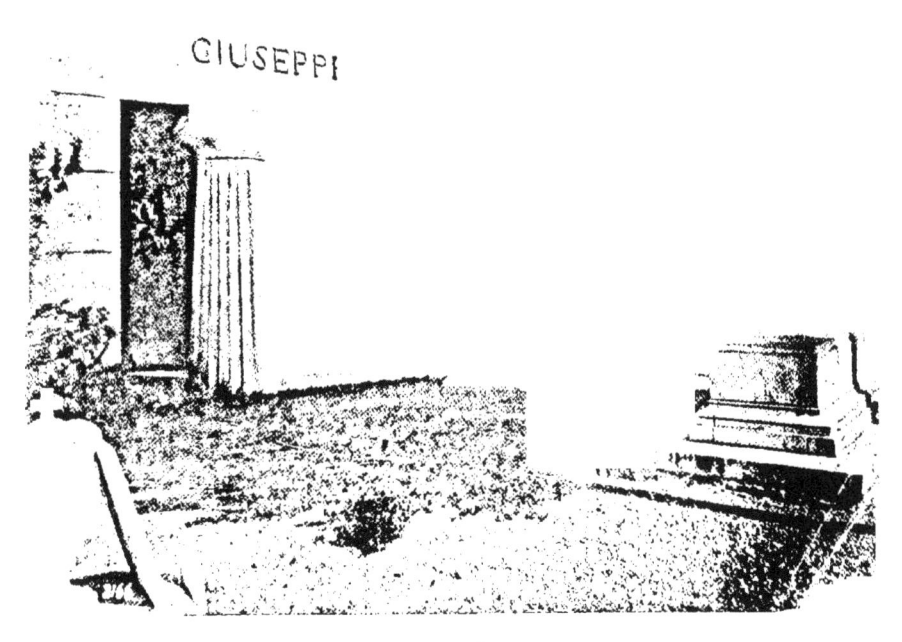

MAZZINI'S TOMB

INDEX

NOTE.—The name of Joseph Mazzini has not been indexed, as it recurs on almost every page.

ABERCROMBY, SIR RALPH, 104, 111, 116, 156, 170, 181
Aberdeen, Lord, 49 (*note*), 67, 68, 74, 81
Agostini, 221
Aguyar, 201
Albert, Prince, 33, 230
Albini, 269
Alduino, Colonel, 74
Alfieri, 132
Ambiveri, 321
Anelli, Rev. Luigi, 159, 165, 174
Antonini, Paolo, 169
Anzani, 170
Arago, Emanuel, 210, 211
Arcioni, Pietro, 154
Arduino, King, 2
Argyll, Duke of, 334
Armellini, 188, 189, 198
Arnaldo da Brescia, 145
Arnold, Matthew, 123
Ashburton, Lord, 58
Ashley, Lord, 29, 86, 89

Ashurst family, 103, 110, 150, 155, 183, 245
Ashurst, Mrs., 223, 326
Ashurst, Caroline (Mrs. Stansfeld), 87, 93, 144, 217, 222, 239
Ashurst, Emily (Mrs. Hawkes, then Venturi), 44, 57, 92, 93, 110, 121, 122, 129, 217, 222, 238, 239
Ashurst, Matilda (Mrs. Biggs), 121, 130, 222, 230, 239
Ashurst, Eliza (Mrs. Bardon), 92, 122, 217, 219, 222
Ashurst, William, 87, 92, 107, 129, 219, 326, 327
Aspre, General d', 157, 176
Austria, Emperor of, 2, 284, 286
Avezzana, General, 189, 190, 193, 200
Azeglio, Emanuele d', 272, 285, 333
Azeglio, Massimo d', 102, 243, 244, 251, 283, 284, 288, 301, 302

INDEX

Balbo, Conte Cesare, 102, 127, 148
Baldaccone, Rev. —, 63
Ballerio, Giuditta, *see* Sidoli, Giuditta
Bandiera, Admiral, 67, 69
Bandiera, Attilio, 67, 68, 69, 70, 71, 72, 73, 75, 76, 78, 79, 80, 83, 101, 124, 301
Bandiera, Baroness, 72
Bandiera, Emilio, 69, 70, 71, 72, 73, 74, 75, 76, 78, 79, 80, 83, 101, 124, 301
Barbès, Armand, 212
Baring, Lady Harriet, 55, 56, 58, 59
Baring, Mr., 58
Barrot, Odillon, 194, 197, 211, 219, 229
Basile, Dr., 328, 336, 337
Bassi, Paolo, 175
Bassi, Father Ugo, 184, 191
Bastide, Minister, 171, 177
Bava, General, 161, 172
Bcart, Constance, 275
Beauharnais, Prince Eugène, 63
Belgiojoso, Princess, 197
Belgium, King of, 285
Benedetta, Mazzini's old nurse, 104
Benedetti, 298
Benoit, 64, 65
Bentham, Jeremy, 34, 35
Bentinck, Lord George, 96, 138
Bentivegna, Baron, 264
Berchet, 9
Beretta, 325
Berry, Duchess of, 219
Bertani, Dr., 176, 196, 200, 255, 256, 264, 295, 300, 304, 306, 319, 324, 328
Berti, 80
Bertola, Count, 92
Bertolotti, 99
Bettini, 240
Bianchi, Nicomede, 133
Biggs, Lizzie, 121, 144
Bini, Carlo, 4, 10
Bismarck, Prince, 247, 338, 339
Bixio, French Ambassador, 156
Bixio, Nino, 118, 295, 300, 303, 321
Blanc, Louis, 212, 217, 233, 234, 235, 237, 335
Boccheciampi, spy, 79, 80
Bolza, 165
Bonaparte-Wyse, Letizia (Mme. Ratazzi), 329.
Borel, Joseph, *see* Garibaldi, Giuseppe, General
Botta, 137
Bourbon, Charles of, 128
Bowring, Dr., 26, 28, 65, 66, 67, 81, 89, 101, 115
Bozzelli, 142
Brignole, Marquis, 149
Brodie, Sir Benjamin, 259
Brofferio, Angelo, 5, 166, 290
Brougham, Lord, 58, 208
Brown, English Consul, 272
Browning, Bertino, 251
Browning, Mrs., 98, 123, 250, 251
Browning, Robert, 97, 98, 123, 150, 251
Brunetti, Angelo - Ciceruacchio, 184

INDEX

Brunswick, Duke of, 65
Buller, Charles, 47, 55, 89
Buller, Mrs., 47
Buol, Count, 243, 244
Byron, Lady, 53
Byron, Lord, 30, 46, 86, 98, 106

CADORNA, CARLO, 5
Cadorna, General, 307
Cairoli, Brothers, 340
Calvi, Pietro Fortunato, 254, 258
Campanella, Federico, 10, 11 (*note*), 257, 315, 317
Campbell, Consul, 173
Campbell, 98
Cane, Sir J., 186
Cantù, Cesare, 68, 133 (*note*)
Capponi, Gino, 129
Carcassi, 272
Carlyle, Thomas, 29, 31, 32, 33, 34, 35, 36, 37, 38, 40, 41, 42, 45, 46, 47, 48, 51, 53, 56, 58, 82, 83, 89, 100, 123, 126, 186, 203, 219, 220
Carlyle, Mrs., 33, 38, 41, 42, 43, 44, 45, 46, 48, 49, 50, 52, 53, 54, 55, 59, 60, 61, 123, 126, 219
Carpenter, W., 107
Casati, Count Gabrio, 159, 160, 162, 165, 166
Cass, American Consul, 206
Cassati, Governor of Mantua, 258
Castagneto, Count, 119
Castagnino, Dr., spy, 16
Castelcicala, Prince of, 114

Cattaneo, Carlo, 152, 165, 172, 177, 221, 269, 272, 325
Cavaignac, General, 41, 171, 179, 180, 187
Cavour, Count Camillo, 127, 163, 244, 247, 255, 259, 261, 267, 272, 273, 274, 277, 278, 279, 280, 281, 282, 283, 284, 285, 287, 288, 291, 292, 293, 295, 296, 297, 298, 299, 300, 301, 302, 304, 307, 310, 311, 312, 316, 317, 342
Ceccopieri, General, 155
Cecilia, 18, 81
Cernuschi, 201, 202, 221
Cerrutti, 149
Changarnier, General, 219, 229
Charles Albert, King, 3, 5, 6, 7, 8, 9, 10, 12, 13, 15, 21, 39, 40, 54, 95, 102, 103, 104, 111, 112, 116, 117, 118, 119, 120, 126, 133, 134, 147, 148, 150, 152, 153, 155, 156, 158, 159, 161, 162, 165, 167, 168, 169, 170, 172, 173, 174, 175, 176, 179, 182, 184, 188, 254, 271
Charles Felix, King, 15
Chiala, 287
Ciacchi, Cardinal, 111
Cialdini, General, 152, 279, 323, 324
Cianciolo, 139
Ciani, Brothers, 22
Cipriani, Leone, 290, 292
Cironi, 258
Civinini, 271
Cleombroto, *see* Garibaldi, General Giuseppe
Clotilde, Princess, 277, 279

345

INDEX

Cobden, 91, 95, 96, 114, 115, 327
Collegno, Marquis, 152
Compagnoni, spy, 79
Comte, 35
Confalonieri, Count Federico, 3 (*note*)
Consiglio, 73
Cook, Eliza, 130
Coombe, George, 114
Cooper, Th., 107
"Cornelia," 149
Corsini, Don Neri, 282, 312
Cosenz, General, 264, 279, 304, 321
Cosenza, 238
Cottin, spy, 4
Courbet, 233, 234, 237
Courtaulds, 91
Cousin, 5, 249
Cowen, Jos., 89, 90, 245, 266
Cowley, Lord, 280
Cowper, 98
Crispi, 139, 244, 299, 305, 314
Cromwell, 37, 45, 47, 131
Cugia, General, 323
Culiolo, Captain "Leggiero," 205
Cuneo, G. B., 23

Dabormida, General, 255
Dall' Ungaro, poet, 115, 178, 274
Dandolo, Enrico, 167
Dante, 25, 38, 46, 47, 145
Davis, Captain J., 238
Dawkins, Consul, 111
Dawson, George, 130
De Ferrari, Marquis, 323
Del Carretto, 79

Della Rocca, General, 286
De Majo, 140
Derby, Lord, 276, 334
Dickens, Charles, 91, 92, 130
Dillon, Frank, 89
Disraeli, 96
Dobson-Collett, 145
Dolfi, Beppe, 289, 314
Dragone, 268
Drouhyn de Lhuis, 227
Dufferin, Marquis, 334
Duncombe, Th., 66, 67, 68, 81, 85, 86, 107
Durando, General Giacomo, 5 (*note*), 155, 157, 158, 160, 176
Durini, Count, 159

Elia, Colonel, 45, 46
Elliott, 311
Emerson, 123, 144
Emiliani, 18, 81
Epps, Dr., 107
Eugénie, Empress, 279, 287, 322

Fabrizi, Dr. Nicola, 54, 69, 71, 75, 76, 77, 134, 142, 249, 257, 264
Failly, General, 240
Falcone, 270
Falloux, Minister, 215
Fanelli, 268
Fanti, General, 152, 172, 175, 289, 291, 292, 307
Farini, 288, 289, 299
Fava, Baron, 165
Ferrari, Napoleone, 221, 238, 240

INDEX

Fife, Sir John, 228
Fletcher, Mrs., 89
Fleury, General, 284, 286
Forbes, Colonel, 161, 204
Foscolo, Ugo, 23, 87, 336
Fox, Robert Barclay, 35
Fox, W. J., 107
Frost, 33, 34
Froude, 55
Fuller, Margaret, Contessa d'Ossoli, 129, 197, 251

GALILEI, GALILEO, 38
Gambini, Dr. Andrea, 13, 19, 57, 104
Garibaldi, Anita, 168, 204
Garibaldi, Giuseppe, 22, 23, 55 (*note*), 81, 102, 153, 168, 169, 170, 175, 176, 182, 184, 187, 189, 190, 191, 192, 193, 195, 196, 197, 199, 200, 201, 204, 205, 206, 245, 246, 247, 248, 249, 250, 251, 253, 254, 255, 256, 257, 262, 263, 264, 265, 266, 267, 268, 270, 277, 279, 280, 283, 289, 291, 292, 294, 295, 296, 298, 299, 300, 301, 302, 303, 304, 305, 306, 307, 308, 309, 310, 313, 314, 315, 316, 317, 318, 319, 320, 321, 322, 323, 324, 325, 326, 327, 328, 329, 330, 331, 332, 333, 334, 335, 336, 337, 339, 340, 342
Garibaldi, Menotti, 330, 337
Garibaldi, Ricciotti, 253, 260
Garibaldi, Teresita, 328
Garrison, Lloyd, 92

Gavioli, 18, 19, 65
Geneys, Admiral de, 23
Genoa, Duke of, 172, 174, 182
Ghio, Colonel, 270
Giannone, 93
Gillman family, 129
Gioberti, Vincenzo, 69, 102 (*note*), 158, 163, 166, 188
Gisquet, 64, 65
Gladstone, Mrs., 256
Gladstone, William, 49, 228, 229, 290, 334, 336
Goethe, 30, 46, 50, 52
Gorzkowsky, General, 205
Graham, Sir James, 49 (*note*), 67, 68, 74, 81, 82, 83, 84, 85, 86, 91
Grammont, Duc de, 296
Granville, Lord, 244
Graziana, Marianna Bandiera, 72, 73
Grazioli, 258
Greco, 331
Gregory XVI., Pope, 101, 202
Grey, Lord, 96, 228
Griffini, Romolo, 164, 176
Grisi, Madame, 110, 122
Guadagnoli, 204
Guerrazzi, Domenico, 4 (*note*), 34, 185, 187
Guerrieri-Gonzaga, Marchese Anselmo, 159, 171, 179
Guerzoni, 169
Guiccioli family, 205
Guizot, 5, 63, 113, 144, 146, 182

HARNEY, JULIAN, 186, 246

347

INDEX

Hartington, Lord, 276
Hartmann, Moritz, 219, 229 (*note*)
Haussonville, Marquis D', 302
Hawkes, Sidney, 92, 93, 107, 129
Haynau, General, 227, 258
Henry V., King, 219
Herwig family, 258
Herzen, 335
Hess, Marshal, 175, 286
Holland, Lady, 256
Holland, Lord, 256
Holyoake, 187
Horne, R. H., 130
Hosman, Hatty, 251
Howden, Lord, 231
Howitts family, 130
Hudson, Sir James, 255, 272, 273, 288, 294, 295, 296, 297, 298, 312
Hugo, Victor, 30, 209, 210, 211, 266
Hume, 91

IMBRIANI, MATTEO RENATO, 256

JELLACIČ, GENERAL, 155
Jerrold, Douglas, 107, 130
Joly, lawyer, 211

KELLERSBERG, COLONEL, 280
Kinglake, 230, 312
Klapka, 155
Kleber, General, 216
Konarsky, 38
Kosciuszko, 9

Kossuth, 179, 214, 222, 226, 227, 230, 241, 242, 247, 248, 254, 317
Krzanowsky, 188
Kuhn, General, 339

LA FARINA, 299, 301
Lafayette, General, 5
Lamarmora, General, 167, 279, 292
Lamartine, 30, 145, 146, 147, 179
Lamberti, 10, 11, 12, 14, 16, 22, 24, 69, 93, 118
Lamennais, 29, 30, 35, 64, 126, 211
Lamoricière, 307
Lazzareschi, 18, 81
Lecchi, General, 154
Ledru-Rollin, 146, 147, 209, 212, 222, 234, 235, 237, 335
Leigh-Smith, Barbara, 251
Lemmi, Adriano, 222, 266
Leo XIII., Pope (Cardinal Pecci), 283
Leroux, Pierre, 126, 234, 237
Lesseps, 192, 193, 194, 208
Lewes, G. H., 228
Liechtenberg, Prince, 63
Liechtenstein, Prince, 170, 192
Lieven, Princess, 59
Linton, G. W., 106, 107, 145
Linton, W. L., 89
Litta, Conte Pompeo, 153, 159, 165, 170, 174
Little, Doctor, 253, 259
Lockhart, 36
Lonsdale, Lord, 228

INDEX

Louis Philippe, 7, 63, 100, 111, 113, 144, 182, 184, 194, 233
Lupatelli, 80
Lyons, Captain, 140, 141

MACAULAY, LORD, 96
Macchiavelli, 145, 146
Mackintosh, 138
Macready, 228
Maestri, Pietro, 164, 172
Maffei, 337
Malleson, 91
Malmesbury, Earl of, 244, 279, 334
Mameli, Goffredo, 148, 188, 189, 196, 203
Mamiani della Rovere, Conte Terenzio, 149, 183
Manara, Luciano, 154, 155, 200, 201, 222
Mandrot, Madeleine de, 26
Manessi, 80
Manin, Lodovico, 167, 168, 178, 181, 247, 249
Manners, Lord John, 130
Maria Pia, Princess, 328
Marie Louise, Empress, 128
Mario, Alberto, 238, 244, 266, 269, 276, 289, 293, 294, 319, 325, 328
Mario (Singer), 110, 111, 122
Martin, Stone, and Martin, bankers, 220
Martineau, Miss Harriet, 41
Martini, Count Enrico, 168
Masini, 17
Masson, David, 228

Mastei-Ferretti, Cardinal, *vide* Pius IX.
Mattina, 269
Maximilian, Archduke, 261, 285, 307
Mayer, Enrico, 11, 129
Mayne-Reid, Captain, 241
Mayor, Edw., 267
Mazzini, Francesca, 28
Mazzini, Doctor Giacomo, 3, 28, 55, 84, 85, 95, 136
Mazzini, Maria, *née* Drago, 3, 17, 19, 44, 57, 62, 150, 163, 182, 206, 238
Mazzuchelli, 99
Medici, General, 20, 153, 169, 170, 173, 188, 201, 255, 263, 264, 266, 278, 279, 295, 300, 302, 304, 306, 321, 339
Melegari, 26, 28
Menotti, Achille, 150
Menotti, Ciro, 11, 150
Menotti, Massimiliano, 150
Meteyard, Miss, 130
Metternich, Prince, 2, 79, 101, 104, 111, 113, 115, 116, 128, 148, 152, 182, 187, 247, 342
Mezzacapo, General, 188
Miall, Edward, 130, 228
Micciarelli, T. V., spy, 71, 73, 74
Miceli, 314
Milano, Agesilao, 274
Mill, John Stuart, 29, 34, 35, 36, 56, 58, 89
Miller, 79
Milner-Gibson, Mr., 89, 277
Milner-Gibson, Mrs., 110
Minghetti, Marco, 313

INDEX

Minto, Earl of, 113, 115, 135, 141, 142, 144
Mirafiori, Rosina, Countess of, 315
Modena, Duke of, 7, 20, 69, 128, 248, 281, 303
Modena, Julia, 197
Monckton-Milnes, 58, 81, 130
Montanara, Guido, 232, 258
Montanelli, 3 (*note*), 221
Montecchi, 188
Mordini, 314, 335
Morgan, Lady, 42
Moro, Domenico, 70, 72, 76, 77, 79, 80
Morpeth, Lord, 96
Moses, 12
Mosto, 266, 272, 319
Murat, Prince, 267
Musolino, 314

NAPIER, Loan, 140, 142
Naples, King of, 134, 138, 140, 142, 182, 190, 229, 255, 261, 264, 266, 270, 271, 281, 282, 290, 301, 302, 303, 307, 310
Napoleon I., Emperor, 1, 2, 9, 13, 21, 63, 108, 145, 146, 153, 189, 233
Napoleon III., Emperor, 12, 98, 147, 186, 187, 191, 194, 207, 208, 218, 229, 233, 235, 236, 237, 247, 268, 273, 274, 277, 278, 279, 282, 283, 286, 288, 289, 290, 292, 293, 296, 297, 302, 303, 307, 310, 311, 312, 316, 317, 318, 319, 322, 327, 331, 335, 339, 340

Napoleon, Prince, 277, 278, 279, 280, 282, 284, 291, 316
Nardi, Anacarsi, 79, 80, 125
Nathan family, 88, 130
Nathan, Rosselli Janet, 341
Nathan, Mrs. Sarina, 89, 246
Negri, Laura de, 16
Nelaton, Doctor, 328
Nencioni, Enrico, 45
Newman, Professor, 228
Niccolini, 129
Nichol, Professor, 228
Nickerson, James, 238
Nicotera, 268, 270, 271, 275, 299
Niel, Marshal, 278
Nivari, Battistino, spy, 79
Normanby, Lord, 156, 179, 207, 229, 230
Nugent, General, 67, 157, 160, 161
Nullo, 320, 321

O'CONNELL, 63
O'Connor, 186
Oddo, 139
Ogareff, 335
Oliphant, Lawrence, 298
Olivier, Dominic, 12, 17
Olivier, Emile, 12
Orange, William of, 33
Orsini, 139, 248, 250, 257, 258, 277
Osmani, 80
Oudinot, General, 180, 187, 190, 191, 192, 193, 194, 196, 199, 209
Overden, Lord, 256

INDEX

Pacchioni, 80
Pacifico, Don, 227
Paleocapa, 167
Pallavicino, Colonel, 323, 324
Pallavicini, Marquis Giorgio, 264, 309, 322, 323
Palmerston, Lady, 256, 330, 334
Palmerston, Lord, 96, 99, 100, 102, 111, 112, 113, 114, 116, 128, 135, 141, 144, 146, 153, 156, 157, 170, 171, 172, 173, 178, 179, 180, 181, 187, 207, 208, 224, 226, 227, 228, 229, 230, 231, 236, 247, 256, 276, 284, 285, 286, 290, 305, 333, 334, 335
Panizzi, Doctor, 255, 256, 295
Pantelleria, Prince of, 139
Paolucci, Admiral, 67, 73, 75
Papoff, 321
Pareto, Marquess, 147, 148, 166, 275
Parkes, 268
Parkins, Doctor, 327
Parma, Duke of, 128, 303
Parry, J. H., 107
Partesotti, Attilio, spy, 76, 78
Pasolini, Count, 325
Patterson, Thomas, 238
Pecchio, Giuseppe, 6 (*note*)
Peel, Sir Robert, 49, 95, 96, 227
Pellico, Silvio, 3 (*note*), 78
Pepe, General, 155
Périer, Casimir, 8
Persano, Admiral, 301, 303
Persigny, Count of, 284, 285
Pescantini, 127 (*note*)
Pianciani, 306
Pick, R., 238

Picozzi, 241
Pilo, Rosalino, 139, 256, 264, 266, 268, 269, 299, 300, 305, 306
Pimodan, General, 154
Pinelli, General, 321
Piolti, 241
Pisacane, Carlo, 189, 197, 199, 256, 263, 266, 267, 268, 269, 270, 271, 275, 277, 299, 301, 304
Pisani, 269
Pistrucci, Scipione, 21, 61, 64, 85, 206
Pius IX., Pope, 97, 101, 115, 116, 117, 118, 119, 120, 133, 134, 135, 141, 157, 158, 183, 184, 185, 194, 208, 209, 210, 211, 234, 258, 283, 310
Poerio, 256
Poma, Doctor, 232, 258
Ponsonby, Lord, 113, 156, 172, 224, 226
Portugal, King of, 328
Prati, 167
Proudhon, 233
Prussia, King of, 338, 339
Purchase, H., 238

Quadrio, Maurizio, 244, 257, 271

Radetzky, General, 55, 73, 75, 128, 150, 153, 155, 156, 157, 161, 170, 171, 172, 173, 174, 175, 177, 179, 181, 183, 188, 242, 245
Radnor, Earl of, 130

INDEX

Rainieri, Archduke, 13, 75, 79
Ramorino, General, 21, 22, 249
Rattazzi, Urbano, 244, 287, 295, 296, 297, 299, 315, 317, 319, 320, 329
Restelli, 167, 172
Ribotti, Admiral, 5 (*note*)
Ricasoli, Barone Bettino, 282, 284, 289, 291, 292, 312, 313, 316, 317, 341
Ricci, Marquess, 166, 179
Ricciotti, 76, 77, 80
Ripari, Doctor, 255, 322
Rizzio, 38
Robertson, 29, 30, 36
Rocca, 80
Roebuck, 227, 273
Rogers, 97
Rosales, Marquess, 22, 25
Rosazza, Giacomo, 10
Rosselli family, 88, 130
Rosselli, General, 189, 192, 199, 200, 249
Rossi, Count Pellegrino, 111, 182, 183, 184
Rothschild, 62
Routledge, George, 257
Rubattino, Raffaele, 302, 303.
Rudinì, Marquess, 139
Ruffini, Agostino, 17, 28, 40, 62, 122, 127, 147
Ruffini, Brothers, 24, 25, 27
Ruffini, Giovanni, 10, 17, 25, 40, 43, 44, 45, 47, 48, 62, 64, 122, 127, 147, 149, 163, 166
Ruffini, Jacopo, 5, 10, 14, 15, 16, 17, 62, 127, 206, 326
Ruffini, Madame, 18, 24, 47, 48, 62

Ruffini, Nina, 48
Ruffini, Ottavio, 16, 17
Ruffini, Vittorio, 16
Ruge, Arnold, 222
Russell, Lord John, 95, 96, 186, 187, 189, 230, 231, 259, 285, 286, 290, 295, 296, 297, 298, 311, 312, 333, 334
Russell, Lord Odo, 280

SACCHI, GENERAL, 192, 301, 302, 321
Saffi, Aurelio, 185, 189, 198, 206, 241, 244, 245, 265, 335
Salasco, General, 175
Saliceti, 188, 221
Sand, Georges, 30, 62, 92, 98, 122, 123, 125, 126, 212, 213, 214, 216, 218, 235, 236
Santarosa, Conte, 249
Sarpi, Fra Paolo, 30
Sauget, General de, 139, 140
Savi, 249
Savoia-Carignano, Prince of, 282
Savoie, 211
Savoy, Duke of, *vide* Victor Emmanuel II.
Schwarzenberg, Prince of, 225, 231
Scuri, 91, 92
Settembrini, Luigi, 256
Settembrini, Raffaele, 256
Settimo, Ruggero, 139, 141, 182
Shaen, W., 89, 94, 107, 111, 129, 144, 245, 266
Shaftesbury, Earl of, 334
Shakespeare, 98, 99
Shamyl, 119

INDEX

Scholefield, 228
Shelley, 99
Sidoli, Achille, 188
Sidoli, Giuditta, 10, 11, 12, 16, 17, 18, 19, 24, 25, 26, 27, 28, 45, 188
Simeoni, 271
Sirtori, General, 163, 164, 178, 228, 304, 321
Sivori, 100
Smith, George, publisher, 329
Somerset, Duke of, 276, 333
Spaur, Count, 185
Spaventa, Silvio, 256
Speri, Tito, 232, 258
Spring, Marcus, 129
Stallo, 266
Stanley, Lord, 227
Stansfeld, Joseph, 92, 93, 94, 99, 106, 107, 130, 145, 217, 220, 237, 242, 245, 246, 254, 259, 266, 275, 277, 278, 290, 293, 294, 295, 296, 305, 311, 326, 327, 328, 329, 330, 331, 335, 336
Staton, Lord, 74
Sterbini, 189
Stockmar, Baron, 230
Stone, Frank, 130
Stuart, Lord D. C., 228
Stuart, Mary, 38
Sutherland, Duchess of, 334
Sutherland, Duke of, 333, 335, 337

TALLEYRAND, 2
Tancione, 40, 43, 100
Tancione, Susanna, 40, 41, 43, 59, 100, 150

Taylor, Mrs. P. A., 57, 90, 130
Taylor, P. A., senior, 107
Taylor, Peter, 90, 91, 106, 107, 228, 245, 266
Tazzoli, Don Enrico, 232, 258
Temple, Sir W., 255, 256
Tennyson, Alfred, 98
Tesei, 79
Thiers, Adolphe, 30, 100, 147, 209, 218, 219, 229
Thouvenel, 296, 297
Thurn and Taxis, Prince, 160
Tocqueville, 194, 215, 229
Tola, Effisio, 15
Tommaseo, 167, 168
Torresani, 165
Toynbee, Joseph, 89, 107, 130
Trevelyan, Arthur, 228
Tuscany, Duke of, 281

ULIVIERI, GENERAL, 173
Urbino, spy, 165
Usiglio, Angelo, 17, 26, 33, 48

VAILLANT, MARSHAL, 286
Valerio, Lorenzo, 166, 325
Vecchi, Luigi, 169
Venerucci, 80
Verità, Don Giovanni, 205
Victor Emmanuel I., 6, 7
Victor Emmanuel II., 172, 188, 243, 259, 267, 278, 279, 280, 282, 283, 284, 286, 287, 288, 289, 290, 291, 292, 293, 300, 301, 302, 308, 310, 315, 316, 318, 319, 320, 322, 323, 329, 331, 341, 342

INDEX

Victoria, Queen, 29, 33, 34, 230, 231
Villamarina, Marquess, 268, 273
Vincent, H., 107

WALES, PRINCE OF, 337
Walewsky, Count, 230, 279, 296
Walpole, 29
Washington, 9
Wate, 268
Watson, J., 107
Welden, General, 155, 178, 181
Wellington, Duke of, 49, 186

Wilmer, John, 238
Winkworth, Miss, 111
Wollf, spy, 341
Worcell, 90
Wreford, Harry, 270
Wurtemberg, King of, 303

ZAMBECCARI, LIVIO, 192
Zambianchi, Colonel, 304, 306
Zamoysky, Count, 227
Zanetti, Professor, 329, 330
Zerbini, Isabella " Nina," 237
Zucchi, General, 69, 70, 174, 188

Lightning Source UK Ltd.
Milton Keynes UK
UKHW02f2211080818
326964UK00012B/1187/P